10 NEW ACTUAL, OFFICIAL
LSAT **PREPTESTS**
WITH COMPARATIVE READING™

A Publication of the Law School Admission Council,
Newtown, PA

FROM THE EDITOR

Although these PrepTests are presented to you in paper form, the LSAT® and LSAT Writing® are now delivered electronically. Please visit LSAC.org for the most up-to-date information about these tests.

The Law School Admission Council's mission is to advance law and justice by encouraging diverse and talented individuals to study law and by supporting their enrollment and learning journeys from prelaw through practice. See https://www.lsac.org/about.

ISBN-13: 978-0-9846360-0-6

Print number
15 14 13 12 11

TABLE OF CONTENTS

INTRODUCTION TO THE LSAT

The Law School Admission Test (LSAT) is designed to measure skills considered essential for success in law school: the reading and comprehension of complex texts with accuracy and insight; the organization and management of information and the ability to draw reasonable inferences from it; the ability to think critically; and the analysis and evaluation of the reasoning and arguments of others.

The LSAT provides a standard measure of acquired reading and verbal reasoning skills that law schools can use as one of several factors in assessing applicants.

For up-to-date information about LSAC's services, go to our website, LSAC.org.

SCORING

Your LSAT score is based on the number of questions you answer correctly (the raw score). There is no deduction for incorrect answers, and all questions count equally. In other words, there is no penalty for guessing.

Test Score Accuracy—Reliability and Standard Error of Measurement

Candidates perform at different levels on different occasions for reasons quite unrelated to the characteristics of a test itself. The accuracy of test scores is best described by the use of two related statistical terms: reliability and standard error of measurement.

Reliability is a measure of how consistently a test measures the skills being assessed. The higher the reliability coefficient for a test, the more certain we can be that test takers would get very similar scores if they took the test again.

LSAC reports an internal consistency measure of reliability for every test form. Reliability can vary from 0.00 to 1.00, and a test with no measurement error would have a reliability coefficient of 1.00 (never attained in practice). Reliability coefficients for past LSAT forms have ranged from .90 to .95, indicating a high degree of consistency for these tests. LSAC expects the reliability of the LSAT to continue to fall within the same range.

LSAC also reports the amount of measurement error associated with each test form, a concept known as the *standard error of measurement* (SEM). The SEM, which is usually about 2.6 points, indicates how close a test taker's observed score is likely to be to his or her true score. True scores are theoretical scores that would be obtained from perfectly reliable tests with no measurement error—scores never known in practice.

Score bands, or ranges of scores that contain a test taker's true score a certain percentage of the time, can be derived using the SEM. LSAT score bands are constructed by adding and subtracting the (rounded) SEM to and from an actual LSAT score (e.g., the LSAT score, plus or minus 3 points).

Scores near 120 or 180 have asymmetrical bands. Score bands constructed in this manner will contain an individual's true score approximately 68 percent of the time.

Measurement error also must be taken into account when comparing the LSAT scores of two test takers. It is likely that small differences in scores are due to measurement error rather than to meaningful differences in ability. The standard error of score differences provides some guidance as to the importance of differences between two scores. The standard error of score differences is approximately 1.4 times larger than the standard error of measurement for the individual scores.

Thus, a test score should be regarded as a useful but approximate measure of a test taker's abilities as measured by the test, not as an exact determination of his or her abilities. LSAC encourages law schools to examine the range of scores within the interval that probably contains the test taker's true score (e.g., the test taker's score band) rather than solely interpret the reported score alone.

Adjustments for Variation in Test Difficulty

All test forms of the LSAT reported on the same score scale are designed to measure the same abilities, but one test form may be slightly easier or more difficult than another. The scores from different test forms are made comparable through a statistical procedure known as equating. As a result of equating, a given scaled score earned on different test forms reflects the same level of ability.

Research on the LSAT

Summaries of LSAT validity studies and other LSAT research can be found in member law school libraries and at LSAC.org.

THE THREE LSAT MULTIPLE–CHOICE QUESTION TYPES

The multiple-choice questions on the LSAT reflect a broad range of academic disciplines and are intended to give no advantage to candidates from a particular academic background.

The sections of the test contain three different question types. The following material presents a general discussion of the nature of each question type and some strategies that can be used in answering them.

Analytical Reasoning Questions

Analytical Reasoning questions are designed to assess the ability to consider a group of facts and rules, and, given those facts and rules, determine what could or must be true. The specific scenarios associated with these questions are usually unrelated to law, since they are intended to be accessible to a wide range of test takers. However, the skills tested parallel those involved in determining what could or must be the case given a set of regulations, the terms of a contract, or the facts of a legal case in relation to the law. In Analytical Reasoning questions, you are asked to reason deductively from a set of statements and rules or principles that describe relationships among persons, things, or events.

Analytical Reasoning questions appear in sets, with each set based on a single passage. The passage used for each set of questions describes common ordering relationships or grouping relationships, or a combination of both types of relationships. Examples include scheduling employees for work shifts, assigning instructors to class sections, ordering tasks according to priority, and distributing grants for projects.

Analytical Reasoning questions test a range of deductive reasoning skills. These include:

- Comprehending the basic structure of a set of relationships by determining a complete solution to the problem posed (for example, an acceptable seating arrangement of all six diplomats around a table)

- Reasoning with conditional ("if-then") statements and recognizing logically equivalent formulations of such statements

- Inferring what could be true or must be true from given facts and rules

- Inferring what could be true or must be true from given facts and rules together with new information in the form of an additional or substitute fact or rule

- Recognizing when two statements are logically equivalent in context by identifying a condition or rule that could replace one of the original conditions while still resulting in the same possible outcomes

Analytical Reasoning questions reflect the kinds of detailed analyses of relationships and sets of constraints that a law student must perform in legal problem solving. For example, an Analytical Reasoning passage might describe six diplomats being seated around a table, following certain rules of protocol as to who can sit where. You, the test taker, must answer questions about the logical implications of given and new information. For example, you may be asked who can sit between diplomats X and Y, or who cannot sit next to X if W sits next to Y. Similarly, if you were a student in law school, you might be asked to analyze a scenario involving a set of particular circumstances and a set of governing rules in the form of constitutional provisions, statutes, administrative codes, or prior rulings that have been upheld. You might then be asked to determine the

legal options in the scenario: what is required given the scenario, what is permissible given the scenario, and what is prohibited given the scenario. Or you might be asked to develop a "theory" for the case: when faced with an incomplete set of facts about the case, you must fill in the picture based on what is implied by the facts that are known. The problem could be elaborated by the addition of new information or hypotheticals.

No formal training in logic is required to answer these questions correctly. Analytical Reasoning questions are intended to be answered using knowledge, skills, and reasoning ability generally expected of college students and graduates.

Suggested Approach

Some people may prefer to answer first those questions about a passage that seem less difficult and then those that seem more difficult. In general, it is best to finish one passage before starting on another, because much time can be lost in returning to a passage and reestablishing familiarity with its relationships. However, if you are having great difficulty on one particular set of questions and are spending too much time on them, it may be to your advantage to skip that set of questions and go on to the next passage, returning to the problematic set of questions after you have finished the other questions in the section.

Do not assume that because the conditions for a set of questions look long or complicated, the questions based on those conditions will be especially difficult.

Read the passage carefully. Careful reading and analysis are necessary to determine the exact nature of the relationships involved in an Analytical Reasoning passage. Some relationships are fixed (for example, P and R must always work on the same project). Other relationships are variable (for example, Q must be assigned to either team 1 or team 3). Some relationships that are not stated explicitly in the conditions are implied by and can be deduced from those that are stated (for example, if one condition about paintings in a display specifies that Painting K must be to the left of Painting Y, and another specifies that Painting W must be to the left of Painting K, then it can be deduced that Painting W must be to the left of Painting Y).

In reading the conditions, do not introduce unwarranted assumptions. For instance, in a set of questions establishing relationships of height and weight among the members of a team, do not assume that a person who is taller than another person must weigh more than that person. As another example, suppose a set involves ordering and a question in the set asks what must be true if both X and Y must be earlier than Z; in this case, do not assume that X must be earlier than Y merely because X is mentioned before Y. All the information needed to answer each question is provided in the passage and the question itself.

The conditions are designed to be as clear as possible. Do not interpret the conditions as if they were intended to trick you. For example, if a question asks how many people could be eligible to serve on a committee, consider only those people named in the passage unless directed otherwise. When in doubt, read the conditions in their most obvious sense. Remember, however, that the language in the conditions is intended to be read for precise meaning. It is essential to pay particular attention to words that describe or limit relationships, such as "only," "exactly," "never," "always," "must be," "cannot be," and the like.

The result of this careful reading will be a clear picture of the structure of the relationships involved, including the kinds of relationships permitted, the participants in the relationships, and the range of possible actions or attributes for these participants.

Keep in mind question independence. Each question should be considered separately from the other questions in its set. No information, except what is given in the original conditions, should be carried over from one question to another.

In some cases a question will simply ask for conclusions to be drawn from the conditions as originally given. Some questions may, however, add information to the original conditions or temporarily suspend or replace one of the original conditions for the purpose of that question only. For example, if Question 1 adds the supposition "if P is sitting at table 2 ...," this supposition should NOT be carried over to any other question in the set.

Logical Reasoning Questions

Arguments are a fundamental part of the law, and analyzing arguments is a key element of legal analysis. Training in the law builds on a foundation of basic reasoning skills. Law students must draw on the skills of analyzing, evaluating, constructing, and refuting arguments. They need to be able to identify what information is relevant to an issue or argument and what impact further evidence might have. They need to be able to reconcile opposing positions and use arguments to persuade others.

Logical Reasoning questions evaluate the ability to analyze, critically evaluate, and complete arguments as they occur in ordinary language. The questions are based on short arguments drawn from a wide variety of sources, including newspapers, general interest magazines, scholarly publications, advertisements, and informal discourse. These arguments mirror legal reasoning in the types of arguments presented and in their complexity, though few of the arguments actually have law as a subject matter.

Each Logical Reasoning question requires you to read and comprehend a short passage, then answer one question (or, rarely, two questions) about it. The questions are designed to assess a wide range of skills involved in thinking critically, with an emphasis on skills that are central to legal reasoning. These skills include:

- Recognizing the parts of an argument and their relationships

- Recognizing similarities and differences between patterns of reasoning

- Drawing well-supported conclusions

- Reasoning by analogy

- Recognizing misunderstandings or points of disagreement

- Determining how additional evidence affects an argument

- Detecting assumptions made by particular arguments

- Identifying and applying principles or rules

- Identifying flaws in arguments

- Identifying explanations

The questions do not presuppose specialized knowledge of logical terminology. For example, you will not be expected to know the meaning of specialized terms such as "ad hominem" or "syllogism." On the other hand, you will be expected to understand and critique the reasoning contained in arguments. This requires that you possess a university-level understanding of widely used concepts such as argument, premise, assumption, and conclusion.

Suggested Approach

Read each question carefully. Make sure that you understand the meaning of each part of the question. Make sure that you understand the meaning of each answer choice and the ways in which it may or may not relate to the question posed.

Do not pick a response simply because it is a true statement. Although true, it may not answer the question posed.

Answer each question on the basis of the information that is given, even if you do not agree with it. Work within the context provided by the passage. LSAT questions do not involve any tricks or hidden meanings.

Reading Comprehension Questions

Both law school and the practice of law revolve around extensive reading of highly varied, dense, argumentative, and expository texts (for example, cases, codes, contracts, briefs, decisions, evidence). This reading must be exacting, distinguishing precisely what is said from what is not said. It involves comparison, analysis, synthesis, and application (for example, of principles and rules). It involves drawing appropriate inferences and applying ideas and arguments to new contexts. Law school reading also requires the ability to grasp unfamiliar subject matter and the ability to penetrate difficult and challenging material.

The purpose of LSAT Reading Comprehension questions is to measure the ability to read, with understanding and insight, examples of lengthy and complex materials similar to those commonly encountered in law school. The Reading Comprehension section of the LSAT contains four sets of reading questions, each set consisting of a selection of reading material followed by five to eight questions. The reading selection in three of the four sets consists of a single reading passage; the other set contains two related shorter passages. Sets with two passages are a variant of Reading Comprehension called Comparative Reading, which was introduced in June 2007.

Comparative Reading questions concern the relationships between the two passages, such as those of generalization/instance, principle/application, or point/counterpoint. Law school work often requires reading two or more texts in conjunction with each other and understanding their relationships. For example, a law student may read a trial court decision together with an appellate court decision that overturns it, or identify the fact pattern from a hypothetical suit together with the potentially controlling case law.

Reading selections for LSAT Reading Comprehension questions are drawn from a wide range of subjects in the humanities, the social sciences, the biological and physical sciences, and areas related to the law. Generally, the selections are densely written, use high-level vocabulary, and contain sophisticated argument or complex rhetorical structure (for example, multiple points of view). Reading Comprehension questions require you to read carefully and accurately, to determine the relationships among the various parts of the reading selection, and to draw reasonable inferences from the material in the selection. The questions may ask about the following characteristics of a passage or pair of passages:

- The main idea or primary purpose

- Information that is explicitly stated

- Information or ideas that can be inferred

- The meaning or purpose of words or phrases as used in context

- The organization or structure

- The application of information in the selection to a new context

- Principles that function in the selection

- Analogies to claims or arguments in the selection

- An author's attitude as revealed in the tone of a passage or the language used

- The impact of new information on claims or arguments in the selection

Suggested Approach

Since reading selections are drawn from many different disciplines and sources, you should not be discouraged if you encounter material with which you are not familiar. It is important to remember that questions are to be answered exclusively on the basis of the information provided in the selection. There is no particular knowledge that you are expected to bring to the test, and you should not make inferences based on any prior knowledge of a subject that you may have. You may, however, wish to defer working on a set of questions that seems particularly difficult or unfamiliar until after you have dealt with sets you find easier.

Strategies. One question that often arises in connection with Reading Comprehension has to do with the most effective and efficient order in which to read the selections and questions. Possible approaches include:

- reading the selection very closely and then answering the questions;

- reading the questions first, reading the selection closely, and then returning to the questions; or

- skimming the selection and questions very quickly, then rereading the selection closely and answering the questions.

Test takers are different, and the best strategy for one might not be the best strategy for another. In preparing for the test, therefore, you might want to experiment with the different strategies and decide what works most effectively for you. Remember that your strategy must be effective under timed conditions. For this reason, the first strategy—reading the selection very closely and then answering the questions—may be the most effective for you. Nonetheless, if you believe that one of the other strategies might be more effective for you, you should try it out and assess your performance using it.

Reading the selection. Whatever strategy you choose, you should give the passage or pair of passages at least one careful reading before answering the questions. Try to distinguish main ideas from supporting ideas, and opinions or attitudes from factual, objective information. Note transitions from one idea to the next and identify the relationships among the different ideas or parts of a passage, or between the two passages in Comparative Reading sets. Consider how and why an author makes points and draws conclusions. Be sensitive to implications of what the passages say.

You may find it helpful to mark key parts of passages. For example, you might underline main ideas or important arguments, and you might circle transitional words—"although," "nevertheless," "correspondingly," and the like—that will help you map the structure of a passage. Also, you might note descriptive words that will help you identify an author's attitude toward a particular idea or person.

Answering the Questions

- Always read all the answer choices before selecting the best answer. The best answer choice is the one that most accurately and completely answers the question being posed.

- Respond to the specific question being asked. Do not pick an answer choice simply because it is a true statement. For example, picking a true statement might yield an incorrect answer to a question in which you are asked to identify an author's position on an issue, since you are not being asked to evaluate the truth of the author's position but only to correctly identify what that position is.

- Answer the questions only on the basis of the information provided in the selection. Your own views, interpretations, or opinions, and those you have heard from others, may sometimes conflict with those expressed in a reading selection; however, you are expected to work within the context provided by the reading selection. You should not expect to agree with everything you encounter in Reading Comprehension passages.

THE WRITING SAMPLE*

You will be asked to write one sample essay. LSAC does not score the writing sample, but copies are sent to all law schools to which you apply. According to a 2006 LSAC survey of 157 United States and Canadian law schools, almost all use the writing sample in evaluating at least some applications for admission. Failure to respond to writing sample prompts and frivolous responses have been used by law schools as grounds for rejection of applications for admission.

In developing and implementing the writing sample portion of the LSAT, LSAC has operated on the following premises: First, law schools and the legal profession value highly the ability to communicate effectively in writing. Second, it is important to encourage potential law students to develop effective writing skills. Third, a sample of an applicant's writing, produced under controlled conditions, is a potentially useful indication of that person's writing ability. Fourth, the writing sample can serve as an independent check on other writing submitted by applicants as part

---

*Note: The writing sample is now administered on a secure, proctored online platform at a time and place of your choosing. Visit LSAC.org for more details.

of the admission process. Finally, writing samples may be useful for diagnostic purposes related to improving a candidate's writing.

The writing prompt presents a decision problem. You are asked to make a choice between two positions or courses of action. Both of the choices are defensible, and you are given criteria and facts on which to base your decision. There is no "right" or "wrong" position to take on the topic, so the quality of each test taker's response is a function not of which choice is made, but of how well or poorly the choice is supported and how well or poorly the other choice is criticized.

The LSAT writing prompt was designed and validated by legal education professionals. Since it involves writing based on fact sets and criteria, the writing sample gives applicants the opportunity to demonstrate the type of argumentative writing that is required in law school, although the topics are usually nonlegal.

You will have 35 minutes in which to plan and write an essay on the topic you receive. Read the topic and the accompanying directions carefully. You will probably find it best to spend a few minutes considering the topic and organizing your thoughts before you begin writing. In your essay, be sure to develop your ideas fully, leaving time, if possible, to review what you have written. Do not write on a topic other than the one specified. Writing on a topic of your own choice is not acceptable.

No special knowledge is required or expected for this writing exercise. Law schools are interested in the reasoning, clarity, organization, language usage, and writing mechanics displayed in your essay. How well you write is more important than how much you write.

TAKING THE PREPTESTS UNDER SIMULATED LSAT CONDITIONS

One important way to prepare for the LSAT is to simulate the day of the test by taking a practice test under actual time constraints. Taking a practice test under timed conditions helps you to estimate the amount of time you can afford to spend on each question in a section and to determine the question types on which you may need additional practice.

Since the LSAT is a timed test, it is important to use your allotted time wisely. During the test, you may work only on the section designated by the test supervisor. You cannot devote extra time to a difficult section and make up that time on a section you find easier. In pacing yourself, and checking your answers, you should think of each section of the test as a separate minitest.

Be sure that you answer every question on the test. When you do not know the correct answer to a question, first eliminate the responses that you know are incorrect, then make your best guess among the remaining choices. Do not be afraid to guess as there is no penalty for incorrect answers.

When you take a practice test, abide by all the

requirements specified in the directions and keep strictly within the specified time limits. Work without a rest period. When you take an actual test, you will have a short break between two of the sections.

When taken under conditions as much like actual testing conditions as possible, a practice test provides very useful preparation for taking the LSAT.

Official directions for the four multiple-choice sections and the writing samples are included in these PrepTests so that you can approximate actual testing conditions as you practice.

To take the test:

- Set a timer for 35 minutes. Answer all the questions in Section I. Stop working on that section when the 35 minutes have elapsed.

- Repeat, allowing yourself 35 minutes each for Sections II, III, and IV.

- Set the timer again for 35 minutes, then prepare your response to the writing sample topic at the end of each PrepTest.

- Refer to the "Computing Your Score" section at the end of each PrepTest for instruction on evaluating your performance. An answer key is provided for that purpose.

The Official LSAT PrepTest

52

- September 2007
  PrepTest 52

- Form 7LSN73

SECTION I

Time—35 minutes

25 Questions

<u>Directions:</u> The questions in this section are based on the reasoning contained in brief statements or passages. For some questions, more than one of the choices could conceivably answer the question. However, you are to choose the <u>best</u> answer; that is, the response that most accurately and completely answers the question. You should not make assumptions that are by commonsense standards implausible, superfluous, or incompatible with the passage. After you have chosen the best answer, blacken the corresponding space on your answer sheet.

1. Certain companies require their managers to rank workers in the groups they supervise from best to worst, giving each worker a unique ranking based on job performance. The top 10 percent of the workers in each group are rewarded and the bottom 10 percent are penalized or fired. But this system is unfair to workers. Good workers could receive low rankings merely because they belong to groups of exceptionally good workers. Furthermore, managers often give the highest rankings to workers who share the manager's interests outside of work.

   Which one of the following most accurately expresses the conclusion drawn in the argument?

   (A) Some companies require their managers to give unique rankings to the workers they supervise.
   (B) Under the ranking system, the top 10 percent of the workers in each group are rewarded and the bottom 10 percent are penalized or fired.
   (C) The ranking system is not a fair way to determine penalties or rewards for workers.
   (D) Workers in exceptionally strong work groups are unfairly penalized under the ranking system.
   (E) Managers often give the highest rankings to workers who share the manager's outside interests.

2. Psychologist: A study of 436 university students found that those who took short naps throughout the day suffered from insomnia more frequently than those who did not. Moreover, people who work on commercial fishing vessels often have irregular sleep patterns that include frequent napping, and they also suffer from insomnia. So it is very likely that napping tends to cause insomnia.

   The reasoning in the psychologist's argument is most vulnerable to criticism on the grounds that the argument

   (A) presumes, without providing justification, that university students suffer from insomnia more frequently than do members of the general population
   (B) presumes that all instances of insomnia have the same cause
   (C) fails to provide a scientifically respectable definition for the term "napping"
   (D) fails to consider the possibility that frequent daytime napping is an effect rather than a cause of insomnia
   (E) presumes, without providing justification, that there is such a thing as a regular sleep pattern for someone working on a commercial fishing vessel

GO ON TO THE NEXT PAGE.

3. Whenever Joe's car is vacuumed, the employees of K & L Auto vacuum it; they are the only people who ever vacuum Joe's car. If the employees of K & L Auto vacuumed Joe's car, then Joe took his car to K & L Auto to be fixed. Joe's car was recently vacuumed. Therefore, Joe took his car to K & L Auto to be fixed.

The pattern of reasoning exhibited by the argument above is most similar to that exhibited by which one of the following?

(A) Emily's water glass is wet and it would be wet only if she drank water from it this morning. Since the only time she drinks water in the morning is when she takes her medication, Emily took her medication this morning.

(B) Lisa went to the hair salon today since either she went to the hair salon today or she went to the bank this morning, but Lisa did not go to the bank this morning.

(C) There are no bills on John's kitchen table. Since John gets at least one bill per day and he always puts his bills on his kitchen table, someone else must have checked John's mail today.

(D) Linda is grumpy only if she does not have her coffee in the morning, and Linda does not have her coffee in the morning only if she runs out of coffee. Therefore, Linda runs out of coffee only on days that she is grumpy.

(E) Jeff had to choose either a grapefruit or cereal for breakfast this morning. Given that Jeff is allergic to grapefruit, Jeff must have had cereal for breakfast this morning.

4. Editorialist: In a large corporation, one of the functions of the corporation's president is to promote the key interests of the shareholders. Therefore, the president has a duty to keep the corporation's profits high.

Which one of the following, if true, would most strengthen the editorialist's argument?

(A) Shareholders sometimes will be satisfied even if dividends paid to them from company profits are not high.

(B) The president and the board of directors of a corporation are jointly responsible for advancing the key interests of the shareholders.

(C) Keeping a corporation's profits high is likely to advance the important interests of the corporation's shareholders.

(D) In considering where to invest, most potential shareholders are interested in more than just the profitability of a corporation.

(E) The president of a corporation has many functions besides advancing the important interests of the corporation's shareholders.

5. Everyone in Biba's neighborhood is permitted to swim at Barton Pool at some time during each day that it is open. No children under the age of 6 are permitted to swim at Barton Pool between noon and 5 P.M. From 5 P.M. until closing, Barton Pool is reserved for adults only.

If all the sentences above are true, then which one of the following must be true?

(A) Few children under the age of 6 live in Biba's neighborhood.

(B) If Biba's next-door neighbor has a child under the age of 6, then Barton Pool is open before noon.

(C) If most children who swim in Barton Pool swim in the afternoon, then the pool is generally less crowded after 5 P.M.

(D) On days when Barton Pool is open, at least some children swim there in the afternoon.

(E) Any child swimming in Barton Pool before 5 P.M. must be breaking Barton Pool rules.

6. Beck: Our computer program estimates municipal automotive use based on weekly data. Some staff question the accuracy of the program's estimates. But because the figures it provides are remarkably consistent from week to week, we can be confident of its accuracy.

The reasoning in Beck's argument is flawed in that it

(A) fails to establish that consistency is a more important consideration than accuracy

(B) fails to consider the program's accuracy in other tasks that it may perform

(C) takes for granted that the program's output would be consistent even if its estimates were inaccurate

(D) regards accuracy as the sole criterion for judging the program's value

(E) fails to consider that the program could produce consistent but inaccurate output

GO ON TO THE NEXT PAGE.

7. Inertia affects the flow of water pumped through a closed system of pipes. When the pump is first switched on, the water, which has mass, takes time to reach full speed. When the pump is switched off, inertia causes the decrease in the water flow to be gradual. The effects of inductance in electrical circuits are similar to the effects of inertia in water pipes.

The information above provides the most support for which one of the following?

(A) The rate at which electrical current flows is affected by inductance.
(B) The flow of electrical current in a circuit requires inertia.
(C) Inertia in the flow of water pumped by an electrically powered pump is caused by inductance in the pump's circuits.
(D) Electrical engineers try to minimize the effects of inductance in electrical circuits.
(E) When a water pump is switched off it continues to pump water for a second or two.

8. Journalist: To reconcile the need for profits sufficient to support new drug research with the moral imperative to provide medicines to those who most need them but cannot afford them, some pharmaceutical companies feel justified in selling a drug in rich nations at one price and in poor nations at a much lower price. But this practice is unjustified. A nation with a low average income may still have a substantial middle class better able to pay for new drugs than are many of the poorer citizens of an overall wealthier nation.

Which one of the following principles, if valid, most helps to justify the journalist's reasoning?

(A) People who are ill deserve more consideration than do healthy people, regardless of their relative socioeconomic positions.
(B) Wealthy institutions have an obligation to expend at least some of their resources to assist those incapable of assisting themselves.
(C) Whether one deserves special consideration depends on one's needs rather than on characteristics of the society to which one belongs.
(D) The people in wealthy nations should not have better access to health care than do the people in poorer nations.
(E) Unequal access to health care is more unfair than an unequal distribution of wealth.

9. Robert: The school board is considering adopting a year-round academic schedule that eliminates the traditional three-month summer vacation. This schedule should be adopted, since teachers need to cover more new material during the school year than they do now.

Samantha: The proposed schedule will not permit teachers to cover more new material. Even though the schedule eliminates summer vacation, it adds six new two-week breaks, so the total number of school days will be about the same as before.

Which one of the following, if true, is a response Robert could make that would counter Samantha's argument?

(A) Teachers would be willing to accept elimination of the traditional three-month summer vacation as long as the total vacation time they are entitled to each year is not reduced.
(B) Most parents who work outside the home find it difficult to arrange adequate supervision for their school-age children over the traditional three-month summer vacation.
(C) In school districts that have adopted a year-round schedule that increases the number of school days per year, students show a deeper understanding and better retention of new material.
(D) Teachers spend no more than a day of class time reviewing old material when students have been away from school for only a few weeks, but have to spend up to a month of class time reviewing after a three-month summer vacation.
(E) Students prefer taking a long vacation from school during the summer to taking more frequent but shorter vacations spread throughout the year.

GO ON TO THE NEXT PAGE.

10. In order to reduce traffic congestion and raise revenue for the city, the mayor plans to implement a charge of $10 per day for driving in the downtown area. Payment of this charge will be enforced using a highly sophisticated system that employs digital cameras and computerized automobile registration. This system will not be ready until the end of next year. Without this system, however, mass evasion of the charge will result. Therefore, when the mayor's plan is first implemented, payment of the charge will not be effectively enforced.

Which one of the following is an assumption on which the argument depends for its conclusion to be properly drawn?

(A) The mayor's plan to charge for driving downtown will be implemented before the end of next year.
(B) The city will incur a budget deficit if it does not receive the revenue it expects to raise from the charge for driving downtown.
(C) The plan to charge for driving downtown should be implemented as soon as payment of the charge can be effectively enforced.
(D) Raising revenue is a more important consideration for the city than is reducing traffic congestion.
(E) A daily charge for driving downtown is the most effective way to reduce traffic congestion.

11. A recent study revealed that the percentage of people treated at large, urban hospitals who recover from their illnesses is lower than the percentage for people treated at smaller, rural hospitals.

Each of the following, if true, contributes to an explanation of the difference in recovery rates EXCEPT:

(A) Because there are fewer patients to feed, nutritionists at small hospitals are better able to tailor meals to the dietary needs of each patient.
(B) The less friendly, more impersonal atmosphere of large hospitals can be a source of stress for patients at those hospitals.
(C) Although large hospitals tend to draw doctors trained at the more prestigious schools, no correlation has been found between the prestige of a doctor's school and patients' recovery rate.
(D) Because space is relatively scarce in large hospitals, doctors are encouraged to minimize the length of time that patients are held for observation following a medical procedure.
(E) Doctors at large hospitals tend to have a greater number of patients and consequently less time to explain to staff and to patients how medications are to be administered.

12. Perry: Worker-owned businesses require workers to spend time on management decision-making and investment strategy, tasks that are not directly productive. Also, such businesses have less extensive divisions of labor than do investor-owned businesses. Such inefficiencies can lead to low profitability, and thus increase the risk for lenders. Therefore, lenders seeking to reduce their risk should not make loans to worker-owned businesses.

Which one of the following, if true, most seriously weakens Perry's argument?

(A) Businesses with the most extensive divisions of labor sometimes fail to make the fullest use of their most versatile employees' potential.
(B) Lenders who specialize in high-risk loans are the largest source of loans for worker-owned businesses.
(C) Investor-owned businesses are more likely than worker-owned businesses are to receive start-up loans.
(D) Worker-owned businesses have traditionally obtained loans from cooperative lending institutions established by coalitions of worker-owned businesses.
(E) In most worker-owned businesses, workers compensate for inefficiencies by working longer hours than do workers in investor-owned businesses.

13. Some paleontologists believe that certain species of dinosaurs guarded their young in protective nests long after the young hatched. As evidence, they cite the discovery of fossilized hadrosaur babies and adolescents in carefully designed nests. But similar nests for hatchlings and adolescents are constructed by modern crocodiles, even though crocodiles guard their young only for a very brief time after they hatch. Hence, _____.

Which one of the following most logically completes the argument?

(A) paleontologists who believe that hadrosaurs guarded their young long after the young hatched have no evidence to support this belief
(B) we will never be able to know the extent to which hadrosaurs guarded their young
(C) hadrosaurs guarded their young for at most very brief periods after hatching
(D) it is unclear whether what we learn about hadrosaurs from their fossilized remains tells us anything about other dinosaurs
(E) the construction of nests for hatchlings and adolescents is not strong evidence for the paleontologists' belief

14. For one academic year all the students at a high school were observed. The aim was to test the hypothesis that studying more increased a student's chances of earning a higher grade. It turned out that the students who spent the most time studying did not earn grades as high as did many students who studied less. Nonetheless, the researchers concluded that the results of the observation supported the initial hypothesis.

Which one of the following, if true, most helps to explain why the researchers drew the conclusion described above?

(A) The students who spent the most time studying earned higher grades than did some students who studied for less time than the average.

(B) The students tended to get slightly lower grades as the academic year progressed.

(C) In each course, the more a student studied, the better his or her grade was in that course.

(D) The students who spent the least time studying tended to be students with no more than average involvement in extracurricular activities.

(E) Students who spent more time studying understood the course material better than other students did.

15. Researchers had three groups of professional cyclists cycle for one hour at different levels of intensity. Members of groups A, B, and C cycled at rates that sustained, for an hour, pulses of about 60 percent, 70 percent, and 85 percent, respectively, of the recommended maximum pulse rate for recreational cyclists. Most members of Group A reported being less depressed and angry afterward. Most members of Group B did not report these benefits. Most members of Group C reported feeling worse in these respects than before the exercise.

Which one of the following is most strongly supported by the information above?

(A) The higher the pulse rate attained in sustained exercise, the less psychological benefit the exercise tends to produce.

(B) The effect that a period of cycling has on the mood of professional cyclists tends to depend at least in part on how intense the cycling is.

(C) For professional cyclists, the best exercise from the point of view of improving mood is cycling that pushes the pulse no higher than 60 percent of the maximum pulse rate.

(D) Physical factors, including pulse rate, contribute as much to depression as do psychological factors.

(E) Moderate cycling tends to benefit professional cyclists physically as much or more than intense cycling.

16. Anyone who believes in extraterrestrials believes in UFOs. But the existence of UFOs has been conclusively refuted. Therefore a belief in extraterrestrials is false as well.

Which one of the following arguments contains flawed reasoning most similar to that in the argument above?

(A) Anyone who believes in unicorns believes in centaurs. But it has been demonstrated that there are no centaurs, so there are no unicorns either.

(B) Anyone who believes in unicorns believes in centaurs. But you do not believe in centaurs, so you do not believe in unicorns either.

(C) Anyone who believes in unicorns believes in centaurs. But you do not believe in unicorns, so you do not believe in centaurs either.

(D) Anyone who believes in unicorns believes in centaurs. But there is no good reason to believe in centaurs, so a belief in unicorns is unjustified as well.

(E) Anyone who believes in unicorns believes in centaurs. But it has been conclusively proven that there is no such thing as a unicorn, so a belief in centaurs is mistaken as well.

17. People want to be instantly and intuitively liked. Those persons who are perceived as forming opinions of others only after cautiously gathering and weighing the evidence are generally resented. Thus, it is imprudent to appear prudent.

Which one of the following, if assumed, enables the argument's conclusion to be properly drawn?

(A) People who act spontaneously are well liked.

(B) Imprudent people act instantly and intuitively.

(C) People resent those less prudent than themselves.

(D) People who are intuitive know instantly when they like someone.

(E) It is imprudent to cause people to resent you.

GO ON TO THE NEXT PAGE.

18. Journalist: Recent studies have demonstrated that a regular smoker who has just smoked a cigarette will typically display significantly better short-term memory skills than a nonsmoker, whether or not the nonsmoker has also just smoked a cigarette for the purposes of the study. Moreover, the majority of those smokers who exhibit this superiority in short-term memory skills will do so for at least eight hours after having last smoked.

If the journalist's statements are true, then each of the following could be true EXCEPT:

(A) The short-term memory skills exhibited by a nonsmoker who has just smoked a cigarette are usually substantially worse than the short-term memory skills exhibited by a nonsmoker who has not recently smoked a cigarette.

(B) The short-term memory skills exhibited by a nonsmoker who has just smoked a cigarette are typically superior to those exhibited by a regular smoker who has just smoked a cigarette.

(C) The short-term memory skills exhibited by a nonsmoker who has just smoked a cigarette are typically superior to those exhibited by a regular smoker who has not smoked for more than eight hours.

(D) A regular smoker who, immediately after smoking a cigarette, exhibits short-term memory skills no better than those typically exhibited by a nonsmoker is nevertheless likely to exhibit superior short-term memory skills in the hours following a period of heavy smoking.

(E) The short-term memory skills exhibited by a regular smoker who last smoked a cigarette five hours ago are typically superior to those exhibited by a regular smoker who has just smoked a cigarette.

19. Educator: It has been argued that our professional organization should make decisions about important issues—such as raising dues and taking political stands—by a direct vote of all members rather than by having members vote for officers who in turn make the decisions. This would not, however, be the right way to decide these matters, for the vote of any given individual is much more likely to determine organizational policy by influencing the election of an officer than by influencing the result of a direct vote on a single issue.

Which one of the following principles would, if valid, most help to justify the educator's reasoning?

(A) No procedure for making organizational decisions should allow one individual's vote to weigh more than that of another.

(B) Outcomes of organizational elections should be evaluated according to their benefit to the organization as a whole, not according to the fairness of the methods by which they are produced.

(C) Important issues facing organizations should be decided by people who can devote their full time to mastering the information relevant to the issues.

(D) An officer of an organization should not make a particular decision on an issue unless a majority of the organization's members would approve of that decision.

(E) An organization's procedures for making organizational decisions should maximize the power of each member of the organization to influence the decisions made.

GO ON TO THE NEXT PAGE.

20. Neural connections carrying signals from the cortex (the brain region responsible for thought) down to the amygdala (a brain region crucial for emotions) are less well developed than connections carrying signals from the amygdala up to the cortex. Thus, the amygdala exerts a greater influence on the cortex than vice versa.

The argument's conclusion follows logically if which one of the following is assumed?

(A) The influence that the amygdala exerts on the rest of the brain is dependent on the influence that the cortex exerts on the rest of the brain.

(B) No other brain region exerts more influence on the cortex than does the amygdala.

(C) The region of the brain that has the most influence on the cortex is the one that has the most highly developed neural connections to the cortex.

(D) The amygdala is not itself controlled by one or more other regions of the brain.

(E) The degree of development of a set of neural connections is directly proportional to the influence transmitted across those connections.

21. The *Iliad* and the *Odyssey* were both attributed to Homer in ancient times. But these two poems differ greatly in tone and vocabulary and in certain details of the fictional world they depict. So they are almost certainly not the work of the same poet.

Which one of the following statements, if true, most weakens the reasoning above?

(A) Several hymns that were also attributed to Homer in ancient times differ more from the *Iliad* in the respects mentioned than does the *Odyssey*.

(B) Both the *Iliad* and the *Odyssey* have come down to us in manuscripts that have suffered from minor copying errors and other textual corruptions.

(C) Works known to have been written by the same modern writer are as different from each other in the respects mentioned as are the *Iliad* and the *Odyssey*.

(D) Neither the *Iliad* nor the *Odyssey* taken by itself is completely consistent in all of the respects mentioned.

(E) Both the *Iliad* and the *Odyssey* were the result of an extended process of oral composition in which many poets were involved.

22. Moralist: A statement is wholly truthful only if it is true and made without intended deception. A statement is a lie if it is intended to deceive or if its speaker, upon learning that the statement was misinterpreted, refrains from clarifying it.

Which one of the following judgments most closely conforms to the principles stated by the moralist?

(A) Ted's statement to the investigator that he had been abducted by extraterrestrial beings was wholly truthful even though no one has ever been abducted by extraterrestrial beings. After all, Ted was not trying to deceive the investigator.

(B) Tony was not lying when he told his granddaughter that he did not wear dentures, for even though Tony meant to deceive his granddaughter, she made it clear to Tony that she did not believe him.

(C) Siobhan did not tell a lie when she told her supervisor that she was ill and hence would not be able to come to work for an important presentation. However, even though her statement was true, it was not wholly truthful.

(D) Walter's claim to a potential employer that he had done volunteer work was a lie. Even though Walter had worked without pay in his father's factory, he used the phrase "volunteer work" in an attempt to deceive the interviewer into thinking he had worked for a socially beneficial cause.

(E) The tour guide intended to deceive the tourists when he told them that the cabin they were looking at was centuries old. Still, his statement about the cabin's age was not a lie, for if he thought that this statement had been misinterpreted, he would have tried to clarify it.

GO ON TO THE NEXT PAGE.

23. Principle: It is healthy for children to engage in an activity that promotes their intellectual development only if engaging in that activity does not detract from their social development.

Application: Although Megan's frequent reading stimulates her intellectually, it reduces the amount of time she spends interacting with other people. Therefore, it is not healthy for her to read as much as she does.

The application of the principle is most vulnerable to criticism on which one of the following grounds?

(A) It misinterprets the principle as a universal claim intended to hold in all cases without exception, rather than as a mere generalization.
(B) It overlooks the possibility that the benefits of a given activity may sometimes be important enough to outweigh the adverse health effects.
(C) It misinterprets the principle to be, at least in part, a claim about what is unhealthy, rather than solely a claim about what is healthy.
(D) It takes for granted that any decrease in the amount of time a child spends interacting with others detracts from that child's social development.
(E) It takes a necessary condition for an activity's being healthy as a sufficient condition for its being so.

24. In response to several bacterial infections traced to its apple juice, McElligott now flash pasteurizes its apple juice by quickly heating and immediately rechilling it. Intensive pasteurization, in which juice is heated for an hour, eliminates bacteria more effectively than does any other method, but is likely to destroy the original flavor. However, because McElligott's citrus juices have not been linked to any bacterial infections, they remain unpasteurized.

The statements above, if true, provide the most support for which one of the following claims?

(A) McElligott's citrus juices contain fewer infectious bacteria than do citrus juices produced by other companies.
(B) McElligott's apple juice is less likely to contain infectious bacteria than are McElligott's citrus juices.
(C) McElligott's citrus juices retain more of the juices' original flavor than do any pasteurized citrus juices.
(D) The most effective method for eliminating bacteria from juice is also the method most likely to destroy flavor.
(E) Apple juice that undergoes intensive pasteurization is less likely than McElligott's apple juice is to contain bacteria.

25. Sociologist: Widespread acceptance of the idea that individuals are incapable of looking after their own welfare is injurious to a democracy. So legislators who value democracy should not propose any law prohibiting behavior that is not harmful to anyone besides the person engaging in it. After all, the assumptions that appear to guide legislators will often become widely accepted.

The sociologist's argument requires the assumption that

(A) democratically elected legislators invariably have favorable attitudes toward the preservation of democracy
(B) people tend to believe what is believed by those who are prominent and powerful
(C) legislators often seem to be guided by the assumption that individuals are incapable of looking after their own welfare, even though these legislators also seem to value democracy
(D) in most cases, behavior that is harmful to the person who engages in it is harmful to no one else
(E) a legislator proposing a law prohibiting an act that can harm only the person performing the act will seem to be assuming that individuals are incapable of looking after their own welfare

S T O P

IF YOU FINISH BEFORE TIME IS CALLED, YOU MAY CHECK YOUR WORK ON THIS SECTION ONLY.
DO NOT WORK ON ANY OTHER SECTION IN THE TEST.

SECTION II

Time—35 minutes

23 Questions

Directions: Each group of questions in this section is based on a set of conditions. In answering some of the questions, it may be useful to draw a rough diagram. Choose the response that most accurately and completely answers each question and blacken the corresponding space on your answer sheet.

Questions 1–7

Workers at a water treatment plant open eight valves—G, H, I, K, L, N, O, and P—to flush out a system of pipes that needs emergency repairs. To maximize safety and efficiency, each valve is opened exactly once, and no two valves are opened at the same time. The valves are opened in accordance with the following conditions:

Both K and P are opened before H.
O is opened before L but after H.
L is opened after G.
N is opened before H.
I is opened after K.

1. Which one of the following could be the order, from first to last, in which the valves are opened?

    (A)   P, I, K, G, N, H, O, L
    (B)   P, G, K, N, L, H, O, I
    (C)   G, K, I, P, H, O, N, L
    (D)   N, K, P, H, O, I, L, G
    (E)   K, I, N, G, P, H, O, L

2. Each of the following could be the fifth valve opened EXCEPT:

    (A)   H
    (B)   I
    (C)   K
    (D)   N
    (E)   O

3. If I is the second valve opened, then each of the following could be true EXCEPT:

    (A)   G is the third valve opened.
    (B)   H is the fourth valve opened.
    (C)   P is the fifth valve opened.
    (D)   O is the sixth valve opened.
    (E)   G is the seventh valve opened.

4. If L is the seventh valve opened, then each of the following could be the second valve opened EXCEPT:

    (A)   G
    (B)   I
    (C)   K
    (D)   N
    (E)   P

5. Which one of the following must be true?

    (A)   At least one valve is opened before P is opened.
    (B)   At least two valves are opened before G is opened.
    (C)   No more than two valves are opened after O is opened.
    (D)   No more than three valves are opened after H is opened.
    (E)   No more than four valves are opened before N is opened.

6. If K is the fourth valve opened, then which one of the following could be true?

    (A)   I is the second valve opened.
    (B)   N is the third valve opened.
    (C)   G is the fifth valve opened.
    (D)   O is the fifth valve opened.
    (E)   P is the sixth valve opened.

7. If G is the first valve opened and I is the third valve opened, then each of the following must be true EXCEPT:

    (A)   K is the second valve opened.
    (B)   N is the fourth valve opened.
    (C)   H is the sixth valve opened.
    (D)   O is the seventh valve opened.
    (E)   L is the eighth valve opened.

GO ON TO THE NEXT PAGE.

Questions 8–12

On a field trip to the Museum of Natural History, each of six children—Juana, Kyle, Lucita, Salim, Thanh, and Veronica—is accompanied by one of three adults—Ms. Margoles, Mr. O'Connell, and Ms. Podorski. Each adult accompanies exactly two of the children, consistent with the following conditions:

If Ms. Margoles accompanies Juana, then Ms. Podorski accompanies Lucita.

If Kyle is not accompanied by Ms. Margoles, then Veronica is accompanied by Mr. O'Connell.

Either Ms. Margoles or Mr. O'Connell accompanies Thanh.

Juana is not accompanied by the same adult as Kyle; nor is Lucita accompanied by the same adult as Salim; nor is Thanh accompanied by the same adult as Veronica.

8. Which one of the following could be an accurate matching of the adults to the children they accompany?

(A) Ms. Margoles: Juana, Thanh; Mr. O'Connell: Lucita, Veronica; Ms. Podorski: Kyle, Salim

(B) Ms. Margoles: Kyle, Thanh; Mr. O'Connell: Juana, Salim; Ms. Podorski: Lucita, Veronica

(C) Ms. Margoles: Lucita, Thanh; Mr. O'Connell: Juana, Salim; Ms. Podorski: Kyle, Veronica

(D) Ms. Margoles: Kyle, Veronica; Mr. O'Connell: Juana, Thanh; Ms. Podorski: Lucita, Salim

(E) Ms. Margoles: Salim, Veronica; Mr. O'Connell: Kyle, Lucita; Ms. Podorski: Juana, Thanh

9. If Ms. Margoles accompanies Lucita and Thanh, then which one of the following must be true?

(A) Juana is accompanied by the same adult as Veronica.

(B) Kyle is accompanied by the same adult as Salim.

(C) Juana is accompanied by Mr. O'Connell.

(D) Kyle is accompanied by Ms. Podorski.

(E) Salim is accompanied by Ms. Podorski.

10. If Ms. Podorski accompanies Juana and Veronica, then Ms. Margoles could accompany which one of the following pairs of children?

(A) Kyle and Salim

(B) Kyle and Thanh

(C) Lucita and Salim

(D) Lucita and Thanh

(E) Salim and Thanh

11. Ms. Podorski CANNOT accompany which one of the following pairs of children?

(A) Juana and Lucita

(B) Juana and Salim

(C) Kyle and Salim

(D) Salim and Thanh

(E) Salim and Veronica

12. Mr. O'Connell CANNOT accompany which one of the following pairs of children?

(A) Juana and Lucita

(B) Juana and Veronica

(C) Kyle and Thanh

(D) Lucita and Thanh

(E) Salim and Veronica

GO ON TO THE NEXT PAGE.

Questions 13–17

Three short seminars—Goals, Objections, and Persuasion—and three long seminars—Humor, Negotiating, and Telemarketing—will be scheduled for a three-day sales training conference. On each day, two of the seminars will be given consecutively. Each seminar will be given exactly once. The schedule must conform to the following conditions:

   Exactly one short seminar and exactly one long seminar will be given each day.
   Telemarketing will not be given until both Goals and Objections have been given.
   Negotiating will not be given until Persuasion has been given.

13. Which one of the following could be an accurate schedule for the sales training conference?

   (A)   first day: Persuasion followed by Negotiating
         second day: Objections followed by Telemarketing
         third day: Goals followed by Humor
   (B)   first day: Objections followed by Humor
         second day: Goals followed by Telemarketing
         third day: Persuasion followed by Negotiating
   (C)   first day: Objections followed by Negotiating
         second day: Persuasion followed by Humor
         third day: Goals followed by Telemarketing
   (D)   first day: Objections followed by Goals
         second day: Telemarketing followed by Persuasion
         third day: Negotiating followed by Humor
   (E)   first day: Goals followed by Humor
         second day: Persuasion followed by Telemarketing
         third day: Objections followed by Negotiating

14. If Goals is given on the first day of the sales training conference, then which one of the following could be true?

   (A)   Negotiating is given on the first day.
   (B)   Objections is given on the first day.
   (C)   Persuasion is given on the first day.
   (D)   Humor is given on the second day.
   (E)   Telemarketing is given on the second day.

15. If Negotiating is given at some time before Objections, then which one of the following must be true?

   (A)   Negotiating is given at some time before Goals.
   (B)   Persuasion is given at some time before Goals.
   (C)   Persuasion is given at some time before Objections.
   (D)   Humor is given at some time before Objections.
   (E)   Negotiating is given at some time before Humor.

16. Which one of the following CANNOT be the second seminar given on the second day of the sales training conference?

   (A)   Humor
   (B)   Persuasion
   (C)   Objections
   (D)   Negotiating
   (E)   Goals

17. If Humor is given on the second day of the sales training conference, then which one of the following could be true?

   (A)   Telemarketing is given on the first day.
   (B)   Negotiating is given on the second day.
   (C)   Telemarketing is given on the second day.
   (D)   Objections is given on the third day.
   (E)   Persuasion is given on the third day.

GO ON TO THE NEXT PAGE.

Questions 18–23

A bread truck makes exactly one bread delivery to each of six restaurants in succession—Figueroa's, Ginsberg's, Harris's, Kanzaki's, Leacock's, and Malpighi's—though not necessarily in that order. The following conditions must apply:

> Ginsberg's delivery is earlier than Kanzaki's but later than Figueroa's.
> Harris's delivery is earlier than Ginsberg's.
> If Figueroa's delivery is earlier than Malpighi's, then Leacock's delivery is earlier than Harris's.
> Either Malpighi's delivery is earlier than Harris's or it is later than Kanzaki's, but not both.

18. Which one of the following accurately represents an order in which the deliveries could occur, from first to last?

    (A)   Harris's, Figueroa's, Leacock's, Ginsberg's, Kanzaki's, Malpighi's
    (B)   Leacock's, Harris's, Figueroa's, Ginsberg's, Malpighi's, Kanzaki's
    (C)   Malpighi's, Figueroa's, Harris's, Ginsberg's, Leacock's, Kanzaki's
    (D)   Malpighi's, Figueroa's, Kanzaki's, Harris's, Ginsberg's, Leacock's
    (E)   Malpighi's, Figueroa's, Ginsberg's, Kanzaki's, Harris's, Leacock's

19. If Figueroa's delivery is fourth, then which one of the following must be true?

    (A)   Ginsberg's delivery is fifth.
    (B)   Harris's delivery is second.
    (C)   Harris's delivery is third.
    (D)   Leacock's delivery is second.
    (E)   Malpighi's delivery is first.

20. If Malpighi's delivery is first and Leacock's delivery is third, then which one of the following must be true?

    (A)   Figueroa's delivery is second.
    (B)   Harris's delivery is second.
    (C)   Harris's delivery is fourth.
    (D)   Kanzaki's delivery is fifth.
    (E)   Kanzaki's delivery is last.

21. Which one of the following must be true?

    (A)   Figueroa's delivery is earlier than Leacock's.
    (B)   Ginsberg's delivery is earlier than Leacock's.
    (C)   Harris's delivery is earlier than Kanzaki's.
    (D)   Leacock's delivery is earlier than Ginsberg's.
    (E)   Malpighi's delivery is earlier than Harris's.

22. If Kanzaki's delivery is earlier than Leacock's, then which one of the following could be true?

    (A)   Figueroa's delivery is first.
    (B)   Ginsberg's delivery is third.
    (C)   Harris's delivery is third.
    (D)   Leacock's delivery is fifth.
    (E)   Malpighi's delivery is second.

23. Which one of the following must be false?

    (A)   Figueroa's delivery is first.
    (B)   Ginsberg's delivery is fifth.
    (C)   Harris's delivery is third.
    (D)   Leacock's delivery is second.
    (E)   Malpighi's delivery is fourth.

S T O P

IF YOU FINISH BEFORE TIME IS CALLED, YOU MAY CHECK YOUR WORK ON THIS SECTION ONLY.
DO NOT WORK ON ANY OTHER SECTION IN THE TEST.

SECTION III

Time—35 minutes

25 Questions

<u>Directions:</u> The questions in this section are based on the reasoning contained in brief statements or passages. For some questions, more than one of the choices could conceivably answer the question. However, you are to choose the <u>best</u> answer; that is, the response that most accurately and completely answers the question. You should not make assumptions that are by commonsense standards implausible, superfluous, or incompatible with the passage. After you have chosen the best answer, blacken the corresponding space on your answer sheet.

1. Any museum that owns the rare stamp that features an airplane printed upside down should not display it. Ultraviolet light causes red ink to fade, and a substantial portion of the stamp is red. If the stamp is displayed, it will be damaged. It should be kept safely locked away, even though this will deny the public the chance to see it.

   The reasoning above most closely conforms to which one of the following principles?

   (A) The public should judge the quality of a museum by the rarity of the objects in its collection.

   (B) Museum display cases should protect their contents from damage caused by ultraviolet light.

   (C) Red ink should not be used on items that will not be exposed to ultraviolet light.

   (D) A museum piece that would be damaged by display should not be displayed.

   (E) The primary purpose of a museum is to educate the public.

2. Dietitian: Many diet-conscious consumers are excited about new "fake fat" products designed to give food the flavor and consistency of fatty foods, yet without fat's harmful effects. Consumers who expect the new fat substitute to help them lose weight are likely to be disappointed, however. Research has shown that when people knowingly or unknowingly eat foods containing "fake fat," they tend to take in at least as many additional calories as are saved by eating "fake fat."

   Which one of the following most accurately expresses the conclusion of the dietitian's argument?

   (A) People tend to take in a certain number of daily calories, no matter what types of food they eat.

   (B) Most consumers who think that foods with "fake fat" are more nutritious than fatty foods are destined to be disappointed.

   (C) "Fake fat" products are likely to contribute to obesity more than do other foods.

   (D) "Fake fat" in foods is probably not going to help consumers meet weight loss goals.

   (E) "Fake fat" in foods is indistinguishable from genuine fat by most consumers on the basis of taste alone.

3. Banking analyst: Banks often offer various services to new customers at no charge. But this is not an ideal business practice, since regular, long-term customers, who make up the bulk of the business for most banks, are excluded from these special offers.

   Which one of the following, if true, most strengthens the banking analyst's argument?

   (A) Most banks have similar charges for most services and pay similar interest rates on deposits.

   (B) Banks do best when offering special privileges only to their most loyal customers.

   (C) Offering services at no charge to all of its current customers would be prohibitively expensive for a bank.

   (D) Once they have chosen a bank, people tend to remain loyal to that bank.

   (E) Some banks that offer services at no charge to new customers are very successful.

GO ON TO THE NEXT PAGE.

4. Panelist: Medical research articles cited in popular newspapers or magazines are more likely than other medical research articles to be cited in subsequent medical research. Thus, it appears that medical researchers' judgments of the importance of prior research are strongly influenced by the publicity received by that research and do not strongly correspond to the research's true importance.

The panelist's argument is most vulnerable to criticism on the grounds that it

(A) presents counterarguments to a view that is not actually held by any medical researcher

(B) fails to consider the possibility that popular newspapers and magazines do a good job of identifying the most important medical research articles

(C) takes for granted that coverage of medical research in the popular press is more concerned with the eminence of the scientists involved than with the content of their research

(D) fails to consider the possibility that popular newspapers and magazines are able to review only a minuscule percentage of medical research articles

(E) draws a conclusion that is logically equivalent to its premise

5. Lahar: We must now settle on a procedure for deciding on meeting agendas. Our club's constitution allows three options: unanimous consent, majority vote, or assigning the task to a committee. Unanimous consent is unlikely. Forming a committee has usually led to factionalism and secret deals. Clearly, we should subject meeting agendas to majority vote.

Lahar's argument does which one of the following?

(A) rejects suggested procedures on constitutional grounds

(B) claims that one procedure is the appropriate method for reaching every decision in the club

(C) suggests a change to a constitution on the basis of practical considerations

(D) recommends a choice based on the elimination of alternative options

(E) supports one preference by arguing against those who have advocated alternatives

6. Mayor: Local antitobacco activists are calling for expanded antismoking education programs paid for by revenue from heavily increased taxes on cigarettes sold in the city. Although the effectiveness of such education programs is debatable, there is strong evidence that the taxes themselves would produce the sought-after reduction in smoking. Surveys show that cigarette sales drop substantially in cities that impose stiff tax increases on cigarettes.

Which one of the following, if true, most undermines the reasoning in the argument above?

(A) A city-imposed tax on cigarettes will substantially reduce the amount of smoking in the city if the tax is burdensome to the average cigarette consumer.

(B) Consumers are more likely to continue buying a product if its price increases due to higher taxes than if its price increases for some other reason.

(C) Usually, cigarette sales will increase substantially in the areas surrounding a city after that city imposes stiff taxes on cigarettes.

(D) People who are well informed about the effects of long-term tobacco use are significantly less likely to smoke than are people who are not informed.

(E) Antismoking education programs that are funded by taxes on cigarettes will tend to lose their funding if they are successful.

GO ON TO THE NEXT PAGE.

7. Gotera: Infants lack the motor ability required to voluntarily produce particular sounds, but produce various babbling sounds randomly. Most children are several years old before they can voluntarily produce most of the vowel and consonant sounds of their language. We can conclude that speech acquisition is entirely a motor control process rather than a process that is abstract or mental.

Which one of the following is an assumption required by Gotera's argument?

(A) Speech acquisition is a function only of one's ability to produce the sounds of spoken language.
(B) During the entire initial babbling stage, infants cannot intentionally move their tongues while they are babbling.
(C) The initial babbling stage is completed during infancy.
(D) The initial babbling stage is the first stage of the speech acquisition process.
(E) Control of tongue and mouth movements requires a sophisticated level of mental development.

8. Caldwell: The government recently demolished a former naval base. Among the complex's facilities were a gymnasium, a swimming pool, office buildings, gardens, and housing for hundreds of people. Of course the government was legally permitted to use these facilities as it wished. But clearly, using them for the good of the community would have benefited everyone, and thus the government's actions were not only inefficient but immoral.

Caldwell's argument is most vulnerable to criticism on the grounds that it

(A) fails to consider that an action may be morally permissible even if an alternative course of action is to everyone's advantage
(B) presumes, without providing justification, that the actual consequences of an action are irrelevant to the action's moral permissibility
(C) presumes, without providing justification, that the government never acts in the most efficient manner
(D) presumes, without providing justification, that any action that is efficient is also moral
(E) inappropriately treats two possible courses of action as if they were the only options

9. Reducing stress lessens a person's sensitivity to pain. This is the conclusion reached by researchers who played extended audiotapes to patients before they underwent surgery and afterward while they were recovering. One tape consisted of conversation; the other consisted of music. Those who listened only to the latter tape required less anesthesia during surgery and fewer painkillers afterward than those who listened only to the former tape.

Which one of the following is an assumption on which the researchers' reasoning depends?

(A) All of the patients in the study listened to the same tape before surgery as they listened to after surgery.
(B) Anticipating surgery is no less stressful than recovering from surgery.
(C) Listening to music reduces stress.
(D) The psychological effects of music are not changed by anesthesia or painkillers.
(E) Both anesthesia and painkillers tend to reduce stress.

10. Samuel: Because communication via computer is usually conducted privately and anonymously between people who would otherwise interact in person, it contributes to the dissolution, not the creation, of lasting communal bonds.

Tova: You assume that communication via computer replaces more intimate forms of communication and interaction, when more often it replaces asocial or even antisocial behavior.

On the basis of their statements, Samuel and Tova are committed to disagreeing about which one of the following?

(A) A general trend of modern life is to dissolve the social bonds that formerly connected people.
(B) All purely private behavior contributes to the dissolution of social bonds.
(C) Face-to-face communication is more likely to contribute to the creation of social bonds than is anonymous communication.
(D) It is desirable that new social bonds be created to replace the ones that have dissolved.
(E) If people were not communicating via computer, they would most likely be engaged in activities that create stronger social bonds.

GO ON TO THE NEXT PAGE.

11. Spreading iron particles over the surface of the earth's oceans would lead to an increase in phytoplankton, decreasing the amount of carbon dioxide in the atmosphere and thereby counteracting the greenhouse effect. But while counteracting the greenhouse effect is important, the side effects of an iron-seeding strategy have yet to be studied. Since the oceans represent such an important resource, this response to the greenhouse effect should not be implemented immediately.

The reasoning above most closely conforms to which one of the following principles?

(A) A problem-solving strategy should be implemented if the side effects of the strategy are known.

(B) Implementing a problem-solving strategy that alters an important resource is impermissible if the consequences are not adequately understood.

(C) We should not implement a problem-solving strategy if the consequences of doing so are more serious than the problem itself.

(D) We should not implement a problem-solving strategy if that strategy requires altering an important resource.

(E) As long as there is a possibility that a strategy for solving a problem may instead exacerbate that problem, such a solution should not be adopted.

12. No matter how conscientious they are, historians always have biases that affect their work. Hence, rather than trying to interpret historical events, historians should instead interpret what the people who participated in historical events thought about those events.

The reasoning in the argument is most vulnerable to criticism on the grounds that the argument fails to consider the possibility that

(A) historians who have different biases often agree about many aspects of some historical events

(B) scholars in disciplines other than history also risk having their biases affect their work

(C) many of the ways in which historians' biases affect their work have been identified

(D) not all historians are aware of the effect that their particular biases have on their work

(E) the proposed shift in focus is unlikely to eliminate the effect that historians' biases have on their work

13. Humanitarian considerations aside, sheer economics dictates that country X should institute, as country Y has done, a nationwide system of air and ground transportation for conveying seriously injured persons to specialized trauma centers. Timely access to the kind of medical care that only specialized centers can provide could save the lives of many people. The earnings of these people would result in a substantial increase in country X's gross national product, and the taxes paid on those earnings would substantially augment government revenues.

The argument depends on the assumption that

(A) lifetime per-capita income is roughly the same in country X as it is in country Y

(B) there are no specialized trauma centers in country X at present

(C) the treatment of seriously injured persons in trauma centers is not more costly than treatment elsewhere

(D) there would be a net increase in employment in country X if more persons survived serious injury

(E) most people seriously injured in automobile accidents in country X do not now receive treatment in specialized trauma centers

14. Early urban societies could not have been maintained without large-scale farming nearby. This is because other methods of food acquisition, such as foraging, cannot support populations as dense as urban ones. Large-scale farming requires irrigation, which remained unfeasible in areas far from rivers or lakes until more recent times.

Which one of the following is most strongly supported by the information above?

(A) Most peoples who lived in early times lived in areas near rivers or lakes.

(B) Only if farming is possible in the absence of irrigation can societies be maintained in areas far from rivers or lakes.

(C) In early times it was not possible to maintain urban societies in areas far from rivers or lakes.

(D) Urban societies with farms near rivers or lakes do not have to rely upon irrigation to meet their farming needs.

(E) Early rural societies relied more on foraging than on agriculture for food.

GO ON TO THE NEXT PAGE.

15. Economist: A country's rapid emergence from an economic recession requires substantial new investment in that country's economy. Since people's confidence in the economic policies of their country is a precondition for any new investment, countries that put collective goals before individuals' goals cannot emerge quickly from an economic recession.

Which one of the following, if assumed, enables the economist's conclusion to be properly drawn?

(A) No new investment occurs in any country that does not emerge quickly from an economic recession.

(B) Recessions in countries that put collective goals before individuals' goals tend not to affect the country's people's support for their government's policies.

(C) If the people in a country that puts individuals' goals first are willing to make new investments in their country's economy, their country will emerge quickly from an economic recession.

(D) People in countries that put collective goals before individuals' goals lack confidence in the economic policies of their countries.

(E) A country's economic policies are the most significant factor determining whether that country's economy will experience a recession.

16. The average length of stay for patients at Edgewater Hospital is four days, compared to six days at University Hospital. Since studies show that recovery rates at the two hospitals are similar for patients with similar illnesses, University Hospital could decrease its average length of stay without affecting quality of care.

The reasoning in the argument is most vulnerable to criticism on the grounds that the argument

(A) equates the quality of care at a hospital with patients' average length of stay

(B) treats a condition that will ensure the preservation of quality of care as a condition that is required to preserve quality of care

(C) fails to take into account the possibility that patients at Edgewater Hospital tend to be treated for different illnesses than patients at University Hospital

(D) presumes, without providing justification, that the length of time patients stay in the hospital is never relevant to the recovery rates of these patients

(E) fails to take into account the possibility that patients at University Hospital generally prefer longer hospital stays

17. Philosopher: Graham argues that since a person is truly happy only when doing something, the best life is a life that is full of activity. But we should not be persuaded by Graham's argument. People sleep, and at least sometimes when sleeping, they are truly happy, even though they are not doing anything.

Which one of the following most accurately describes the role played in the philosopher's argument by the claim that at least sometimes when sleeping, people are truly happy, even though they are not doing anything?

(A) It is a premise of Graham's argument.

(B) It is an example intended to show that a premise of Graham's argument is false.

(C) It is an analogy appealed to by Graham but that the philosopher rejects.

(D) It is an example intended to disprove the conclusion of Graham's argument.

(E) It is the main conclusion of the philosopher's argument.

GO ON TO THE NEXT PAGE.

18. Historian: In rebuttal of my claim that West influenced Stuart, some people point out that West's work is mentioned only once in Stuart's diaries. But Stuart's diaries mention several meetings with West, and Stuart's close friend, Abella, studied under West. Furthermore, Stuart's work often uses West's terminology which, though now commonplace, none of Stuart's contemporaries used.

Which one of the following propositions is most supported by the historian's statements, if those statements are true?

(A) Stuart's discussions with Abella were one of the means by which West influenced Stuart.

(B) It is more likely that Stuart influenced West than that West influenced Stuart.

(C) Stuart's contemporaries were not influenced by West.

(D) Stuart's work was not entirely free from West's influence.

(E) Because of Stuart's influence on other people, West's terminology is now commonplace.

19. One theory to explain the sudden extinction of all dinosaurs points to "drug overdoses" as the cause. Angiosperms, a certain class of plants, first appeared at the time that dinosaurs became extinct. These plants produce amino-acid-based alkaloids that are psychoactive agents. Most plant-eating mammals avoid these potentially lethal poisons because they taste bitter. Moreover, mammals have livers that help detoxify such drugs. However, dinosaurs could neither taste the bitterness nor detoxify the substance once it was ingested. This theory receives its strongest support from the fact that it helps explain why so many dinosaur fossils are found in unusual and contorted positions.

Which one of the following, if true, would most undermine the theory presented above?

(A) Many fossils of large mammals are found in contorted positions.

(B) Angiosperms provide a great deal of nutrition.

(C) Carnivorous dinosaurs mostly ate other, vegetarian, dinosaurs that fed on angiosperms.

(D) Some poisonous plants do not produce amino-acid-based alkaloids.

(E) Mammals sometimes die of drug overdoses from eating angiosperms.

20. There are two ways to manage an existing transportation infrastructure: continuous maintenance at adequate levels, and periodic radical reconstruction. Continuous maintenance dispenses with the need for radical reconstruction, and radical reconstruction is necessitated by failing to perform continuous maintenance. Over the long run, continuous maintenance is far less expensive; nevertheless, it almost never happens.

Which one of the following, if true, most contributes to an explanation of why the first alternative mentioned is almost never adopted?

(A) Since different parts of the transportation infrastructure are the responsibility of different levels of government, radical reconstruction projects are very difficult to coordinate efficiently.

(B) When funds for transportation infrastructure maintenance are scarce, they are typically distributed in proportion to the amount of traffic that is borne by different elements of the infrastructure.

(C) If continuous maintenance is performed at less-than-adequate levels, the need for radical reconstruction will often arise later than if maintenance had been restricted to responding to emergencies.

(D) Radical reconstruction projects are, in general, too costly to be paid for from current revenue.

(E) For long periods, the task of regular maintenance lacks urgency, since the consequences of neglecting it are very slow to manifest themselves.

GO ON TO THE NEXT PAGE.

21. A good way to get over one's fear of an activity one finds terrifying is to do it repeatedly. For instance, over half of people who have parachuted only once report being extremely frightened by the experience, while less than 1 percent of those who have parachuted ten times or more report being frightened by it.

The reasoning in the argument is most vulnerable to criticism on the grounds that the argument

(A) takes for granted that the greater the number of dangerous activities one engages in the less one is frightened by any one of them

(B) neglects to consider those people who have parachuted more than once but fewer than ten times

(C) takes for granted that people do not know how frightening something is unless they have tried it

(D) fails to take into account the possibility that people would be better off if they did not do things that terrify them

(E) overlooks the possibility that most people who have parachuted many times did not find it frightening initially

22. Most economists believe that reducing the price of any product generally stimulates demand for it. However, most wine merchants have found that reducing the price of domestic wines to make them more competitive with imported wines with which they were previously comparably priced is frequently followed by an increase in sales of those imported wines.

Which one of the following, if true, most helps to reconcile the belief of most economists with the consequences observed by most wine merchants?

(A) Economists' studies of the prices of grocery items and their rates of sales rarely cover alcoholic beverages.

(B) Few merchants of any kind have detailed knowledge of economic theories about the relationship between item prices and sales rates.

(C) Consumers are generally willing to forgo purchasing other items they desire in order to purchase a superior wine.

(D) Imported wines in all price ranges are comparable in quality to domestic wines that cost less.

(E) An increase in the demand for a consumer product is compatible with an increase in demand for a competing product.

23. Certain bacteria that produce hydrogen sulfide as a waste product would die if directly exposed to oxygen. The hydrogen sulfide reacts with oxygen, removing it and so preventing it from harming the bacteria. Furthermore, the hydrogen sulfide tends to kill other organisms in the area, thereby providing the bacteria with a source of food. As a result, a dense colony of these bacteria produces for itself an environment in which it can continue to thrive indefinitely.

Which one of the following is most strongly supported by the information above?

(A) A dense colony of the bacteria can indefinitely continue to produce enough hydrogen sulfide to kill other organisms in the area and to prevent oxygen from harming the bacteria.

(B) The hydrogen sulfide produced by the bacteria kills other organisms in the area by reacting with and removing oxygen.

(C) Most organisms, if killed by the hydrogen sulfide produced by the bacteria, can provide a source of food for the bacteria.

(D) The bacteria can continue to thrive indefinitely only in an environment in which the hydrogen sulfide they produce has removed all oxygen and killed other organisms in the area.

(E) If any colony of bacteria produces hydrogen sulfide as a waste product, it thereby ensures that it is both provided with a source of food and protected from harm by oxygen.

GO ON TO THE NEXT PAGE.

24. Books that present a utopian future in which the inequities and sufferings of the present are replaced by more harmonious and rational social arrangements will always find enthusiastic buyers. Since gloomy books predicting that even more terrifying times await us are clearly not of this genre, they are unlikely to be very popular.

The questionable pattern of reasoning in which one of the following arguments is most similar to that in the argument above?

(A) Art that portrays people as happy and contented has a tranquilizing effect on the viewer, an effect that is appealing to those who are tense or anxious. Thus, people who dislike such art are neither tense nor anxious.

(B) People who enjoy participating in activities such as fishing or hiking may nevertheless enjoy watching such spectator sports as boxing or football. Thus, one cannot infer from someone's participating in vigorous contact sports that he or she is not also fond of less violent forms of recreation.

(C) Action movies that involve complicated and dangerous special-effects scenes are enormously expensive to produce. Hence, since traditional dramatic or comedic films contain no such scenes, it is probable that they are relatively inexpensive to produce.

(D) Adults usually feel a pleasant nostalgia when hearing the music they listened to as adolescents, but since adolescents often like music specifically because they think it annoys their parents, adults rarely appreciate the music that their children will later listen to with nostalgia.

(E) All self-employed businesspeople have salaries that fluctuate with the fortunes of the general economy, but government bureaucrats are not self-employed. Therefore, not everyone with an income that fluctuates with the fortunes of the general economy is a government bureaucrat.

25. Some people mistakenly believe that since we do not have direct access to the distant past we cannot learn much about it. Contemporary historians and archaeologists find current geography, geology, and climate to be rich in clues about a given region's distant history. However, the more distant the period we are studying is, the less useful the study of the present becomes.

Of the following, which one most closely conforms to the principle that the passage illustrates?

(A) Astronomers often draw inferences about the earlier years of our solar system on the basis of recently collected data. Unfortunately, they have been able to infer comparatively little about the origin of our solar system.

(B) Much can be learned about the perpetrator of a crime by applying scientific methods of investigation to the crime scene. But the more the crime scene has been studied the less likely anything will be learned from further study.

(C) To understand a literary text one needs to understand the author's world view. However, the farther that world view gets from one's own the less one will be able to appreciate the text.

(D) We often extrapolate from ordinary sensory experience to things beyond such experience and form a rash judgment, such as the claim that the earth is the center of the universe because it appears that way to us.

(E) One crucial clue to the extent of the ancient Egyptians' mathematical knowledge came from studying the pyramids. The more we studied such structures, the more impressed we were by how much the Egyptians knew.

S T O P

IF YOU FINISH BEFORE TIME IS CALLED, YOU MAY CHECK YOUR WORK ON THIS SECTION ONLY.
DO NOT WORK ON ANY OTHER SECTION IN THE TEST.

SECTION IV

Time—35 minutes

27 Questions

Directions: Each set of questions in this section is based on a single passage or a pair of passages. The questions are to be answered on the basis of what is stated or implied in the passage or pair of passages. For some of the questions, more than one of the choices could conceivably answer the question. However, you are to choose the best answer; that is, the response that most accurately and completely answers the question, and blacken the corresponding space on your answer sheet.

Many critics agree that the primary characteristic of Senegalese filmmaker Ousmane Sembène's work is its sociopolitical commitment. Sembène was trained in Moscow in the cinematic methods of socialist
(5) realism, and he asserts that his films are not meant to entertain his compatriots, but rather to raise their awareness of the past and present realities of their society. But his originality as a filmmaker lies most strikingly in his having successfully adapted film,
(10) originally a Western cultural medium, to the needs, pace, and structures of West African culture. In particular, Sembène has found within African oral culture techniques and strategies that enable him to express his views and to reach both literate and
(15) nonliterate Senegalese viewers.

A number of Sembène's characters and motifs can be traced to those found in traditional West African storytelling. The tree, for instance, which in countless West African tales symbolizes knowledge, life, death,
(20) and rebirth, is a salient motif in *Emitaï*. The trickster, usually a dishonest individual who personifies antisocial traits, appears in *Borom Sarret*, *Mandabi*, and *Xala* as a thief, a corrupted civil servant, and a member of the elite, respectively. In fact, most of
(25) Sembène's characters, like those of many oral West African narratives, are types embodying collective ideas or attitudes. And in the oral tradition, these types face archetypal predicaments, as is true, for example, of the protagonist of *Borom Sarret*, who has
(30) no name and is recognizable instead by his trade—he is a street merchant—and by the difficulties he encounters but is unable to overcome.

Moreover, many of Sembène's films derive their structure from West African dilemma tales, the
(35) outcomes of which are debated and decided by their audiences. The open-endedness of most of his plots reveals that Sembène similarly leaves it to his viewers to complete his narratives: in such films as *Borom Sarret*, *Mandabi*, and *Ceddo*, for example, he
(40) provides his spectators with several alternatives as the films end. The openness of his narratives is also evidenced by his frequent use of freeze-frames, which carry the suggestion of continued action.

Finally, like many West African oral tales,
(45) Sembène's narratives take the form of initiatory journeys that bring about a basic change in the worldview of the protagonist and ultimately, Sembène hopes, in that of the viewer. His films denounce social and political injustice, and his protagonists'
(50) social consciousness emerges from an acute self-
consciousness brought about by the juxtaposition of opposites within the films' social context: good versus evil, powerlessness versus power, or poverty versus wealth. Such binary oppositions are used analogously
(55) in West African tales, and it seems likely that these dialectical elements are related to African oral storytelling more than, as many critics have supposed, to the Marxist components of his ideology.

1. Which one of the following most accurately states the main point of the passage?

(A) Sembène's originality as a filmmaker lies in his adaptation of traditional archetypal predicaments and open-ended plots, both of which are derived from West African oral tales.

(B) Many of the characters in Sembène's films are variations on character types common to traditional West African storytelling.

(C) Sembène's films derive their distinctive characteristics from oral narrative traditions that had not previously been considered suitable subject matter for films.

(D) Sembène's films give vivid expression to the social and political beliefs held by most of the Senegalese people.

(E) Sembène's films are notable in that they use elements derived from traditional West African storytelling to comment critically on contemporary social and political issues.

GO ON TO THE NEXT PAGE.

2. The author says that Sembène does which one of the following in at least some of his films?

   (A) uses animals as symbols
   (B) uses slow motion for artistic effect
   (C) provides oral narration of the film's story
   (D) juxtaposes West African images and Marxist symbols
   (E) leaves part of the story to be filled in by audiences

3. Which one of the following would, if true, most strengthen the claim made by the author in the last sentence of the passage (lines 54–58)?

   (A) Several African novelists who draw upon the oral traditions of West Africa use binary oppositions as fundamental structures in their narratives, even though they have not read Marxist theory.
   (B) Folklorists who have analyzed oral storytelling traditions from across the world have found that the use of binary oppositions to structure narratives is common to many of these traditions.
   (C) When he trained in Moscow, Sembène read extensively in Marxist political theory and worked to devise ways of synthesizing Marxist theory and the collective ideas expressed in West African storytelling.
   (D) Very few filmmakers in Europe or North America make use of binary oppositions to structure their narratives.
   (E) Binary oppositions do not play an essential structuring role in the narratives of some films produced by other filmmakers who subscribe to Marxist principles.

4. Which one of the following inferences about Sembène is most strongly supported by the passage?

   (A) His films have become popular both in parts of Africa and elsewhere.
   (B) He has not received support from government agencies for his film production.
   (C) His films are widely misunderstood by critics in Senegal.
   (D) His characters are drawn from a broad range of social strata.
   (E) His work has been subjected to government censorship.

5. Which one of the following most closely expresses the author's intended meaning in using the word "initiatory" (line 45)?

   (A) beginning a series
   (B) experimental
   (C) transformative
   (D) unprecedented
   (E) prefatory

6. The passage does NOT provide evidence that Sembène exhibits which one of the following attitudes in one or more of his films?

   (A) disenchantment with attempts to reform Senegalese government
   (B) confidence in the aptness of using traditional motifs to comment on contemporary issues
   (C) concern with social justice
   (D) interest in the vicissitudes of ordinary people's lives
   (E) desire to educate his audience

GO ON TO THE NEXT PAGE.

Passage A

Readers, like writers, need to search for answers. Part of the joy of reading is in being surprised, but academic historians leave little to the imagination. The perniciousness of the historiographic approach became
(5) fully evident to me when I started teaching. Historians require undergraduates to read scholarly monographs that sap the vitality of history; they visit on students what was visited on them in graduate school. They assign books with formulaic arguments that transform
(10) history into an abstract debate that would have been unfathomable to those who lived in the past. Aimed so squarely at the head, such books cannot stimulate students who yearn to connect to history emotionally as well as intellectually.
(15) In an effort to address this problem, some historians have begun to rediscover stories. It has even become something of a fad within the profession. This year, the American Historical Association chose as the theme for its annual conference some putative connection to
(20) storytelling: "Practices of Historical Narrative." Predictably, historians responded by adding the word "narrative" to their titles and presenting papers at sessions on "Oral History and the Narrative of Class Identity," and "Meaning and Time: The Problem of
(25) Historical Narrative." But it was still historiography, intended only for other academics. At meetings of historians, we still encounter very few historians telling stories or moving audiences to smiles, chills, or tears.

Passage B

Writing is at the heart of the lawyer's craft, and so,
(30) like it or not, we who teach the law inevitably teach aspiring lawyers how lawyers write. We do this in a few stand-alone courses and, to a greater extent, through the constraints that we impose on their writing throughout the curriculum. Legal writing, because of the purposes
(35) it serves, is necessarily ruled by linear logic, creating a path without diversions, surprises, or reversals. Conformity is a virtue, creativity suspect, humor forbidden, and voice mute.
Lawyers write as they see other lawyers write, and,
(40) influenced by education, profession, economic constraints, and perceived self-interest, they too often write badly. Perhaps the currently fashionable call for attention to narrative in legal education could have an effect on this. It is not yet exactly clear what role
(45) narrative should play in the law, but it is nonetheless true that every case has at its heart a story—of real events and people, of concerns, misfortunes, conflicts, feelings. But because legal analysis strips the human narrative content from the abstract, canonical legal
(50) form of the case, law students learn to act as if there is no such story.
It may well turn out that some of the terminology and public rhetoric of this potentially subversive movement toward attention to narrative will find its

(55) way into the law curriculum, but without producing corresponding changes in how legal writing is actually taught or in how our future colleagues will write. Still, even mere awareness of the value of narrative could perhaps serve as an important corrective.

7. Which one of the following does each of the passages display?

   (A) a concern with the question of what teaching methods are most effective in developing writing skills

   (B) a concern with how a particular discipline tends to represent points of view it does not typically deal with

   (C) a conviction that writing in specialized professional disciplines cannot be creatively crafted

   (D) a belief that the writing in a particular profession could benefit from more attention to storytelling

   (E) a desire to see writing in a particular field purged of elements from other disciplines

8. The passages most strongly support which one of the following inferences regarding the authors' relationships to the professions they discuss?

   (A) Neither author is an active member of the profession that he or she discusses.

   (B) Each author is an active member of the profession he or she discusses.

   (C) The author of passage A is a member of the profession discussed in that passage, but the author of passage B is not a member of either of the professions discussed in the passages.

   (D) Both authors are active members of the profession discussed in passage B.

   (E) The author of passage B, but not the author of passage A, is an active member of both of the professions discussed in the passages.

GO ON TO THE NEXT PAGE.

9. Which one of the following does each passage indicate is typical of writing in the respective professions discussed in the passages?

    (A) abstraction
    (B) hyperbole
    (C) subversion
    (D) narrative
    (E) imagination

10. In which one of the following ways are the passages NOT parallel?

    (A) Passage A presents and rejects arguments for an opposing position, whereas passage B does not.
    (B) Passage A makes evaluative claims, whereas passage B does not.
    (C) Passage A describes specific examples of a phenomenon it criticizes, whereas passage B does not.
    (D) Passage B offers criticism, whereas passage A does not.
    (E) Passage B outlines a theory, whereas passage A does not.

11. The phrase "scholarly monographs that sap the vitality of history" in passage A (lines 6–7) plays a role in that passage's overall argument that is most analogous to the role played in passage B by which one of the following phrases?

    (A) "Writing is at the heart of the lawyer's craft" (line 29)
    (B) "Conformity is a virtue, creativity suspect, humor forbidden, and voice mute" (lines 37–38)
    (C) "Lawyers write as they see other lawyers write" (line 39)
    (D) "every case has at its heart a story" (line 46)
    (E) "Still, even mere awareness of the value of narrative could perhaps serve as an important corrective" (lines 57–59)

12. Suppose that a lawyer is writing a legal document describing the facts that are at issue in a case. The author of passage B would be most likely to expect which one of the following to be true of the document?

    (A) It will be poorly written because the lawyer who is writing it was not given explicit advice by law professors on how lawyers should write.
    (B) It will be crafted to function like a piece of fiction in its description of the characters and motivations of the people involved in the case.
    (C) It will be a concise, well-crafted piece of writing that summarizes most, if not all, of the facts that are important in the case.
    (D) It will not genuinely convey the human dimension of the case, regardless of how accurate the document may be in its details.
    (E) It will neglect to make appropriate connections between the details of the case and relevant legal doctrines.

GO ON TO THE NEXT PAGE.

Traditional theories of animal behavior assert that animal conflict within a species is highly ritualized and does not vary from contest to contest. This species-specific model assumes that repetitive use of
(5) the same visual and vocal displays and an absence of escalated fighting evolved to prevent injury. The contestant that exhibits the "best" display wins the contested resource. Galápagos tortoises, for instance, settle contests on the basis of height: the ritualized
(10) display consists of two tortoises facing one another and stretching their necks skyward; the tortoise perceived as being "taller" wins.

In populations of the spider *Agelenopsis aperta*, however, fighting behavior varies greatly from contest
(15) to contest. In addition, fighting is not limited to displays: biting and shoving are common. Susan Riechert argues that a recently developed model, evolutionary game theory, provides a closer fit to *A. aperta* territorial disputes than does the species-
(20) specific model, because it explains variations in conflict behavior that may result from varying conditions, such as differences in size, age, and experience of combatants. Evolutionary game theory was adapted from the classical game theory that was
(25) developed by von Neumann and Morgenstern to explain human behavior in conflict situations. In both classical and evolutionary game theory, strategies are weighed in terms of maximizing the average payoff against contestants employing both the same and
(30) different strategies. For example, a spider may engage in escalated fighting during a dispute only if the disputed resource is valuable enough to warrant the risk of physical injury. There are, however, two major differences between the classical and evolutionary
(35) theories. First, whereas in classical game theory it is assumed that rational thought is used to determine which action to take, evolutionary game theory assumes that instinct and long-term species advantage ultimately determine the strategies that are exhibited.
(40) The other difference is in the payoffs: in classical game theory, the payoffs are determined by an individual's personal judgment of what constitutes winning; in evolutionary game theory, the payoffs are defined in terms of reproductive success.
(45) In studying populations of *A. aperta* in a grassland habitat and a riparian habitat, Riechert predicts that such factors as the size of the opponents, the potential rate of predation in a habitat, and the probability of winning a subsequent site if the dispute
(50) is lost will all affect the behavior of spiders in territorial disputes. In addition, she predicts that the markedly different levels of competition for web sites in the two habitats will affect the spiders' willingness to engage in escalated fighting. In the grassland,
(55) where 12 percent of the habitat is available for occupation by *A. aperta*, Riechert predicts that spiders will be more willing to engage in escalated fighting than in the riparian habitat, where 90 percent of the habitat is suitable for occupation.

13. Which one of the following best states the main idea of the passage?

(A) Evolutionary game theory and classical game theory can be used to analyze the process of decision-making used by humans and animals in settling disputes.

(B) *A. aperta* in grassland habitats and riparian habitats exhibit an unusually wide variety of fighting behaviors in territorial disputes.

(C) Evolutionary game theory may be useful in explaining the behavior of certain spiders during territorial disputes.

(D) The traditional theory of animal behavior in conflict situations cannot be used to explain the fighting behavior of most species.

(E) Evolutionary game theory, adapted from classical game theory, is currently used by scientists to predict the behavior of spiders in site selection.

14. The author of the passage mentions Galápagos tortoises in the first paragraph most likely in order to

(A) describe a kind of fighting behavior that is used by only a few species

(B) suggest that repetitive use of the same visual and vocal displays is a kind of fighting behavior used by some but not all species

(C) provide evidence to support the claim that fighting behavior does not vary greatly from contest to contest for most species

(D) provide an example of a fighting behavior that is unique to a particular species

(E) provide an example of a ritualized fighting behavior of the kind that traditional theorists assume is the norm for most species

GO ON TO THE NEXT PAGE.

15. Item Removed From Scoring.

16. Which one of the following, if true, is LEAST consistent with Riechert's theory about fighting behavior in spiders?

   (A)   Spiders in the grassland habitat engage in escalated fighting when a disputed site is highly desirable.
   (B)   Spiders in the riparian habitat are not willing to engage in escalated fighting for less-than-suitable sites.
   (C)   Spiders in the riparian habitat confine their fighting to displays more regularly than do spiders in the grassland habitat.
   (D)   Spiders in the riparian habitat are as willing to engage in escalated fighting as are spiders in the grassland habitat.
   (E)   Spiders in the riparian habitat are more likely to withdraw when faced with a larger opponent in territorial disputes than are spiders in the grassland habitat.

17. Which one of the following best states the function of the third paragraph of the passage?

   (A)   It develops a comparison of the two theories that were introduced in the preceding paragraph.
   (B)   It continues a discussion of a controversial theory described in the first two paragraphs of the passage.
   (C)   It describes an experiment that provides support for the theory described in the preceding paragraph.
   (D)   It describes a rare phenomenon that cannot be accounted for by the theory described in the first paragraph.
   (E)   It describes predictions that can be used to test the validity of a theory described in a preceding paragraph.

18. The passage suggests which one of the following about the behavior of *A. aperta* in conflict situations?

   (A)   They exhibit variations in fighting behavior from contest to contest primarily because of the different levels of competition for suitable sites in different habitats.
   (B)   They may confine their fighting behavior to displays if the value of a disputed resource is too low and the risk of physical injury is too great.
   (C)   They exhibit variations in fighting behavior that are similar to those exhibited by members of most other species of animals.
   (D)   They are more likely to engage in escalated fighting during disputes than to limit their fighting behavior to visual and vocal displays.
   (E)   They are more willing to engage in escalated fighting during conflict situations than are members of most other species of animals.

19. The primary purpose of the passage is to

   (A)   present an alternative to a traditional approach
   (B)   describe a phenomenon and provide specific examples
   (C)   evaluate evidence used to support an argument
   (D)   present data that refutes a controversial theory
   (E)   suggest that a new theory may be based on inadequate research

GO ON TO THE NEXT PAGE.

Most people acknowledge that not all governments have a moral right to govern and that there are sometimes morally legitimate reasons for disobeying the law, as when a particular law
(5) prescribes behavior that is clearly immoral. It is also commonly supposed that such cases are special exceptions and that, in general, the fact that something is against the law counts as a moral, as well as legal, ground for not doing it; i.e., we
(10) generally have a moral duty to obey a law simply because it is the law. But the theory known as philosophical anarchism denies this view, arguing instead that people who live under the jurisdiction of governments have no moral duty to those
(15) governments to obey their laws. Some commentators have rejected this position because of what they take to be its highly counterintuitive implications: (1) that no existing government is morally better than any other (since all are, in a sense, equally illegitimate),
(20) and (2) that, lacking any moral obligation to obey any laws, people may do as they please without scruple. In fact, however, philosophical anarchism does not entail these claims.

First, the conclusion that no government is
(25) morally better than any other does not follow from the claim that nobody owes moral obedience to any government. Even if one denies that there is a moral obligation to follow the laws of any government, one can still evaluate the morality of the policies and
(30) actions of various governments. Some governments do more good than harm, and others more harm than good, to their subjects. Some violate the moral rights of individuals more regularly, systematically, and seriously than others. In short, it is perfectly
(35) consistent with philosophical anarchism to hold that governments vary widely in their moral stature.

Second, philosophical anarchists maintain that all individuals have basic, nonlegal moral duties to one another—duties not to harm others in their lives,
(40) liberty, health, or goods. Even if governmental laws have no moral force, individuals still have duties to refrain from those actions that constitute crimes in the majority of legal systems (such as murder, assault, theft, and fraud). Moreover, philosophical anarchists
(45) hold that people have a positive moral obligation to care for one another, a moral obligation that they might even choose to discharge by supporting cooperative efforts by governments to help those in need. And where others are abiding by established
(50) laws, even those laws derived from mere conventions, individuals are morally bound not to violate those laws when doing so would endanger others. Thus, if others obey the law and drive their vehicles on the right, one must not endanger them by driving on the
(55) left, for, even though driving on the left is not inherently immoral, it is morally wrong to deliberately harm the innocent.

20. Which one of the following most accurately expresses the main point of the passage?

(A) Some views that certain commentators consider to be implications of philosophical anarchism are highly counterintuitive.

(B) Contrary to what philosophical anarchists claim, some governments are morally superior to others, and citizens under legitimate governments have moral obligations to one another.

(C) It does not follow logically from philosophical anarchism that no government is morally better than any other or that people have no moral duties toward one another.

(D) Even if, as certain philosophical anarchists claim, governmental laws lack moral force, people still have a moral obligation to refrain from harming one another.

(E) Contrary to what some of its opponents have claimed, philosophical anarchism does not conflict with the ordinary view that one should obey the law because it is the law.

21. The author identifies which one of the following as a commonly held belief?

(A) In most cases we are morally obligated to obey the law simply because it is the law.

(B) All governments are in essence morally equal.

(C) We are morally bound to obey only those laws we participate in establishing.

(D) Most crimes are morally neutral, even though they are illegal.

(E) The majority of existing laws are intended to protect others from harm.

22. The author's stance regarding the theory of philosophical anarchism can most accurately be described as one of

(A) ardent approval of most aspects of the theory

(B) apparent acceptance of some of the basic positions of the theory

(C) concerned pessimism about the theory's ability to avoid certain extreme views

(D) hesitant rejection of some of the central features of the theory

(E) resolute antipathy toward both the theory and certain of its logical consequences

GO ON TO THE NEXT PAGE.

23. By attributing to commentators the view that philosophical anarchism has implications that are "counterintuitive" (line 17), the author most likely means that the commentators believe that

(A) the implications conflict with some commonly held beliefs

(B) there is little empirical evidence that the implications are actually true

(C) common sense indicates that philosophical anarchism does not have such implications

(D) the implications appear to be incompatible with each other

(E) each of the implications contains an internal logical inconsistency

24. Which one of the following scenarios most completely conforms to the views attributed to philosophical anarchists in lines 37–44?

(A) A member of a political party that is illegal in a particular country divulges the names of other members because he fears legal penalties.

(B) A corporate executive chooses to discontinue her company's practice of dumping chemicals illegally when she learns that the chemicals are contaminating the water supply.

(C) A person who knows that a coworker has stolen funds from their employer decides to do nothing because the coworker is widely admired.

(D) A person neglects to pay her taxes, even though it is likely that she will suffer severe legal penalties as a consequence, because she wants to use the money to finance a new business.

(E) A driver determines that it is safe to exceed the posted speed limit, in spite of poor visibility, because there are apparently no other vehicles on the road.

25. It can be inferred that the author would be most likely to agree that

(A) people are subject to more moral obligations than is generally held to be the case

(B) governments that are morally superior recognize that their citizens are not morally bound to obey their laws

(C) one may have good reason to support the efforts of one's government even if one has no moral duty to obey its laws

(D) there are some sound arguments for claiming that most governments have a moral right to require obedience to their laws

(E) the theory of philosophical anarchism entails certain fundamental principles regarding how laws should be enacted and enforced

26. The author's discussion of people's positive moral duty to care for one another (lines 44–49) functions primarily to

(A) demonstrate that governmental efforts to help those in need are superfluous

(B) suggest that philosophical anarchists maintain that laws that foster the common good are extremely rare

(C) imply that the theoretical underpinnings of philosophical anarchism are inconsistent with certain widely held moral truths

(D) indicate that philosophical anarchists recognize that people are subject to substantial moral obligations

(E) illustrate that people are morally obligated to refrain from those actions that are crimes in most legal systems

27. In the passage, the author seeks primarily to

(A) describe the development and theoretical underpinnings of a particular theory

(B) establish that a particular theory conforms to the dictates of common sense

(C) argue that two necessary implications of a particular theory are morally acceptable

(D) defend a particular theory against its critics by showing that their arguments are mistaken

(E) demonstrate that proponents of a particular theory are aware of the theory's defects

S T O P

IF YOU FINISH BEFORE TIME IS CALLED, YOU MAY CHECK YOUR WORK ON THIS SECTION ONLY.
DO NOT WORK ON ANY OTHER SECTION IN THE TEST.

Time: 35 Minutes

General Directions

You will have 35 minutes in which to plan and write an essay on the topic inside. Read the topic and the accompanying directions carefully. You will probably find it best to spend a few minutes considering the topic and organizing your thoughts before you begin writing. In your essay, be sure to develop your ideas fully, leaving time, if possible, to review what you have written. **Do not write on a topic other than the one specified. Writing on a topic of your own choice is not acceptable.**

No special knowledge is required or expected for this writing exercise. Law schools are interested in the reasoning, clarity, organization, language usage, and writing mechanics displayed in your essay. How well you write is more important than how much you write.

Confine your essay to the blocked, lined area on the front and back of the separate Writing Sample Response Sheet. Only that area will be reproduced for law schools. Be sure that your writing is legible.

Both this topic sheet and your response sheet must be turned over to the testing staff before you leave the room.

Scratch Paper
Do not write your essay in this space.

LSAT® Writing Sample Topic

Directions: The scenario presented below describes two choices, either one of which can be supported on the basis of the information given. Your essay should consider both choices and argue for one over the other, based on the two specified criteria and the facts provided. There is no "right" or "wrong" choice: a reasonable argument can be made for either.

A neighborhood association is planning to sponsor a public event on the first day of summer—either a walking tour or a 5 kilometer run. Using the facts below, write an essay in which you argue for one event over the other based on the following two criteria:

- The association wants to encourage more neighborhood residents to become association members.
- In order to conduct other activities during the year, the association wants to minimize the time and resources required by the event.

The first event is a free, self-guided walking tour of some of the neighborhood's private homes and historic buildings. The tour would feature the association's promotional table and exhibits of crafts, music, and cooking. Many neighborhood residents have expressed interest in such a tour. Some of the responsibility for organizing the event would be borne by those who own the homes and buildings; the association would be responsible for the remaining details. The costs of this event would consume most of the association's annual budget. Other neighborhood associations that have conducted similar tours report robust neighborhood participation and accompanying increases in membership.

The second event is a 5 kilometer run through the neighborhood. The association has sponsored this yearly event for almost a decade. In recent years, the association has hired a third-party company to manage the race and would do so again. Registration fees collected from race participants would cover administrative costs. In the past the event has led to modest increases in membership for the association. At its peak, almost 1,000 people participated in the race, most of them from out of town. This year more people are expected to participate, because the course has been professionally certified and the race would serve as a qualifying race for a national championship.

WP-O065B

Scratch Paper
Do not write your essay in this space.

COMPUTING YOUR SCORE

Directions:

1. Use the Answer Key on the next page to check your answers.

2. Use the Scoring Worksheet below to compute your raw score.

3. Use the Score Conversion Chart to convert your raw score into the 120–180 scale.

Scoring Worksheet

1. Enter the number of questions you answered correctly in each section.

Number Correct

SECTION I .... _____
SECTION II .... _____
SECTION III .... _____
SECTION IV .... _____

2. Enter the sum here: _____
This is your Raw Score.

Conversion Chart
For Converting Raw Score to the 120–180 LSAT Scaled Score
LSAT Form 7LSN73

Reported Score	Raw Score Lowest	Raw Score Highest
180	97	99
179	—*	—*
178	96	96
177	95	95
176	94	94
175	—*	—*
174	93	93
173	92	92
172	91	91
171	90	90
170	89	89
169	88	88
168	87	87
167	86	86
166	84	85
165	83	83
164	82	82
163	80	81
162	78	79
161	77	77
160	75	76
159	73	74
158	72	72
157	70	71
156	68	69
155	66	67
154	64	65
153	62	63
152	61	61
151	59	60
150	57	58
149	55	56
148	53	54
147	51	52
146	50	50
145	48	49
144	46	47
143	45	45
142	43	44
141	41	42
140	40	40
139	38	39
138	36	37
137	35	35
136	33	34
135	32	32
134	31	31
133	29	30
132	28	28
131	27	27
130	25	26
129	24	24
128	23	23
127	22	22
126	21	21
125	20	20
124	19	19
123	18	18
122	16	17
121	—*	—*
120	0	15

*There is no raw score that will produce this scaled score for this form.

ANSWER KEY

SECTION I

1.	C	8.	C	15.	B	22.	D
2.	D	9.	D	16.	A	23.	D
3.	A	10.	A	17.	E	24.	E
4.	C	11.	C	18.	B	25.	E
5.	B	12.	E	19.	E		
6.	E	13.	E	20.	E		
7.	A	14.	C	21.	C		

SECTION II

1.	E	8.	B	15.	C	22.	C
2.	C	9.	E	16.	B	23.	E
3.	B	10.	A	17.	D		
4.	B	11.	D	18.	C		
5.	E	12.	C	19.	A		
6.	B	13.	B	20.	E		
7.	B	14.	E	21.	C		

SECTION III

1.	D	8.	A	15.	D	22.	E
2.	D	9.	C	16.	C	23.	A
3.	B	10.	E	17.	B	24.	C
4.	B	11.	B	18.	D	25.	A
5.	D	12.	E	19.	A		
6.	C	13.	D	20.	E		
7.	A	14.	C	21.	E		

SECTION IV

1.	E	8.	B	15.	*	22.	B
2.	E	9.	A	16.	D	23.	A
3.	A	10.	C	17.	E	24.	B
4.	D	11.	B	18.	B	25.	C
5.	C	12.	D	19.	A	26.	D
6.	A	13.	C	20.	C	27.	D
7.	D	14.	E	21.	A		

* Item removed from scoring.

The Official LSAT PrepTest

53

- December 2007
  PrepTest 53

- Form 7LSN74

1

SECTION I
Time—35 minutes
25 Questions

Directions: The questions in this section are based on the reasoning contained in brief statements or passages. For some questions, more than one of the choices could conceivably answer the question. However, you are to choose the best answer; that is, the response that most accurately and completely answers the question. You should not make assumptions that are by commonsense standards implausible, superfluous, or incompatible with the passage. After you have chosen the best answer, blacken the corresponding space on your answer sheet.

1. Consumer advocate: Businesses are typically motivated primarily by the desire to make as great a profit as possible, and advertising helps businesses to achieve this goal. But it is clear that the motive of maximizing profits does not impel businesses to present accurate information in their advertisements. It follows that consumers should be skeptical of the claims made in advertisements.

   Each of the following, if true, would strengthen the consumer advocate's argument EXCEPT:

   (A) Businesses know that they can usually maximize their profits by using inaccurate information in their advertisements.
   (B) Businesses have often included inaccurate information in their advertisements.
   (C) Many consumers have a cynical attitude toward advertising.
   (D) Those who create advertisements are less concerned with the accuracy than with the creativity of advertisements.
   (E) The laws regulating truth in advertising are not applicable to many of the most common forms of inaccurate advertising.

2. Elaine: The purpose of art museums is to preserve artworks and make them available to the public. Museums, therefore, should seek to acquire and display the best examples of artworks from each artistic period and genre, even if some of these works are not recognized by experts as masterpieces.

   Frederick: Art museums ought to devote their limited resources to acquiring the works of recognized masters in order to ensure the preservation of the greatest artworks.

   Elaine's and Frederick's statements provide the most support for the claim that they would disagree about whether

   (A) many artistic masterpieces are not recognized as such by art experts
   (B) museums should seek to represent all genres of art in their collections
   (C) art museums should seek to preserve works of art
   (D) an art museum ought to acquire an unusual example of a period or genre if more characteristic examples are prohibitively expensive
   (E) all of the artworks that experts identify as masterpieces are actually masterpieces

3. Science columnist: It is clear why humans have so many diseases in common with cats. Many human diseases are genetically based, and cats are genetically closer to humans than are any other mammals except nonhuman primates. Each of the genes identified so far in cats has an exact counterpart in humans.

   Which one of the following, if true, most weakens the science columnist's explanation for the claim that humans have so many diseases in common with cats?

   (A) Cats have built up resistance to many of the diseases they have in common with humans.
   (B) Most diseases that humans have in common with cats have no genetic basis.
   (C) Cats have more diseases in common with nonhuman primates than with humans.
   (D) Many of the diseases humans have in common with cats are mild and are rarely diagnosed.
   (E) Humans have more genes in common with nonhuman primates than with cats.

4. This region must find new ways to help business grow. After all, shoe manufacturing used to be a major local industry, but recently has experienced severe setbacks due to overseas competition, so there is a need for expansion into new manufacturing areas. Moreover, our outdated public policy generally inhibits business growth.

   Which one of the following most accurately expresses the main conclusion drawn in the argument?

   (A) The region needs to find new ways to enhance business growth.
   (B) Shoe manufacturing is no longer a major source of income in the region.
   (C) Shoe manufacturing in the region has dramatically declined due to overseas competition.
   (D) Business in the region must expand into new areas of manufacturing.
   (E) Outdated public policy inhibits business growth in the region.

GO ON TO THE NEXT PAGE.

5. As a result of modern medicine, more people have been able to enjoy long and pain-free lives. But the resulting increase in life expectancy has contributed to a steady increase in the proportion of the population that is of advanced age. This population shift is creating potentially devastating financial problems for some social welfare programs.

Which one of the following propositions is most precisely exemplified by the situation presented above?

(A) Technical or scientific innovation cannot be the solution to all problems.

(B) Implementing technological innovations should be delayed until the resulting social changes can be managed.

(C) Every enhancement of the quality of life has unavoidable negative consequences.

(D) All social institutions are affected by a preoccupation with prolonging life.

(E) Solving one set of problems can create a different set of problems.

6. Since Jackie is such a big fan of Moral Vacuum's music, she will probably like The Cruel Herd's new album. Like Moral Vacuum, The Cruel Herd on this album plays complex rock music that employs the acoustic instrumentation and harmonic sophistication of early sixties jazz. The Cruel Herd also has very witty lyrics, full of puns and sardonic humor, like some of Moral Vacuum's best lyrics.

Which one of the following, if true, most strengthens the argument?

(A) Jackie has not previously cared for The Cruel Herd, but on the new album The Cruel Herd's previous musical arranger has been replaced by Moral Vacuum's musical arranger.

(B) Though The Cruel Herd's previous albums' production quality was not great, the new album is produced by one of the most widely employed producers in the music industry.

(C) Like Moral Vacuum, The Cruel Herd regularly performs in clubs popular with many students at the university that Jackie attends.

(D) All of the music that Jackie prefers to listen to on a regular basis is rock music.

(E) Jackie's favorite Moral Vacuum songs have lyrics that are somber and marked by a strong political awareness.

7. Superconductors are substances that conduct electricity without resistance at low temperatures. Their use, however, will never be economically feasible, unless there is a substance that superconducts at a temperature above minus 148 degrees Celsius. If there is such a substance, that substance must be an alloy of niobium and germanium. Unfortunately, such alloys superconduct at temperatures no higher than minus 160 degrees Celsius.

If the statements above are true, which one of the following must also be true?

(A) The use of superconductors will never be economically feasible.

(B) If the alloys of niobium and germanium do not superconduct at temperatures above minus 148 degrees Celsius, then there are other substances that will do so.

(C) The use of superconductors could be economically feasible if there is a substance that superconducts at temperatures below minus 148 degrees Celsius.

(D) Alloys of niobium and germanium do not superconduct at temperatures below minus 160 degrees Celsius.

(E) No use of alloys of niobium and germanium will ever be economically feasible.

8. Doctor: In three separate studies, researchers compared children who had slept with night-lights in their rooms as infants to children who had not. In the first study, the children who had slept with night-lights proved more likely to be nearsighted, but the later studies found no correlation between night-lights and nearsightedness. However, the children in the first study were younger than those in the later studies. This suggests that if night-lights cause nearsightedness, the effect disappears with age.

Which one of the following, if true, would most weaken the doctor's argument?

(A) A fourth study comparing infants who were currently sleeping with night-lights to infants who were not did not find any correlation between night-lights and nearsightedness.

(B) On average, young children who are already very nearsighted are no more likely to sleep with night-lights than young children who are not already nearsighted.

(C) In a study involving children who had not slept with night-lights as infants but had slept with night-lights when they were older, most of the children studied were not nearsighted.

(D) The two studies in which no correlation was found did not examine enough children to provide significant support for any conclusion regarding a causal relationship between night-lights and nearsightedness.

(E) In a fourth study involving 100 children who were older than those in any of the first three studies, several of the children who had slept with night-lights as infants were nearsighted.

GO ON TO THE NEXT PAGE.

9. Global surveys estimate the earth's population of nesting female leatherback turtles has fallen by more than two-thirds in the past 15 years. Any species whose population declines by more than two-thirds in 15 years is in grave danger of extinction, so the leatherback turtle is clearly in danger of extinction.

Which one of the following is an assumption that the argument requires?

(A) The decline in the population of nesting female leatherback turtles is proportional to the decline in the leatherback turtle population as a whole.

(B) If the global population of leatherback turtles falls by more than two-thirds over the next 15 years, the species will eventually become extinct.

(C) The global population of leatherback turtles consists in roughly equal numbers of females and males.

(D) Very few leatherback turtles exist in captivity.

(E) The only way to ensure the continued survival of leatherback turtles in the wild is to breed them in captivity.

10. Public health experts have waged a long-standing educational campaign to get people to eat more vegetables, which are known to help prevent cancer. Unfortunately, the campaign has had little impact on people's diets. The reason is probably that many people simply dislike the taste of most vegetables. Thus, the campaign would probably be more effective if it included information on ways to make vegetables more appetizing.

Which one of the following, if true, most strengthens the argument?

(A) The campaign to get people to eat more vegetables has had little impact on the diets of most people who love the taste of vegetables.

(B) Some ways of making vegetables more appetizing diminish vegetables' ability to help prevent cancer.

(C) People who find a few vegetables appetizing typically do not eat substantially more vegetables than do people who dislike the taste of most vegetables.

(D) People who dislike the taste of most vegetables would eat many more vegetables if they knew how to make them more appetizing.

(E) The only way to make the campaign to get people to eat more vegetables more effective would be to ensure that anyone who at present dislikes the taste of certain vegetables learns to find those vegetables appetizing.

11. Pure science—research with no immediate commercial or technological application—is a public good. Such research requires a great amount of financial support and does not yield profits in the short term. Since private corporations will not undertake to support activities that do not yield short-term profits, a society that wants to reap the benefits of pure science ought to use public funds to support such research.

The claim about private corporations serves which one of the following functions in the argument?

(A) It expresses the conclusion of the argument.

(B) It explains what is meant by the expression "pure research" in the context of the argument.

(C) It distracts attention from the point at issue by introducing a different but related goal.

(D) It supports the conclusion by ruling out an alternative way of achieving the benefits mentioned.

(E) It illustrates a case where unfortunate consequences result from a failure to accept the recommendation offered.

12. Melinda: Hazard insurance decreases an individual's risk by judiciously spreading the risk among many policyholders.

Jack: I disagree. It makes sense for me to buy fire insurance for my house, but I don't see how doing so lessens the chances that my house will burn down.

Jack's response most clearly trades on an ambiguity in which one of the following expressions used by Melinda?

(A) judiciously spreading
(B) many policyholders
(C) risk
(D) decreases
(E) hazard insurance

GO ON TO THE NEXT PAGE.

13. Some doctors believe that a certain drug reduces the duration of episodes of vertigo, claiming that the average duration of vertigo for people who suffer from it has decreased since the drug was introduced. However, during a recent three-month shortage of the drug, there was no significant change in the average duration of vertigo. Thus, we can conclude that the drug has no effect on the duration of vertigo.

Which one of the following is an assumption required by the argument?

(A) If a drug made a difference in the duration of vertigo, a three-month shortage of that drug would have caused a significant change in the average duration of vertigo.

(B) If there were any change in the average duration of vertigo since the introduction of the drug, it would have demonstrated that the drug has an effect on the duration of vertigo.

(C) A period of time greater than three months would not have been better to use in judging whether the drug has an effect on the duration of vertigo.

(D) Changes in diet and smoking habits are not responsible for any change in the average duration of vertigo since the introduction of the drug.

(E) There are various significant factors other than drugs that decrease the duration of vertigo for many people who suffer from it.

14. It has been suggested that a television set should be thought of as nothing more than "a toaster with pictures" and that since we let market forces determine the design of kitchen appliances we can let them determine what is seen on television. But that approach is too simple. Some governmental control is needed, since television is so important politically and culturally. It is a major source of commercial entertainment. It plays an important political role because it is the primary medium through which many voters obtain information about current affairs. It is a significant cultural force in that in the average home it is on for more than five hours a day.

Which one of the following most accurately expresses the role played in the argument by the claim that television is so important politically and culturally?

(A) It states a view that the argument as a whole is designed to discredit.

(B) It is an intermediate conclusion that is offered in support of the claim that a television set should be thought of as nothing more than "a toaster with pictures" and for which the claim that we can let market forces determine what is seen on television is offered as support.

(C) It is a premise that is offered in support of the claim that we let market forces determine the design of kitchen appliances.

(D) It is an intermediate conclusion that is offered in support of the claim that some governmental control of television is needed and for which the claim that the television is on for more than five hours a day in the average home is offered as partial support.

(E) It is a premise that is offered in support of the claim that television is the primary medium through which many voters obtain information about current affairs.

GO ON TO THE NEXT PAGE.

15. Earthworms, vital to the health of soil, prefer soil that is approximately neutral on the acid-to-alkaline scale. Since decomposition of dead plants makes the top layer of soil highly acidic, application of crushed limestone, which is highly alkaline, to the soil's surface should make the soil more attractive to earthworms.

Which one of the following is an assumption on which the argument depends?

(A) As far as soil health is concerned, aiding the decomposition of dead plants is the most important function performed by earthworms.

(B) After its application to the soil's surface, crushed limestone stays in the soil's top layer long enough to neutralize some of the top layer's acidity.

(C) Crushed limestone contains available calcium and magnesium, both of which are just as vital as earthworms to healthy soil.

(D) By itself, acidity of soil does nothing to hasten decomposition of dead plants.

(E) Alkaline soil is significantly more likely to benefit from an increased earthworm population than is highly acidic soil.

16. Jurist: A nation's laws must be viewed as expressions of a moral code that transcends those laws and serves as a measure of their adequacy. Otherwise, a society can have no sound basis for preferring any given set of laws to all others. Thus, any moral prohibition against the violation of statutes must leave room for exceptions.

Which one of the following can be properly inferred from the jurist's statements?

(A) Those who formulate statutes are not primarily concerned with morality when they do so.

(B) Sometimes criteria other than the criteria derived from a moral code should be used in choosing one set of laws over another.

(C) Unless it is legally forbidden ever to violate some moral rules, moral behavior and compliance with laws are indistinguishable.

(D) There is no statute that a nation's citizens have a moral obligation to obey.

(E) A nation's laws can sometimes come into conflict with the moral code they express.

17. An association between two types of conditions does not establish that conditions of one type cause conditions of the other type. Even persistent and inviolable association is inconclusive; such association is often due to conditions of both types being effects of the same kind of cause.

Which one of the following judgments most closely conforms to the principle stated above?

(A) Some people claim that rapid growth of the money supply is what causes inflation. But this is a naive view. What these people do not realize is that growth in the money supply and inflation are actually one and the same phenomenon.

(B) People who have high blood pressure tend to be overweight. But before we draw any inferences, we should consider that an unhealthy lifestyle can cause high blood pressure, and weight gain can result from living unhealthily.

(C) In some areas, there is a high correlation between ice cream consumption and the crime rate. Some researchers have proposed related third factors, but we cannot rule out that the correlation is purely coincidental.

(D) People's moods seem to vary with the color of the clothes they wear. Dark colors are associated with gloomy moods, and bright colors are associated with cheerful moods. This correlation resolves nothing, however. We cannot say whether it is the colors that cause the moods or the converse.

(E) Linguists propose that the similarities between Greek and Latin are due to their common descent from an earlier language. But how are we to know that the similarities are not actually due to the two languages having borrowed structures from one another, as with the languages Marathi and Telegu?

GO ON TO THE NEXT PAGE.

18. Salesperson: When a salesperson is successful, it is certain that that person has been in sales for at least three years. This is because to succeed as a salesperson, one must first establish a strong client base, and studies have shown that anyone who spends at least three years developing a client base can eventually make a comfortable living in sales.

The reasoning in the salesperson's argument is vulnerable to criticism on the grounds that it fails to consider the possibility that

(A) salespeople who have spent three years developing a client base might not yet be successful in sales

(B) some salespeople require fewer than three years in which to develop a strong client base

(C) a salesperson who has not spent three years developing a client base may not succeed in sales

(D) it takes longer than three years for a salesperson to develop a strong client base

(E) few salespeople can afford to spend three years building a client base

19. People who have habitually slept less than six hours a night and then begin sleeping eight or more hours a night typically begin to feel much less anxious. Therefore, most people who sleep less than six hours a night can probably cause their anxiety levels to fall by beginning to sleep at least eight hours a night.

The reasoning in which one of the following arguments is most similar to that in the argument above?

(A) When a small company first begins to advertise on the Internet, its financial situation generally improves. This shows that most small companies that have never advertised on the Internet can probably improve their financial situation by doing so.

(B) Certain small companies that had never previously advertised on the Internet have found that their financial situations began to improve after they started to do so. So most small companies can probably improve their financial situations by starting to advertise on the Internet.

(C) It must be true that any small company that increases its Internet advertising will improve its financial situation, since most small companies that advertise on the Internet improved their financial situations soon after they first began to do so.

(D) Usually, the financial situation of a small company that has never advertised on the Internet will improve only if that company starts to advertise on the Internet. Therefore, a typical small company that has never advertised on the Internet can probably improve its financial situation by doing so.

(E) A small company's financial situation usually improves soon after that company first begins to advertise on the Internet. Thus, most small companies that have never advertised on the Internet could probably become financially strong.

GO ON TO THE NEXT PAGE.

20. Biologist: Lions and tigers are so similar to each other anatomically that their skeletons are virtually indistinguishable. But their behaviors are known to be quite different: tigers hunt only as solitary individuals, whereas lions hunt in packs. Thus, paleontologists cannot reasonably infer solely on the basis of skeletal anatomy that extinct predatory animals, such as certain dinosaurs, hunted in packs.

The conclusion is properly drawn if which one of the following is assumed?

(A)   The skeletons of lions and tigers are at least somewhat similar in structure in certain key respects to the skeletons of at least some extinct predatory animals.

(B)   There have existed at least two species of extinct predatory dinosaurs that were so similar to each other that their skeletal anatomy is virtually indistinguishable.

(C)   If skeletal anatomy alone is ever an inadequate basis for inferring a particular species' hunting behavior, then it is never reasonable to infer, based on skeletal anatomy alone, that a species of animals hunted in packs.

(D)   If any two animal species with virtually indistinguishable skeletal anatomy exhibit quite different hunting behaviors, then it is never reasonable to infer, based solely on the hunting behavior of those species, that the two species have the same skeletal anatomy.

(E)   If it is unreasonable to infer, solely on the basis of differences in skeletal anatomy, that extinct animals of two distinct species differed in their hunting behavior, then the skeletal remains of those two species are virtually indistinguishable.

21. The trees always blossom in May if April rainfall exceeds 5 centimeters. If April rainfall exceeds 5 centimeters, then the reservoirs are always full on May 1. The reservoirs were not full this May 1 and thus the trees will not blossom this May.

Which one of the following exhibits a flawed pattern of reasoning most similar to the flawed pattern of reasoning in the argument above?

(A)   If the garlic is in the pantry, then it is still fresh. And the potatoes are on the basement stairs if the garlic is in the pantry. The potatoes are not on the basement stairs, so the garlic is not still fresh.

(B)   The jar reaches optimal temperature if it is held over the burner for 2 minutes. The contents of the jar liquefy immediately if the jar is at optimal temperature. The jar was held over the burner for 2 minutes, so the contents of the jar must have liquefied immediately.

(C)   A book is classified "special" if it is more than 200 years old. If a book was set with wooden type, then it is more than 200 years old. This book is not classified "special," so it is not printed with wooden type.

(D)   The mower will operate only if the engine is not flooded. The engine is flooded if the foot pedal is depressed. The foot pedal is not depressed, so the mower will operate.

(E)   If the kiln is too hot, then the plates will crack. If the plates crack, then the artisan must redo the order. The artisan need not redo the order. Thus, the kiln was not too hot.

22. Doctor: Being overweight has long been linked with a variety of health problems, such as high blood pressure and heart disease. But recent research conclusively shows that people who are slightly overweight are healthier than those who are considerably underweight. Therefore, to be healthy, it suffices to be slightly overweight.

The argument's reasoning is flawed because the argument

(A)   ignores medical opinions that tend to lead to a conclusion contrary to the one drawn

(B)   never adequately defines what is meant by "healthy"

(C)   does not take into account the fact that appropriate weight varies greatly from person to person

(D)   holds that if a person lacks a property that would suffice to make the person unhealthy, then that person must be healthy

(E)   mistakes a merely relative property for one that is absolute

GO ON TO THE NEXT PAGE.

23. Robust crops not only withstand insect attacks more successfully than other crops, they are also less likely to be attacked in the first place, since insects tend to feed on weaker plants. Killing insects with pesticides does not address the underlying problem of inherent vulnerability to damage caused by insect attacks. Thus, a better way to reduce the vulnerability of agricultural crops to insect pest damage is to grow those crops in good soil—soil with adequate nutrients, organic matter, and microbial activity.

Which one of the following is an assumption on which the argument depends?

(A)   The application of nutrients and organic matter to farmland improves the soil's microbial activity.
(B)   Insects never attack crops grown in soil containing adequate nutrients, organic matter, and microbial activity.
(C)   The application of pesticides to weak crops fails to reduce the extent to which they are damaged by insect pests.
(D)   Crops that are grown in good soil tend to be more robust than other crops.
(E)   Growing crops without the use of pesticides generally produces less robust plants than when pesticides are used.

24. People perceive color by means of certain photopigments in the retina that are sensitive to certain wavelengths of light. People who are color-blind are unable to distinguish between red and green, for example, due to an absence of certain photopigments. What is difficult to explain, however, is that in a study of people who easily distinguish red from green, 10 to 20 percent failed to report distinctions between many shades of red that the majority of the subjects were able to distinguish.

Each of the following, if true, helps to explain the result of the study cited above EXCEPT:

(A)   People with abnormally low concentrations of the photopigments for perceiving red can perceive fewer shades of red than people with normal concentrations.
(B)   Questions that ask subjects to distinguish between different shades of the same color are difficult to phrase with complete clarity.
(C)   Some people are uninterested in fine gradations of color and fail to notice or report differences they do not care about.
(D)   Some people are unable to distinguish red from green due to an absence in the retina of the photopigment sensitive to green.
(E)   Some people fail to report distinctions between certain shades of red because they lack the names for those shades.

25. Occultist: The issue of whether astrology is a science is easily settled: it is both an art and a science. The scientific components are the complicated mathematics and the astronomical knowledge needed to create an astrological chart. The art is in the synthesis of a multitude of factors and symbols into a coherent statement of their relevance to an individual.

The reasoning in the occultist's argument is most vulnerable to criticism on the grounds that the argument

(A)   presumes, without providing justification, that any science must involve complicated mathematics
(B)   incorrectly infers that a practice is a science merely from the fact that the practice has some scientific components
(C)   denies the possibility that astrology involves components that are neither artistic nor scientific
(D)   incorrectly infers that astronomical knowledge is scientific merely from the fact that such knowledge is needed to create an astrological chart
(E)   presumes, without providing justification, that any art must involve the synthesis of a multitude of factors and symbols

S T O P

IF YOU FINISH BEFORE TIME IS CALLED, YOU MAY CHECK YOUR WORK ON THIS SECTION ONLY.
DO NOT WORK ON ANY OTHER SECTION IN THE TEST.

SECTION II

Time—35 minutes

23 Questions

Directions: Each group of questions in this section is based on a set of conditions. In answering some of the questions, it may be useful to draw a rough diagram. Choose the response that most accurately and completely answers each question and blacken the corresponding space on your answer sheet.

Questions 1–5

Five performers—Traugott, West, Xavier, Young, and Zinser—are recruited by three talent agencies—Fame Agency, Premier Agency, and Star Agency. Each performer signs with exactly one of the agencies and each agency signs at least one of the performers. The performers' signing with the agencies is in accord with the following:

Xavier signs with Fame Agency.
Xavier and Young do not sign with the same agency as each other.
Zinser signs with the same agency as Young.
If Traugott signs with Star Agency, West also signs with Star Agency.

1. Which one of the following could be a complete and accurate list of the performers who sign with each agency?

   (A) Fame Agency: Xavier
   Premier Agency: West
   Star Agency: Traugott, Young, Zinser
   (B) Fame Agency: Xavier
   Premier Agency: Traugott, West
   Star Agency: Young, Zinser
   (C) Fame Agency: Xavier
   Premier Agency: Traugott, Young
   Star Agency: West, Zinser
   (D) Fame Agency: Young, Zinser
   Premier Agency: Xavier
   Star Agency: Traugott, West
   (E) Fame Agency: Xavier, Young, Zinser
   Premier Agency: Traugott
   Star Agency: West

2. Which one of the following could be true?

   (A) West is the only performer who signs with Star Agency.
   (B) West, Young, and Zinser all sign with Premier Agency.
   (C) Xavier signs with the same agency as Zinser.
   (D) Zinser is the only performer who signs with Star Agency.
   (E) Three of the performers sign with Fame Agency.

3. Which one of the following must be true?

   (A) West and Zinser do not sign with the same agency as each other.
   (B) Fame Agency signs at most two of the performers.
   (C) Fame Agency signs the same number of the performers as Star Agency.
   (D) Traugott signs with the same agency as West.
   (E) West does not sign with Fame Agency.

4. The agency with which each of the performers signs is completely determined if which one of the following is true?

   (A) Traugott signs with Fame Agency.
   (B) Traugott signs with Star Agency.
   (C) West signs with Premier Agency.
   (D) Xavier signs with Fame Agency.
   (E) Zinser signs with Premier Agency.

5. If Zinser signs with Star Agency, which one of the following must be false?

   (A) Premier Agency signs exactly one performer.
   (B) Star Agency signs exactly three of the performers.
   (C) Traugott signs with Star Agency.
   (D) West signs with Star Agency.
   (E) None of the other performers signs with the same agency as Xavier.

GO ON TO THE NEXT PAGE.

Questions 6–11

A competition is being held to select a design for Yancy College's new student union building. Each of six architects—Green, Jackson, Liu, Mertz, Peete, and Valdez—has submitted exactly one design. There are exactly six designs, and they are presented one at a time to the panel of judges, each design being presented exactly once, consistent with the following conditions:

Mertz's design is presented at some time before Liu's and after Peete's.

Green's design is presented either at some time before Jackson's or at some time after Liu's, but not both.

Valdez's design is presented either at some time before Green's or at some time after Peete's, but not both.

6. Which one of the following could be the order in which the designs are presented, from first to last?

    (A)   Jackson's, Peete's, Mertz's, Green's, Valdez's, Liu's
    (B)   Peete's, Jackson's, Liu's, Mertz's, Green's, Valdez's
    (C)   Peete's, Mertz's, Jackson's, Liu's, Green's, Valdez's
    (D)   Peete's, Mertz's, Valdez's, Green's, Liu's, Jackson's
    (E)   Valdez's, Liu's, Jackson's, Peete's, Mertz's, Green's

7. Mertz's design CANNOT be presented

    (A)   sixth
    (B)   fifth
    (C)   fourth
    (D)   third
    (E)   second

8. If Liu's design is presented sixth, then which one of the following must be true?

    (A)   Green's design is presented at some time before Jackson's.
    (B)   Jackson's design is presented at some time before Mertz's.
    (C)   Peete's design is presented at some time before Green's.
    (D)   Peete's design is presented at some time before Valdez's.
    (E)   Valdez's design is presented at some time before Green's.

9. If Jackson's design is presented at some time before Mertz's, then each of the following could be true EXCEPT:

    (A)   Jackson's design is presented second.
    (B)   Peete's design is presented third.
    (C)   Peete's design is presented fourth.
    (D)   Jackson's design is presented fifth.
    (E)   Liu's design is presented fifth.

10. Which one of the following designs CANNOT be the design presented first?

    (A)   Green's
    (B)   Jackson's
    (C)   Liu's
    (D)   Peete's
    (E)   Valdez's

11. Which one of the following could be an accurate partial list of the architects, each matched with his or her design's place in the order in which the designs are presented?

    (A)   first: Mertz; fourth: Liu; fifth: Green
    (B)   second: Green; third: Peete; fourth: Jackson
    (C)   second: Mertz; fifth: Green; sixth: Jackson
    (D)   fourth: Peete; fifth: Liu; sixth: Jackson
    (E)   fourth: Valdez; fifth: Green; sixth: Liu

GO ON TO THE NEXT PAGE.

Questions 12–17

Detectives investigating a citywide increase in burglaries questioned exactly seven suspects—S, T, V, W, X, Y, and Z—each on a different one of seven consecutive days. Each suspect was questioned exactly once. Any suspect who confessed did so while being questioned. The investigation conformed to the following:

> T was questioned on day three.
> The suspect questioned on day four did not confess.
> S was questioned after W was questioned.
> Both X and V were questioned after Z was questioned.
> No suspects confessed after W was questioned.
> Exactly two suspects confessed after T was questioned.

12. Which one of the following could be true?

(A) X was questioned on day one.
(B) V was questioned on day two.
(C) Z was questioned on day four.
(D) W was questioned on day five.
(E) S was questioned on day six.

13. If Z was the second suspect to confess, then each of the following statements could be true EXCEPT:

(A) T confessed.
(B) T did not confess.
(C) V did not confess.
(D) X confessed.
(E) Y did not confess.

14. If Y was questioned after V but before X, then which one of the following could be true?

(A) V did not confess.
(B) Y confessed.
(C) X did not confess.
(D) X was questioned on day four.
(E) Z was questioned on day two.

15. Which one of the following suspects must have been questioned before T was questioned?

(A) V
(B) W
(C) X
(D) Y
(E) Z

16. If X and Y both confessed, then each of the following could be true EXCEPT:

(A) V confessed.
(B) X was questioned on day five.
(C) Y was questioned on day one.
(D) Z was questioned on day one.
(E) Z did not confess.

17. If neither X nor V confessed, then which one of the following must be true?

(A) T confessed.
(B) V was questioned on day two.
(C) X was questioned on day four.
(D) Y confessed.
(E) Z did not confess.

GO ON TO THE NEXT PAGE.

Questions 18–23

The three highest-placing teams in a high school debate tournament are the teams from Fairview, Gillom, and Hilltop high schools. Each team has exactly two members. The individuals on these three teams are Mei, Navarro, O'Rourke, Pavlovich, Sethna, and Tsudama. The following is the case:

Sethna is on the team from Gillom High.
Tsudama is on the second-place team.
Mei and Pavlovich are not on the same team.
Pavlovich's team places higher than Navarro's team.
The team from Gillom High places higher than the team from Hilltop High.

18. Which one of the following could be an accurate list of the members of each of the three highest-placing teams?

(A)   first place: Mei and O'Rourke
        second place: Pavlovich and Sethna
        third place: Navarro and Tsudama
(B)   first place: Mei and Pavlovich
        second place: Sethna and Tsudama
        third place: Navarro and O'Rourke
(C)   first place: Navarro and Sethna
        second place: Pavlovich and Tsudama
        third place: Mei and O'Rourke
(D)   first place: O'Rourke and Pavlovich
        second place: Navarro and Tsudama
        third place: Mei and Sethna
(E)   first place: Pavlovich and Sethna
        second place: O'Rourke and Tsudama
        third place: Mei and Navarro

19. If Pavlovich is on the team from Hilltop High, then which one of the following could be true?

(A)   O'Rourke is on the first-place team.
(B)   Pavlovich is on the first-place team.
(C)   Mei is on the second-place team.
(D)   Navarro is on the second-place team.
(E)   Sethna is on the second-place team.

20. If O'Rourke is on the second-place team, then which one of the following could be true?

(A)   Mei is on the team from Gillom High.
(B)   Navarro is on the team from Fairview High.
(C)   O'Rourke is on the team from Gillom High.
(D)   Pavlovich is on the team from Hilltop High.
(E)   Tsudama is on the team from Gillom High.

21. If Pavlovich and Tsudama are teammates, then for how many of the individuals can it be exactly determined where his or her team places?

(A)   two
(B)   three
(C)   four
(D)   five
(E)   six

22. If Mei is on a team that places higher than the Hilltop team, then which one of the following could be true?

(A)   The Fairview team places first.
(B)   The Gillom team places second.
(C)   Navarro is on the second-place team.
(D)   O'Rourke is on the first-place team.
(E)   Pavlovich is on the first-place team.

23. Sethna's teammate could be any one of the following EXCEPT:

(A)   Mei
(B)   Navarro
(C)   O'Rourke
(D)   Pavlovich
(E)   Tsudama

S T O P

IF YOU FINISH BEFORE TIME IS CALLED, YOU MAY CHECK YOUR WORK ON THIS SECTION ONLY.
DO NOT WORK ON ANY OTHER SECTION IN THE TEST.

SECTION III
Time—35 minutes
25 Questions

Directions: The questions in this section are based on the reasoning contained in brief statements or passages. For some questions, more than one of the choices could conceivably answer the question. However, you are to choose the <u>best</u> answer; that is, the response that most accurately and completely answers the question. You should not make assumptions that are by commonsense standards implausible, superfluous, or incompatible with the passage. After you have chosen the best answer, blacken the corresponding space on your answer sheet.

1. At many electronics retail stores, the consumer has the option of purchasing product warranties that extend beyond the manufacturer's warranty. However, consumers are generally better off not buying extended warranties. Most problems with electronic goods occur within the period covered by the manufacturer's warranty.

   Which one of the following, if true, most strengthens the argument?

   (A) Problems with electronic goods that occur after the manufacturer's warranty expires are generally inexpensive to fix in comparison with the cost of an extended warranty.

   (B) Because problems are so infrequent after the manufacturer's warranty expires, extended warranties on electronic goods are generally inexpensive.

   (C) Most of those who buy extended warranties on electronic goods do so because special circumstances make their item more likely to break than is usually the case.

   (D) Some extended warranties on electronic goods cover the product for the period covered by the manufacturer's warranty as well as subsequent years.

   (E) Retail stores sell extended warranties in part because consumers who purchase them are likely to purchase other products from the same store.

2. Since the 1970s, environmentalists have largely succeeded in convincing legislators to enact extensive environmental regulations. Yet, as environmentalists themselves not only admit but insist, the condition of the environment is worsening, not improving. Clearly, more environmental regulations are not the solution to the environment's problems.

   The argument's reasoning is flawed because the argument

   (A) attacks the environmentalists themselves instead of their positions

   (B) presumes, without providing warrant, that only an absence of environmental regulations could prevent environmental degradation

   (C) fails to consider the possibility that the condition of the environment would have worsened even more without environmental regulations

   (D) fails to justify its presumption that reducing excessive regulations is more important than preserving the environment

   (E) fails to consider the views of the environmentalists' opponents

GO ON TO THE NEXT PAGE.

3. Although it is unwise to take a developmental view of an art like music—as if Beethoven were an advance over Josquin, or Miles Davis an advance over Louis Armstrong—there are ways in which it makes sense to talk about musical knowledge growing over time. We certainly know more about certain sounds than was known five centuries ago; that is, we understand how sounds that earlier composers avoided can be used effectively in musical compositions. For example, we now know how the interval of the third, which is considered dissonant, can be used in compositions to create consonant musical phrases.

Which one of the following most accurately expresses the main conclusion of the argument?

(A) Sounds that were never used in past musical compositions are used today.

(B) Sounds that were once considered dissonant are more pleasing to modern listeners.

(C) It is inappropriate to take a developmental view of music.

(D) It is unwise to say that one composer is better than another.

(E) Our understanding of music can improve over the course of time.

4. A recent test of an electric insect control device discovered that, of the more than 300 insects killed during one 24-hour period, only 12 were mosquitoes. Thus this type of device may kill many insects, but will not significantly aid in controlling the potentially dangerous mosquito population.

Which one of the following, if true, most seriously weakens the argument?

(A) A careful search discovered no live mosquitoes in the vicinity of the device after the test.

(B) A very large proportion of the insects that were attracted to the device were not mosquitoes.

(C) The device is more likely to kill beneficial insects than it is to kill harmful insects.

(D) Many of the insects that were killed by the device are mosquito-eating insects.

(E) The device does not succeed in killing all of the insects that it attracts.

5. Brain-scanning technology provides information about processes occurring in the brain. For this information to help researchers understand how the brain enables us to think, however, researchers must be able to rely on the accuracy of the verbal reports given by subjects while their brains are being scanned. Otherwise brain-scan data gathered at a given moment might not contain information about what the subject reports thinking about at that moment, but instead about some different set of thoughts.

Which one of the following most accurately expresses the main conclusion of the argument?

(A) It is unlikely that brain-scanning technology will ever enable researchers to understand how the brain enables us to think.

(B) There is no way that researchers can know for certain that subjects whose brains are being scanned are accurately reporting what they are thinking.

(C) Because subjects whose brains are being scanned may not accurately report what they are thinking, the results of brain-scanning research should be regarded with great skepticism.

(D) Brain scans can provide information about the accuracy of the verbal reports of subjects whose brains are being scanned.

(E) Information from brain scans can help researchers understand how the brain enables us to think only if the verbal reports of those whose brains are being scanned are accurate.

GO ON TO THE NEXT PAGE.

6. Ornithologist: This bird species is widely thought to subsist primarily on vegetation, but my research shows that this belief is erroneous. While concealed in a well-camouflaged blind, I have observed hundreds of these birds every morning over a period of months, and I estimate that over half of what they ate consisted of insects and other animal food sources.

The reasoning in the ornithologist's argument is most vulnerable to criticism on the grounds that the argument

(A) assumes, without providing justification, that the feeding behavior of the birds observed was not affected by the ornithologist's act of observation

(B) fails to specify the nature of the animal food sources, other than insects, that were consumed by the birds

(C) adopts a widespread belief about the birds' feeding habits without considering the evidence that led to the belief

(D) neglects the possibility that the birds have different patterns of food consumption during different parts of the day and night

(E) fails to consider the possibility that the birds' diet has changed since the earlier belief about their diet was formed

7. Educator: Only those students who are genuinely curious about a topic can successfully learn about that topic. They find the satisfaction of their curiosity intrinsically gratifying, and appreciate the inherent rewards of the learning process itself. However, almost no child enters the classroom with sufficient curiosity to learn successfully all that the teacher must instill. A teacher's job, therefore, _____.

Which one of the following most logically completes the educator's argument?

(A) requires for the fulfillment of its goals the stimulation as well as the satisfaction of curiosity

(B) necessitates the creative use of rewards that are not inherent in the learning process itself

(C) is to focus primarily on those topics that do not initially interest the students

(D) is facilitated by students' taking responsibility for their own learning

(E) becomes easier if students realize that some learning is not necessarily enjoyable

8. Environmentalist: When bacteria degrade household cleaning products, vapors that are toxic to humans are produced. Unfortunately, household cleaning products are often found in landfills. Thus, the common practice of converting landfills into public parks is damaging human health.

Which one of the following is an assumption the environmentalist's argument requires?

(A) In at least some landfills that have been converted into public parks there are bacteria that degrade household cleaning products.

(B) Converting a landfill into a public park will cause no damage to human health unless toxic vapors are produced in that landfill and humans are exposed to them.

(C) If a practice involves the exposure of humans to vapors from household cleaning products, then it causes at least some damage to human health.

(D) When landfills are converted to public parks, measures could be taken that would prevent people using the parks from being exposed to toxic vapors.

(E) If vapors toxic to humans are produced by the degradation of household cleaning products by bacteria in any landfill, then the health of at least some humans will suffer.

9. Tea made from camellia leaves is a popular beverage. However, studies show that regular drinkers of camellia tea usually suffer withdrawal symptoms if they discontinue drinking the tea. Furthermore, regular drinkers of camellia tea are more likely than people in general to develop kidney damage. Regular consumption of this tea, therefore, can result in a heightened risk of kidney damage.

Which one of the following, if true, most seriously weakens the argument?

(A) Several other popular beverages contain the same addictive chemical that is found in camellia tea.

(B) Addictive chemicals are unlikely to cause kidney damage solely by virtue of their addictive qualities.

(C) Some people claim that regular consumption of camellia tea helps alleviate their stress.

(D) Most people who regularly drink camellia tea do not develop kidney damage.

(E) Many people who regularly consume camellia tea also regularly consume other beverages suspected of causing kidney damage.

GO ON TO THE NEXT PAGE.

10. Artist: Avant-garde artists intend their work to challenge a society's mainstream beliefs and initiate change. And some art collectors claim that an avant-garde work that becomes popular in its own time is successful. However, a society's mainstream beliefs do not generally show any significant changes over a short period of time. Therefore, when an avant-garde work becomes popular it is a sign that the work is not successful, since it does not fulfil the intentions of its creator.

The reference to the claim of certain art collectors plays which one of the following roles in the artist's argument?

(A) It serves to bolster the argument's main conclusion.

(B) It identifies a view that is ultimately disputed by the argument.

(C) It identifies a position supported by the initial premise in the argument.

(D) It provides support for the initial premise in the argument.

(E) It provides support for a counterargument to the initial premise.

11. A recent epidemiological study found that businesspeople who travel internationally on business are much more likely to suffer from chronic insomnia than are businesspeople who do not travel on business. International travelers experience the stresses of dramatic changes in climate, frequent disruption of daily routines, and immersion in cultures other than their own, stresses not commonly felt by those who do not travel. Thus, it is likely that these stresses cause the insomnia.

Which one of the following would, if true, most strengthen the reasoning above?

(A) Most international travel for the sake of business occurs between countries with contiguous borders.

(B) Some businesspeople who travel internationally greatly enjoy the changes in climate and immersion in another culture.

(C) Businesspeople who already suffer from chronic insomnia are no more likely than businesspeople who do not to accept assignments from their employers that require international travel.

(D) Experiencing dramatic changes in climate and disruption of daily routines through international travel can be beneficial to some people who suffer from chronic insomnia.

(E) Some businesspeople who once traveled internationally but no longer do so complain of various sleep-related ailments.

12. Many mountain climbers regard climbing Mount Everest as the ultimate achievement. But climbers should not attempt this climb since the risk of death or serious injury in an Everest expedition is very high. Moreover, the romantic notion of gaining "spiritual discovery" atop Everest is dispelled by climbers' reports that the only profound experiences they had at the top were of exhaustion and fear.

Which one of the following principles, if valid, most helps to justify the reasoning above?

(A) Projects undertaken primarily for spiritual reasons ought to be abandoned if the risks are great.

(B) Dangerous activities that are unlikely to result in significant spiritual benefits for those undertaking them should be avoided.

(C) Activities that are extremely dangerous ought to be legally prohibited unless they are necessary to produce spiritual enlightenment.

(D) Profound spiritual experiences can be achieved without undergoing the serious danger involved in mountain climbing.

(E) Mountain climbers and other athletes should carefully examine the underlying reasons they have for participating in their sports.

13. Each of the smallest particles in the universe has an elegantly simple structure. Since these particles compose the universe, we can conclude that the universe itself has an elegantly simple structure.

Each of the following arguments exhibits flawed reasoning similar to that in the argument above EXCEPT:

(A) Each part of this car is nearly perfectly engineered. Therefore this car is nearly perfect, from an engineering point of view.

(B) Each part of this desk is made of metal. Therefore this desk is made of metal.

(C) Each brick in this wall is rectangular. Therefore this wall is rectangular.

(D) Each piece of wood in this chair is sturdy. Therefore this chair is sturdy.

(E) Each sentence in this novel is well constructed. Therefore this is a well-constructed novel.

GO ON TO THE NEXT PAGE.

14. Criminologist: A judicial system that tries and punishes criminals without delay is an effective deterrent to violent crime. Long, drawn-out trials and successful legal maneuvering may add to criminals' feelings of invulnerability. But if potential violent criminals know that being caught means prompt punishment, they will hesitate to break the law.

Which one of the following, if true, would most seriously weaken the criminologist's argument?

(A) It is in the nature of violent crime that it is not premeditated.
(B) About one-fourth of all suspects first arrested for a crime are actually innocent.
(C) Many violent crimes are committed by first-time offenders.
(D) Everyone accused of a crime has the right to a trial.
(E) Countries that promptly punish suspected lawbreakers have lower crime rates than countries that allow long trials.

15. Journalist: Many people object to mandatory retirement at age 65 as being arbitrary, arguing that people over 65 make useful contributions. However, if those who reach 65 are permitted to continue working indefinitely, we will face unacceptable outcomes. First, young people entering the job market will not be able to obtain decent jobs in the professions for which they were trained, resulting in widespread dissatisfaction among the young. Second, it is not fair for those who have worked 40 or more years to deprive others of opportunities. Therefore, mandatory retirement should be retained.

The journalist's argument depends on assuming which one of the following?

(A) Anyone who has worked 40 years is at least 65 years old.
(B) All young people entering the job market are highly trained professionals.
(C) It is unfair for a person not to get a job in the profession for which that person was trained.
(D) If people are forced to retire at age 65, there will be much dissatisfaction among at least some older people.
(E) If retirement ceases to be mandatory at age 65, at least some people will choose to work past age 65.

16. Editorial: Contrary to popular belief, teaching preschoolers is not especially difficult, for they develop strict systems (e.g., for sorting toys by shape), which help them to learn, and they are always intensely curious about something new in their world.

Which one of the following, if true, most seriously weakens the editorial's argument?

(A) Preschoolers have a tendency to imitate adults, and most adults follow strict routines.
(B) Children intensely curious about new things have very short attention spans.
(C) Some older children also develop strict systems that help them learn.
(D) Preschoolers ask as many creative questions as do older children.
(E) Preschool teachers generally report lower levels of stress than do other teachers.

17. Lawyer: A body of circumstantial evidence is like a rope, and each item of evidence is like a strand of that rope. Just as additional pieces of circumstantial evidence strengthen the body of evidence, adding strands to the rope strengthens the rope. And if one strand breaks, the rope is not broken nor is its strength much diminished. Thus, even if a few items of a body of circumstantial evidence are discredited, the overall body of evidence retains its basic strength.

The reasoning in the lawyer's argument is most vulnerable to criticism on the grounds that the argument

(A) takes for granted that no items in a body of circumstantial evidence are significantly more critical to the strength of the evidence than other items in that body
(B) presumes, without providing justification, that the strength of a body of evidence is less than the sum of the strengths of the parts of that body
(C) fails to consider the possibility that if many items in a body of circumstantial evidence were discredited, the overall body of evidence would be discredited
(D) offers an analogy in support of a conclusion without indicating whether the two types of things compared share any similarities
(E) draws a conclusion that simply restates a claim presented in support of that conclusion

GO ON TO THE NEXT PAGE.

18. Ethicist: Many environmentalists hold that the natural environment is morally valuable for its own sake, regardless of any benefits it provides us. However, even if nature has no moral value, nature can be regarded as worth preserving simply on the grounds that people find it beautiful. Moreover, because it is philosophically disputable whether nature is morally valuable but undeniable that it is beautiful, an argument for preserving nature that emphasizes nature's beauty will be less vulnerable to logical objections than one that emphasizes its moral value.

The ethicist's reasoning most closely conforms to which one of the following principles?

(A) An argument in favor of preserving nature will be less open to logical objections if it avoids the issue of what makes nature worth preserving.

(B) If an argument for preserving nature emphasizes a specific characteristic of nature and is vulnerable to logical objections, then that characteristic does not provide a sufficient reason for preserving nature.

(C) If it is philosophically disputable whether nature has a certain characteristic, then nature would be more clearly worth preserving if it did not have that characteristic.

(D) Anything that has moral value is worth preserving regardless of whether people consider it to be beautiful.

(E) An argument for preserving nature will be less open to logical objections if it appeals to a characteristic that can be regarded as a basis for preserving nature and that philosophically indisputably belongs to nature.

19. An editor is compiling a textbook containing essays by several different authors. The book will contain essays by Lind, Knight, or Jones, but it will not contain essays by all three. If the textbook contains an essay by Knight, then it will also contain an essay by Jones.

If the statements above are true, which one of the following must be true?

(A) If the textbook contains an essay by Lind, then it will not contain an essay by Knight.

(B) The textbook will contain an essay by only one of Lind, Knight, and Jones.

(C) The textbook will not contain an essay by Knight.

(D) If the textbook contains an essay by Lind, then it will also contain an essay by Jones.

(E) The textbook will contain an essay by Lind.

20. The ability of mammals to control their internal body temperatures is a factor in the development of their brains and intelligence. This can be seen from the following facts: the brain is a chemical machine, all chemical reactions are temperature dependent, and any organism that can control its body temperature can assure that these reactions occur at the proper temperatures.

Which one of the following is an assumption on which the argument depends?

(A) Organisms unable to control their body temperatures do not have the capacity to generate internal body heat without relying on external factors.

(B) Mammals are the only animals that have the ability to control their internal body temperatures.

(C) The brain cannot support intelligence if the chemical reactions within it are subject to uncontrolled temperatures.

(D) The development of intelligence in mammals is not independent of the chemical reactions in their brains taking place at the proper temperatures.

(E) Organisms incapable of controlling their internal body temperatures are subject to unpredictable chemical processes.

21. People who object to the proposed hazardous waste storage site by appealing to extremely implausible scenarios in which the site fails to contain the waste safely are overlooking the significant risks associated with delays in moving the waste from its present unsafe location. If we wait to remove the waste until we find a site certain to contain it safely, the waste will remain in its current location for many years, since it is currently impossible to guarantee that any site can meet that criterion. Yet keeping the waste at the current location for that long clearly poses unacceptable risks.

The statements above, if true, most strongly support which one of the following?

(A) The waste should never have been stored in its current location.

(B) The waste should be placed in the most secure location that can ever be found.

(C) Moving the waste to the proposed site would reduce the threat posed by the waste.

(D) Whenever waste must be moved, one should limit the amount of time allotted to locating alternative waste storage sites.

(E) Any site to which the waste could be moved will be safer than its present site.

GO ON TO THE NEXT PAGE.

22. A recent survey indicates that the average number of books read annually per capita has declined in each of the last three years. However, it also found that most bookstores reported increased profits during the same period.

Each of the following, if true, helps to resolve the survey's apparently paradoxical results EXCEPT:

(A) Recent cutbacks in government spending have forced public libraries to purchase fewer popular contemporary novels.

(B) Due to the installation of sophisticated new antitheft equipment, the recent increase in shoplifting that has hit most retail businesses has left bookstores largely unaffected.

(C) Over the past few years many bookstores have capitalized on the lucrative coffee industry by installing coffee bars.

(D) Bookstore owners reported a general shift away from the sale of inexpensive paperback novels and toward the sale of lucrative hardback books.

(E) Citing a lack of free time, many survey respondents indicated that they had canceled magazine subscriptions in favor of purchasing individual issues at bookstores when time permits.

23. Naturalist: A species can survive a change in environment, as long as the change is not too rapid. Therefore, the threats we are creating to woodland species arise not from the fact that we are cutting down trees, but rather from the rate at which we are doing so.

The reasoning in which one of the following is most similar to that in the naturalist's argument?

(A) The problem with burning fossil fuels is that the supply is limited; so, the faster we expend these resources, the sooner we will be left without an energy source.

(B) Many people gain more satisfaction from performing a job well—regardless of whether they like the job—than from doing merely adequately a job they like; thus, people who want to be happy should choose jobs they can do well.

(C) Some students who study thoroughly do well in school. Thus, what is most important for success in school is not how much time a student puts into studying, but rather how thoroughly the student studies.

(D) People do not fear change if they know what the change will bring; so, our employees' fear stems not from our company's undergoing change, but from our failing to inform them of what the changes entail.

(E) Until ten years ago, we had good soil and our agriculture flourished. Therefore, the recent decline of our agriculture is a result of our soil rapidly eroding and there being nothing that can replace the good soil we lost.

GO ON TO THE NEXT PAGE.

24. Professor: A person who can select a beverage from among 50 varieties of cola is less free than one who has only these 5 choices: wine, coffee, apple juice, milk, and water. It is clear, then, that meaningful freedom cannot be measured simply by the number of alternatives available; the extent of the differences among the alternatives is also a relevant factor.

The professor's argument proceeds by

(A) supporting a general principle by means of an example

(B) drawing a conclusion about a particular case on the basis of a general principle

(C) supporting its conclusion by means of an analogy

(D) claiming that whatever holds for each member of a group must hold for the whole group

(E) inferring one general principle from another, more general, principle

25. Principle: Meetings should be kept short, addressing only those issues relevant to a majority of those attending. A person should not be required to attend a meeting if none of the issues to be addressed at the meeting are relevant to that person.

Application: Terry should not be required to attend today's two o'clock meeting.

Which one of the following, if true, most justifies the stated application of the principle?

(A) The only issues on which Terry could make a presentation at the meeting are issues irrelevant to at least a majority of those who could attend.

(B) If Terry makes a presentation at the meeting, the meeting will not be kept short.

(C) No issue relevant to Terry could be relevant to a majority of those attending the meeting.

(D) If Terry attends the meeting a different set of issues will be relevant to a majority of those attending than if Terry does not attend.

(E) The majority of the issues to be addressed at the meeting are not relevant to Terry.

S T O P

IF YOU FINISH BEFORE TIME IS CALLED, YOU MAY CHECK YOUR WORK ON THIS SECTION ONLY.
DO NOT WORK ON ANY OTHER SECTION IN THE TEST.

SECTION IV

Time—35 minutes

27 Questions

<u>Directions:</u> Each set of questions in this section is based on a single passage or a pair of passages. The questions are to be answered on the basis of what is <u>stated</u> or <u>implied</u> in the passage or pair of passages. For some of the questions, more than one of the choices could conceivably answer the question. However, you are to choose the <u>best</u> answer; that is, the response that most accurately and completely answers the question, and blacken the corresponding space on your answer sheet.

Asian American poetry from Hawaii, the Pacific island state of the United States, is generally characterizable in one of two ways: either as portraying a model multicultural paradise, or as
(5) exemplifying familiar Asian American literary themes such as generational conflict. In this light, the recent work of Wing Tek Lum in *Expounding the Doubtful Points* is striking for its demand to be understood on its own terms. Lum offers no romanticized notions of
(10) multicultural life in Hawaii, and while he does explore themes of family, identity, history, and literary tradition, he does not do so at the expense of attempting to discover and retain a local sensibility. For Lum such a sensibility is informed by the fact
(15) that Hawaii's population, unlike that of the continental U.S., has historically consisted predominantly of people of Asian and Pacific island descent, making the experience of its Asian Americans somewhat different than that of mainland
(20) Asian Americans.

In one poem, Lum meditates on the ways in which a traditional Chinese lunar celebration he is attending at a local beach both connects him to and separates him from the past. In the company of new
(25) Chinese immigrants, the speaker realizes that while ties to the homeland are comforting and necessary, it is equally important to have "a sense of new family" in this new land of Hawaii, and hence a new identity—one that is sensitive to its new environment.
(30) The role of immigrants in this poem is significant in that, through their presence, Lum is able to refer both to the traditional culture of his ancestral homeland as well as to the flux within Hawaiian society that has been integral to its heterogeneity. Even in a laudatory
(35) poem to famous Chinese poet Li Po (701–762 A.D.), which partly serves to place Lum's work within a distinguished literary tradition, Lum refuses to offer a stereotypical nostalgia for the past, instead pointing out the often elitist tendencies inherent in the work of
(40) some traditionally acclaimed Chinese poets.

Lum closes his volume with a poem that further points to the complex relationships between heritage and local culture in determining one's identity. Pulling together images and figures as vastly
(45) disparate as a famous Chinese American literary character and an old woman selling bread, Lum avoids an excessively romantic vision of U.S. culture, while simultaneously acknowledging the dream of this culture held by many newly arrived immigrants.
(50) The central image of a communal pot where each

person chooses what she or he wishes to eat but shares with others the "sweet soup / spooned out at the end of the meal" is a hopeful one; however, it also appears to caution that the strong cultural
(55) emphasis in the U.S. on individual drive and success that makes retaining a sense of homeland tradition difficult should be identified and responded to in ways that allow for a healthy new sense of identity to be formed.

1. Which one of the following most accurately expresses the main point of the passage?

(A) The poetry of Lum departs from other Asian American poetry from Hawaii in that it acknowledges its author's heritage but also expresses the poet's search for a new local identity.

(B) Lum's poetry is in part an expression of the conflict between a desire to participate in a community with shared traditions and values and a desire for individual success.

(C) Lum writes poetry that not only rejects features of the older literary tradition in which he participates but also rejects the popular literary traditions of Hawaiian writers.

(D) The poetry of Lum illustrates the extent to which Asian American writers living in Hawaii have a different cultural perspective than those living in the continental U.S.

(E) Lum's poetry is an unsuccessful attempt to manage the psychological burdens of reconciling a sense of tradition with a healthy sense of individual identity.

GO ON TO THE NEXT PAGE.

2. Given the information in the passage, which one of the following is Lum most likely to believe?

(A) Images in a poem should be explained in that poem so that their meaning will be widely understood.

(B) The experience of living away from one's homeland is necessary for developing a healthy perspective on one's cultural traditions.

(C) It is important to reconcile the values of individual achievement and enterprise with the desire to retain one's cultural traditions.

(D) One's identity is continually in transition and poetry is a way of developing a static identity.

(E) One cannot both seek a new identity and remain connected to one's cultural traditions.

3. The author of the passage uses the phrase "the flux within Hawaiian society" (line 33) primarily in order to

(A) describe the social tension created by the mix of attitudes exhibited by citizens of Hawaii

(B) deny that Hawaiian society is culturally distinct from that of the continental U.S.

(C) identify the process by which immigrants learn to adapt to their new communities

(D) refer to the constant change to which the culture in Hawaii is subject due to its diverse population

(E) emphasize the changing attitudes of many immigrants to Hawaii toward their traditional cultural norms

4. According to the passage, some Asian American literature from Hawaii has been characterized as which one of the following?

(A) inimical to the process of developing a local sensibility

(B) centered on the individual's drive to succeed

(C) concerned with conflicts between different age groups

(D) focused primarily on retaining ties to one's homeland

(E) tied to a search for a new sense of family in a new land

5. The author of the passage describes *Expounding the Doubtful Points* as "striking" (lines 7–8) primarily in order to

(A) underscore the forceful and contentious tone of the work

(B) indicate that the work has not been properly analyzed by literary critics

(C) stress the radical difference between this work and Lum's earlier work

(D) emphasize the differences between this work and that of other Asian American poets from Hawaii

(E) highlight the innovative nature of Lum's experiments with poetic form

6. With which one of the following statements regarding Lum's poetry would the author of the passage be most likely to agree?

(A) It cannot be used to support any specific political ideology.

(B) It is an elegant demonstration of the poet's appreciation of the stylistic contributions of his literary forebears.

(C) It is most fruitfully understood as a meditation on the choice between new and old that confronts any human being in any culture.

(D) It conveys thoughtful assessments of both his ancestral homeland tradition and the culture in which he is attempting to build a new identity.

(E) It conveys Lum's antipathy toward tradition by juxtaposing traditional and nontraditional images.

GO ON TO THE NEXT PAGE.

In England the burden of history weighs heavily on common law, that unwritten code of time-honored laws derived largely from English judicial custom and precedent. Students of contemporary British law are

(5) frequently required to study medieval cases, to interpret archaic Latin maxims, or to confront doctrinal principles whose validity is based solely on their being part of the "timeless reason" of the English legal tradition. Centuries-old custom serves as

(10) the basis both for the divisions of law school subject matter and for much of the terminology of legal redress. Connected not only with legal history but also with the cultural history of the English people, common law cannot properly be understood without

(15) taking a long historical view.

Yet the academic study of jurisprudence has seldom treated common law as a constantly evolving phenomenon rooted in history; those interpretive theories that do acknowledge the antiquity of

(20) common law ignore the practical contemporary significance of its historical forms. The reasons for this omission are partly theoretical and partly political. In theoretical terms, modern jurisprudence has consistently treated law as a unified system of

(25) rules that can be studied at any given moment in time as a logical whole. The notion of jurisprudence as a system of norms or principles deemphasizes history in favor of the coherence of a system. In this view, the past of the system is conceived as no more than

(30) the continuous succession of its states of presence. In political terms, believing in the logic of law is a necessary part of believing in its fairness; even if history shows the legal tradition to be far from unitary and seldom logical, the prestige of the legal

(35) institution requires that jurisprudence treat the tradition as if it were, in essence, the application of known rules to objectively determined facts. To suggest otherwise would be dispiriting for the student and demoralizing for the public.

(40) Legal historian Peter Goodrich has argued, however, that common law is most fruitfully studied as a continually developing tradition rather than as a set of rules. Taking his cue from the study of literature, Goodrich sees common law as a sort of

(45) literary text, with history and tradition serving as the text's narrative development. To study the common law historically, says Goodrich, is to study a text in which fiction is as influential as analysis, perception as significant as rule, and the play of memory as

(50) strong as the logic of argument. The concept of tradition, for Goodrich, implies not only the preservation and transmission of existing forms, but also the continuous rewriting of those forms to adapt them to contemporary legal circumstances.

7. Which one of the following statements best expresses the main idea of the passage?

(A) The residual influences of common law explain not only the divisions of subject matter but also the terminology associated with many legal procedures.

(B) In the academic study of jurisprudence, theoretical interpretations of common law have traditionally been at odds with political interpretations of common law.

(C) Common law, while often treated as an oral history of the English people, would, according to one scholar, be more fruitfully studied as a universally adaptable and constantly changing system of rules.

(D) Although obviously steeped in history and tradition, common law has seldom been studied in relation to its development, as one theorist proposes that it be understood.

(E) Although usually studied as a unitary and logical system of rules and norms, the history of common law shows that body of law to be anything but consistent and fair.

8. It can be inferred that the author of the passage believes which one of the following about the history of law in relation to modern jurisprudence?

(A) Modern jurisprudence misinterprets the nature of the legal tradition.

(B) The history of law proves the original forms of common law to be antiquated and irrelevant to modern jurisprudence.

(C) The history of law, if it is to be made applicable to modern jurisprudence, is best studied as a system of rules rather than as a literary text.

(D) Mainstream theories of modern jurisprudence overlook the order and coherence inherent in legal history.

(E) Mainstream theories of modern jurisprudence, by and large devoid of a sense of legal history, are unnecessarily dispiriting to students and the public alike.

GO ON TO THE NEXT PAGE.

9. Which one of the following would best exemplify the kind of interpretive theory referred to in the first sentence of the second paragraph of the passage?

(A) a theory that traced modern customs involving property ownership to their origins in medieval practice

(B) a theory that relied on a comparison between modern courtroom procedures and medieval theatrical conventions

(C) a theory that analyzed medieval marriage laws without examining their relationship to modern laws

(D) a theory that compared the development of English common law in the twentieth century with simultaneous developments in German common law without examining the social repercussions of either legal system

(E) a theory that compared rules of evidence in civil courts with those in criminal courts

10. It can be inferred from the passage that Peter Goodrich would be most likely to agree with which one of the following statements concerning common law?

(A) Common law is more fruitfully studied as a relic of the history of the English people than as a legal code.

(B) The "text" of common law has degenerated from an early stage of clarity to a current state of incoherence.

(C) Without the public's belief in the justness of common law, the legal system cannot be perpetuated.

(D) While rich in literary significance, the "text" of common law has only a very limited applicability to modern life.

(E) The common law "text" inherited by future generations will differ from the one currently in use.

11. Which one of the following best defines the word "political" as it is used in the second paragraph of the passage?

(A) concerned with the ways by which people seek to advance themselves in a profession

(B) concerned with the covert and possibly unethical methods by which governments achieve their goals

(C) having to do with the maintenance of ethical standards between professions and the citizenry

(D) having to do with the maintenance of an institution's effectiveness

(E) having to do with the manner in which institutions are perceived by radical theorists

12. The passage states that students of British law are frequently required to study

(A) histories of English politics
(B) episodes of litigation from the Middle Ages
(C) treatises on political philosophy
(D) histories of ancient Roman jurisprudence
(E) essays on narrative development

13. Which one of the following best describes the author's opinion of most modern academic theories of common law?

(A) They are overly detailed and thus stultifying to both the student and the public.

(B) They lack an essential dimension that would increase their accuracy.

(C) They overemphasize the practical aspects of the common law at the expense of the theoretical.

(D) They excuse students of the law from the study of important legal disputes of the past.

(E) They routinely treat the study of the law as an art rather than as a science.

14. The primary purpose of the passage is to

(A) explain a paradoxical situation and discuss a new view of the situation

(B) supply a chronological summary of the history of an idea

(C) trace the ideas of an influential theorist and evaluate the theorist's ongoing work

(D) contrast the legal theories of past eras with those of today and suggest how these theories should be studied

(E) advocate a traditional school of thought while criticizing a new trend

GO ON TO THE NEXT PAGE.

The passages discuss relationships between business interests and university research.

Passage A

As university researchers working in a "gift economy" dedicated to collegial sharing of ideas, we have long been insulated from market pressures. The recent tendency to treat research findings as
(5) commodities, tradable for cash, threatens this tradition and the role of research as a public good.

The nurseries for new ideas are traditionally universities, which provide an environment uniquely suited to the painstaking testing and revision of
(10) theories. Unfortunately, the market process and values governing commodity exchange are ill suited to the cultivation and management of new ideas. With their shareholders impatient for quick returns, businesses are averse to wide-ranging experimentation. And, what
(15) is even more important, few commercial enterprises contain the range of expertise needed to handle the replacement of shattered theoretical frameworks.

Further, since entrepreneurs usually have little affinity for adventure of the intellectual sort, they can
(20) buy research and bury its products, hiding knowledge useful to society or to their competitors. The growth of industrial biotechnology, for example, has been accompanied by a reduction in the free sharing of research methods and results—a high price to pay for
(25) the undoubted benefits of new drugs and therapies.

Important new experimental results once led university scientists to rush down the hall and share their excitement with colleagues. When instead the rush is to patent lawyers and venture capitalists, I
(30) worry about the long-term future of scientific discovery.

Passage B

The fruits of pure science were once considered primarily a public good, available for society as a whole. The argument for this view was that most of
(35) these benefits were produced through government support of universities, and thus no individual was entitled to restrict access to them.

Today, however, the critical role of science in the modern "information economy" means that what was
(40) previously seen as a public good is being transformed into a market commodity. For example, by exploiting the information that basic research has accumulated about the detailed structures of cells and genes, the biotechnology industry can derive profitable
(45) pharmaceuticals or medical screening technologies. In this context, assertion of legal claims to "intellectual property"—not just in commercial products but in the underlying scientific knowledge—becomes crucial.

Previously, the distinction between a scientific
(50) "discovery" (which could not be patented) and a technical "invention" (which could) defined the limits of industry's ability to patent something. Today, however, the speed with which scientific discoveries can be turned into products and the large profits
(55) resulting from this transformation have led to a blurring of both the legal distinction between discovery and invention and the moral distinction between what should and should not be patented.

Industry argues that if it has supported—either in
(60) its own laboratories or in a university—the makers of a scientific discovery, then it is entitled to seek a return on its investment, either by charging others for using the discovery or by keeping it for its own exclusive use.

15. Which one of the following is discussed in passage B but not in passage A?

(A) the blurring of the legal distinction between discovery and invention
(B) the general effects of the market on the exchange of scientific knowledge
(C) the role of scientific research in supplying public goods
(D) new pharmaceuticals that result from industrial research
(E) industry's practice of restricting access to research findings

16. Both passages place in opposition the members of which one of the following pairs?

(A) commercially successful research and commercially unsuccessful research
(B) research methods and research results
(C) a marketable commodity and a public good
(D) a discovery and an invention
(E) scientific research and other types of inquiry

GO ON TO THE NEXT PAGE.

17. Both passages refer to which one of the following?

    (A) theoretical frameworks
    (B) venture capitalists
    (C) physics and chemistry
    (D) industrial biotechnology
    (E) shareholders

18. It can be inferred from the passages that the authors believe that the increased constraint on access to scientific information and ideas arises from

    (A) the enormous increase in the volume of scientific knowledge that is being generated
    (B) the desire of individual researchers to receive credit for their discoveries
    (C) the striving of commercial enterprises to gain a competitive advantage in the market
    (D) moral reservations about the social impact of some scientific research
    (E) a drastic reduction in government funding for university research

19. Which one of the following statements is most strongly supported by both passages?

    (A) Many scientific researchers who previously worked in universities have begun to work in the biotechnology industry.
    (B) Private biotechnology companies have invalidly patented the basic research findings of university researchers.
    (C) Because of the nature of current scientific research, patent authorities no longer consider the distinction between discoveries and inventions to be clear-cut.
    (D) In the past, scientists working in industry had free access to the results of basic research conducted in universities.
    (E) Government-funded research in universities has traditionally been motivated by the goals of private industry.

GO ON TO THE NEXT PAGE.

Sometimes there is no more effective means of controlling an agricultural pest than giving free rein to its natural predators. A case in point is the cyclamen mite, a pest whose population can be
(5) effectively controlled by a predatory mite of the genus *Typhlodromus*. Cyclamen mites infest strawberry plants; they typically establish themselves in a strawberry field shortly after planting, but their populations do not reach significantly damaging
(10) levels until the plants' second year. *Typhlodromus* mites usually invade the strawberry fields during the second year, rapidly subdue the cyclamen mite populations, and keep them from reaching significantly damaging levels.

(15) *Typhlodromus* owes its effectiveness as a predator to several factors in addition to its voracious appetite. Its population can increase as rapidly as that of its prey. Both species reproduce by parthenogenesis—a mode of reproduction in which unfertilized eggs
(20) develop into fertile females. Cyclamen mites lay three eggs per day over the four or five days of their reproductive life span; *Typhlodromus* lay two or three eggs per day for eight to ten days. Seasonal synchrony of *Typhlodromus* reproduction with the
(25) growth of prey populations and ability to survive at low prey densities also contribute to the predatory efficiency of *Typhlodromus*. During winter, when cyclamen mite populations dwindle to a few individuals hidden in the crevices and folds of leaves
(30) in the crowns of the strawberry plants, the predatory mites subsist on the honeydew produced by aphids and white flies. They do not reproduce except when they are feeding on the cyclamen mites. These features, which make *Typhlodromus* well-suited for
(35) exploiting the seasonal rises and falls of its prey, are common among predators that control prey populations.

Greenhouse experiments have verified the importance of *Typhlodromus* predation for keeping
(40) cyclamen mites in check. One group of strawberry plants was stocked with both predator and prey mites; a second group was kept predator-free by regular application of parathion, an insecticide that kills the predatory species but does not affect the cyclamen
(45) mite. Throughout the study, populations of cyclamen mites remained low in plots shared with *Typhlodromus*, but their infestation attained significantly damaging proportions on predator-free plants.

(50) Applying parathion in this instance is a clear case in which using a pesticide would do far more harm than good to an agricultural enterprise. The results were similar in field plantings of strawberries, where cyclamen mites also reached damaging levels when
(55) predators were eliminated by parathion, but they did not attain such levels in untreated plots. When cyclamen mite populations began to increase in an untreated planting, the predator populations quickly responded to reduce the outbreak. On average,
(60) cyclamen mites were about 25 times more abundant in the absence of predators than in their presence.

20. Which one of the following most accurately expresses the main point of the passage?

(A) Control of agricultural pests is most effectively and safely accomplished without the use of pesticides, because these pesticides can kill predators that also control the pests.

(B) Experimental verification is essential in demonstrating the effectiveness of natural controls of agricultural pests.

(C) The relationship between *Typhlodromus* and cyclamen mites demonstrates how natural predation can keep a population of agricultural pests in check.

(D) Predation by *Typhlodromus* is essential for the control of cyclamen mite populations in strawberry fields.

(E) Similarity in mode and timing of reproduction is what enables *Typhlodromus* effectively to control populations of cyclamen mites in fields of strawberry plants.

21. Based on the passage, the author would probably hold that which one of the following principles is fundamental to long-term predatory control of agricultural pests?

(A) The reproduction of the predator population should be synchronized with that of the prey population, so that the number of predators surges just prior to a surge in prey numbers.

(B) The effectiveness of the predatory relationship should be experimentally demonstrable in greenhouse as well as field applications.

(C) The prey population should be able to survive in times of low crop productivity, so that the predator population will not decrease to very low levels.

(D) The predator population's level of consumption of the prey species should be responsive to variations in the size of the prey population.

(E) The predator population should be vulnerable only to pesticides to which the prey population is also vulnerable.

22. Which one of the following is mentioned in the passage as a factor contributing to the effectiveness of *Typhlodromus* as a predator?

(A) its ability to withstand most insecticides except parathion

(B) its lack of natural predators in strawberry fields

(C) its ability to live in different climates in different geographic regions

(D) its constant food supply in cyclamen mite populations

(E) its ability to survive when few prey are available

GO ON TO THE NEXT PAGE.

23. Suppose that pesticide X drastically slows the reproductive rate of cyclamen mites and has no other direct effect on cyclamen mites or *Typhlodromus*. Based on the information in the passage, which one of the following would most likely have occurred if, in the experiments mentioned in the passage, pesticide X had been used instead of parathion, with all other conditions affecting the experiments remaining the same?

(A) In both treated and untreated plots inhabited by both *Typhlodromus* and cyclamen mites, the latter would have been effectively controlled.

(B) Cyclamen mite populations in all treated plots from which *Typhlodromus* was absent would have been substantially lower than in untreated plots inhabited by both kinds of mites.

(C) In the treated plots, slowed reproduction in cyclamen mites would have led to a loss of reproductive synchrony between *Typhlodromus* and cyclamen mites.

(D) In the treated plots, *Typhlodromus* populations would have decreased temporarily and would have eventually increased.

(E) In the treated plots, cyclamen mite populations would have reached significantly damaging levels more slowly, but would have remained at those levels longer, than in untreated plots.

24. It can be inferred from the passage that the author would be most likely to agree with which one of the following statements about the use of predators to control pest populations?

(A) If the use of predators to control cyclamen mite populations fails, then parathion should be used to control these populations.

(B) Until the effects of the predators on beneficial insects that live in strawberry fields are assessed, such predators should be used with caution to control cyclamen mite populations.

(C) Insecticides should be used to control certain pest populations in fields of crops only if the use of natural predators has proven inadequate.

(D) If an insecticide can effectively control pest populations as well as predator populations, then it should be used instead of predators to control pest populations.

(E) Predators generally control pest populations more effectively than pesticides because they do not harm the crops that their prey feed on.

25. The author mentions the egg-laying ability of each kind of mite (lines 20–23) primarily in order to support which one of the following claims?

(A) Mites that reproduce by parthenogenesis do so at approximately equal rates.

(B) Predatory mites typically have a longer reproductive life span than do cyclamen mites.

(C) *Typhlodromus* can lay their eggs in synchrony with cyclamen mites.

(D) *Typhlodromus* can reproduce at least as quickly as cyclamen mites.

(E) The egg-laying rate of *Typhlodromus* is slower in the presence of cyclamen mites than it is in their absence.

26. Which one of the following would, if true, most strengthen the author's position regarding the practical applicability of the information about predatory mites presented in the passage?

(A) The individual *Typhlodromus* mites that have the longest reproductive life spans typically also lay the greatest number of eggs per day.

(B) The insecticides that are typically used for mite control on strawberry plants kill both predatory and nonpredatory species of mites.

(C) In areas in which strawberry plants become infested by cyclamen mites, winters tend to be short and relatively mild.

(D) *Typhlodromus* are sometimes preyed upon by another species of mites that is highly susceptible to parathion.

(E) *Typhlodromus* easily tolerate the same range of climatic conditions that strawberry plants do.

27. Information in the passage most strongly supports which one of the following statements?

(A) Strawberry crops can support populations of both cyclamen mites and *Typhlodromus* mites without significant damage to those crops.

(B) For control of cyclamen mites by another mite species to be effective, it is crucial that the two species have the same mode of reproduction.

(C) Factors that make *Typhlodromus* effective against cyclamen mites also make it effective against certain other pests of strawberry plants.

(D) When *Typhlodromus* is relied on to control cyclamen mites in strawberry crops, pesticides may be necessary to prevent significant damage during the first year.

(E) Strawberry growers have unintentionally caused cyclamen mites to become a serious crop pest by the indiscriminate use of parathion.

S T O P

IF YOU FINISH BEFORE TIME IS CALLED, YOU MAY CHECK YOUR WORK ON THIS SECTION ONLY.
DO NOT WORK ON ANY OTHER SECTION IN THE TEST.

Acknowledgment is made to the following sources from which material has been adapted for use in this test booklet:

Brenda Kwon, review of *Expanding the Doubtful Points* by Wing Tek Lum. ©1995 by the Regents of the University of California.

Robert E. Ricklefs and Gary L. Miller, *Ecology*, Third Edition. ©1990 by W.H. Freeman and Company.

Edward Rothstein, *Emblems of Mind*. ©1995 by Edward Rothstein.

Wait for the supervisor's instructions before you open the page to the topic.
Please print and sign your name and write the date in the designated spaces below.

Time: 35 Minutes

General Directions

You will have 35 minutes in which to plan and write an essay on the topic inside. Read the topic and the accompanying directions carefully. You will probably find it best to spend a few minutes considering the topic and organizing your thoughts before you begin writing. In your essay, be sure to develop your ideas fully, leaving time, if possible, to review what you have written. **Do not write on a topic other than the one specified. Writing on a topic of your own choice is not acceptable.**

No special knowledge is required or expected for this writing exercise. Law schools are interested in the reasoning, clarity, organization, language usage, and writing mechanics displayed in your essay. How well you write is more important than how much you write.

Confine your essay to the blocked, lined area on the front and back of the separate Writing Sample Response Sheet. Only that area will be reproduced for law schools. Be sure that your writing is legible.

Both this topic sheet and your response sheet must be turned over to the testing staff before you leave the room.

Topic Code	Print Your Full Name Here		
	Last	First	M.I.
068386			

Date	Sign Your Name Here
/ /	

Scratch Paper
Do not write your essay in this space.

LSAT® Writing Sample Topic

Directions: The scenario presented below describes two choices, either one of which can be supported on the basis of the information given. Your essay should consider both choices and argue for one over the other, based on the two specified criteria and the facts provided. There is no "right" or "wrong" choice: a reasonable argument can be made for either.

Dennis, a photographer and local historian, has been commissioned to write a book about the preservation of photographs. He has worked out two different approaches to completing the book, which must be finished in two years. Using the facts below, write an essay in which you argue for one approach over the other based on the following two criteria:

- Dennis would like to improve his knowledge of photographic preservation through practical, hands-on experience.
- Dennis wants to produce a draft of the book as soon as possible.

One approach is for Dennis to take a two-year, part-time position at the photographic archives of a prestigious portrait gallery. He would help people locate visual images for publication, exhibition, research, or personal use from the archives. He would also perform various administrative tasks. Over the two-year period, Dennis would learn a great deal about the methodologies and techniques relating to photographic preservation through routine contact with professional archivists and visiting researchers. He would also enjoy extensive access to the portrait gallery's resources during that time.

Alternatively, Dennis can take a one-year, full-time position with the local public archives, which has a vast collection of photographs from the surrounding region dating back to 1865. Dennis would be helping to complete the cataloging and scanning of those photographs for inclusion in an online system. His extensive responsibilities would include entering historic photographs into a web-based database, determining the street address or location of scenes depicted in the photographs, transferring historic photographic negatives to acid-free storage, and retouching scanned images. He would work alongside skilled archivists and would gain a working knowledge of photographic conservation-preservation procedures.

WP-O068B

Scratch Paper
Do not write your essay in this space.

EliteView™ forms by NCS Pearson EM-252259-6:654321   Printed in U.S.A.

LAST NAME (Print)

FIRST NAME (Print)

SSN/ SIN

L

MI

TEST CENTER NO.

SIGNATURE

M   M   D   D   Y   Y
TEST DATE

LSAC ACCOUNT NO.

TOPIC CODE

Writing Sample Response Sheet

DO NOT WRITE IN THIS SPACE

**Begin your essay in the lined area below.
Continue on the back if you need more space.**

COMPUTING YOUR SCORE

Directions:

1. Use the Answer Key on the next page to check your answers.

2. Use the Scoring Worksheet below to compute your raw score.

3. Use the Score Conversion Chart to convert your raw score into the 120–180 scale.

Scoring Worksheet

1. Enter the number of questions you answered correctly in each section.

	Number Correct
SECTION I.................	_____
SECTION II...............	_____
SECTION III..............	_____
SECTION IV	_____

2. Enter the sum here: _____
   This is your Raw Score.

Conversion Chart
For Converting Raw Score to the 120–180 LSAT Scaled Score
LSAT Form 7LSN74

Reported Score	Raw Score Lowest	Raw Score Highest
180	98	100
179	97	97
178	96	96
177	—*	—*
176	95	95
175	94	94
174	93	93
173	92	92
172	91	91
171	90	90
170	89	89
169	88	88
168	87	87
167	86	86
166	84	85
165	83	83
164	81	82
163	80	80
162	78	79
161	77	77
160	75	76
159	73	74
158	71	72
157	70	70
156	68	69
155	66	67
154	64	65
153	62	63
152	61	61
151	59	60
150	57	58
149	55	56
148	53	54
147	52	52
146	50	51
145	48	49
144	46	47
143	45	45
142	43	44
141	41	42
140	40	40
139	38	39
138	36	37
137	35	35
136	33	34
135	32	32
134	30	31
133	29	29
132	28	28
131	26	27
130	25	25
129	24	24
128	22	23
127	21	21
126	20	20
125	19	19
124	18	18
123	17	17
122	16	16
121	15	15
120	0	14

*There is no raw score that will produce this scaled score for this form.

ANSWER KEY

SECTION I

1.	C	8.	D	15.	B	22.	E
2.	B	9.	A	16.	E	23.	D
3.	B	10.	D	17.	B	24.	D
4.	A	11.	D	18.	B	25.	B
5.	E	12.	C	19.	A		
6.	A	13.	A	20.	C		
7.	A	14.	D	21.	A		

SECTION II

1.	B	8.	A	15.	E	22.	E
2.	A	9.	D	16.	A	23.	B
3.	B	10.	C	17.	D		
4.	B	11.	B	18.	E		
5.	C	12.	B	19.	A		
6.	C	13.	E	20.	B		
7.	A	14.	A	21.	C		

SECTION III

1.	A	8.	A	15.	E	22.	B
2.	C	9.	E	16.	B	23.	D
3.	E	10.	B	17.	A	24.	A
4.	A	11.	C	18.	E	25.	C
5.	E	12.	B	19.	A		
6.	D	13.	B	20.	D		
7.	A	14.	A	21.	C		

SECTION IV

1.	A	8.	A	15.	A	22.	E
2.	C	9.	C	16.	C	23.	A
3.	D	10.	E	17.	D	24.	C
4.	C	11.	D	18.	C	25.	D
5.	D	12.	B	19.	D	26.	E
6.	D	13.	B	20.	C	27.	A
7.	D	14.	A	21.	D		

The Official LSAT PrepTest

54

- June 2008
  PrepTest 54

- Form 9LSN79

SECTION I

Time—35 minutes

27 Questions

<u>Directions:</u> Each set of questions in this section is based on a single passage or a pair of passages. The questions are to be answered on the basis of what is <u>stated</u> or <u>implied</u> in the passage or pair of passages. For some of the questions, more than one of the choices could conceivably answer the question. However, you are to choose the <u>best</u> answer; that is, the response that most accurately and completely answers the question, and blacken the corresponding space on your answer sheet.

This passage was adapted from an article published in 1996.

The Internet is a system of computer networks that allows individuals and organizations to communicate freely with other Internet users throughout the world. As a result, an astonishing
(5) variety of information is able to flow unimpeded across national and other political borders, presenting serious difficulties for traditional approaches to legislation and law enforcement, to which such borders are crucial.
(10) Control over physical space and the objects located in it is a defining attribute of sovereignty. Lawmaking presupposes some mechanism for enforcement, i.e., the ability to control violations. But jurisdictions cannot control the information and
(15) transactions flowing across their borders via the Internet. For example, a government might seek to intercept transmissions that propagate the kinds of consumer fraud that it regulates within its jurisdiction. But the volume of electronic communications
(20) crossing its territorial boundaries is too great to allow for effective control over individual transmissions. In order to deny its citizens access to specific materials, a government would thus have to prevent them from using the Internet altogether. Such a draconian
(25) measure would almost certainly be extremely unpopular, since most affected citizens would probably feel that the benefits of using the Internet decidedly outweigh the risks.
One legal domain that is especially sensitive to
(30) geographical considerations is that governing trademarks. There is no global registration of trademarks; international protection requires registration in each country. Moreover, within a country, the same name can sometimes be used
(35) proprietarily by businesses of different kinds in the same locality, or by businesses of the same kind in different localities, on the grounds that use of the trademark by one such business does not affect the others. But with the advent of the Internet, a business
(40) name can be displayed in such a way as to be accessible from any computer connected to the Internet anywhere in the world. Should such a display advertising a restaurant in Norway be deemed to infringe a trademark in Brazil just because it can be
(45) accessed freely from Brazil? It is not clear that any particular country's trademark authorities possess, or should possess, jurisdiction over such displays. Otherwise, any use of a trademark on the Internet

could be subject to the jurisdiction of every country
(50) simultaneously.
The Internet also gives rise to situations in which regulation is needed but cannot be provided within the existing framework. For example, electronic communications, which may pass through many
(55) different territorial jurisdictions, pose perplexing new questions about the nature and adequacy of privacy protections. Should French officials have lawful access to messages traveling via the Internet from Canada to Japan? This is just one among many
(60) questions that collectively challenge the notion that the Internet can be effectively controlled by the existing system of territorial jurisdictions.

1. Which one of the following most accurately expresses the main point of the passage?

   (A) The high-volume, global nature of activity on the Internet undermines the feasibility of controlling it through legal frameworks that presuppose geographic boundaries.

   (B) The system of Internet communications simultaneously promotes and weakens the power of national governments to control their citizens' speech and financial transactions.

   (C) People value the benefits of their participation on the Internet so highly that they would strongly oppose any government efforts to regulate their Internet activity.

   (D) Internet communications are responsible for a substantial increase in the volume and severity of global crime.

   (E) Current Internet usage and its future expansion pose a clear threat to the internal political stability of many nations.

GO ON TO THE NEXT PAGE.

2. The author mentions French officials in connection with messages traveling between Canada and Japan (lines 57–59) primarily to

   (A) emphasize that the Internet allows data to be made available to users worldwide
   (B) illustrate the range of languages that might be used on the Internet
   (C) provide an example of a regulatory problem arising when an electronic communication intended for a particular destination passes through intermediate jurisdictions
   (D) show why any use of a trademark on the Internet could be subject to the jurisdiction of every country simultaneously
   (E) highlight the kind of international cooperation that made the Internet possible

3. According to the passage, which one of the following is an essential property of political sovereignty?

   (A) control over business enterprises operating across territorial boundaries
   (B) authority over communicative exchanges occurring within a specified jurisdiction
   (C) power to regulate trademarks throughout a circumscribed geographic region
   (D) control over the entities included within a designated physical space
   (E) authority over all commercial transactions involving any of its citizens

4. Which one of the following words employed by the author in the second paragraph is most indicative of the author's attitude toward any hypothetical measure a government might enact to deny its citizens access to the Internet?

   (A) benefits
   (B) decidedly
   (C) unpopular
   (D) draconian
   (E) risks

5. What is the main purpose of the fourth paragraph?

   (A) to call into question the relevance of the argument provided in the second paragraph
   (B) to provide a practical illustration that questions the general claim made in the first paragraph
   (C) to summarize the arguments provided in the second and third paragraphs
   (D) to continue the argument that begins in the third paragraph
   (E) to provide an additional argument in support of the general claim made in the first paragraph

GO ON TO THE NEXT PAGE.

Passage A

Drilling fluids, including the various mixtures known as drilling muds, play essential roles in oil-well drilling. As they are circulated down through the drill pipe and back up the well itself, they lubricate the
(5) drill bit, bearings, and drill pipe; clean and cool the drill bit as it cuts into the rock; lift rock chips (cuttings) to the surface; provide information about what is happening downhole, allowing the drillers to monitor the behavior, flow rate, pressure, and
(10) composition of the drilling fluid; and maintain well pressure to control cave-ins.

Drilling muds are made of bentonite and other clays and polymers, mixed with a fluid to the desired viscosity. By far the largest ingredient of drilling
(15) muds, by weight, is barite, a very heavy mineral of density 4.3 to 4.6. It is also used as an inert filler in some foods and is more familiar in its medical use as the "barium meal" administered before X-raying the digestive tract.
(20) Over the years individual drilling companies and their expert drillers have devised proprietary formulations, or mud "recipes," to deal with specific types of drilling jobs. One problem in studying the effects of drilling waste discharges is that the drilling
(25) fluids are made from a range of over 1,000, sometimes toxic, ingredients—many of them known, confusingly, by different trade names, generic descriptions, chemical formulae, and regional or industry slang words, and many of them kept secret by companies or individual
(30) formulators.

Passage B

Drilling mud, cuttings, and associated chemicals are normally released only during the drilling phase of a well's existence. These discharges are the main environmental concern in offshore oil production, and
(35) their use is tightly regulated. The discharges are closely monitored by the offshore operator, and releases are controlled as a condition of the operating permit.

One type of mud—water-based mud (WBM)—is a mixture of water, bentonite clay, and chemical
(40) additives, and is used to drill shallow parts of wells. It is not particularly toxic to marine organisms and disperses readily. Under current regulations, it can be dumped directly overboard. Companies typically recycle WBMs until their properties are no longer
(45) suitable and then, over a period of hours, dump the entire batch into the sea.

For drilling deeper wells, oil-based mud (OBM) is normally used. The typical difference from WBM is the high content of mineral oil (typically 30 percent).
(50) OBMs also contain greater concentrations of barite, a powdered heavy mineral, and a number of additives. OBMs have a greater potential for negative environmental impact, partly because they do not disperse as readily. Barite may impact some
(55) organisms, particularly scallops, and the mineral oil may have toxic effects. Currently only the residues of OBMs adhering to cuttings that remain after the cuttings are sieved from the drilling fluids may be discharged overboard, and then only mixtures up to a
(60) specified maximum oil content.

6. A primary purpose of each of the passages is to

(A) provide causal explanations for a type of environmental pollution
(B) describe the general composition and properties of drilling muds
(C) point out possible environmental impacts associated with oil drilling
(D) explain why oil-well drilling requires the use of drilling muds
(E) identify difficulties inherent in the regulation of oil-well drilling operations

7. Which one of the following is a characteristic of barite that is mentioned in both of the passages?

(A) It does not disperse readily in seawater.
(B) It is not found in drilling muds containing bentonite.
(C) Its use in drilling muds is tightly regulated.
(D) It is the most commonly used ingredient in drilling muds.
(E) It is a heavy mineral.

8. Each of the following is supported by one or both of the passages EXCEPT:

(A) Clay is an important constituent of many, if not all, drilling muds.
(B) At least one type of drilling mud is not significantly toxic to marine life.
(C) There has been some study of the environmental effects of drilling-mud discharges.
(D) Government regulations allow drilling muds to contain 30 percent mineral oil.
(E) During the drilling of an oil well, drilling mud is continuously discharged into the sea.

GO ON TO THE NEXT PAGE.

9. Which one of the following can be most reasonably inferred from the two passages taken together, but not from either one individually?

(A) Barite is the largest ingredient of drilling muds, by weight, and also the most environmentally damaging.

(B) Although barite can be harmful to marine organisms, it can be consumed safely by humans.

(C) Offshore drilling is more damaging to the environment than is land-based drilling.

(D) The use of drilling muds needs to be more tightly controlled by government.

(E) If offshore drilling did not generate cuttings, it would be less harmful to the environment.

10. Each of the following is supported by one or both of the passages EXCEPT:

(A) Drillers monitor the suitability of the mud they are using.

(B) The government requires drilling companies to disclose all ingredients used in their drilling muds.

(C) In certain quantities, barite is not toxic to humans.

(D) Oil reserves can be found within or beneath layers of rock.

(E) Drilling deep oil wells requires the use of different mud recipes than does drilling shallow oil wells.

11. Based on information in the passages, which one of the following, if true, provides the strongest support for a prediction that the proportion of oil-well drilling using OBMs will increase in the future?

(A) The cost of certain ingredients in WBMs is expected to increase steadily over the next several decades.

(B) The deeper an offshore oil well, the greater the concentration of barite that must be used in the drilling mud.

(C) Oil reserves at shallow depths have mostly been tapped, leaving primarily much deeper reserves for future drilling.

(D) It is unlikely that oil drillers will develop more efficient ways of removing OBM residues from cuttings that remain after being sieved from drilling fluids.

(E) Barite is a common mineral, the availability of which is virtually limitless.

12. According to passage B, one reason OBMs are potentially more environmentally damaging than WBMs is that OBMs

(A) are slower to disperse
(B) contain greater concentrations of bentonite
(C) contain a greater number of additives
(D) are used for drilling deeper wells
(E) cannot be recycled

GO ON TO THE NEXT PAGE.

Aida Overton Walker (1880–1914), one of the most widely acclaimed African American performers of the early twentieth century, was known largely for popularizing a dance form known as the cakewalk
(5) through her choreographing, performance, and teaching of the dance. The cakewalk was originally developed prior to the United States Civil War by African Americans, for whom dance was a means of maintaining cultural links within a slave society. It
(10) was based on traditional West African ceremonial dances, and like many other African American dances, it retained features characteristic of African dance forms, such as gliding steps and an emphasis on improvisation.
(15) To this African-derived foundation, the cakewalk added certain elements from European dances: where African dances feature flexible body postures, large groups and separate-sex dancing, the cakewalk developed into a high-kicking walk performed by a
(20) procession of couples. Ironically, while these modifications later enabled the cakewalk to appeal to European Americans and become one of the first cultural forms to cross the racial divide in North America, they were originally introduced with satiric
(25) intent. Slaves performed the grandiloquent walks in order to parody the processional dances performed at slave owners' balls and, in general, the self-important manners of slave owners. To add a further irony, by the end of the nineteenth century, the cakewalk was
(30) itself being parodied by European American stage performers, and these parodies in turn helped shape subsequent versions of the cakewalk.
While this complex evolution meant that the cakewalk was not a simple cultural phenomenon—
(35) one scholar has characterized this layering of parody upon parody with the phrase "mimetic vertigo"—it is in fact what enabled the dance to attract its wide audience. In the cultural and socioeconomic flux of the turn-of-the-century United States, where
(40) industrialization, urbanization, mass immigration, and rapid social mobility all reshaped the cultural landscape, an art form had to be capable of being many things to many people in order to appeal to a large audience.
(45) Walker's remarkable success at popularizing the cakewalk across otherwise relatively rigid racial boundaries rested on her ability to address within her interpretation of it the varying and sometimes conflicting demands placed on the dance. Middle-
(50) class African Americans, for example, often denounced the cakewalk as disreputable, a complaint reinforced by the parodies circulating at the time. Walker won over this audience by refining the cakewalk and emphasizing its fundamental grace.
(55) Meanwhile, because middle- and upper-class European Americans often felt threatened by the tremendous cultural flux around them, they prized what they regarded as authentic art forms as bastions of stability; much of Walker's success with this

(60) audience derived from her distillation of what was widely acclaimed as the most authentic cakewalk. Finally, Walker was able to gain the admiration of many newly rich industrialists and financiers, who found in the grand flourishes of her version of the
(65) cakewalk a fitting vehicle for celebrating their newfound social rank.

13. Which one of the following most accurately expresses the main point of the passage?

(A) Walker, who was especially well known for her success in choreographing, performing, and teaching the cakewalk, was one of the most widely recognized African American performers of the early twentieth century.

(B) In spite of the disparate influences that shaped the cakewalk, Walker was able to give the dance broad appeal because she distilled what was regarded as the most authentic version in an era that valued authenticity highly.

(C) Walker popularized the cakewalk by capitalizing on the complex cultural mix that had developed from the dance's original blend of satire and cultural preservation, together with the effects of later parodies.

(D) Whereas other versions of the cakewalk circulating at the beginning of the twentieth century were primarily parodic in nature, the version popularized by Walker combined both satire and cultural preservation.

(E) Because Walker was able to recognize and preserve the characteristics of the cakewalk as African Americans originally performed it, it became the first popular art form to cross the racial divide in the United States.

14. The author describes the socioeconomic flux of the turn-of-the-century United States in the third paragraph primarily in order to

(A) argue that the cakewalk could have become popular only in such complex social circumstances

(B) detail the social context that prompted performers of the cakewalk to fuse African and European dance forms

(C) identify the target of the overlapping parodic layers that characterized the cakewalk

(D) indicate why a particular cultural environment was especially favorable for the success of the cakewalk

(E) explain why European American parodies of the cakewalk were able to reach wide audiences

GO ON TO THE NEXT PAGE.

15. Which one of the following is most analogous to the author's account in the second paragraph of how the cakewalk came to appeal to European Americans?

(A) Satirical versions of popular music songs are frequently more popular than the songs they parody.

(B) A style of popular music grows in popularity among young listeners because it parodies the musical styles admired by older listeners.

(C) A style of music becomes admired among popular music's audience in part because of elements that were introduced in order to parody popular music.

(D) A once popular style of music wins back its audience by incorporating elements of the style of music that is currently most popular.

(E) After popular music begins to appropriate elements of a traditional style of music, interest in that traditional music increases.

16. The passage asserts which one of the following about the cakewalk?

(A) It was largely unknown outside African American culture until Walker popularized it.

(B) It was mainly a folk dance, and Walker became one of only a handful of people to perform it professionally.

(C) Its performance as parody became uncommon as a result of Walker's popularization of its authentic form.

(D) Its West African origins became commonly known as a result of Walker's work.

(E) It was one of the first cultural forms to cross racial lines in the United States.

17. It can be inferred from the passage that the author would be most likely to agree with which one of the following statements?

(A) Because of the broad appeal of humor, satiric art forms are often among the first to cross racial or cultural divisions.

(B) The interactions between African American and European American cultural forms often result in what is appropriately characterized as "mimetic vertigo."

(C) Middle-class European Americans who valued the cakewalk's authenticity subsequently came to admire other African American dances for the same reason.

(D) Because of the influence of African dance forms, some popular dances that later emerged in the United States featured separate-sex dancing.

(E) Some of Walker's admirers were attracted to her version of the cakewalk as a means for bolstering their social identities.

18. The passage most strongly suggests that the author would be likely to agree with which one of the following statements about Walker's significance in the history of the cakewalk?

(A) Walker broadened the cakewalk's appeal by highlighting elements that were already present in the dance.

(B) Walker's version of the cakewalk appealed to larger audiences than previous versions did because she accentuated its satiric dimension.

(C) Walker popularized the cakewalk by choreographing various alternative interpretations of it, each tailored to the interests of a different cultural group.

(D) Walker added a "mimetic vertigo" to the cakewalk by inserting imitations of other performers' cakewalking into her dance routines.

(E) Walker revitalized the cakewalk by disentangling its complex admixture of African and European elements.

19. The passage provides sufficient information to answer which one of the following questions?

(A) What were some of the attributes of African dance forms that were preserved in the cakewalk?

(B) Who was the first performer to dance the cakewalk professionally?

(C) What is an aspect of the cakewalk that was preserved in other North American dance forms?

(D) What features were added to the original cakewalk by the stage parodies circulating at the end of the nineteenth century?

(E) For about how many years into the twentieth century did the cakewalk remain widely popular?

GO ON TO THE NEXT PAGE.

In principle, a cohesive group—one whose members generally agree with one another and support one another's judgments—can do a much better job at decision making than it could if it were
(5) noncohesive. When cohesiveness is low or lacking entirely, compliance out of fear of recrimination is likely to be strongest. To overcome this fear, participants in the group's deliberations need to be confident that they are members in good standing and
(10) that the others will continue to value their role in the group, whether or not they agree about a particular issue under discussion. As members of a group feel more accepted by the others, they acquire greater freedom to say what they really think, becoming less
(15) likely to use deceitful arguments or to play it safe by dancing around the issues with vapid or conventional comments. Typically, then, the more cohesive a group becomes, the less its members will deliberately censor what they say out of fear of being punished socially
(20) for antagonizing their fellow members.

But group cohesiveness can have pitfalls as well: while the members of a highly cohesive group can feel much freer to deviate from the majority, their desire for genuine concurrence on every important
(25) issue often inclines them not to use this freedom. In a highly cohesive group of decision makers, the danger is not that individuals will conceal objections they harbor regarding a proposal favored by the majority, but that they will think the proposal is a good one
(30) without attempting to carry out a critical scrutiny that could reveal grounds for strong objections. Members may then decide that any misgivings they feel are not worth pursuing—that the benefit of any doubt should be given to the group consensus. In this way, they
(35) may fall victim to a syndrome known as "groupthink," which one psychologist concerned with collective decision making has defined as "a deterioration of mental efficiency, reality testing, and moral judgment that results from in-group pressures."
(40) Based on analyses of major fiascoes of international diplomacy and military decision making, researchers have identified groupthink behavior as a recurring pattern that involves several factors: overestimation of the group's power and morality,
(45) manifested, for example, in an illusion of invulnerability, which creates excessive optimism; closed-mindedness to warnings of problems and to alternative viewpoints; and unwarranted pressures toward uniformity, including self-censorship with
(50) respect to doubts about the group's reasoning and a concomitant shared illusion of unanimity concerning group decisions. Cohesiveness of the decision-making group is an essential antecedent condition for this syndrome but not a sufficient one, so it is important
(55) to work toward identifying the additional factors that determine whether group cohesiveness will deteriorate into groupthink or allow for effective decision making.

20. Which one of the following most accurately expresses the main point of the passage?

(A) Despite its value in encouraging frank discussion, high cohesion can lead to a debilitating type of group decision making called groupthink.

(B) Group members can guard against groupthink if they have a good understanding of the critical role played by cohesion.

(C) Groupthink is a dysfunctional collective decision-making pattern that can occur in diplomacy and military affairs.

(D) Low cohesion in groups is sometimes desirable when higher cohesion involves a risk of groupthink behavior.

(E) Future efforts to guard against groupthink will depend on the results of ongoing research into the psychology of collective decision making.

21. A group of closely associated colleagues has made a disastrous diplomatic decision after a series of meetings marked by disagreement over conflicting alternatives. It can be inferred from the passage that the author would be most likely to say that this scenario

(A) provides evidence of chronic indecision, thus indicating a weak level of cohesion in general

(B) indicates that the group's cohesiveness was coupled with some other factor to produce a groupthink fiasco

(C) provides no evidence that groupthink played a role in the group's decision

(D) provides evidence that groupthink can develop even in some groups that do not demonstrate an "illusion of unanimity"

(E) indicates that the group probably could have made its decision-making procedure more efficient by studying the information more thoroughly

GO ON TO THE NEXT PAGE.

22. Which one of the following, if true, would most support the author's contentions concerning the conditions under which groupthink takes place?

(A) A study of several groups, each made up of members of various professions, found that most fell victim to groupthink.

(B) There is strong evidence that respectful dissent is more likely to occur in cohesive groups than in groups in which there is little internal support.

(C) Extensive analyses of decisions made by a large number of groups found no cases of groupthink in groups whose members generally distrust one another's judgments.

(D) There is substantial evidence that groupthink is especially likely to take place when members of a group develop factions whose intransigence prolongs the group's deliberations.

(E) Ample research demonstrates that voluntary deference to group opinion is not a necessary factor for the formation of groupthink behavior.

23. The passage mentions which one of the following as a component of groupthink?

(A) unjustified suspicions among group members regarding an adversary's intentions

(B) strong belief that the group's decisions are right

(C) group members working under unusually high stress, leading to illusions of invulnerability

(D) the deliberate use of vapid, clichéd arguments

(E) careful consideration of objections to majority positions

24. It can be inferred from the passage that both the author of the passage and the researchers mentioned in the passage would be most likely to agree with which one of the following statements about groupthink?

(A) Groupthink occurs in all strongly cohesive groups, but its contribution to collective decision making is not fully understood.

(B) The causal factors that transform group cohesion into groupthink are unique to each case.

(C) The continued study of cohesiveness of groups is probably fruitless for determining what factors elicit groupthink.

(D) Outside information cannot influence group decisions once they have become determined by groupthink.

(E) On balance, groupthink cannot be expected to have a beneficial effect in a group's decision making.

25. In the passage, the author says which one of the following about conformity in decision-making groups?

(A) Enforced conformity may be appropriate in some group decision situations.

(B) A high degree of conformity is often expected of military decision-making group members.

(C) Inappropriate group conformity can result from inadequate information.

(D) Voluntary conformity occurs much less frequently than enforced conformity.

(E) Members of noncohesive groups may experience psychological pressure to conform.

26. In line 5, the author mentions low group cohesiveness primarily in order to

(A) contribute to a claim that cohesiveness can be conducive to a freer exchange of views in groups

(B) establish a comparison between groupthink symptoms and the attributes of low-cohesion groups

(C) suggest that there may be ways to make both cohesive and noncohesive groups more open to dissent

(D) indicate that both cohesive and noncohesive groups may be susceptible to groupthink dynamics

(E) lay the groundwork for a subsequent proposal for overcoming the debilitating effects of low cohesion

27. Based on the passage, it can be inferred that the author would be most likely to agree with which one of the following?

(A) Highly cohesive groups are more likely to engage in confrontational negotiating styles with adversaries than are those with low cohesion.

(B) It is difficult for a group to examine all relevant options critically in reaching decisions unless it has a fairly high degree of cohesiveness.

(C) A group with varied viewpoints on a given issue is less likely to reach a sound decision regarding that issue than is a group whose members are unified in their outlook.

(D) Intense stress and high expectations are the key factors in the formation of groupthink.

(E) Noncohesive groups can, under certain circumstances, develop all of the symptoms of groupthink.

S T O P

IF YOU FINISH BEFORE TIME IS CALLED, YOU MAY CHECK YOUR WORK ON THIS SECTION ONLY.
DO NOT WORK ON ANY OTHER SECTION IN THE TEST.

SECTION II

Time—35 minutes

26 Questions

<u>Directions:</u> The questions in this section are based on the reasoning contained in brief statements or passages. For some questions, more than one of the choices could conceivably answer the question. However, you are to choose the <u>best</u> answer; that is, the response that most accurately and completely answers the question. You should not make assumptions that are by commonsense standards implausible, superfluous, or incompatible with the passage. After you have chosen the best answer, blacken the corresponding space on your answer sheet.

1. Executive: Our company is proud of its long history of good relations with its employees. In fact, a recent survey of our retirees proves that we treat our employees fairly, since 95 percent of the respondents reported that they had always been treated fairly during the course of their careers with us.

   The executive's argument is flawed in that it

   (A) presents as its sole premise a claim that one would accept as true only if one already accepted the truth of the conclusion
   (B) relies on evidence that cannot be verified
   (C) equivocates on the word "fairly"
   (D) bases a generalization on a sample that may not be representative
   (E) presumes, without providing justification, that older methods of managing employees are superior to newer ones

2. Many of those who are most opposed to cruelty to animals in the laboratory, in the slaughterhouse, or on the farm are people who truly love animals and who keep pets. The vast majority of domestic pets, however, are dogs and cats, and both of these species are usually fed meat. Therefore, many of those who are most opposed to cruelty to animals do, in fact, contribute to such cruelty.

   Which one of the following is an assumption made by the argument?

   (A) Loving pets requires loving all forms of animal life.
   (B) Many of those who are opposed to keeping dogs and cats as pets are also opposed to cruelty to animals.
   (C) Some people who work in laboratories, in slaughterhouses, or on farms are opposed to cruelty to animals.
   (D) Many popular pets are not usually fed meat.
   (E) Feeding meat to pets contributes to cruelty to animals.

3. Statistics from the National Booksellers Association indicate that during the last five years most bookstores have started to experience declining revenues from the sale of fiction, despite national campaigns to encourage people to read more fiction. Therefore, these reading campaigns have been largely unsuccessful.

   Which one of the following statements, if true, most seriously weakens the argument?

   (A) Mail order book clubs have enjoyed substantial growth in fiction sales throughout the last five years.
   (B) During the last five years the most profitable items in bookstores have been newspapers and periodicals rather than novels.
   (C) Fierce competition has forced booksellers to make drastic markdowns on the cover price of best-selling biographies.
   (D) Due to the poor economic conditions that have prevailed during the last five years, most libraries report substantial increases in the number of patrons seeking books on changing careers and starting new businesses.
   (E) The National Booksellers Association statistics do not include profits from selling novels by mail to overseas customers.

4. People who consume a lot of honey tend to have fewer cavities than others have. Yet, honey is high in sugar, and sugar is one of the leading causes of tooth decay.

   Which one of the following, if true, most helps to resolve the apparent paradox described above?

   (A) People who eat a lot of honey tend to consume very little sugar from other sources.
   (B) Many people who consume a lot of honey consume much of it dissolved in drinks.
   (C) People's dental hygiene habits vary greatly.
   (D) Refined sugars have been linked to more health problems than have unrefined sugars.
   (E) Honey contains bacteria that inhibit the growth of the bacteria that cause tooth decay.

GO ON TO THE NEXT PAGE.

5. Byrne: One of our club's bylaws specifies that any officer who fails to appear on time for any one of the quarterly board meetings, or who misses two of our monthly general meetings, must be suspended. Thibodeaux, an officer, was recently suspended. But Thibodeaux has never missed a monthly general meeting. Therefore, Thibodeaux must have failed to appear on time for a quarterly board meeting.

The reasoning in Byrne's argument is flawed in that the argument

(A) fails to consider the possibility that Thibodeaux has arrived late for two or more monthly general meetings
(B) presumes, without providing justification, that if certain events each produce a particular result, then no other event is sufficient to produce that result
(C) takes for granted that an assumption required to establish the argument's conclusion is sufficient to establish that conclusion
(D) fails to specify at what point someone arriving at a club meeting is officially deemed late
(E) does not specify how long Thibodeaux has been an officer

6. Manufacturers of writing paper need to add mineral "filler" to paper pulp if the paper made from the pulp is to look white. Without such filler, paper products look grayish. To make writing paper that looks white from recycled paper requires more filler than is required to make such paper from other sources. Therefore, barring the more efficient use of fillers in paper manufacturing or the development of paper-whitening technologies that do not require mineral fillers, if writing paper made from recycled paper comes to replace other types of writing paper, paper manufacturers will have to use more filler than they now use.

Which one of the following is an assumption on which the argument depends?

(A) Certain kinds of paper cannot be manufactured from recycled paper.
(B) The fillers that are used to make paper white are harmful to the environment.
(C) Grayish writing paper will not be a universally acceptable alternative to white writing paper.
(D) Beyond a certain limit, increasing the amount of filler added to paper pulp does not increase the whiteness of the paper made from the pulp.
(E) The total amount of writing paper manufactured worldwide will increase significantly in the future.

7. Environmentalist: The excessive atmospheric buildup of carbon dioxide, which threatens the welfare of everyone in the world, can be stopped only by reducing the burning of fossil fuels. Any country imposing the strict emission standards on the industrial burning of such fuels that this reduction requires, however, would thereby reduce its gross national product. No nation will be willing to bear singlehandedly the costs of an action that will benefit everyone. It is obvious, then, that the catastrophic consequences of excessive atmospheric carbon dioxide are unavoidable unless _____.

Which one of the following most logically completes the argument?

(A) all nations become less concerned with pollution than with the economic burdens of preventing it
(B) multinational corporations agree to voluntary strict emission standards
(C) international agreements produce industrial emission standards
(D) distrust among nations is eliminated
(E) a world government is established

8. A clear advantage of digital technology over traditional printing is that digital documents, being patterns of electronic signals rather than patterns of ink on paper, do not generate waste in the course of their production and use. However, because patterns of electronic signals are necessarily ephemeral, a digital document can easily be destroyed and lost forever.

The statements above best illustrate which one of the following generalizations?

(A) A property of a technology may constitute an advantage in one set of circumstances and a disadvantage in others.
(B) What at first appears to be an advantage of a technology may create more problems than it solves.
(C) It is more important to be able to preserve information than it is for information to be easily accessible.
(D) Innovations in document storage technologies sometimes decrease, but never eliminate, the risk of destroying documents.
(E) Advances in technology can lead to increases in both convenience and environmental soundness.

GO ON TO THE NEXT PAGE.

9. Museum visitor: The national government has mandated a 5 percent increase in the minimum wage paid to all workers. This mandate will adversely affect the museum-going public. The museum's revenue does not currently exceed its expenses, and since the mandate will significantly increase the museum's operating expenses, the museum will be forced either to raise admission fees or to decrease services.

Which one of the following is an assumption required by the museum visitor's argument?

(A) Some of the museum's employees are not paid significantly more than the minimum wage.
(B) The museum's revenue from admission fees has remained constant over the past five years.
(C) Some of the museum's employees are paid more than the current minimum wage.
(D) The annual number of visitors to the museum has increased steadily.
(E) Not all visitors to the museum are required to pay an admission fee.

10. Helen: Reading a book is the intellectual equivalent of investing money: you're investing time, thereby foregoing other ways of spending that time, in the hope that what you learn will later afford you more opportunities than you'd get by spending the time doing something other than reading that book.

Randi: But that applies only to vocational books. Reading fiction is like watching a sitcom: it's just wasted time.

Which one of the following most accurately describes the technique Randi uses in responding to Helen's claims?

(A) questioning how the evidence Helen uses for a claim was gathered
(B) disputing the scope of Helen's analogy by presenting another analogy
(C) arguing that Helen's reasoning ultimately leads to an absurd conclusion
(D) drawing an analogy to an example presented by Helen
(E) denying the relevance of an example presented by Helen

11. Contrary to recent speculations, no hardware store will be opening in the shopping plaza. If somebody were going to open a store there, they would already have started publicizing it. But there has been no such publicity.

Which one of the following most accurately expresses the conclusion drawn in the argument?

(A) Some people have surmised that a hardware store will be opening in the shopping plaza.
(B) A hardware store will not be opening in the shopping plaza.
(C) If somebody were going to open a hardware store in the shopping plaza, that person would already have started publicizing it.
(D) It would be unwise to open a hardware store in the shopping plaza.
(E) There has been no publicity concerning the opening of a hardware store in the shopping plaza.

12. Ethicist: Although science is frequently said to be morally neutral, it has a traditional value system of its own. For example, scientists sometimes foresee that a line of theoretical research they are pursuing will yield applications that could seriously harm people, animals, or the environment. Yet, according to science's traditional value system, such consequences do not have to be considered in deciding whether to pursue that research. Ordinary morality, in contrast, requires that we take the foreseeable consequences of our actions into account whenever we are deciding what to do.

The ethicist's statements, if true, most strongly support which one of the following?

(A) Scientists should not be held responsible for the consequences of their research.
(B) According to the dictates of ordinary morality, scientists doing research that ultimately turns out to yield harmful applications are acting immorally.
(C) Science is morally neutral because it assigns no value to the consequences of theoretical research.
(D) It is possible for scientists to both adhere to the traditional values of their field and violate a principle of ordinary morality.
(E) The uses and effects of scientifically acquired knowledge can never be adequately foreseen.

GO ON TO THE NEXT PAGE.

13. Consumers seek to purchase the highest quality at the lowest prices. Companies that do not offer products that attract consumers eventually go bankrupt. Therefore, companies that offer neither the best quality nor the lowest price will eventually go bankrupt.

The conclusion above follows logically if which one of the following is assumed?

(A)   No company succeeds in producing a product that is both highest in quality and lowest in price.

(B)   Products that are neither highest in quality nor lowest in price do not attract consumers.

(C)   Any company that offers either the highest quality or the lowest price will avoid bankruptcy.

(D)   Some consumers will not continue to patronize a company purely out of brand loyalty.

(E)   No company is driven from the market for reasons other than failing to meet consumer demands.

14. The number of serious traffic accidents (accidents resulting in hospitalization or death) that occurred on Park Road from 1986 to 1990 was 35 percent lower than the number of serious accidents from 1981 to 1985. The speed limit on Park Road was lowered in 1986. Hence, the reduction of the speed limit led to the decrease in serious accidents.

Which one of the following statements, if true, most weakens the argument?

(A)   The number of speeding tickets issued annually on Park Road remained roughly constant from 1981 to 1990.

(B)   Beginning in 1986, police patrolled Park Road much less frequently than in 1985 and previous years.

(C)   The annual number of vehicles using Park Road decreased significantly and steadily from 1981 to 1990.

(D)   The annual number of accidents on Park Road that did not result in hospitalization remained roughly constant from 1981 to 1990.

(E)   Until 1986 accidents were classified as "serious" only if they resulted in an extended hospital stay.

15. Humans are supposedly rational: in other words, they have a capacity for well-considered thinking and behavior. This is supposedly the difference that makes them superior to other animals. But humans knowingly pollute the world's precious air and water and, through bad farming practices, deplete the soil that feeds them. Thus, humans are not rational after all, so it is absurd to regard them as superior to other animals.

The reasoning above is flawed in that it

(A)   relies crucially on an internally contradictory definition of rationality

(B)   takes for granted that humans are aware that their acts are irrational

(C)   neglects to show that the irrational acts perpetrated by humans are not also perpetrated by other animals

(D)   presumes, without offering justification, that humans are no worse than other animals

(E)   fails to recognize that humans may possess a capacity without displaying it in a given activity

16. "Good hunter" and "bad hunter" are standard terms in the study of cats. Good hunters can kill prey that weigh up to half their body weight. All good hunters have a high muscle-to-fat ratio. Most wild cats are good hunters, but some domestic cats are good hunters as well.

If the statements above are true, which one of the following must also be true?

(A)   Some cats that have a high muscle-to-fat ratio are not good hunters.

(B)   A smaller number of domestic cats than wild cats have a high muscle-to-fat ratio.

(C)   All cats that are bad hunters have a low muscle-to-fat ratio.

(D)   Some cats that have a high muscle-to-fat ratio are domestic.

(E)   All cats that have a high muscle-to-fat ratio can kill prey that weigh up to half their body weight.

GO ON TO THE NEXT PAGE.

17. Ethicist: The penalties for drunk driving are far more severe when the drunk driver accidentally injures people than when no one is injured. Moral responsibility for an action depends solely on the intentions underlying the action and not on the action's results. Therefore, legal responsibility, depending as it does in at least some cases on factors other than the agent's intentions, is different than moral responsibility.

The claim that the penalties for drunk driving are far more severe when the drunk driver accidentally injures people than when no one is injured plays which one of the following roles in the ethicist's argument?

(A) It is a premise offered in support of the claim that legal responsibility for an action is based solely upon features of the action that are generally unintended by the agent.

(B) It is offered as an illustration of the claim that the criteria of legal responsibility for an action include but are not the same as those for moral responsibility.

(C) It is offered as an illustration of the claim that people may be held morally responsible for an action for which they are not legally responsible.

(D) It is a premise offered in support of the claim that legal responsibility depends in at least some cases on factors other than the agent's intentions.

(E) It is a premise offered in support of the claim that moral responsibility depends solely on the intentions underlying the action and not on the action's result.

18. Columnist: Taking a strong position on an issue makes one likely to misinterpret or ignore additional evidence that conflicts with one's stand. But in order to understand an issue fully, it is essential to consider such evidence impartially. Thus, it is best not to take a strong position on an issue unless one has already considered all important evidence conflicting with that position.

The columnist's reasoning most closely conforms to which one of the following principles?

(A) It is reasonable to take a strong position on an issue if one fully understands the issue and has considered the evidence regarding that issue impartially.

(B) To ensure that one has impartially considered the evidence regarding an issue on which one has taken a strong position, one should avoid misinterpreting or ignoring evidence regarding that issue.

(C) Anyone who does not understand an issue fully should avoid taking a strong position on it.

(D) One should try to understand an issue fully if doing so will help one to avoid misinterpreting or ignoring evidence regarding that issue.

(E) It is reasonable to take a strong position on an issue only if there is important evidence conflicting with that position.

GO ON TO THE NEXT PAGE.

19. The coach of the Eagles used a computer analysis to determine the best combinations of players for games. The analysis revealed that the team has lost only when Jennifer was not playing. Although no computer was needed to discover this information, this sort of information is valuable, and in this case it confirms that Jennifer's presence in the game will ensure that the Eagles will win.

The argument above is most vulnerable to criticism on the grounds that it

(A) infers from the fact that a certain factor is sufficient for a result that the absence of that factor is necessary for the opposite result

(B) presumes, without providing justification, that a player's contribution to a team's win or loss can be reliably quantified and analyzed by computer

(C) draws conclusions about applications of computer analyses to sports from the evidence of a single case

(D) presumes, without providing justification, that occurrences that have coincided in the past must continue to coincide

(E) draws a conclusion about the value of computer analyses from a case in which computer analysis provided no facts beyond what was already known

20. Of the various food containers made of recycled Styrofoam, egg cartons are among the easiest to make. Because egg shells keep the actual food to be consumed from touching the Styrofoam, used Styrofoam need not be as thoroughly cleaned when made into egg cartons as when made into other food containers.

Which one of the following is most strongly supported by the information above?

(A) No food containers other than egg cartons can safely be made of recycled Styrofoam that has not been thoroughly cleaned.

(B) There are some foods that cannot be packaged in recycled Styrofoam no matter how the Styrofoam is recycled.

(C) The main reason Styrofoam must be thoroughly cleaned when recycled is to remove any residual food that has come into contact with the Styrofoam.

(D) Because they are among the easiest food containers to make from recycled Styrofoam, most egg cartons are made from recycled Styrofoam.

(E) Not every type of food container made of recycled Styrofoam is effectively prevented from coming into contact with the food it contains.

GO ON TO THE NEXT PAGE.

21. Most people who become migraine sufferers as adults were prone to bouts of depression as children. Hence it stands to reason that a child who is prone to bouts of depression is likely to suffer migraines during adulthood.

The flawed pattern of reasoning in the argument above is most parallel to that in which one of the following?

(A) Most good-tempered dogs were vaccinated against rabies as puppies. Therefore, a puppy that is vaccinated against rabies is likely to become a good-tempered dog.

(B) Most vicious dogs were ill-treated when young. Hence it can be concluded that a pet owner whose dog is vicious is likely to have treated the dog badly when it was young.

(C) Most well-behaved dogs have undergone obedience training. Thus, if a dog has not undergone obedience training, it will not be well behaved.

(D) Most of the pets taken to veterinarians are dogs. Therefore, it stands to reason that dogs are more prone to illness or accident than are other pets.

(E) Most puppies are taken from their mothers at the age of eight weeks. Thus, a puppy that is older than eight weeks is likely to have been taken from its mother.

22. Student: The publications of Professor Vallejo on the origins of glassblowing have reopened the debate among historians over whether glassblowing originated in Egypt or elsewhere. If Professor Vallejo is correct, there is insufficient evidence for claiming, as most historians have done for many years, that glassblowing began in Egypt. So, despite the fact that the traditional view is still maintained by the majority of historians, if Professor Vallejo is correct, we must conclude that glassblowing originated elsewhere.

Which one of the following is an error in the student's reasoning?

(A) It draws a conclusion that conflicts with the majority opinion of experts.

(B) It presupposes the truth of Professor Vallejo's claims.

(C) It fails to provide criteria for determining adequate historical evidence.

(D) It mistakes the majority view for the traditional view.

(E) It confuses inadequate evidence for truth with evidence for falsity.

23. At Southgate Mall, mattresses are sold only at Mattress Madness. Every mattress at Mattress Madness is on sale at a 20 percent discount. So every mattress for sale at Southgate Mall is on sale at a 20 percent discount.

Which one of the following arguments is most similar in its reasoning to the argument above?

(A) The only food in Diane's apartment is in her refrigerator. All the food she purchased within the past week is in her refrigerator. Therefore, she purchased all the food in her apartment within the past week.

(B) Diane's refrigerator, and all the food in it, is in her apartment. Diane purchased all the food in her refrigerator within the past week. Therefore, she purchased all the food in her apartment within the past week.

(C) All the food in Diane's apartment is in her refrigerator. Diane purchased all the food in her refrigerator within the past week. Therefore, she purchased all the food in her apartment within the past week.

(D) The only food in Diane's apartment is in her refrigerator. Diane purchased all the food in her refrigerator within the past week. Therefore, all the food she purchased within the past week is in her apartment.

(E) The only food that Diane has purchased within the past week is in her refrigerator. All the food that she has purchased within the past week is in her apartment. Therefore, all the food in her apartment is in her refrigerator.

GO ON TO THE NEXT PAGE.

24. There are 1.3 billion cows worldwide, and this population is growing to keep pace with the demand for meat and milk. These cows produce trillions of liters of methane gas yearly, and this methane contributes to global warming. The majority of the world's cows are given relatively low-quality diets even though cows produce less methane when they receive better-quality diets. Therefore, methane production from cows could be kept in check if cows were given better-quality diets.

Which one of the following, if true, adds the most support for the conclusion of the argument?

(A) Cows given good-quality diets produce much more meat and milk than they would produce otherwise.

(B) Carbon and hydrogen, the elements that make up methane, are found in abundance in the components of all types of cow feed.

(C) Most farmers would be willing to give their cows high-quality feed if the cost of that feed were lower.

(D) Worldwide, more methane is produced by cows raised for meat production than by those raised for milk production.

(E) Per liter, methane contributes more to global warming than does carbon dioxide, a gas that is thought to be the most significant contributor to global warming.

25. To face danger solely because doing so affords one a certain pleasure does not constitute courage. Real courage is manifested only when a person, in acting to attain a goal, perseveres in the face of fear prompted by one or more dangers involved.

Which one of the following statements can be properly inferred from the statements above?

(A) A person who must face danger in order to avoid future pain cannot properly be called courageous for doing so.

(B) A person who experiences fear of some aspects of a dangerous situation cannot be said to act courageously in that situation.

(C) A person who happens to derive pleasure from some dangerous activities is not a courageous person.

(D) A person who faces danger in order to benefit others is acting courageously only if the person is afraid of the danger.

(E) A person who has no fear of the situations that everyone else would fear cannot be said to be courageous in any situation.

26. The government will purchase and install new severe weather sirens for this area next year if replacement parts for the old sirens are difficult to obtain. The newspaper claims that public safety in the event of severe weather would be enhanced if new sirens were to be installed. The local company from which replacement parts were purchased last year has since gone out of business. So, if the newspaper is correct, the public will be safer during severe weather in the future.

The argument's conclusion follows logically from its premises if which one of the following is assumed?

(A) If public safety in the event of severe weather is enhanced next year, it will be because new sirens have been purchased.

(B) The newspaper was correct in claiming that public safety in the event of severe weather would be enhanced if new sirens were purchased.

(C) The local company from which replacement parts for the old sirens were purchased last year was the only company in the area that sold them.

(D) Replacement parts for the old sirens will be difficult to obtain if the government cannot obtain them from the company it purchased them from last year.

(E) Because the local company from which replacement parts had been purchased went out of business, the only available parts are of such inferior quality that use of them would make the sirens less reliable.

S T O P

IF YOU FINISH BEFORE TIME IS CALLED, YOU MAY CHECK YOUR WORK ON THIS SECTION ONLY.
DO NOT WORK ON ANY OTHER SECTION IN THE TEST.

SECTION III

Time—35 minutes

23 Questions

Directions: Each group of questions in this section is based on a set of conditions. In answering some of the questions, it may be useful to draw a rough diagram. Choose the response that most accurately and completely answers each question and blacken the corresponding space on your answer sheet.

Questions 1–5

A dance is being choreographed for six dancers: three men—Felipe, Grant, and Hassan—and three women—Jaclyn, Keiko, and Lorena. At no time during the dance will anyone other than the dancers be on stage. Who is on stage and who is off stage at any particular time in the dance is determined by the following constraints:

If Jaclyn is on stage, Lorena is off stage.
If Lorena is off stage, Jaclyn is on stage.
If Felipe is off stage, Jaclyn is also off stage.
If any of the women are on stage, Grant is also on stage.

1. Which one of the following is a list of all of the dancers who could be on stage at a particular time?

(A) Grant
(B) Keiko, Lorena
(C) Grant, Hassan, Lorena
(D) Grant, Hassan, Jaclyn
(E) Felipe, Grant, Jaclyn, Lorena

2. Which one of the following CANNOT be true at any time during the dance?

(A) Felipe and Grant are the only men on stage.
(B) Grant and Hassan are the only men on stage.
(C) Jaclyn is the only woman on stage.
(D) Keiko is the only woman on stage.
(E) Jaclyn and Keiko are the only women on stage.

3. Which one of the following is a complete and accurate list of the dancers any one of whom could be off stage when Jaclyn is on stage?

(A) Lorena
(B) Felipe, Lorena
(C) Hassan, Lorena
(D) Hassan, Keiko
(E) Hassan, Keiko, Lorena

4. If there are more women than men on stage, then exactly how many dancers must be on stage?

(A) five
(B) four
(C) three
(D) two
(E) one

5. What is the minimum number of dancers that must be on stage at any given time?

(A) zero
(B) one
(C) two
(D) three
(E) four

GO ON TO THE NEXT PAGE.

Questions 6–12

A critic has prepared a review of exactly six music CDs—
Headstrong, In Flight, Nice, Quasi, Reunion, and *Sounds
Good.* Each CD received a rating of either one, two, three, or
four stars, with each CD receiving exactly one rating.
Although the ratings were meant to be kept secret until the
review was published, the following facts have been leaked to
the public:

> For each of the ratings, at least one but no more than two
> of the CDs received that rating.
> *Headstrong* received exactly one more star than *Nice* did.
> Either *Headstrong* or *Reunion* received the same number
> of stars as *In Flight* did.
> At most one CD received more stars than *Quasi* did.

6. Which one of the following could be an accurate
   matching of ratings to the CDs that received those
   ratings?

   (A)   one star: *In Flight, Reunion;* two stars: *Nice;*
         three stars: *Headstrong;* four stars: *Quasi,*
         Sounds Good
   (B)   one star: *In Flight, Reunion;* two stars: *Quasi,*
         Sounds Good; three stars: *Nice;* four stars:
         Headstrong
   (C)   one star: *Nice;* two stars: *Headstrong;*
         three stars: *In Flight, Sounds Good;* four stars:
         Quasi, Reunion
   (D)   one star: *Nice, Sounds Good;* two stars: *In Flight,*
         Reunion; three stars: *Quasi;* four stars:
         Headstrong
   (E)   one star: *Sounds Good;* two stars: *Reunion;*
         three stars: *Nice, Quasi;* four stars:
         Headstrong, In Flight

7. If *Headstrong* is the only CD that received a rating of
   two stars, then which one of the following must be true?

   (A)   *In Flight* received a rating of three stars.
   (B)   *Nice* received a rating of three stars.
   (C)   *Quasi* received a rating of three stars.
   (D)   *Reunion* received a rating of one star.
   (E)   *Sounds Good* received a rating of one star.

8. If *Reunion* received the same rating as *Sounds Good,*
   then which one of the following must be true?

   (A)   *Headstrong* received a rating of two stars.
   (B)   *In Flight* received a rating of three stars.
   (C)   *Nice* received a rating of two stars.
   (D)   *Quasi* received a rating of four stars.
   (E)   *Sounds Good* received a rating of one star.

9. If *Nice* and *Reunion* each received a rating of one star,
   then which one of the following could be true?

   (A)   *Headstrong* received a rating of three stars.
   (B)   *Headstrong* received a rating of four stars.
   (C)   *In Flight* received a rating of three stars.
   (D)   *Sounds Good* received a rating of two stars.
   (E)   *Sounds Good* received a rating of three stars.

10. Which one of the following CANNOT be true?

    (A)   *Quasi* is the only CD that received a rating of
          three stars.
    (B)   *Quasi* is the only CD that received a rating of
          four stars.
    (C)   *Reunion* is the only CD that received a rating of
          one star.
    (D)   *Reunion* is the only CD that received a rating of
          two stars.
    (E)   *Reunion* is the only CD that received a rating of
          three stars.

11. If *Reunion* is the only CD that received a rating of one
    star, then which one of the following could be true?

    (A)   *Headstrong* received a rating of four stars.
    (B)   *In Flight* received a rating of two stars.
    (C)   *Nice* received a rating of three stars.
    (D)   *Quasi* received a rating of three stars.
    (E)   *Sounds Good* received a rating of two stars.

12. Which one of the following CANNOT have received a
    rating of four stars?

    (A)   *Headstrong*
    (B)   *In Flight*
    (C)   *Quasi*
    (D)   *Reunion*
    (E)   *Sounds Good*

GO ON TO THE NEXT PAGE.

Questions 13–17

A cake has exactly six layers—lemon, marzipan, orange, raspberry, strawberry, and vanilla. There is exactly one bottom layer (the first layer), and each succeeding layer (from second through sixth) completely covers the layer beneath it. The following conditions must apply:

The raspberry layer is neither immediately above nor immediately below the strawberry layer.

The marzipan layer is immediately above the lemon layer.

The orange layer is above the marzipan layer but below the strawberry layer.

13. Which one of the following could be an accurate list of the layers of the cake, from bottom to top?

    (A) lemon, marzipan, orange, strawberry, vanilla, raspberry
    (B) lemon, marzipan, orange, strawberry, raspberry, vanilla
    (C) marzipan, lemon, raspberry, vanilla, orange, strawberry
    (D) raspberry, lemon, marzipan, vanilla, strawberry, orange
    (E) raspberry, orange, lemon, marzipan, strawberry, vanilla

14. If the strawberry layer is not immediately above the orange layer, then which one of the following could be true?

    (A) The raspberry layer is immediately above the vanilla layer.
    (B) The raspberry layer is immediately above the orange layer.
    (C) The raspberry layer is immediately below the marzipan layer.
    (D) The raspberry layer is the second layer.
    (E) The raspberry layer is the top layer.

15. If the strawberry layer is not the top layer, then which one of the following is a complete and accurate list of the layers that could be the vanilla layer?

    (A) the first, the second, the third, the fourth, the fifth, the sixth
    (B) the second, the third, the fourth, the fifth, the sixth
    (C) the third, the fourth, the fifth, the sixth
    (D) the fourth, the fifth, the sixth
    (E) the fifth, the sixth

16. If the lemon layer is third, then which one of the following could be true?

    (A) The vanilla layer is fifth.
    (B) The vanilla layer is immediately above the raspberry layer.
    (C) The orange layer is not immediately above the marzipan layer.
    (D) The raspberry layer is above the marzipan layer.
    (E) The strawberry layer is not the top layer.

17. Which one of the following could be an accurate list of the two lowest layers of the cake, listed in order from the bottom up?

    (A) lemon, raspberry
    (B) vanilla, raspberry
    (C) marzipan, raspberry
    (D) raspberry, marzipan
    (E) raspberry, strawberry

GO ON TO THE NEXT PAGE.

Questions 18–23

A panel reviews six contract bids—H, J, K, R, S, and T. No two bids have the same cost. Exactly one of the bids is accepted. The following conditions must hold:

The accepted bid is either K or R and is either the second or the third lowest in cost.

H is lower in cost than each of J and K.

If J is the fourth lowest in cost, then J is lower in cost than each of S and T.

If J is not the fourth lowest in cost, then J is higher in cost than each of S and T.

Either R or S is the fifth lowest in cost.

18. Which one of the following could be an accurate list of the bids in order from lowest to highest in cost?

(A) T, K, H, S, J, R
(B) H, T, K, S, R, J
(C) H, S, T, K, R, J
(D) H, K, S, J, R, T
(E) H, J, K, R, S, T

19. Which one of the following bids CANNOT be the fourth lowest in cost?

(A) H
(B) J
(C) K
(D) R
(E) T

20. Which one of the following bids CANNOT be the second lowest in cost?

(A) H
(B) J
(C) K
(D) R
(E) T

21. If R is the accepted bid, then which one of the following must be true?

(A) T is the lowest in cost.
(B) K is the second lowest in cost.
(C) R is the third lowest in cost.
(D) S is the fifth lowest in cost.
(E) J is the highest in cost.

22. Which one of the following must be true?

(A) H is lower in cost than S.
(B) H is lower in cost than T.
(C) K is lower in cost than J.
(D) S is lower in cost than J.
(E) S is lower in cost than K.

23. If R is the lowest in cost, then which one of the following could be false?

(A) J is the highest in cost.
(B) S is the fifth lowest in cost.
(C) K is the third lowest in cost.
(D) H is the second lowest in cost.
(E) K is the accepted bid.

S T O P

IF YOU FINISH BEFORE TIME IS CALLED, YOU MAY CHECK YOUR WORK ON THIS SECTION ONLY.
DO NOT WORK ON ANY OTHER SECTION IN THE TEST.

SECTION IV

Time—35 minutes

25 Questions

Directions: The questions in this section are based on the reasoning contained in brief statements or passages. For some questions, more than one of the choices could conceivably answer the question. However, you are to choose the best answer; that is, the response that most accurately and completely answers the question. You should not make assumptions that are by commonsense standards implausible, superfluous, or incompatible with the passage. After you have chosen the best answer, blacken the corresponding space on your answer sheet.

1. Editorialist: Advertisers devote millions of dollars to the attempt to instill attitudes and desires that lead people to purchase particular products, and advertisers' techniques have been adopted by political strategists in democratic countries, who are paid to manipulate public opinion in every political campaign. Thus, the results of elections in democratic countries cannot be viewed as representing the unadulterated preferences of the people.

Which one of the following, if true, most strengthens the editorialist's argument?

(A) Public opinion can be manipulated more easily by officials of nondemocratic governments than by those of democratic governments.

(B) Advertisers' techniques are often apparent to the people to whom the advertisements are directed.

(C) Many democratic countries have laws limiting the amount that may be spent on political advertisements in any given election.

(D) People who neither watch television nor read any print media are more likely to vote than people who do one or both of these activities.

(E) Unlike advertisements for consumer products, most of which only reinforce existing beliefs, political advertisements often change voters' beliefs.

2. Kris: Years ago, the chemical industry claimed that technological progress cannot occur without pollution. Today, in the name of technological progress, the cellular phone industry manufactures and promotes a product that causes environmental pollution in the form of ringing phones and loud conversations in public places. Clearly, the cellular industry must be regulated, just as the chemical industry is now regulated.

Terry: That's absurd. Chemical pollution can cause physical harm, but the worst harm that cellular phones can cause is annoyance.

Terry responds to Kris's argument by doing which one of the following?

(A) questioning the reliability of the source of crucial information in Kris's argument

(B) attacking the accuracy of the evidence about the chemical industry that Kris puts forward

(C) arguing that an alleged cause of a problem is actually an effect of that problem

(D) questioning the strength of the analogy on which Kris's argument is based

(E) rejecting Kris's interpretation of the term "technological progress"

GO ON TO THE NEXT PAGE.

3. Researcher: Any country can determine which type of public school system will work best for it by investigating the public school systems of other countries. Nationwide tests could be given in each country and other countries could adopt the system of the country that has the best scores on these tests.

    Which one of the following is an assumption required by the researcher's argument?

    (A) A type of school system that works well in one country will work well in any other country.
    (B) A number of children in each country in the research sample are educated in private schools.
    (C) If two countries performed differently on these nationwide tests, further testing could determine what features of the school systems account for the differences.
    (D) Most countries in the research sample already administer nationwide tests to their public school students.
    (E) The nationwide testing in the research sample will target as closely as possible grade levels that are comparable in the different countries in the research sample.

4. Ray: Cynthia claims that her car's trunk popped open because the car hit a pothole. Yet, she also acknowledged that the trunk in that car had popped open on several other occasions, and that on none of those other occasions had the car hit a pothole. Therefore, Cynthia mistakenly attributed the trunk's popping open to the car's having hit a pothole.

    The reasoning in Ray's argument is most vulnerable to criticism in that the argument

    (A) fails to consider the possibility that the trunks of other cars may pop open when those cars hit potholes
    (B) fails to consider the possibility that potholes can have negative effects on a car's engine
    (C) presumes, without providing justification, that if one event causes another, it cannot also cause a third event
    (D) fails to consider the possibility that one type of event can be caused in many different ways
    (E) presumes the truth of the claim that it is trying to establish

5. Journalists agree universally that lying is absolutely taboo. Yet, while many reporters claim that spoken words ought to be quoted verbatim, many others believe that tightening a quote from a person who is interviewed is legitimate on grounds that the speaker's remarks would have been more concise if the speaker had written them instead. Also, many reporters believe that, to expose wrongdoing, failing to identify oneself as a reporter is permissible, while others condemn such behavior as a type of lying.

    Which one of the following is most supported by the information above?

    (A) Reporters make little effort to behave ethically.
    (B) There is no correct answer to the question of whether lying in a given situation is right or wrong.
    (C) Omission of the truth is the same thing as lying.
    (D) Since lying is permissible in some situations, reporters are mistaken to think that it is absolutely taboo.
    (E) Reporters disagree on what sort of behavior qualifies as lying.

6. Wood-frame houses withstand earthquakes far better than masonry houses do, because wooden frames have some flexibility; their walls can better handle lateral forces. In a recent earthquake, however, a wood-frame house was destroyed, while the masonry house next door was undamaged.

    Which one of the following, if true, most helps to explain the results of the earthquake described above?

    (A) In earthquake-prone areas, there are many more wood-frame houses than masonry houses.
    (B) In earthquake-prone areas, there are many more masonry houses than wood-frame houses.
    (C) The walls of the wood-frame house had once been damaged in a flood.
    (D) The masonry house was far more expensive than the wood-frame house.
    (E) No structure is completely impervious to the destructive lateral forces exerted by earthquakes.

GO ON TO THE NEXT PAGE.

7. In an experiment, biologists repeatedly shone a bright light into a tank containing a sea snail and simultaneously shook the tank. The snail invariably responded by tensing its muscular "foot," a typical reaction in sea snails to ocean turbulence. After several repetitions of this procedure, the snail tensed its "foot" whenever the biologists shone the light into its tank, even when the tank was not simultaneously shaken. Therefore, the snail must have learned to associate the shining of the bright light with the shaking of the tank.

Which one of the following is an assumption required by the argument?

(A) All sea snails react to ocean turbulence in the same way as the sea snail in the experiment did.

(B) Sea snails are not ordinarily exposed to bright lights such as the one used in the biologists' experiment.

(C) The sea snail used in the experiment did not differ significantly from other members of its species in its reaction to external stimuli.

(D) The appearance of a bright light alone would ordinarily not result in the sea snail's tensing its "foot."

(E) Tensing of the muscular "foot" in sea snails is an instinctual rather than a learned response to ocean turbulence.

8. The university's purchasing department is highly efficient overall. We must conclude that each of its twelve staff members is highly efficient.

Which one of the following arguments exhibits flawed reasoning most similar to that exhibited by the argument above?

(A) The employees at this fast-food restaurant are the youngest and most inexperienced of any fast-food workers in the city. Given this, it seems obvious that customers will have to wait longer for their food at this restaurant than at others.

(B) The outside audit of our public relations department has exposed serious deficiencies in the competence of each member of that department. We must conclude that the department is inadequate for our needs.

(C) This supercomputer is the most sophisticated—and the most expensive—ever built. It must be that each of its components is the most sophisticated and expensive available.

(D) Literature critics have lavished praise on every chapter of this book. In light of their reviews, one must conclude that the book is excellent.

(E) Passing a driving test is a condition of employment at the city's transportation department. It follows that each of the department's employees has passed the test.

9. The Jacksons regularly receive wrong-number calls for Sara, whose phone number was misprinted in a directory. Sara contacted the Jacksons, informing them of the misprint and her correct number. The Jacksons did not lead Sara to believe that they would pass along the correct number, but it would be helpful to Sara and of no difficulty for them to do so. Thus, although it would not be wrong for the Jacksons to tell callers trying to reach Sara merely that they have dialed the wrong number, it would be laudable if the Jacksons passed along Sara's correct number.

Which one of the following principles, if valid, most helps to justify the reasoning in the argument?

(A) It is always laudable to do something helpful to someone, but not doing so would be wrong only if one has led that person to believe one would do it.

(B) Being helpful to someone is laudable whenever it is not wrong to do so.

(C) If one can do something that would be helpful to someone else and it would be easy to do, then it is laudable and not wrong to do so.

(D) Doing something for someone is laudable only if it is difficult for one to do so and it is wrong for one not to do so.

(E) The only actions that are laudable are those that it would not be wrong to refrain from doing, whether or not it is difficult to do so.

GO ON TO THE NEXT PAGE.

10. Albert: The government has proposed new automobile emissions regulations designed to decrease the amount of polycyclic aromatic hydrocarbons (PAHs) released into the atmosphere by automobile exhaust. I don't see the need for such regulations; although PAHs are suspected of causing cancer, a causal link has never been proven.

Erin: Scientists also blame PAHs for 10,000 premature deaths in this country each year from lung and heart disease. So the proposed regulations would save thousands of lives.

Which one of the following, if true, is the logically strongest counter that Albert can make to Erin's argument?

(A) Most automobile manufacturers are strongly opposed to additional automobile emissions regulations.

(B) It is not known whether PAHs are a causal factor in any diseases other than heart and lung disease and cancer.

(C) Even if no new automobile emissions regulations are enacted, the amount of PAHs released into the atmosphere will decrease if automobile usage declines.

(D) Most of the PAHs released into the atmosphere are the result of wear and tear on automobile tires.

(E) PAHs are one of several components of automobile exhaust that scientists suspect of causing cancer.

11. Australia has considerably fewer species of carnivorous mammals than any other continent does but about as many carnivorous reptile species as other continents do. This is probably a consequence of the unusual sparseness of Australia's ecosystems. To survive, carnivorous mammals must eat much more than carnivorous reptiles need to; thus carnivorous mammals are at a disadvantage in ecosystems in which there is relatively little food.

Which one of the following most accurately expresses the main conclusion of the argument?

(A) Australia has considerably fewer species of carnivorous mammals than any other continent does but about as many carnivorous reptile species as other continents do.

(B) In ecosystems in which there is relatively little food carnivorous mammals are at a disadvantage relative to carnivorous reptiles.

(C) The unusual sparseness of Australia's ecosystems is probably the reason Australia has considerably fewer carnivorous mammal species than other continents do but about as many carnivorous reptile species.

(D) The reason that carnivorous mammals are at a disadvantage in ecosystems in which there is relatively little food is that they must eat much more in order to survive than carnivorous reptiles need to.

(E) Because Australia's ecosystems are unusually sparse, carnivorous mammals there are at a disadvantage relative to carnivorous reptiles.

12. Linguist: The Sapir-Whorf hypothesis states that a society's world view is influenced by the language or languages its members speak. But this hypothesis does not have the verifiability of hypotheses of physical science, since it is not clear that the hypothesis could be tested.

If the linguist's statements are accurate, which one of the following is most supported by them?

(A) The Sapir-Whorf hypothesis is probably false.
(B) Only the hypotheses of physical science are verifiable.
(C) Only verifiable hypotheses should be seriously considered.
(D) We do not know whether the Sapir-Whorf hypothesis is true or false.
(E) Only the hypotheses of physical science should be taken seriously.

GO ON TO THE NEXT PAGE.

13. The highest mountain ranges are formed by geological forces that raise the earth's crust: two continent-bearing tectonic plates of comparable density collide and crumple upward, causing a thickening of the crust. The erosive forces of wind and precipitation inexorably wear these mountains down. Yet the highest mountain ranges tend to be found in places where these erosive forces are most prevalent.

Which one of the following, if true, most helps to reconcile the apparent conflict described above?

(A) Patterns of extreme wind and precipitation often result from the dramatic differences in elevation commonly found in the highest mountain ranges.

(B) The highest mountain ranges have less erosion-reducing vegetation near their peaks than do other mountain ranges.

(C) Some lower mountain ranges are formed by a different collision process, whereby one tectonic plate simply slides beneath another of lesser density.

(D) The amount of precipitation that a given region of the earth receives may vary considerably over the lifetime of an average mountain range.

(E) The thickening of the earth's crust associated with the formation of the highest mountain ranges tends to cause the thickened portion of the crust to sink over time.

14. Expert: A group of researchers claims to have shown that for an antenna to work equally well at all frequencies, it must be symmetrical in shape and have what is known as a fractal structure. Yet the new antenna developed by these researchers, which satisfies both of these criteria, in fact works better at frequencies below 250 megahertz than at frequencies above 250 megahertz. Hence, their claim is incorrect.

The reasoning in the expert's argument is flawed because the argument

(A) fails to provide a definition of the technical term "fractal"

(B) contradicts itself by denying in its conclusion the claim of scientific authorities that it relies on in its premises

(C) concludes that a claim is false merely on the grounds that there is insufficient evidence that it is true

(D) interprets an assertion that certain conditions are necessary as asserting that those conditions are sufficient

(E) takes for granted that there are only two possible alternatives, either below or above 250 megahertz

15. Singletary: We of Citizens for Cycling Freedom object to the city's new ordinance requiring bicyclists to wear helmets. If the city wanted to become a safer place for cyclists, it would not require helmets. Instead, it would construct more bicycle lanes and educate drivers about bicycle safety. Thus, passage of the ordinance reveals that the city is more concerned with the appearance of safety than with bicyclists' actual safety.

Which one of the following most accurately describes the role played in Singletary's argument by the statement that mentions driver education?

(A) It is cited as evidence for the claim that the city misunderstands the steps necessary for ensuring bicyclists' safety.

(B) It is used as partial support for a claim about the motivation of the city.

(C) It is offered as evidence of the total ineffectiveness of the helmet ordinance.

(D) It is offered as an example of further measures the city will take to ensure bicyclists' safety.

(E) It is presented as an illustration of the city's overriding interest in its public image.

16. Max: Although doing so would be very costly, humans already possess the technology to build colonies on the Moon. As the human population increases and the amount of unoccupied space available for constructing housing on Earth diminishes, there will be a growing economic incentive to construct such colonies to house some of the population. Thus, such colonies will almost certainly be built and severe overcrowding on Earth relieved.

Max's argument is most vulnerable to criticism on which one of the following grounds?

(A) It takes for granted that the economic incentive to construct colonies on the Moon will grow sufficiently to cause such a costly project to be undertaken.

(B) It takes for granted that the only way of relieving severe overcrowding on Earth is the construction of colonies on the Moon.

(C) It overlooks the possibility that colonies will be built on the Moon regardless of any economic incentive to construct such colonies to house some of the population.

(D) It overlooks the possibility that colonies on the Moon might themselves quickly become overcrowded.

(E) It takes for granted that none of the human population would prefer to live on the Moon unless Earth were seriously overcrowded.

GO ON TO THE NEXT PAGE.

17. Ethicist: An action is wrong if it violates a rule of the society in which the action is performed and that rule promotes the general welfare of people in the society. An action is right if it is required by a rule of the society in which the action is performed and the rule promotes the general welfare of the people in that society.

Which one of the following judgments most closely conforms to the principle cited by the ethicist?

(A) Amelia's society has a rule against lying. However, she lies anyway in order to protect an innocent person from being harmed. While the rule against lying promotes the general welfare of people in the society, Amelia's lie is not wrong because she is preventing harm.

(B) Jordan lives in a society that requires its members to eat certain ceremonial foods during festivals. Jordan disobeys this rule. Because the rule is not detrimental to the general welfare of people in her society, Jordan's disobedience is wrong.

(C) Elgin obeys a certain rule of his society. Because Elgin knows that this particular rule is detrimental to the general welfare of the people in his society, his obedience is wrong.

(D) Dahlia always has a cup of coffee before getting dressed in the morning. Dahlia's action is right because it does not violate any rule of the society in which she lives.

(E) Edward's society requires children to take care of their aged parents. Edward's taking care of his aged parents is the right thing for him to do because the rule requiring this action promotes the general welfare of people in the society.

18. Teresa: If their goal is to maximize profits, film studios should concentrate on producing big-budget films rather than small-budget ones. For, unlike big-budget films, small-budget films never attract mass audiences. While small-budget films are less expensive to produce and, hence, involve less risk of unprofitability than big-budget films, low production costs do not guarantee the highest possible profits.

Which one of the following is an assumption required by Teresa's argument?

(A) Each big-budget film is guaranteed to attract a mass audience.

(B) A film studio cannot make both big-budget films and small-budget films.

(C) A film studio will not maximize its profits unless at least some of its films attract mass audiences.

(D) It is impossible to produce a big-budget film in a financially efficient manner.

(E) A film studio's primary goal should be to maximize profits.

19. Cyclists in the Tour de France are extremely physically fit: all of the winners of this race have had abnormal physiological constitutions. Typical of the abnormal physiology of these athletes are exceptional lung capacity and exceptionally powerful hearts. Tests conducted on last year's winner did not reveal an exceptionally powerful heart. That cyclist must, therefore, have exceptional lung capacity.

The reasoning in the argument is most vulnerable to criticism on the grounds that it overlooks the possibility that

(A) having exceptional lung capacity and an exceptionally powerful heart is an advantage in cycling

(B) some winners of the Tour de France have neither exceptional lung capacity nor exceptionally powerful hearts

(C) cyclists with normal lung capacity rarely have exceptionally powerful hearts

(D) the exceptional lung capacity and exceptionally powerful hearts of Tour de France winners are due to training

(E) the notions of exceptional lung capacity and exceptional heart function are relative to the physiology of most cyclists

20. TV meteorologist: Our station's weather forecasts are more useful and reliable than those of the most popular news station in the area. After all, the most important question for viewers in this area is whether it will rain, and on most of the occasions when we have forecast rain for the next day, we have been right. The same cannot be said for either of our competitors.

Which one of the following, if true, most strengthens the meteorologist's argument?

(A) The meteorologist's station forecast rain more often than did the most popular news station in the area.

(B) The less popular of the competing stations does not employ any full-time meteorologists.

(C) The most popular news station in the area is popular because of its investigative news reports.

(D) The meteorologist's station has a policy of not making weather forecasts more than three days in advance.

(E) On most of the occasions when the meteorologist's station forecast that it would not rain, at least one of its competitors also forecast that it would not rain.

GO ON TO THE NEXT PAGE.

21. In an experiment, volunteers witnessed a simulated crime. After they witnessed the simulation the volunteers were first questioned by a lawyer whose goal was to get them to testify inaccurately about the event. They were then cross-examined by another lawyer whose goal was to cause them to correct the inaccuracies in their testimony. The witnesses who gave testimony containing fewer inaccurate details than most of the other witnesses during the first lawyer's questioning also gave testimony containing a greater number of inaccurate details than most of the other witnesses during cross-examination.

Which one of the following, if true, most helps to resolve the apparent conflict in the results concerning the witnesses who gave testimony containing fewer inaccurate details during the first lawyer's questioning?

(A) These witnesses were more observant about details than were most of the other witnesses.
(B) These witnesses had better memories than did most of the other witnesses.
(C) These witnesses were less inclined than most of the other witnesses to be influenced in their testimony by the nature of the questioning.
(D) These witnesses were unclear about the details at first but then began to remember more accurately as they answered questions.
(E) These witnesses tended to give testimony containing more details than most of the other witnesses.

22. The short-term and long-term interests of a business often conflict; when they do, the morally preferable act is usually the one that serves the long-term interest. Because of this, businesses often have compelling reasons to execute the morally preferable act.

Which one of the following, if assumed, enables the conclusion of the argument to be properly drawn?

(A) A business's moral interests do not always provide compelling reasons for executing an act.
(B) A business's long-term interests often provide compelling reasons for executing an act.
(C) The morally preferable act for a business to execute and the long-term interests of the business seldom conflict.
(D) The morally preferable act for a business to execute and the short-term interests of the business usually conflict.
(E) When a business's short-term and long-term interests conflict, morality alone is rarely the overriding consideration.

23. Politician: The current crisis in mathematics education must be overcome if we are to remain competitive in the global economy. Alleviating this crisis requires the employment of successful teaching methods. No method of teaching a subject can succeed that does not get students to spend a significant amount of time outside of class studying that subject.

Which one of the following statements follows logically from the statements above?

(A) If students spend a significant amount of time outside of class studying mathematics, the current crisis in mathematics education will be overcome.
(B) The current crisis in mathematics education will not be overcome unless students spend a significant amount of time outside of class studying mathematics.
(C) Few subjects are as important as mathematics to the effort to remain competitive in the global economy.
(D) Only if we succeed in remaining competitive in the global economy will students spend a significant amount of time outside of class studying mathematics.
(E) Students' spending a significant amount of time outside of class studying mathematics would help us to remain competitive in the global economy.

GO ON TO THE NEXT PAGE.

24. Downtown Petropolis boasted over 100 large buildings 5 years ago. Since then, 60 of those buildings have been demolished. Since the number of large buildings in a downtown is an indicator of the economic health of that downtown, it is clear that downtown Petropolis is in a serious state of economic decline.

Which one of the following is an assumption required by the argument?

(A) The demolitions that have taken place during the past 5 years have been evenly spread over that period.

(B) There have never been significantly more than 100 large buildings in downtown Petropolis.

(C) Most of the buildings demolished during the past 5 years were torn down because they were structurally unsound.

(D) The large buildings demolished over the past 5 years have been replaced with small buildings built on the same sites.

(E) Significantly fewer than 60 new large buildings have been built in downtown Petropolis during the past 5 years.

25. To get the free dessert, one must order an entree and a salad. But anyone who orders either an entree or a salad can receive a free soft drink. Thus, anyone who is not eligible for a free soft drink is not eligible for a free dessert.

The reasoning in the argument above is most similar to the reasoning in which one of the following arguments?

(A) To get an executive position at Teltech, one needs a university diploma and sales experience. But anyone who has worked at Teltech for more than six months who does not have sales experience has a university diploma. Thus, one cannot get an executive position at Teltech unless one has worked there for six months.

(B) To be elected class president, one must be well liked and well known. Anyone who is well liked or well known has something better to do than run for class president. Therefore, no one who has something better to do will be elected class president.

(C) To grow good azaleas, one needs soil that is both rich in humus and low in acidity. Anyone who has soil that is rich in humus or low in acidity can grow blueberries. So, anyone who cannot grow blueberries cannot grow good azaleas.

(D) To drive to Weller, one must take the highway or take Old Mill Road. Anyone who drives to Weller on the highway will miss the beautiful scenery. Thus, one cannot see the beautiful scenery without taking Old Mill Road to Weller.

(E) To get a discount on ice cream, one must buy frozen raspberries and ice cream together. Anyone who buys ice cream or raspberries will get a coupon for a later purchase. So, anyone who does not get the discount on ice cream will not get a coupon for a later purchase.

S T O P

IF YOU FINISH BEFORE TIME IS CALLED, YOU MAY CHECK YOUR WORK ON THIS SECTION ONLY.
DO NOT WORK ON ANY OTHER SECTION IN THE TEST.

Wait for the supervisor's instructions before you open the page to the topic.
Please print and sign your name and write the date in the designated spaces below.
Time: 35 Minutes

General Directions

You will have 35 minutes in which to plan and write an essay on the topic inside. Read the topic and the accompanying directions carefully. You will probably find it best to spend a few minutes considering the topic and organizing your thoughts before you begin writing. In your essay, be sure to develop your ideas fully, leaving time, if possible, to review what you have written. **Do not write on a topic other than the one specified. Writing on a topic of your own choice is not acceptable.**

No special knowledge is required or expected for this writing exercise. Law schools are interested in the reasoning, clarity, organization, language usage, and writing mechanics displayed in your essay. How well you write is more important than how much you write.

Confine your essay to the blocked, lined area on the front and back of the separate Writing Sample Response Sheet. Only that area will be reproduced for law schools. Be sure that your writing is legible.

Both this topic sheet and your response sheet must be turned over to the testing staff before you leave the room.

Scratch Paper
Do not write your essay in this space.

LSAT® Writing Sample Topic

<u>Directions</u>: The scenario presented below describes two choices, either one of which can be supported on the basis of the information given. Your essay should consider both choices and argue for one over the other, based on the two specified criteria and the facts provided. There is no "right" or "wrong" choice: a reasonable argument can be made for either.

Carol Hudson, the concert coordinator for Jordan Arena, a very large entertainment venue, must schedule one of two musical groups to perform on an open date in the arena's schedule. Using the facts below, write an essay in which you argue for one group over the other based on the following two criteria:

- Carol wants to continue Jordan Arena's long-standing record of sold-out concerts.
- Carol wants to attract an audience at least a third of whom are aged 14 to 24.

The first group, The Mustangs, plays cutting-edge music of a sort popular with the 14- to 24-year-old demographic. The Mustangs, gradually growing in popularity, have filled steadily larger venues. The group recently sold out in record time its largest venue ever, the Midvale Arena, located in a large metropolitan area. Jordan Arena, which is located in a different large metropolitan area, has twice the seating capacity of Midvale Arena. The Mustangs' video of the cover song for their debut album is scheduled for release a few weeks before the Jordan Arena concert date. If the music video is a success, as many expect, The Mustangs' popularity will rapidly soar.

The second group, Radar Love, is an aging but well-established hard rock band, which has consistently appealed to a wide-ranging audience. It has sold out all appearances for the past 20 years, including venues considerably larger than Jordan Arena. A song on the group's latest album quickly became a runaway hit among the 14- to 24-year-old demographic, the first time the group has appealed to this extent to this audience. Twenty percent of the audience at the group's most recent concert, which featured songs from the group's latest album, constituted 14- to 24-year-olds, a significant increase from prior concerts.

WP-P077

Scratch Paper
Do not write your essay in this space.

LAST NAME (Print)

FIRST NAME (Print)

SSN/ SIN

L

MI

TEST CENTER NO.

SIGNATURE

M M D D Y Y
TEST DATE

LSAC ACCOUNT NO.

TOPIC CODE

Writing Sample Response Sheet

DO NOT WRITE IN THIS SPACE

**Begin your essay in the lined area below.
Continue on the back if you need more space.**

COMPUTING YOUR SCORE

Directions:

1. Use the Answer Key on the next page to check your answers.

2. Use the Scoring Worksheet below to compute your raw score.

3. Use the Score Conversion Chart to convert your raw score into the 120–180 scale.

Scoring Worksheet

1. Enter the number of questions you answered correctly in each section.

	Number Correct
SECTION I................	_____
SECTION II...............	_____
SECTION III..............	_____
SECTION IV	_____

2. Enter the sum here: _____
   This is your Raw Score.

Conversion Chart
For Converting Raw Score to the 120–180 LSAT Scaled Score
LSAT Form 9LSN79

Reported Score	Raw Score Lowest	Raw Score Highest
180	99	101
179	98	98
178	—*	—*
177	97	97
176	96	96
175	95	95
174	—*	—*
173	94	94
172	93	93
171	92	92
170	91	91
169	90	90
168	89	89
167	88	88
166	87	87
165	85	86
164	84	84
163	83	83
162	81	82
161	80	80
160	78	79
159	76	77
158	75	75
157	73	74
156	71	72
155	69	70
154	67	68
153	66	66
152	64	65
151	62	63
150	60	61
149	58	59
148	56	57
147	54	55
146	52	53
145	50	51
144	49	49
143	47	48
142	45	46
141	43	44
140	42	42
139	40	41
138	38	39
137	37	37
136	35	36
135	33	34
134	32	32
133	30	31
132	29	29
131	28	28
130	26	27
129	25	25
128	24	24
127	23	23
126	21	22
125	20	20
124	19	19
123	18	18
122	16	17
121	—*	—*
120	0	15

*There is no raw score that will produce this scaled score for this form.

ANSWER KEY

SECTION I

1.	A	8.	E	15.	C	22.	C
2.	C	9.	B	16.	E	23.	B
3.	D	10.	B	17.	E	24.	E
4.	D	11.	C	18.	A	25.	E
5.	E	12.	A	19.	A	26.	A
6.	B	13.	C	20.	A	27.	B
7.	E	14.	D	21.	C		

SECTION II

1.	D	8.	A	15.	E	22.	E
2.	E	9.	A	16.	D	23.	C
3.	A	10.	B	17.	D	24.	A
4.	E	11.	B	18.	C	25.	D
5.	B	12.	D	19.	D	26.	D
6.	C	13.	B	20.	E		
7.	C	14.	C	21.	A		

SECTION III

1.	C	8.	D	15.	E	22.	C
2.	D	9.	E	16.	B	23.	A
3.	E	10.	D	17.	B		
4.	C	11.	E	18.	B		
5.	C	12.	B	19.	A		
6.	A	13.	A	20.	B		
7.	A	14.	B	21.	D		

SECTION IV

1.	E	8.	C	15.	B	22.	B
2.	D	9.	A	16.	A	23.	B
3.	A	10.	D	17.	E	24.	E
4.	D	11.	C	18.	C	25.	C
5.	E	12.	D	19.	B		
6.	C	13.	A	20.	A		
7.	D	14.	D	21.	C		

The Official LSAT PrepTest

- October 2008
  PrepTest 55

- Form 8LSN77

SECTION I

Time—35 minutes

25 Questions

<u>Directions</u>: The questions in this section are based on the reasoning contained in brief statements or passages. For some questions, more than one of the choices could conceivably answer the question. However, you are to choose the <u>best</u> answer; that is, the response that most accurately and completely answers the question. You should not make assumptions that are by commonsense standards implausible, superfluous, or incompatible with the passage. After you have chosen the best answer, blacken the corresponding space on your answer sheet.

1. The editor of a magazine has pointed out several errors of spelling and grammar committed on a recent TV program. But she can hardly be trusted to pass judgment on such matters: similar errors have been found in her own magazine.

   The flawed reasoning in the argument above is most similar to that in which one of the following?

   (A) Your newspaper cannot be trusted with the prerogative to criticize the ethics of our company: you misspelled our president's name.
   (B) Your news program cannot be trusted to judge our hiring practices as unfair: you yourselves unfairly discriminate in hiring and promotion decisions.
   (C) Your regulatory agency cannot condemn our product as unsafe: selling it is allowed under an existing-product clause.
   (D) Your coach cannot be trusted to judge our swimming practices: he accepted a lucrative promotional deal from a soft-drink company.
   (E) Your teen magazine should not run this feature on problems afflicting modern high schools: your revenue depends on not alienating the high school audience.

2. Soaking dried beans overnight before cooking them reduces cooking time. However, cooking without presoaking yields plumper beans. Therefore, when a bean dish's quality is more important than the need to cook that dish quickly, beans should not be presoaked.

   Which one of the following is an assumption required by the argument?

   (A) Plumper beans enhance the quality of a dish.
   (B) There are no dishes whose quality improves with faster cooking.
   (C) A dish's appearance is as important as its taste.
   (D) None of the other ingredients in the dish need to be presoaked.
   (E) The plumper the bean, the better it tastes.

3. Durth: Increasingly, businesses use direct mail advertising instead of paying for advertising space in newspapers, in magazines, or on billboards. This practice is annoying and also immoral. Most direct mail advertisements are thrown out without ever being read, and the paper on which they are printed is wasted. If anyone else wasted this much paper, it would be considered unconscionable.

   Which one of the following most accurately describes Durth's method of reasoning?

   (A) presenting a specific counterexample to the contention that direct mail advertising is not immoral
   (B) asserting that there would be very undesirable consequences if direct mail advertising became a more widespread practice than it is now
   (C) claiming that direct mail advertising is immoral because one of its results would be deemed immoral in other contexts
   (D) basing a conclusion on the claim that direct mail advertising is annoying to those who receive it
   (E) asserting that other advertising methods do not have the negative effects of direct mail advertising

GO ON TO THE NEXT PAGE.

4. Among the various models of Delta vacuum cleaners, one cannot accurately predict how effectively a particular model cleans simply by determining how powerful its motor is. The efficiency of dust filtration systems varies significantly, even between models of Delta vacuum cleaners equipped with identically powerful motors.

The argument's conclusion is properly drawn if which one of the following is assumed?

(A)   For each Delta vacuum cleaner, the efficiency of its dust filtration system has a significant impact on how effectively it cleans.

(B)   One can accurately infer how powerful a Delta vacuum cleaner's motor is from the efficiency of the vacuum cleaner's dust filtration system.

(C)   All Delta vacuum cleaners that clean equally effectively have identically powerful motors.

(D)   For any two Delta vacuum cleaners with equally efficient dust filtration systems, the one with the more powerful motor cleans more effectively.

(E)   One cannot accurately assess how effectively any Delta vacuum cleaner cleans without knowing how powerful that vacuum cleaner's motor is.

5. Many scientists believe that bipedal locomotion (walking on two feet) evolved in early hominids in response to the move from life in dense forests to life in open grasslands. Bipedalism would have allowed early hominids to see over tall grasses, helping them to locate food and to detect and avoid predators. However, because bipedalism also would have conferred substantial advantages upon early hominids who never left the forest—in gathering food found within standing reach of the forest floor, for example—debate continues concerning its origins. It may even have evolved, like the upright threat displays of many large apes, because it bettered an individual's odds of finding a mate.

Which one of the following statements is most supported by the information above?

(A)   For early hominids, forest environments were generally more hospitable than grassland environments.

(B)   Bipedal locomotion would have helped early hominids gather food.

(C)   Bipedal locomotion actually would not be advantageous to hominids living in open grassland environments.

(D)   Bipedal locomotion probably evolved among early hominids who exclusively inhabited forest environments.

(E)   For early hominids, gathering food was more relevant to survival than was detecting and avoiding predators.

6. Mathematics teacher: Teaching students calculus before they attend university may significantly benefit them. Yet if students are taught calculus before they are ready for the level of abstraction involved, they may abandon the study of mathematics altogether. So if we are going to teach pre-university students calculus, we must make sure they can handle the level of abstraction involved.

Which one of the following principles most helps to justify the mathematics teacher's argument?

(A)   Only those who, without losing motivation, can meet the cognitive challenges that new intellectual work involves should be introduced to it.

(B)   Only those parts of university-level mathematics that are the most concrete should be taught to pre-university students.

(C)   Cognitive tasks that require exceptional effort tend to undermine the motivation of those who attempt them.

(D)   Teachers who teach university-level mathematics to pre-university students should be aware that students are likely to learn effectively only when the application of mathematics to concrete problems is shown.

(E)   The level of abstraction involved in a topic should not be considered in determining whether that topic is appropriate for pre-university students.

GO ON TO THE NEXT PAGE.

7. In 1955, legislation in a certain country gave the government increased control over industrial workplace safety conditions. Among the high-risk industries in that country, the likelihood that a worker will suffer a serious injury has decreased since 1955. The legislation, therefore, has increased overall worker safety within high-risk industries.

Which one of the following, if true, most weakens the argument above?

(A) Because of technological innovation, most workplaces in the high-risk industries do not require as much unprotected interaction between workers and heavy machinery as they did in 1955.

(B) Most of the work-related injuries that occurred before 1955 were the result of worker carelessness.

(C) The annual number of work-related injuries has increased since the legislation took effect.

(D) The number of work-related injuries occurring within industries not considered high-risk has increased annually since 1955.

(E) Workplace safety conditions in all industries have improved steadily since 1955.

8. Economist: Historically, sunflower seed was one of the largest production crops in Kalotopia, and it continues to be a major source of income for several countries. The renewed growing of sunflowers would provide relief to Kalotopia's farming industry, which is quite unstable. Further, sunflower oil can provide a variety of products, both industrial and consumer, at little cost to Kalotopia's already fragile environment.

The economist's statements, if true, most strongly support which one of the following?

(A) Kalotopia's farming industry will deteriorate if sunflowers are not grown there.

(B) Stabilizing Kalotopia's farming industry would improve the economy without damaging the environment.

(C) Kalotopia's farming industry would be better off now if it had never ceased to grow any of the crops that historically were large production crops.

(D) A crop that was once a large production crop in Kalotopia would, if it were grown there again, benefit that country's farmers and general economy.

(E) Sunflower seed is a better crop for Kalotopia from both the environmental and the economic viewpoints than are most crops that could be grown there.

9. Several major earthquakes have occurred in a certain region over the last ten years. But a new earthquake prediction method promises to aid local civil defense officials in deciding exactly when to evacuate various towns. Detected before each of these major quakes were certain changes in the electric current in the earth's crust.

Which one of the following, if true, most weakens the argument?

(A) Scientists do not fully understand what brought about the changes in the electric current in the earth's crust that preceded each of the major quakes in the region over the last ten years.

(B) Most other earthquake prediction methods have been based on a weaker correlation than that found between the changes in the electric current in the earth's crust and the subsequent earthquakes.

(C) The frequency of major earthquakes in the region has increased over the last ten years.

(D) There is considerable variation in the length of time between the changes in the electric current and the subsequent earthquakes.

(E) There is presently only one station in the region that is capable of detecting the electric current in the earth's crust.

10. Unlike many machines that are perfectly useful in isolation from others, fax machines must work with other fax machines. Thus, in the fax industry, the proliferation of incompatible formats, which resulted from the large number of competing manufacturers, severely limited the usefulness—and hence the commercial viability—of fax technology until the manufacturers agreed to adopt a common format for their machines.

The information above provides the most support for which one of the following propositions?

(A) Whenever machines are dependent on other machines of the same type, competition among manufacturers is damaging to the industry.

(B) In some industries it is in the interest of competitors to cooperate to some extent with one another.

(C) The more competitors there are in a high-tech industry, the more they will have to cooperate in determining the basic design of their product.

(D) Some cooperation among manufacturers in the same industry is more beneficial than is pure competition.

(E) Cooperation is beneficial only in industries whose products depend on other products of the same type.

GO ON TO THE NEXT PAGE.

11. In comparing different methods by which a teacher's performance can be evaluated and educational outcomes improved, researchers found that a critique of teacher performance leads to enhanced educational outcomes if the critique is accompanied by the information that teacher performance is merely one of several factors that, in concert with other factors, determines the educational outcomes.

Which one of the following best illustrates the principle illustrated by the finding of the researchers?

(A) Children can usually be taught to master subject matter in which they have no interest if they believe that successfully mastering it will earn the respect of their peers.

(B) People are generally more willing to accept a negative characterization of a small group of people if they do not see themselves as members of the group being so characterized.

(C) An actor can more effectively evaluate the merits of her own performance if she can successfully convince herself that she is really evaluating the performance of another actor.

(D) The opinions reached by a social scientist in the study of a society can be considered as more reliable and objective if that social scientist is not a member of that society.

(E) It is easier to correct the mistakes of an athlete if it is made clear to him that the criticism is part of an overarching effort to rectify the shortcomings of the entire team on which he plays.

12. Critic: A novel cannot be of the highest quality unless most readers become emotionally engaged with the imaginary world it describes. Thus shifts of narrative point of view within a novel, either between first and third person or of some other sort, detract from the merit of the work, since such shifts tend to make most readers focus on the author.

Which one of the following is an assumption necessary for the critic's conclusion to be properly drawn?

(A) Most readers become emotionally engaged with the imaginary world described by a novel only if the novel is of the highest quality.

(B) A novel is generally not considered to be of high quality unless it successfully engages the imagination of most readers.

(C) Most readers cannot become emotionally involved with a novel's imaginary world if they focus on the author.

(D) Most readers regard a novel's narrative point of view as representing the perspective of the novel's author.

(E) Shifts in narrative point of view serve no literary purpose.

13. People aged 46 to 55 spend more money per capita than people of any other age group. So it is puzzling that when companies advertise consumer products on television, they focus almost exclusively on people aged 25 and under. Indeed, those who make decisions about television advertising think that the value of a television advertising slot depends entirely on the number of people aged 25 and under who can be expected to be watching at that time.

Which one of the following, if true, most helps to explain the puzzling facts stated above?

(A) The expense of television advertising slots makes it crucial for companies to target people who are most likely to purchase their products.

(B) Advertising slots during news programs almost always cost far less than advertising slots during popular sitcoms whose leading characters are young adults.

(C) When television executives decide which shows to renew, they do so primarily in terms of the shows' ratings among people aged 25 and under.

(D) Those who make decisions about television advertising believe that people older than 25 almost never change their buying habits.

(E) When companies advertise consumer products in print media, they focus primarily on people aged 26 and over.

14. Eighteenth-century moralist: You should never make an effort to acquire expensive new tastes, since they are a drain on your purse and in the course of acquiring them you may expose yourself to sensations that are obnoxious to you. Furthermore, the very effort that must be expended in their acquisition attests their superfluity.

The moralist's reasoning is most vulnerable to criticism on the grounds that the moralist

(A) draws a conclusion that simply restates a claim presented in support of that conclusion

(B) takes for granted that the acquisition of expensive tastes will lead to financial irresponsibility

(C) uses the inherently vague term "sensations" without providing a definition of that term

(D) mistakes a cause of acquisition of expensive tastes for an effect of acquisition of such tastes

(E) rejects trying to achieve a goal because of the cost of achieving it, without considering the benefits of achieving it

GO ON TO THE NEXT PAGE.

15. Zack's Coffeehouse schedules free poetry readings almost every Wednesday. Zack's offers half-priced coffee all day on every day that a poetry reading is scheduled.

Which one of the following can be properly inferred from the information above?

(A)   Wednesday is the most common day on which Zack's offers half-priced coffee all day.

(B)   Most free poetry readings given at Zack's are scheduled for Wednesdays.

(C)   Free poetry readings are scheduled on almost every day that Zack's offers half-priced coffee all day.

(D)   Zack's offers half-priced coffee all day on most if not all Wednesdays.

(E)   On some Wednesdays Zack's does not offer half-priced coffee all day.

16. Philosopher: An event is intentional if it is a human action performed on the basis of a specific motivation. An event is random if it is not performed on the basis of a specific motivation and it is not explainable by normal physical processes.

Which one of the following inferences conforms most closely to the philosopher's position?

(A)   Tarik left the keys untouched on the kitchen counter, but he did not do so on the basis of a specific motivation. Therefore, the keys' remaining on the kitchen counter was a random event.

(B)   Ellis tore the envelope open in order to read its contents, but the envelope was empty. Nevertheless, because Ellis acted on the basis of a specific motivation, tearing the envelope open was an intentional event.

(C)   Judith's hailing a cab distracted a driver in the left lane. She performed the action of hailing the cab on the basis of a specific motivation, so the driver's becoming distracted was an intentional event.

(D)   Yasuko continued to breathe regularly throughout the time that she was asleep. This was a human action, but it was not performed on the basis of a specific motivation. Therefore, her breathing was a random event.

(E)   Henry lost his hold on the wrench and dropped it because the handle was slippery. This was a human action and is explainable by normal physical processes, so it was an intentional event.

17. It is a mistake to conclude, as some have, that ancient people did not know what moral rights were simply because no known ancient language has an expression correctly translatable as "a moral right." This would be like saying that a person who discovers a wild fruit tree and returns repeatedly to harvest from it and study it has no idea what the fruit is until naming it or learning its name.

Which one of the following is an assumption required by the argument?

(A)   To know the name of something is to know what that thing is.

(B)   People who first discover what something is know it better than do people who merely know the name of the thing.

(C)   The name or expression that is used to identify something cannot provide any information about the nature of the thing that is identified.

(D)   A person who repeatedly harvests from a wild fruit tree and studies it has some idea of what the fruit is even before knowing a name for the fruit.

(E)   One need not know what something is before one can name it.

18. There is little plausibility to the claim that it is absurd to criticize anyone for being critical. Obviously, people must assess one another and not all assessments will be positive. However, there is wisdom behind the injunction against being judgmental. To be judgmental is not merely to assess someone negatively, but to do so prior to a serious effort at understanding.

Which one of the following most accurately expresses the main conclusion drawn in the argument?

(A)   To be judgmental is to assess someone negatively prior to making a serious effort at understanding.

(B)   It is absurd to criticize anyone for being critical.

(C)   There is some plausibility to the claim that it is absurd to criticize anyone for being critical.

(D)   Not all assessments people make of one another will be positive.

(E)   There is wisdom behind the injunction against being judgmental.

GO ON TO THE NEXT PAGE.

19. Even those who believe that the art of each age and culture has its own standards of beauty must admit that some painters are simply superior to others in the execution of their artistic visions. But this superiority must be measured in light of the artist's purposes, since the high merits, for example, of Jose Rey Toledo's work and his extraordinary artistic skills are not in doubt, despite the fact that his paintings do not literally resemble what they represent.

The claim that some painters are superior to others in the execution of their artistic visions plays which one of the following roles in the argument?

(A) It is a hypothesis that the argument attempts to refute.

(B) It is a generalization, one sort of objection to which the argument illustrates by giving an example.

(C) It is a claim that, according to the argument, is to be understood in a manner specified by the conclusion.

(D) It is a claim that the argument derives from another claim and that it uses to support its conclusion.

(E) It is a generalization that the argument uses to justify the relevance of the specific example it cites.

20. A study of rabbits in the 1940s convinced many biologists that parthenogenesis—reproduction without fertilization of an egg—sometimes occurs in mammals. However, the study's methods have since been shown to be flawed, and no other studies have succeeded in demonstrating mammalian parthenogenesis. Thus, since parthenogenesis is known to occur in a wide variety of nonmammalian vertebrates, there must be something about mammalian chromosomes that precludes the possibility of parthenogenesis.

A flaw in the reasoning of the argument is that the argument

(A) takes for granted that something that has not been proven to be true is for that reason shown to be false

(B) infers that a characteristic is shared by all nonmammalian vertebrate species merely because it is shared by some nonmammalian vertebrate species

(C) rules out an explanation of a phenomenon merely on the grounds that there is another explanation that can account for the phenomenon

(D) confuses a necessary condition for parthenogenesis with a sufficient condition for it

(E) assumes that the methods used in a study of one mammalian species were flawed merely because the study's findings cannot be generalized to all other mammalian species

21. Advertiser: Most TV shows depend on funding from advertisers and would be canceled without such funding. However, advertisers will not pay to have their commercials aired during a TV show unless many people watching the show buy the advertised products as a result. So if people generally fail to buy the products advertised during their favorite shows, these shows will soon be canceled. Thus, anyone who feels that a TV show is worth preserving ought to buy the products advertised during that show.

The advertiser's reasoning most closely conforms to which one of the following principles?

(A) If a TV show that one feels to be worth preserving would be canceled unless one took certain actions, then one ought to take those actions.

(B) If a TV show would be canceled unless many people took certain actions, then everyone who feels that the show is worth preserving ought to take those actions.

(C) If a TV show is worth preserving, then everyone should take whatever actions are necessary to prevent that show from being canceled.

(D) If one feels that a TV show is worth preserving, then one should take at least some actions to reduce the likelihood that the show will be canceled.

(E) If a TV show would be canceled unless many people took certain actions, then those who feel most strongly that it is worth preserving should take those actions.

GO ON TO THE NEXT PAGE.

22. Psychologist: It is well known that becoming angry often induces temporary incidents of high blood pressure. A recent study further showed, however, that people who are easily angered are significantly more likely to have permanently high blood pressure than are people who have more tranquil personalities. Coupled with the long-established fact that those with permanently high blood pressure are especially likely to have heart disease, the recent findings indicate that heart disease can result from psychological factors.

Which one of the following would, if true, most weaken the psychologist's argument?

(A) Those who are easily angered are less likely to recover fully from episodes of heart disease than are other people.

(B) Medication designed to control high blood pressure can greatly affect the moods of those who use it.

(C) People with permanently high blood pressure who have tranquil personalities virtually never develop heart disease.

(D) Those who discover that they have heart disease tend to become more easily frustrated by small difficulties.

(E) The physiological factors that cause permanently high blood pressure generally make people quick to anger.

23. A professor of business placed a case-study assignment for her class on her university's computer network. She later found out that instead of reading the assignment on the computer screen, 50 out of the 70 students printed it out on paper. Thus, it is not the case that books delivered via computer will make printed books obsolete.

Which one of the following, if true, most strengthens the argument?

(A) Several colleagues of the professor have found that, in their non-business courses, several of their students behave similarly in relation to assignments placed on the computer network.

(B) Studies consistently show that most computer users will print reading material that is more than a few pages in length rather than read it on the computer screen.

(C) Some people get impaired vision from long periods of reading printed matter on computer screens, even if they use high quality computer screens.

(D) Scanning technology is very poor, causing books delivered via computer to be full of errors unless editors carefully read the scanned versions.

(E) Books on cassette tape have only a small fraction of the sales of printed versions of the same books, though sales of videos of books that have been turned into movies remain strong.

GO ON TO THE NEXT PAGE.

24. Advertisement: Researchers studied a group of people trying to lose weight and discovered that those in the group who lost the most weight got more calories from protein than from carbohydrates and ate their biggest meal early in the day. So anyone who follows our diet, which provides more calories from protein than from anything else and which requires that breakfast be the biggest meal of the day, is sure to lose weight.

The reasoning in the advertisement is most vulnerable to criticism on the grounds that the advertisement overlooks the possibility that

(A) eating foods that derive a majority of their calories from carbohydrates tends to make one feel fuller than does eating foods that derive a majority of their calories from protein

(B) a few of the people in the group studied who lost significant amounts of weight got nearly all of their calories from carbohydrates and ate their biggest meal at night

(C) the people in the group studied who increased their activity levels lost more weight, on average, than those who did not, regardless of whether they got more calories from protein or from carbohydrates

(D) some people in the group studied lost no weight yet got more calories from protein than from carbohydrates and ate their biggest meal early in the day

(E) people who eat their biggest meal at night tend to snack more during the day and so tend to take in more total calories than do people who eat their biggest meal earlier in the day

25. Some twentieth-century art is great art. All great art involves original ideas, and any art that is not influential cannot be great art.

Each of the following statements follows logically from the set of statements above EXCEPT:

(A) Some influential art involves original ideas.

(B) Some twentieth-century art involves original ideas.

(C) Only art that involves original ideas is influential.

(D) Only art that is influential and involves original ideas is great art.

(E) Some twentieth-century art is influential and involves original ideas.

S T O P

IF YOU FINISH BEFORE TIME IS CALLED, YOU MAY CHECK YOUR WORK ON THIS SECTION ONLY.
DO NOT WORK ON ANY OTHER SECTION IN THE TEST.

SECTION II

Time—35 minutes

27 Questions

<u>Directions:</u> Each set of questions in this section is based on a single passage or a pair of passages. The questions are to be answered on the basis of what is <u>stated</u> or <u>implied</u> in the passage or pair of passages. For some of the questions, more than one of the choices could conceivably answer the question. However, you are to choose the <u>best</u> answer; that is, the response that most accurately and completely answers the question, and blacken the corresponding space on your answer sheet.

Often when a highly skilled and experienced employee leaves one company to work for another, there is the potential for a transfer of sensitive information between competitors. Two basic principles
(5) in such cases appear irreconcilable: the right of the company to its intellectual property—its proprietary data and trade secrets—and the right of individuals to seek gainful employment and to make free use of their abilities. Nevertheless, the courts have often tried to
(10) preserve both parties' legal rights by refusing to prohibit the employee from working for the competitor, but at the same time providing an injunction against disclosure of any of the former employer's secrets. It has been argued that because such measures help
(15) generate suspicions and similar psychological barriers to full and free utilization of abilities in the employee's new situation, they are hardly effective in upholding the individual's rights to free employment decisions. But it is also doubtful that they are effective in
(20) preserving trade secrets.

It is obviously impossible to divest oneself of that part of one's expertise that one has acquired from former employers and coworkers. Nor, in general, can one selectively refrain from its use, given that it has
(25) become an integral part of one's total intellectual capacity. Nevertheless, almost any such information that is not public knowledge may legitimately be claimed as corporate property: normal employment agreements provide for corporate ownership of all
(30) relevant data, including inventions, generated by the employee in connection with the company's business.

Once an employee takes a position with a competitor, the trade secrets that have been acquired by that employee may manifest themselves clearly and
(35) consciously. This is what court injunctions seek to prohibit. But they are far more likely to manifest themselves subconsciously and inconspicuously—for example, in one's daily decisions at the new post, or in the many small contributions one might make to a large
(40) team effort—often in the form of an intuitive sense of what to do or to avoid. Theoretically, an injunction also prohibits such inadvertent "leakage." However, the former employer faces the practical problem of securing evidence of such leakage, for little will
(45) usually be apparent from the public activities of the new employer. And even if the new employee's activities appear suspicious, there is the further problem of distinguishing trade secrets from what may be legitimately asserted as technological skills
(50) developed independently by the employee or already possessed by the new employer. This is a major stumbling block in the attempt to protect trade secrets,

since the proprietor has no recourse against others who independently generate the same information. It is
(55) therefore unlikely that an injunction against disclosure of trade secrets to future employers actually prevents any transfer of information except for the passage of documents and other concrete embodiments of the secrets.

1. Which one of the following most accurately expresses the main point of the passage?

(A)   There are more effective ways than court injunctions to preserve both a company's right to protect its intellectual property and individuals' rights to make free use of their abilities.

(B)   Court injunctions must be strengthened if they are to remain a relevant means of protecting corporations' trade secrets.

(C)   Enforcement of court injunctions designed to protect proprietary information is impossible when employees reveal such information to new employers.

(D)   Court injunctions prohibiting employees from disclosing former employers' trade secrets to new employers probably do not achieve all of their intended objectives.

(E)   The rights of employees to make full use of their talents and previous training are being seriously eroded by the prohibitions placed on them by court injunctions designed to prevent the transfer of trade secrets.

GO ON TO THE NEXT PAGE.

2. Given the passage's content and tone, which one of the following statements would most likely be found elsewhere in a work from which this passage is an excerpt?

(A) Given the law as it stands, corporations concerned about preserving trade secrets might be best served by giving their employees strong incentives to stay in their current jobs.

(B) While difficult to enforce and interpret, injunctions are probably the most effective means of halting the inadvertent transfer of trade secrets while simultaneously protecting the rights of employees.

(C) Means of redress must be made available to companies that suspect, but cannot prove, that former employees are revealing protected information to competitors.

(D) Even concrete materials such as computer disks are so easy to copy and conceal that it will be a waste of time for courts to try to prevent the spread of information through physical theft.

(E) The psychological barriers that an injunction can place on an employee in a new workplace are inevitably so subtle that they have no effect on the employee.

3. The author's primary purpose in the passage is to

(A) suggest that injunctions against the disclosure of trade secrets not only create problems for employees in the workplace, but also are unable to halt the illicit spread of proprietary information

(B) suggest that the information contained in "documents and other concrete embodiments" is usually so trivial that injunctions do little good in protecting intellectual property

(C) argue that new methods must be found to address the delicate balance between corporate and individual rights

(D) support the position that the concept of protecting trade secrets is no longer viable in an age of increasing access to information

(E) argue that injunctions are not necessary for the protection of trade secrets

4. The passage provides the most support for which one of the following assertions?

(A) Injunctions should be imposed by the courts only when there is strong reason to believe that an employee will reveal proprietary information.

(B) There is apparently no reliable way to protect both the rights of companies to protect trade secrets and the rights of employees to seek new employment.

(C) Employees should not be allowed to take jobs with their former employers' competitors when their new job could compromise trade secrets of their former employers.

(D) The multiplicity of means for transferring information in the workplace only increases the need for injunctions.

(E) Some companies seek injunctions as a means of punishing employees who take jobs with their competitors.

5. With which one of the following statements regarding documents and other concrete embodiments mentioned in line 58 would the author be most likely to agree?

(A) While the transfer of such materials would be damaging, even the seemingly innocuous contributions of an employee to a competitor can do more harm in the long run.

(B) Such materials are usually less informative than what the employee may recollect about a previous job.

(C) Injunctions against the disclosure of trade secrets should carefully specify which materials are included in order to focus on the most damaging ones.

(D) Large-scale transfer of documents and other materials cannot be controlled by injunctions.

(E) Such concrete materials lend themselves to control and identification more readily than do subtler means of transferring information.

6. In the passage, the author makes which one of the following claims?

(A) Injunctions against the disclosure of trade secrets limit an employee's chances of being hired by a competitor.

(B) Measures against the disclosure of trade secrets are unnecessary except in the case of documents and other concrete embodiments of the secrets.

(C) Employees who switch jobs to work for a competitor usually unintentionally violate the law by doing so.

(D) Employers are not restricted in the tactics they can use when seeking to secure protected information from new employees.

(E) What may seem like intellectual theft may in fact be an example of independent innovation.

GO ON TO THE NEXT PAGE.

The following passages concern a plant called purple loosestrife. Passage A is excerpted from a report issued by a prairie research council; passage B from a journal of sociology.

Passage A

Purple loosestrife (*Lythrum salicaria*), an aggressive and invasive perennial of Eurasian origin, arrived with settlers in eastern North America in the early 1800s and has spread across the continent's
(5) midlatitude wetlands. The impact of purple loosestrife on native vegetation has been disastrous, with more than 50 percent of the biomass of some wetland communities displaced. Monospecific blocks of this weed have maintained themselves for at least 20 years.
(10) Impacts on wildlife have not been well studied, but serious reductions in waterfowl and aquatic furbearer productivity have been observed. In addition, several endangered species of vertebrates are threatened with further degradation of their
(15) breeding habitats. Although purple loosestrife can invade relatively undisturbed habitats, the spread and dominance of this weed have been greatly accelerated in disturbed habitats. While digging out the plants can temporarily halt their spread, there has been little
(20) research on long-term purple loosestrife control. Glyphosate has been used successfully, but no measure of the impact of this herbicide on native plant communities has been made.

With the spread of purple loosestrife growing
(25) exponentially, some form of integrated control is needed. At present, coping with purple loosestrife hinges on early detection of the weed's arrival in areas, which allows local eradication to be carried out with minimum damage to the native plant community.

Passage B

(30) The war on purple loosestrife is apparently conducted on behalf of nature, an attempt to liberate the biotic community from the tyrannical influence of a life-destroying invasive weed. Indeed, purple loosestrife control is portrayed by its practitioners as
(35) an environmental initiative intended to save nature rather than control it. Accordingly, the purple loosestrife literature, scientific and otherwise, dutifully discusses the impacts of the weed on endangered species—and on threatened biodiversity
(40) more generally. Purple loosestrife is a pollution, according to the scientific community, and all of nature suffers under its pervasive influence.

Regardless of the perceived and actual ecological effects of the purple invader, it is apparent that
(45) popular pollution ideologies have been extended into the wetlands of North America. Consequently, the scientific effort to liberate nature from purple loosestrife has failed to decouple itself from its philosophical origin as an instrument to control nature
(50) to the satisfaction of human desires. Birds, particularly game birds and waterfowl, provide the bulk of the justification for loosestrife management. However, no bird species other than the canvasback has been identified in the literature as endangered by

(55) purple loosestrife. The impact of purple loosestrife on furbearing mammals is discussed at great length, though none of the species highlighted (muskrat, mink) can be considered threatened in North America. What is threatened by purple loosestrife is the
(60) economics of exploiting such preferred species and the millions of dollars that will be lost to the economies of the United States and Canada from reduced hunting, trapping, and recreation revenues due to a decline in the production of the wetland
(65) resource.

7. Both passages explicitly mention which one of the following?

(A) furbearing animals
(B) glyphosate
(C) the threat purple loosestrife poses to economies
(D) popular pollution ideologies
(E) literature on purple loosestrife control

8. Each of the passages contains information sufficient to answer which one of the following questions?

(A) Approximately how long ago did purple loosestrife arrive in North America?
(B) Is there much literature discussing the potential benefit that hunters might derive from purple loosestrife management?
(C) What is an issue regarding purple loosestrife management on which both hunters and farmers agree?
(D) Is the canvasback threatened with extinction due to the spread of purple loosestrife?
(E) What is a type of terrain that is affected in at least some parts of North America by the presence of purple loosestrife?

9. It can be inferred that the authors would be most likely to disagree about which one of the following?

(A) Purple loosestrife spreads more quickly in disturbed habitats than in undisturbed habitats.
(B) The threat posed by purple loosestrife to local aquatic furbearer populations is serious.
(C) Most people who advocate that eradication measures be taken to control purple loosestrife are not genuine in their concern for the environment.
(D) The size of the biomass that has been displaced by purple loosestrife is larger than is generally thought.
(E) Measures should be taken to prevent other non-native plant species from invading North America.

GO ON TO THE NEXT PAGE.

10. Which one of the following most accurately describes the attitude expressed by the author of passage B toward the overall argument represented by passage A?

   (A) enthusiastic agreement
   (B) cautious agreement
   (C) pure neutrality
   (D) general ambivalence
   (E) pointed skepticism

11. It can be inferred that both authors would be most likely to agree with which one of the following statements regarding purple loosestrife?

   (A) As it increases in North America, some wildlife populations tend to decrease.
   (B) Its establishment in North America has had a disastrous effect on native North American wetland vegetation in certain regions.
   (C) It is very difficult to control effectively with herbicides.
   (D) Its introduction into North America was a great ecological blunder.
   (E) When it is eliminated from a given area, it tends to return to that area fairly quickly.

12. Which one of the following is true about the relationship between the two passages?

   (A) Passage A presents evidence that directly counters claims made in passage B.
   (B) Passage B assumes what passage A explicitly argues for.
   (C) Passage B displays an awareness of the arguments touched on in passage A, but not vice versa.
   (D) Passage B advocates a policy that passage A rejects.
   (E) Passage A downplays the seriousness of claims made in passage B.

13. Which one of the following, if true, would cast doubt on the argument in passage B but bolster the argument in passage A?

   (A) Localized population reduction is often a precursor to widespread endangerment of a species.
   (B) Purple loosestrife was barely noticed in North America before the advent of suburban sprawl in the 1950s.
   (C) The amount by which overall hunting, trapping, and recreation revenues would be reduced as a result of the extinction of one or more species threatened by purple loosestrife represents a significant portion of those revenues.
   (D) Some environmentalists who advocate taking measures to eradicate purple loosestrife view such measures as a means of controlling nature.
   (E) Purple loosestrife has never become a problem in its native habitat, even though no effort has been made to eradicate it there.

GO ON TO THE NEXT PAGE.

With their recognition of Maxine Hong Kingston as a major literary figure, some critics have suggested that her works have been produced almost *ex nihilo*, saying that they lack a large traceable body of direct
(5) literary antecedents especially within the Chinese American heritage in which her work is embedded. But these critics, who have examined only the development of written texts, the most visible signs of a culture's narrative production, have overlooked Kingston's
(10) connection to the long Chinese tradition of a highly developed genre of song and spoken narrative known as "talk-story" (*gong gu tsai*).

Traditionally performed in the dialects of various ethnic enclaves, talk-story has been maintained within
(15) the confines of the family and has rarely surfaced into print. The tradition dates back to Sung dynasty (A.D. 970–1279) storytellers in China, and in the United States it is continually revitalized by an overlapping sequence of immigration from China.
(20) Thus, Chinese immigrants to the U.S. had a fully established, sophisticated oral culture, already ancient and capable of producing masterpieces, by the time they began arriving in the early nineteenth century. This transplanted oral heritage simply embraced new
(25) subject matter or new forms of Western discourse, as in the case of Kingston's adaptations written in English.

Kingston herself believes that as a literary artist she is one in a long line of performers shaping a recalcitrant history into talk-story form. She
(30) distinguishes her "thematic" storytelling memory processes, which sift and reconstruct the essential elements of personally remembered stories, from the memory processes of a print-oriented culture that emphasizes the retention of precise sequences of
(35) words. Nor does the entry of print into the storytelling process substantially change her notion of the character of oral tradition. For Kingston, "writer" is synonymous with "singer" or "performer" in the ancient sense of privileged keeper, transmitter, and creator of stories
(40) whose current stage of development can be frozen in print, but which continue to grow both around and from that frozen text.

Kingston's participation in the tradition of talk-story is evidenced in her book *China Men*, which
(45) utilizes forms typical of that genre and common to most oral cultures including: a fixed "grammar" of repetitive themes; a spectrum of stock characters; symmetrical structures, including balanced oppositions (verbal or physical contests, antithetical characters,
(50) dialectical discourse such as question-answer forms and riddles); and repetition. In *China Men*, Kingston also succeeds in investing idiomatic English with the allusive texture and oral-aural qualities of the Chinese language, a language rich in aural and visual puns,
(55) making her work a written form of talk-story.

14. Which one of the following most accurately states the main point of the passage?

(A) Despite some critics' comments, Kingston's writings have significant Chinese American antecedents, which can be found in the traditional oral narrative form known as talk-story.

(B) Analysis of Kingston's writings, especially *China Men*, supports her belief that literary artists can be performers who continue to reconstruct their stories even after they have been frozen in print.

(C) An understanding of Kingston's work and of Chinese American writers in general reveals that critics of ethnic literatures in the United States have been mistaken in examining only written texts.

(D) Throughout her writings Kingston uses techniques typical of the talk-story genre, especially the retention of certain aspects of Chinese speech in the written English text.

(E) The writings of Kingston have rekindled an interest in talk-story, which dates back to the Sung dynasty, and was extended to the United States with the arrival of Chinese immigrants in the nineteenth century.

15. Which one of the following can be most reasonably inferred from the passage?

(A) In the last few years, written forms of talk-story have appeared in Chinese as often as they have in English.

(B) Until very recently, scholars have held that oral storytelling in Chinese ethnic enclaves was a unique oral tradition.

(C) Talk-story has developed in the United States through a process of combining Chinese, Chinese American, and other oral storytelling forms.

(D) Chinese American talk-story relies upon memory processes that do not emphasize the retention of precise sequences of words.

(E) The connection between certain aspects of Kingston's work and talk-story is argued by some critics to be rather tenuous and questionable.

GO ON TO THE NEXT PAGE.

16. It can be inferred from the passage that the author uses the phrase "personally remembered stories" (line 32) primarily to refer to

    (A) a literary genre of first-person storytelling
    (B) a thematically organized personal narrative of one's own past
    (C) partially idiosyncratic memories of narratives
    (D) the retention in memory of precise sequences of words
    (E) easily identifiable thematic issues in literature

17. In which one of the following is the use of cotton fibers or cotton cloth most analogous to Kingston's use of the English language as described in lines 51–55?

    (A) Scraps of plain cotton cloth are used to create a multicolored quilt.
    (B) The surface texture of woolen cloth is simulated in a piece of cotton cloth by a special process of weaving.
    (C) Because of its texture, cotton cloth is used for a certain type of clothes for which linen is inappropriate.
    (D) In making a piece of cloth, cotton fiber is substituted for linen because of the roughly similar texture of the two materials.
    (E) Because of their somewhat similar textures, cotton and linen fibers are woven together in a piece of cloth to achieve a savings in price over a pure linen cloth.

18. The passage most clearly suggests that Kingston believes which one of the following about at least some of the stories contained in her writings?

    (A) Since they are intimately tied to the nature of the Chinese language, they can be approximated, but not adequately expressed, in English.
    (B) They should be thought of primarily as ethnic literature and evaluated accordingly by critics.
    (C) They will likely be retold and altered to some extent in the process.
    (D) Chinese American history is best chronicled by traditional talk-story.
    (E) Their significance and beauty cannot be captured at all in written texts.

19. The author's argument in the passage would be most weakened if which one of the following were true?

    (A) Numerous writers in the United States have been influenced by oral traditions.
    (B) Most Chinese American writers' work is very different from Kingston's.
    (C) Native American storytellers use narrative devices similar to those used in talk-story.
    (D) *China Men* is for the most part atypical of Kingston's literary works.
    (E) Literary critics generally appreciate the authenticity of Kingston's work.

20. The author's specific purpose in detailing typical talk-story forms (lines 43–51) is to

    (A) show why Kingston's book *China Men* establishes her as a major literary figure
    (B) support the claim that Kingston's use of typically oral techniques makes her work a part of the talk-story tradition
    (C) dispute the critics' view that Chinese American literature lacks literary antecedents
    (D) argue for Kingston's view that the literary artist is at best a "privileged keeper" of stories
    (E) provide an alternative to certain critics' view that Kingston's work should be judged primarily as literature

21. Which one of the following most accurately identifies the attitude shown by the author in the passage toward talk-story?

    (A) scholarly appreciation for its longstanding artistic sophistication
    (B) mild disappointment that it has not distinguished itself from other oral traditions
    (C) tentative approval of its resistance to critical evaluations
    (D) clear respect for the diversity of its ancient sources and cultural derivations
    (E) open admiration for the way it uses song to express narrative

GO ON TO THE NEXT PAGE.

In economics, the term "speculative bubble" refers to a large upward move in an asset's price driven not by the asset's fundamentals—that is, by the earnings derivable from the asset—but rather by
(5) mere speculation that someone else will be willing to pay a higher price for it. The price increase is then followed by a dramatic decline in price, due to a loss in confidence that the price will continue to rise, and the "bubble" is said to have burst. According to
(10) Charles Mackay's classic nineteenth-century account, the seventeenth-century Dutch tulip market provides an example of a speculative bubble. But the economist Peter Garber challenges Mackay's view, arguing that there is no evidence that the Dutch tulip
(15) market really involved a speculative bubble.

By the seventeenth century, the Netherlands had become a center of cultivation and development of new tulip varieties, and a market had developed in which rare varieties of bulbs sold at high prices. For
(20) example, a Semper Augustus bulb sold in 1625 for an amount of gold worth about U.S.$11,000 in 1999. Common bulb varieties, on the other hand, sold for very low prices. According to Mackay, by 1636 rapid price rises attracted speculators, and prices of many
(25) varieties surged upward from November 1636 through January 1637. Mackay further states that in February 1637 prices suddenly collapsed; bulbs could not be sold at 10 percent of their peak values. By 1739, the prices of all the most prized kinds of bulbs had fallen
(30) to no more than one two-hundredth of 1 percent of Semper Augustus's peak price.

Garber acknowledges that bulb prices increased dramatically from 1636 to 1637 and eventually reached very low levels. But he argues that this
(35) episode should not be described as a speculative bubble, for the increase and eventual decline in bulb prices can be explained in terms of the fundamentals. Garber argues that a standard pricing pattern occurs for new varieties of flowers. When a particularly
(40) prized variety is developed, its original bulb sells for a high price. Thus, the dramatic rise in the price of some original tulip bulbs could have resulted as tulips in general, and certain varieties in particular, became fashionable. However, as the prized bulbs become
(45) more readily available through reproduction from the original bulb, their price falls rapidly; after less than 30 years, bulbs sell at reproduction cost. But this does not mean that the high prices of original bulbs are irrational, for earnings derivable from the millions
(50) of bulbs descendent from the original bulbs can be very high, even if each individual descendent bulb commands a very low price. Given that an original bulb can generate a reasonable return on investment even if the price of descendent bulbs decreases
(55) dramatically, a rapid rise and eventual fall of tulip bulb prices need not indicate a speculative bubble.

22. Which one of the following most accurately expresses the main point of the passage?

(A) The seventeenth-century Dutch tulip market is widely but mistakenly believed by economists to provide an example of a speculative bubble.

(B) Mackay did not accurately assess the earnings that could be derived from rare and expensive seventeenth-century Dutch tulip bulbs.

(C) A speculative bubble occurs whenever the price of an asset increases substantially followed by a rapid and dramatic decline.

(D) Garber argues that Mackay's classic account of the seventeenth-century Dutch tulip market as a speculative bubble is not supported by the evidence.

(E) A tulip bulb can generate a reasonable return on investment even if the price starts very high and decreases dramatically.

23. Given Garber's account of the seventeenth-century Dutch tulip market, which one of the following is most analogous to someone who bought a tulip bulb of a certain variety in that market at a very high price, only to sell a bulb of that variety at a much lower price?

(A) someone who, after learning that many others had withdrawn their applications for a particular job, applied for the job in the belief that there would be less competition for it

(B) an art dealer who, after paying a very high price for a new painting, sells it at a very low price because it is now considered to be an inferior work

(C) someone who, after buying a box of rare motorcycle parts at a very high price, is forced to sell them at a much lower price because of the sudden availability of cheap substitute parts

(D) a publisher who pays an extremely high price for a new novel only to sell copies at a price affordable to nearly everyone

(E) an airline that, after selling most of the tickets for seats on a plane at a very high price, must sell the remaining tickets at a very low price

GO ON TO THE NEXT PAGE.

24. The passage most strongly supports the inference that Garber would agree with which one of the following statements?

(A) If speculative bubbles occur at all, they occur very rarely.

(B) Many of the owners of high-priced original tulip bulbs could have expected to at least recoup their original investments from sales of the many bulbs propagated from the original bulbs.

(C) If there is not a speculative bubble in a market, then the level of prices in that market is not irrational.

(D) Most people who invested in Dutch tulip bulbs in the seventeenth century were generally rational in all their investments.

(E) Mackay mistakenly infers from the fact that tulip prices dropped rapidly that the very low prices that the bulbs eventually sold for were irrational.

25. The passage states that Mackay claimed which one of the following?

(A) The rapid rise in price of Dutch tulip bulbs was not due to the fashionability of the flowers they produced.

(B) The prices of certain varieties of Dutch tulip bulbs during the seventeenth century were, at least for a time, determined by speculation.

(C) The Netherlands was the only center of cultivation and development of new tulip varieties in the seventeenth century.

(D) The very high prices of bulbs in the seventeenth-century Dutch tulip market were not irrational.

(E) Buyers of rare and very expensive Dutch tulip bulbs were ultimately able to derive earnings from bulbs descendent from the original bulbs.

26. The main purpose of the second paragraph is to

(A) present the facts that are accepted by all experts in the field

(B) identify the mistake that one scholar alleges another scholar made

(C) explain the basis on which one scholar makes an inference with which another scholar disagrees

(D) undermine the case that one scholar makes for the claim with which another scholar disagrees

(E) outline the factual errors that led one scholar to draw the inference that he drew

27. The phrase "standard pricing pattern" as used in line 38 most nearly means a pricing pattern

(A) against which other pricing patterns are to be measured

(B) that conforms to a commonly agreed-upon criterion

(C) that is merely acceptable

(D) that regularly recurs in certain types of cases

(E) that serves as an exemplar

S T O P

IF YOU FINISH BEFORE TIME IS CALLED, YOU MAY CHECK YOUR WORK ON THIS SECTION ONLY.
DO NOT WORK ON ANY OTHER SECTION IN THE TEST.

SECTION III

Time—35 minutes

25 Questions

<u>Directions</u>: The questions in this section are based on the reasoning contained in brief statements or passages. For some questions, more than one of the choices could conceivably answer the question. However, you are to choose the <u>best</u> answer; that is, the response that most accurately and completely answers the question. You should not make assumptions that are by commonsense standards implausible, superfluous, or incompatible with the passage. After you have chosen the best answer, blacken the corresponding space on your answer sheet.

1. Aristophanes' play *The Clouds*, which was written when the philosopher Socrates was in his mid-forties, portrays Socrates as an atheistic philosopher primarily concerned with issues in natural science. The only other surviving portrayals of Socrates were written after Socrates' death at age 70. They portrayed Socrates as having a religious dimension and a strong focus on ethical issues.

    Which one of the following, if true, would most help to resolve the apparent discrepancy between Aristophanes' portrayal of Socrates and the other surviving portrayals?

    (A) Aristophanes' portrayal of Socrates in *The Clouds* was unflattering, whereas the other portrayals were very flattering.
    (B) Socrates' philosophical views and interests changed sometime after his mid-forties.
    (C) Most of the philosophers who lived before Socrates were primarily concerned with natural science.
    (D) Socrates was a much more controversial figure in the years before his death than he was in his mid-forties.
    (E) Socrates had an influence on many subsequent philosophers who were primarily concerned with natural science.

2. Board member: The J Foundation, a philanthropic organization, gave you this grant on the condition that your resulting work not contain any material detrimental to the J Foundation's reputation. But your resulting work never mentions any of the laudable achievements of our foundation. Hence your work fails to meet the conditions under which the grant was made.

    The reasoning in the board member's argument is vulnerable to criticism on the grounds that the argument

    (A) takes for granted that a work that never mentions any laudable achievements cannot be of high intellectual value
    (B) confuses a condition necessary for the receipt of a grant with a condition sufficient for the receipt of a grant
    (C) presumes, without providing justification, that a work that does not mention a foundation's laudable achievements is harmful to that foundation's reputation
    (D) fails to consider that recipients of a grant usually strive to meet a foundation's conditions
    (E) fails to consider the possibility that the work that was produced with the aid of the grant may have met all conditions other than avoiding detriment to the J Foundation's reputation

3. Psychiatrist: Breaking any habit is difficult, especially when it involves an addictive substance. People who break a habit are more likely to be motivated by immediate concerns than by long-term ones. Therefore, people who succeed in breaking their addiction to smoking cigarettes are more likely to be motivated by the social pressure against smoking—which is an immediate concern—than by health concerns, since _____.

    The conclusion of the psychiatrist's argument is most strongly supported if which one of the following completes the argument?

    (A) a habit that involves an addictive substance is likely to pose a greater health threat than a habit that does not involve any addictive substance
    (B) for most people who successfully quit smoking, smoking does not create an immediate health concern at the time they quit
    (C) some courses of action that exacerbate health concerns can also relieve social pressure
    (D) most people who succeed in quitting smoking succeed only after several attempts
    (E) everyone who succeeds in quitting smoking is motivated either by social pressure or by health concerns

GO ON TO THE NEXT PAGE.

4. Cassie: In order to improve the quality of customer service provided by our real estate agency, we should reduce client loads—the number of clients each agent is expected to serve at one time.

   Melvin: Although smaller client loads are desirable, reducing client loads at our agency is simply not feasible. We already find it very difficult to recruit enough qualified agents; recruiting even more agents, which would be necessary in order to reduce client loads, is out of the question.

   Of the following, which one, if true, is the logically strongest counter that Cassie can make to Melvin's argument?

   (A) Since reducing client loads would improve working conditions for agents, reducing client loads would help recruit additional qualified agents to the real estate agency.

   (B) Many of the real estate agency's current clients have expressed strong support for efforts to reduce client loads.

   (C) Several recently conducted studies of real estate agencies have shown that small client loads are strongly correlated with high customer satisfaction ratings.

   (D) Hiring extra support staff for the real estate agency's main office would have many of the same beneficial effects as reducing client loads.

   (E) Over the last several years, it has become increasingly challenging for the real estate agency to recruit enough qualified agents just to maintain current client loads.

5. The star-nosed mole has a nose that ends in a pair of several-pointed stars, or tentacles that are crucial for hunting, as moles are poor-sighted. These tentacles contain receptors that detect electric fields produced by other animals, enabling the moles to detect and catch suitable prey such as worms and insects.

   Which one of the following is most strongly supported by the information above?

   (A) Both worms and insects produce electric fields.

   (B) The star-nosed mole does not rely at all on its eyesight for survival.

   (C) The star-nosed mole does not rely at all on its sense of smell when hunting.

   (D) Only animals that hunt have noses with tentacles that detect electric fields.

   (E) The star-nosed mole does not produce an electric field.

6. In her recent book a psychologist described several cases that exhibit the following pattern: A child, denied something by its parent, initiates problematic behavior such as screaming; the behavior escalates until finally the exasperated parent acquiesces to the child's demand. At this point the child, having obtained the desired goal, stops the problematic behavior, to the parent's relief. This self-reinforcing pattern of misbehavior and accommodation is repeated with steadily increasing levels of misbehavior by the child.

   The cases described by the psychologist illustrate each of the following generalizations EXCEPT:

   (A) A child can develop problematic behavior patterns as a result of getting what it wants.

   (B) A child and parent can mutually influence each other's behavior.

   (C) Parents, by their choices, can inadvertently increase their child's level of misbehavior.

   (D) A child can unintentionally influence a parent's behavior in ways contrary to the child's intended goals.

   (E) A child can get what it wants by doing what its parent doesn't want it to do.

7. Scientist: In our study, chemical R did not cause cancer in laboratory rats. But we cannot conclude from this that chemical R is safe for humans. After all, many substances known to be carcinogenic to humans cause no cancer in rats; this is probably because some carcinogens cause cancer only via long-term exposure and rats are short lived.

   Which one of the following most precisely describes the role played in the scientist's argument by the statement that chemical R did not cause cancer in laboratory rats?

   (A) It is cited as evidence against the conclusion that chemical R is safe for humans.

   (B) It is advanced to support the contention that test results obtained from laboratory rats cannot be extrapolated to humans.

   (C) It illustrates the claim that rats are too short lived to be suitable as test subjects for the carcinogenic properties of substances to which humans are chronically exposed.

   (D) It is used as evidence to support the hypothesis that chemical R causes cancer in humans via long-term exposure.

   (E) It is cited as being insufficient to support the conclusion that chemical R is safe for humans.

GO ON TO THE NEXT PAGE.

8. Department store manager: There is absolutely no reason to offer our customers free gift wrapping again this holiday season. If most customers take the offer, it will be expensive and time-consuming for us. On the other hand, if only a few customers want it, there is no advantage in offering it.

Which one of the following is an assumption required by the department store manager's argument?

(A) Gift wrapping would cost the store more during this holiday season than in previous holiday seasons.

(B) Anything that slows down shoppers during the holiday season costs the store money.

(C) It would be to the store's advantage to charge customers for gift wrapping services.

(D) It would be expensive to inform customers about the free gift wrapping service.

(E) Either few customers would want free gift wrapping or most customers would want it.

9. Among people who have a history of chronic trouble falling asleep, some rely only on sleeping pills to help them fall asleep, and others practice behavior modification techniques and do not take sleeping pills. Those who rely only on behavior modification fall asleep more quickly than do those who rely only on sleeping pills, so behavior modification is more effective than are sleeping pills in helping people to fall asleep.

Which one of the following, if true, most weakens the argument?

(A) People who do not take sleeping pills spend at least as many total hours asleep each night as do the people who take sleeping pills.

(B) Most people who have trouble falling asleep and who use behavior modification techniques fall asleep more slowly than do most people who have no trouble falling asleep.

(C) Many people who use only behavior modification techniques to help them fall asleep have never used sleeping pills.

(D) The people who are the most likely to take sleeping pills rather than practice behavior modification techniques are those who have previously had the most trouble falling asleep.

(E) The people who are the most likely to practice behavior modification techniques rather than take sleeping pills are those who prefer not to use drugs if other treatments are available.

10. Lawyer: This witness acknowledges being present at the restaurant and watching when my client, a famous television personality, was assaulted. Yet the witness claims to recognize the assailant, but not my famous client. Therefore, the witness's testimony should be excluded.

The lawyer's conclusion follows logically if which one of the following is assumed?

(A) If a witness claims to recognize both parties involved in an assault, then the witness's testimony should be included.

(B) There are other witnesses who can identify the lawyer's client as present during the assault.

(C) It is impossible to determine whether the witness actually recognized the assailant.

(D) The testimony of a witness to an assault should be included only if the witness claims to recognize both parties involved in the assault.

(E) It is unlikely that anyone would fail to recognize the lawyer's client.

11. Biologist: Many paleontologists have suggested that the difficulty of adapting to ice ages was responsible for the evolution of the human brain. But this suggestion must be rejected, for most other animal species adapted to ice ages with no evolutionary changes to their brains.

The biologist's argument is most vulnerable to criticism on which one of the following grounds?

(A) It fails to address adequately the possibility that even if a condition is sufficient to produce an effect in a species, it may not be necessary to produce that effect in that species.

(B) It fails to address adequately the possibility that a condition can produce a change in a species even if it does not produce that change in other species.

(C) It overlooks the possibility that a condition that is needed to produce a change in one species is not needed to produce a similar change in other species.

(D) It presumes without warrant that human beings were presented with greater difficulties during ice ages than were individuals of most other species.

(E) It takes for granted that, if a condition coincided with the emergence of a certain phenomenon, that condition must have been causally responsible for the phenomenon.

GO ON TO THE NEXT PAGE.

12. The total number of book titles published annually in North America has approximately quadrupled since television first became available. Retail sales of new titles, as measured in copies, increased rapidly in the early days of television, though the rate of increase has slowed in recent years. Library circulation has been flat or declining in recent years.

Which one of the following is most strongly supported by the information above?

(A) Television has, over the years, brought about a reduction in the amount of per capita reading in North America.

(B) The introduction of television usually brings about a decrease in library use.

(C) Book publishers in North America now sell fewer copies per title than they sold in the early days of television.

(D) The availability of television does not always cause a decline in the annual number of book titles published or in the number of books sold.

(E) The introduction of television expanded the market for books in North America.

13. Botanist: It has long been believed that people with children or pets should keep poinsettia plants out of their homes. Although this belief has been encouraged by child-rearing books, which commonly list poinsettias as poisonous and therefore dangerous, it is mistaken. Our research has shown, conclusively, that poinsettias pose no risk to children or pets.

Which one of the following most accurately expresses the conclusion drawn in the botanist's argument?

(A) Child-rearing books should encourage people with children to put poinsettias in their homes.

(B) Poinsettias are not dangerously poisonous.

(C) According to many child-rearing books, poinsettias are dangerous.

(D) The belief that households with children or pets should not have poinsettias is mistaken.

(E) Poinsettias pose no risk to children or pets.

14. Archaeologist: An ancient stone building at our excavation site was composed of three kinds of stone—quartz, granite, and limestone. Of these, only limestone occurs naturally in the area. Most of the buildings at the site from the same time period had limestone as their only stone component, and most were human dwellings. Therefore, the building we are studying probably was not a dwelling.

Which one of the following, if true, would most strengthen the archaeologist's reasoning?

(A) Most of the buildings that were used as dwellings at the site were made, at least in part, of limestone.

(B) Most of the buildings at the site that were not dwellings were made, at least in part, from types of stone that do not occur naturally in the area.

(C) Most of the buildings that were built from stones not naturally occurring in the area were not built with both quartz and granite.

(D) Most of the buildings at the site were used as dwellings.

(E) No quartz has been discovered on the site other than that found in the building being studied.

GO ON TO THE NEXT PAGE.

15. Theodore will be able to file his tax return on time only in the event that he has an accountant prepare his tax return and the accountant does not ask Theodore for any additional documentation of his business expenses. If he does have an accountant prepare his return, the accountant will necessarily ask Theodore to provide this additional documentation. Therefore, Theodore will not be able to file on time.

The pattern of reasoning in which one of the following arguments most closely parallels the pattern of reasoning in the argument above?

(A) Given the demands of Timothy's job, his next free evening will occur next Friday. Since he spent a lot of money on his last evening out, he will probably decide to spend his next free evening at home. Therefore, Timothy will probably be at home next Friday evening.

(B) Tovah cannot attend the concert next week if she is away on business. If she misses that concert, she will not have another opportunity to attend a concert this month. Since she will be away on business, Tovah will not be able to attend a concert this month.

(C) Mark's children will not be content this weekend unless he lets them play video games some of the time. Mark will let them play video games, but only at times when he has no other activities planned. Therefore, unless Mark and his children take a break from planned activities, Mark's children will not be content this weekend.

(D) If Teresa is not seated in first class on her airline flight, she will be seated in business class. Therefore, since she cannot be seated in first class on that flight, she will necessarily be seated in business class.

(E) Susannah will have a relaxing vacation only if her children behave especially well and she does not start to suspect that they are planning some mischief. Since she will certainly start to suspect that they are planning some mischief if they behave especially well, Susannah's vacation cannot possibly be relaxing.

16. When a threat to life is common, as are automobile and industrial accidents, only unusual instances tend to be prominently reported by the news media. Instances of rare threats, such as product tampering, however, are seen as news by reporters and are universally reported in featured stories. People in general tend to estimate the risk of various threats by how frequently those threats come to their attention.

If the statements above are true, which one of the following is most strongly supported on the basis of them?

(A) Whether governmental action will be taken to lessen a common risk depends primarily on the prominence given to the risk by the news media.

(B) People tend to magnify the risk of a threat if the threat seems particularly dreadful or if those who would be affected have no control over it.

(C) Those who get their information primarily from the news media tend to overestimate the risk of uncommon threats relative to the risk of common threats.

(D) Reporters tend not to seek out information about long-range future threats but to concentrate their attention on the immediate past and future.

(E) The resources that are spent on avoiding product tampering are greater than the resources that are spent on avoiding threats that stem from the weather.

GO ON TO THE NEXT PAGE.

17. Real estate agent: Upon selling a home, the sellers are legally entitled to remove any items that are not permanent fixtures. Legally, large appliances like dishwashers are not permanent fixtures. However, since many prospective buyers of the home are likely to assume that large appliances in the home would be included with its purchase, sellers who will be keeping the appliances are morally obliged either to remove them before showing the home or to indicate in some other way that the appliances are not included.

Which one of the following principles, if valid, most helps to justify the real estate agent's argumentation?

(A) If a home's sellers will be keeping any belongings that prospective buyers of the home might assume would be included with the purchase of the home, the sellers are morally obliged to indicate clearly that those belongings are not included.

(B) A home's sellers are morally obliged to ensure that prospective buyers of the home do not assume that any large appliances are permanent fixtures in the home.

(C) A home's sellers are morally obliged to include with the sale of the home at least some of the appliances that are not permanent fixtures but were in the home when it was shown to prospective buyers.

(D) A home's sellers are morally obliged not to deliberately mislead any prospective buyers of their home about which belongings are included with the sale of the home and which are not.

(E) If a home's sellers have indicated in some way that a large appliance is included with the home's purchase, then they are morally obliged not to remove that appliance after showing the home.

18. Many parents rigorously organize their children's activities during playtime, thinking that doing so will enhance their children's cognitive development. But this belief is incorrect. To thoroughly structure a child's playtime and expect this to produce a creative and resourceful child would be like expecting a good novel to be produced by someone who was told exactly what the plot and characters must be.

The argument is most vulnerable to criticism on which one of the following grounds?

(A) It takes for granted that if something is conducive to a certain goal it cannot also be conducive to some other goal.

(B) It overlooks the possibility that many children enjoy rigorously organized playtime.

(C) It takes a necessary condition for something's enhancing a child's creativity and resourcefulness to be a sufficient condition for its doing so.

(D) It fails to consider the possibility that being able to write a good novel requires something more than creativity and resourcefulness.

(E) It fails to consider the possibility that something could enhance a child's overall cognitive development without enhancing the child's creativity and resourcefulness.

19. Bureaucrat: The primary, constant goal of an ideal bureaucracy is to define and classify all possible problems and set out regulations regarding each eventuality. Also, an ideal bureaucracy provides an appeal procedure for any complaint. If a complaint reveals an unanticipated problem, the regulations are expanded to cover the new issue, and for this reason an ideal bureaucracy will have an ever-expanding system of regulations.

Which one of the following is an assumption the bureaucrat's argument requires?

(A) An ideal bureaucracy will provide an appeal procedure for complaints even after it has defined and classified all possible problems and set out regulations regarding each eventuality.

(B) For each problem that an ideal bureaucracy has defined and classified, the bureaucracy has received at least one complaint revealing that problem.

(C) An ideal bureaucracy will never be permanently without complaints about problems that are not covered by that bureaucracy's regulations.

(D) An ideal bureaucracy can reach its primary goal if, but only if, its system of regulations is always expanding to cover problems that had not been anticipated.

(E) Any complaint that an ideal bureaucracy receives will reveal an unanticipated problem that the bureaucracy is capable of defining and classifying.

GO ON TO THE NEXT PAGE.

20. Scientists studying a common type of bacteria have discovered that most bacteria of that type are in hibernation at any given time. Some microbiologists have concluded from this that bacteria in general are usually in hibernation. This conclusion would be reasonable if all types of bacteria were rather similar. But, in fact, since bacteria are extremely diverse, it is unlikely that most types of bacteria hibernate regularly.

Which one of the following most accurately expresses the overall conclusion of the argument?

(A) Bacteria of most types are usually in hibernation.

(B) It is probably not true that most types of bacteria hibernate regularly.

(C) If bacteria are extremely diverse, it is unlikely that most types of bacteria hibernate regularly.

(D) The conclusion that bacteria in general are usually in hibernation would be reasonable if all types of bacteria were rather similar.

(E) It is likely that only one type of bacteria hibernates regularly.

21. Any student who is not required to hand in written homework based on the reading assignments in a course will not complete all of the reading assignments. Even highly motivated students will neglect their reading assignments if they are not required to hand in written homework. Therefore, if the students in a course are given several reading assignments and no written assignments, no student in that course will receive a high grade for the course.

The conclusion of the argument follows logically if which one of the following is assumed?

(A) No student who completes anything less than all of the reading assignments for a course will earn a high grade for that course.

(B) Any student who completes all of the reading and written assignments for a course will earn a high grade in that course.

(C) All highly motivated students who complete all of the reading assignments for a course will receive high grades for that course.

(D) If highly motivated students are required to hand in written homework on their reading assignments, then they will complete all of their reading assignments.

(E) Some highly motivated students will earn high grades in a course if they are required to hand in written homework on their reading assignments.

22. In a study, one group of volunteers was fed a high-protein, low-carbohydrate diet; another group was fed a low-protein, high-carbohydrate diet. Both diets contained the same number of calories, and each volunteer's diet prior to the experiment had contained moderate levels of proteins and carbohydrates. After ten days, those on the low-carbohydrate diet had lost more weight than those on the high-carbohydrate diet. Thus, the most effective way to lose body fat is to eat much protein and shun carbohydrates.

Which one of the following, if true, most weakens the argument above?

(A) A low-protein, high-carbohydrate diet causes the human body to retain water, the added weight of which largely compensates for the weight of any body fat lost, whereas a high-protein, low-carbohydrate diet does not.

(B) Many people who consume large quantities of protein nevertheless gain significant amounts of body fat.

(C) A high-protein, low-carbohydrate diet will often enable the human body to convert some body fat into muscle, without causing any significant overall weight loss.

(D) In the experiment, the volunteers on the high-carbohydrate diet engaged in regular exercise of a kind known to produce weight loss, and those on the low-carbohydrate diet did not.

(E) Many of the volunteers who had been on the low-carbohydrate diet eventually regained much of the weight they had lost on the diet after returning to their normal diets.

GO ON TO THE NEXT PAGE.

23. Essayist: Computers have the capacity to represent and to perform logical transformations on pieces of information. Since exactly the same applies to the human mind, the human mind is a type of computer.

The flawed pattern of reasoning in which one of the following most closely resembles the flawed pattern of reasoning in the essayist's argument?

(A) Often individual animals sacrifice their lives when the survival of their offspring or close relatives is threatened. It is probable, therefore, that there is a biological basis for the fact that human beings are similarly often willing to sacrifice their own well-being for the good of their community.

(B) In the plastic arts, such as sculpture or painting, no work can depend for its effectiveness upon a verbal narrative that explains it. Since the same can be said of poetry, we cannot consider this characteristic as a reasonable criterion for distinguishing the plastic arts from other arts.

(C) In any organism, the proper functioning of each component depends upon the proper functioning of every other component. Thus, communities belong to the category of organisms, since communities are invariably characterized by this same interdependence of components.

(D) Some vitamins require the presence in adequate amounts of some mineral in order to be fully beneficial to the body. Thus, since selenium is needed to make vitamin E fully active, anyone with a selenium deficiency will have a greater risk of contracting those diseases from which vitamin E provides some measure of protection.

(E) Friendship often involves obligations whose fulfillment can be painful or burdensome. The same can be said of various forms of cooperation that cannot strictly be called friendship. Thus cooperation, like friendship, can require that priority be given to goals other than mere self-interest.

24. It is popularly believed that a poem has whatever meaning is assigned to it by the reader. But objective evaluation of poetry is possible only if this popular belief is false; for the aesthetic value of a poem cannot be discussed unless it is possible for at least two readers to agree on the correct interpretation of the poem.

Which one of the following is an assumption required by the argument?

(A) Only if they find the same meaning in a poem can two people each judge that it has aesthetic value.

(B) If two readers agree about the meaning of a given poem, that ensures that an objective evaluation of the poem can be made.

(C) Discussion of a poem is possible only if it is false that a poem has whatever meaning is assigned to it by the reader.

(D) A given poem can be objectively evaluated only if the poem's aesthetic value can be discussed.

(E) Aesthetic evaluation of literature is best accomplished through discussion by more than two readers.

25. Dean: The mathematics department at our university has said that it should be given sole responsibility for teaching the course Statistics for the Social Sciences. But this course has no more mathematics in it than high school algebra does. The fact that a course has mathematics in it does not mean that it needs to be taught by a mathematics professor, any more than a course approaching its subject from a historical perspective must be taught by a history professor. Such demands by the mathematics department are therefore unjustified.

The dean's argument is most vulnerable to criticism on the grounds that it

(A) presumes, without providing justification, that expertise in a subject does not enable one to teach that subject well

(B) purports to refute a view by showing that one possible reason for that view is insufficient

(C) presumes, without providing justification, that most students are as knowledgeable about mathematics as they are about history

(D) fails to establish that mathematics professors are not capable of teaching Statistics for the Social Sciences effectively

(E) presumes, without providing justification, that any policies that apply to history courses must be justified with respect to mathematics courses

S T O P

IF YOU FINISH BEFORE TIME IS CALLED, YOU MAY CHECK YOUR WORK ON THIS SECTION ONLY.
DO NOT WORK ON ANY OTHER SECTION IN THE TEST.

SECTION IV
Time—35 minutes
23 Questions

<u>Directions</u>: Each group of questions in this section is based on a set of conditions. In answering some of the questions, it may be useful to draw a rough diagram. Choose the response that most accurately and completely answers each question and blacken the corresponding space on your answer sheet.

Questions 1–6

There are exactly six law students—Gambini, Little, Mitchum, Richardson, Saito, and Veracruz—in a trial advocacy class. The class is divided into three trial teams—team 1, team 2, and team 3—of exactly two students each. Each student is on exactly one of the teams. Each student prepares exactly one of either the opening argument or the final argument for his or her team. The teams must be formed according to the following specifications:

    Mitchum is on the same team as either Gambini or Veracruz.

    Little prepares an opening argument.

    Either Gambini or Richardson, but not both, prepares a final argument.

1. Which one of the following could be the composition of each team and the argument each student prepares?

    (A)   team 1: Little, opening; Gambini, final
            team 2: Veracruz, opening; Mitchum, final
            team 3: Saito, opening; Richardson, final
    (B)   team 1: Mitchum, opening; Gambini, final
            team 2: Veracruz, opening; Little, final
            team 3: Richardson, opening; Saito, final
    (C)   team 1: Richardson, opening; Gambini, final
            team 2: Mitchum, opening; Saito, final
            team 3: Little, opening; Veracruz, final
    (D)   team 1: Gambini, opening; Mitchum, final
            team 2: Little, opening; Richardson, final
            team 3: Veracruz, opening; Saito, final
    (E)   team 1: Gambini, opening; Mitchum, final
            team 2: Richardson, opening; Saito, final
            team 3: Little, opening; Veracruz, final

2. If Gambini is on the same team as Mitchum, and if Gambini prepares the final argument for that team, then which one of the following could be true?

    (A)   Little is on the same team as Veracruz, who prepares the opening argument for the team.
    (B)   Richardson is on the same team as Saito, who prepares the opening argument for the team.
    (C)   Richardson is on the same team as Saito, who prepares the final argument for the team.
    (D)   Saito is on the same team as Veracruz, who prepares the opening argument for the team.
    (E)   Saito is on the same team as Veracruz, who prepares the final argument for the team.

3. Which one of the following could be true?

    (A)   Gambini, who prepares a final argument, is on the same team as Richardson.
    (B)   Gambini, who prepares a final argument, is on the same team as Veracruz.
    (C)   Gambini, who prepares an opening argument, is on the same team as Little.
    (D)   Little, who prepares an opening argument, is on the same team as Mitchum.
    (E)   Mitchum, who prepares an opening argument, is on the same team as Saito.

4. If Richardson is on the same team as Veracruz, then for exactly how many of the students can it be determined which of the arguments he or she prepares?

    (A)   one
    (B)   two
    (C)   three
    (D)   four
    (E)   five

5. If Little is on the same team as Richardson, then which one of the following must be true?

    (A)   Saito is on the same team as Veracruz.
    (B)   Gambini is on the same team as Mitchum.
    (C)   Mitchum prepares a final argument.
    (D)   Veracruz prepares a final argument.
    (E)   Gambini prepares an opening argument.

6. If Saito prepares an opening argument, then which one of the following pairs of students could be on the same team as each other?

    (A)   Gambini and Little
    (B)   Gambini and Saito
    (C)   Little and Veracruz
    (D)   Mitchum and Veracruz
    (E)   Richardson and Veracruz

GO ON TO THE NEXT PAGE.

Questions 7–12

While on vacation, Sukanya receives several e-mail messages from work, each message from one of three associates: Hilary, Jerome, and Lula. Sukanya receives at least one and no more than two messages from each of them. Sukanya receives each message on the day it is sent. No more than one message is sent each day. The messages are received in a manner consistent with the following:

The first message is not from Lula.
Both the first and last messages are from the same person.
Exactly once Sukanya receives a message from Jerome on the day after receiving one from Hilary.
Of the first three messages, exactly one is from Jerome.

7. Which one of the following could be an accurate list of the e-mail messages Sukanya receives, identified by the person each message is from and listed in the order she receives them?

(A) Lula, Hilary, Jerome, Hilary, Jerome, Lula
(B) Jerome, Lula, Hilary, Lula, Jerome
(C) Jerome, Lula, Hilary, Jerome, Hilary
(D) Jerome, Lula, Hilary, Hilary, Jerome
(E) Hilary, Lula, Lula, Jerome, Jerome, Hilary

8. What is the maximum possible number of e-mail messages Sukanya receives after Jerome's first message but before Hilary's first message?

(A) zero
(B) one
(C) two
(D) three
(E) four

9. If Sukanya receives exactly four e-mail messages, then which one of the following must be true?

(A) Exactly one of the messages is from Lula.
(B) Exactly two of the messages are from Jerome.
(C) The second message is from Lula.
(D) The third message is from Hilary.
(E) The fourth message is from Jerome.

10. Which one of the following e-mail messages CANNOT be from Lula?

(A) the second message
(B) the third message
(C) the fourth message
(D) the fifth message (if there is a fifth one)
(E) the sixth message (if there is a sixth one)

11. If Sukanya receives six e-mail messages, the fifth of which is from Lula, which one of the following must be true?

(A) The first message is from Jerome.
(B) The second message is from Lula.
(C) The third message is from Hilary.
(D) The fourth message is from Jerome.
(E) The sixth message is from Lula.

12. If Sukanya receives two e-mail messages from Lula, what is the maximum possible number of e-mail messages Sukanya receives after Lula's first message but before Lula's last message?

(A) zero
(B) one
(C) two
(D) three
(E) four

GO ON TO THE NEXT PAGE.

Questions 13–18

Mercotek carried out a study to compare the productivity of its night shift with that of its day shift. Every week the company's six crews—F, G, H, R, S, and T—were ranked from first (most productive) to sixth (least productive). There were no ties. For any given week, either G and T were the two night-shift crews or else S and H were—the four other crews were the day-shift crews for that week. The following relationships held for every week of the study:

    F is more productive than G.
    R is more productive than S.
    R is more productive than T.
    S is more productive than H.
    G is more productive than T.

13. Which one of the following could be an accurate ranking of all the crews, in order from first to sixth, for a given week of the study?

    (A)   F, G, T, R, S, H
    (B)   F, R, G, T, H, S
    (C)   G, R, T, S, H, F
    (D)   R, F, G, S, H, T
    (E)   R, S, H, T, F, G

14. If F is ranked third for a given week of the study, then which one of the following could also be true of that week?

    (A)   G ranks second.
    (B)   H ranks fourth.
    (C)   R ranks second.
    (D)   S ranks fourth.
    (E)   T ranks fourth.

15. Which one of the following CANNOT be the crew ranked fifth for any given week of the study?

    (A)   G
    (B)   H
    (C)   R
    (D)   S
    (E)   T

16. For any given week of the study, the ranking of all the crews is completely determined if which one of the following is true?

    (A)   F ranks second that week.
    (B)   G ranks fifth that week.
    (C)   H ranks third that week.
    (D)   R ranks third that week.
    (E)   S ranks third that week.

17. If the night-shift crews rank fifth and sixth for a given week of the study, then which one of the following could also be true of that week?

    (A)   G ranks fourth.
    (B)   H ranks fifth.
    (C)   R ranks third.
    (D)   S ranks fourth.
    (E)   T ranks fifth.

18. Which one of the following is a complete and accurate list of the crews that CANNOT be ranked third for any given week of the study?

    (A)   G, H, S
    (B)   R, T
    (C)   F, T
    (D)   G, T
    (E)   T

GO ON TO THE NEXT PAGE.

Questions 19–23

A shuttle van stops exactly four times—once at Fundy, once at Los Altos, once at Mineola, and once at Simcoe—not necessarily in that order. The van starts with exactly four passengers on board—Greg, Jasmine, Rosa, and Vijay—each of whom gets off at a different stop. The following conditions hold:

Los Altos is the first or second stop.
Rosa is still on board when the van reaches Mineola.
Jasmine is on board longer than Vijay.
If Jasmine is still on board when the van reaches Fundy, then Greg is still on board when the van reaches Simcoe; otherwise, Greg is not still on board when the van reaches Simcoe.

19. Which one of the following could be a complete and accurate matching of stops, listed in the order in which the van stops at them, to the passengers who get off at them?

(A)   Los Altos: Greg
      Mineola: Vijay
      Fundy: Jasmine
      Simcoe: Rosa
(B)   Simcoe: Vijay
      Mineola: Greg
      Fundy: Rosa
      Los Altos: Jasmine
(C)   Los Altos: Jasmine
      Mineola: Vijay
      Fundy: Greg
      Simcoe: Rosa
(D)   Los Altos: Rosa
      Mineola: Vijay
      Fundy: Jasmine
      Simcoe: Greg
(E)   Los Altos: Vijay
      Fundy: Jasmine
      Mineola: Rosa
      Simcoe: Greg

20. If Mineola is the first stop, which one of the following is a complete and accurate list of the passengers who could possibly get off there?

(A)   Rosa
(B)   Greg, Rosa
(C)   Greg, Vijay
(D)   Greg, Rosa, Vijay
(E)   Jasmine, Rosa, Vijay

21. If Fundy is the first stop, then which one of the following could accurately list the passengers in order from first to last off?

(A)   Greg, Vijay, Jasmine, Rosa
(B)   Rosa, Vijay, Greg, Jasmine
(C)   Vijay, Greg, Rosa, Jasmine
(D)   Vijay, Jasmine, Greg, Rosa
(E)   Vijay, Rosa, Jasmine, Greg

22. Which one of the following must be true if Greg is still on board both when the van reaches Los Altos and when it reaches Simcoe, not necessarily in that order, assuming he is the second one off the van?

(A)   Vijay is on board when the van reaches Simcoe.
(B)   Vijay is on board when the van reaches Los Altos.
(C)   Rosa is on board when the van reaches Simcoe.
(D)   Rosa is on board when the van reaches Fundy.
(E)   Jasmine is on board when the van reaches Mineola.

23. If Greg is not on board when the van reaches Simcoe, then which one of the following must be false?

(A)   Greg is on board when the van reaches Fundy.
(B)   Jasmine is on board when the van reaches Mineola.
(C)   Rosa is on board when the van reaches Fundy.
(D)   Vijay is on board when the van reaches Fundy.
(E)   Vijay is on board when the van reaches Mineola.

S T O P

IF YOU FINISH BEFORE TIME IS CALLED, YOU MAY CHECK YOUR WORK ON THIS SECTION ONLY. DO NOT WORK ON ANY OTHER SECTION IN THE TEST.

Acknowledgment is made to the following sources from which material has been adapted for use in this test booklet:

Peter M. Garber, *Famous First Bubbles: The Fundamentals of Early Manias.* ©2000 by MIT Press.

John Sandlos, "Purple Loosestrife and the 'Bounding' of Nature in North American Wetlands." ©1997 by Electronic Journal of Sociology.

Linda Ching Sledge, "Oral Tradition in Kingston's *China Men.*" ©1990 by The Modern Language Association of America.

Daniel Q. Thompson, Ronald L. Stuckey, and Edith B. Thompson, "Spread, Impact, and Control of Purple Loosestrife (*Lythrum salicaria*) in North American Wetlands." ©1987 by US Fish and Wildlife Service.

Wait for the supervisor's instructions before you open the page to the topic.
Please print and sign your name and write the date in the designated spaces below.
Time: 35 Minutes

General Directions

You will have 35 minutes in which to plan and write an essay on the topic inside. Read the topic and the accompanying directions carefully. You will probably find it best to spend a few minutes considering the topic and organizing your thoughts before you begin writing. In your essay, be sure to develop your ideas fully, leaving time, if possible, to review what you have written. **Do not write on a topic other than the one specified. Writing on a topic of your own choice is not acceptable.**

No special knowledge is required or expected for this writing exercise. Law schools are interested in the reasoning, clarity, organization, language usage, and writing mechanics displayed in your essay. How well you write is more important than how much you write.

Confine your essay to the blocked, lined area on the front and back of the separate Writing Sample Response Sheet. Only that area will be reproduced for law schools. Be sure that your writing is legible.

Both this topic sheet and your response sheet must be turned over to the testing staff before you leave the room.

Topic Code	Print Your Full Name Here		
071292	Last	First	M.I.

Date	Sign Your Name Here
/ /	

Scratch Paper
Do not write your essay in this space.

LSAT® Writing Sample Topic

<u>Directions</u>: The scenario presented below describes two choices, either one of which can be supported on the basis of the information given. Your essay should consider both choices and argue for one over the other, based on the two specified criteria and the facts provided. There is no "right" or "wrong" choice: a reasonable argument can be made for either.

Aña Rodriguez is a shy five-year-old girl. The Rodriguez family must send Aña to either Mercer Preschool or Butte Preschool. The Rodriguezes are equally satisfied with the quality of the teachers and the facilities at both schools. Using the facts below, write an essay in which you argue for one preschool over the other based on the following two criteria:

- The preschool must provide a stimulating social environment for Aña.
- The preschool must be conveniently located.

Aña is an only child who lives on a block with no other children her age. Two children Aña occasionally plays with at the local playground would be in her class at Mercer. The class size at Mercer is eight children. Mercer occupies its students' time, for the most part, with activities for the entire class. There is little unstructured time. Mercer is within easy walking distance of the Rodriguez home. Parking near Mercer is nearly impossible. After the infrequent winter snowstorms, snow is typically left to melt rather than shoveled. Walking can be difficult at such times.

Aña's best friend will be attending Butte. Aña knows none of the other children who would be in her class. The class size at Butte is 12 children. Most of the students' time is not formally structured. The children are free to participate in a number of optional activities with or without their classmates. The few structured activities all involve small groups of two or three children. Butte is a 10-minute drive, or 20-minute bus ride, from the Rodriguez house. Parking is always available since Butte has its own lot. Aña's younger cousin Pablo, who lives on her block, will be attending a different class at Butte.

WP-Q071A

Scratch Paper
Do not write your essay in this space.

LAST NAME (Print)

FIRST NAME (Print)

SSN/ SIN

L

MI

TEST CENTER NO.

SIGNATURE

M M D D Y Y
TEST DATE

LSAC ACCOUNT NO.

TOPIC CODE

Writing Sample Response Sheet

DO NOT WRITE
IN THIS SPACE

Begin your essay in the lined area below.
Continue on the back if you need more space.

COMPUTING YOUR SCORE

Directions:

1. Use the Answer Key on the next page to check your answers.

2. Use the Scoring Worksheet below to compute your raw score.

3. Use the Score Conversion Chart to convert your raw score into the 120–180 scale.

Scoring Worksheet

1. Enter the number of questions you answered correctly in each section.

	Number Correct
SECTION I.................	_____
SECTION II................	_____
SECTION III...............	_____
SECTION IV	_____

2. Enter the sum here: _____
   This is your Raw Score.

Conversion Chart
For Converting Raw Score to the 120–180 LSAT Scaled Score
LSAT Form 8LSN77

Reported Score	Raw Score Lowest	Raw Score Highest
180	99	100
179	98	98
178	97	97
177	96	96
176	—*	—*
175	95	95
174	94	94
173	—*	—*
172	93	93
171	92	92
170	91	91
169	90	90
168	89	89
167	87	88
166	86	86
165	85	85
164	83	84
163	82	82
162	81	81
161	79	80
160	77	78
159	76	76
158	74	75
157	72	73
156	70	71
155	69	69
154	67	68
153	65	66
152	63	64
151	61	62
150	59	60
149	58	58
148	56	57
147	54	55
146	52	53
145	50	51
144	48	49
143	47	47
142	45	46
141	43	44
140	41	42
139	40	40
138	38	39
137	36	37
136	35	35
135	33	34
134	32	32
133	30	31
132	29	29
131	27	28
130	26	26
129	25	25
128	24	24
127	22	23
126	21	21
125	20	20
124	19	19
123	18	18
122	17	17
121	16	16
120	0	15

*There is no raw score that will produce this scaled score for this form.

ANSWER KEY

SECTION I

1.	B	8.	D	15.	D	22.	E
2.	A	9.	D	16.	B	23.	B
3.	C	10.	B	17.	D	24.	D
4.	A	11.	E	18.	E	25.	C
5.	B	12.	C	19.	C		
6.	A	13.	D	20.	A		
7.	A	14.	E	21.	B		

SECTION II

1.	D	8.	E	15.	D	22.	D
2.	A	9.	B	16.	C	23.	D
3.	A	10.	E	17.	B	24.	B
4.	B	11.	A	18.	C	25.	B
5.	E	12.	C	19.	D	26.	C
6.	E	13.	A	20.	B	27.	D
7.	A	14.	A	21.	A		

SECTION III

1.	B	8.	E	15.	E	22.	A
2.	C	9.	D	16.	C	23.	C
3.	B	10.	D	17.	A	24.	D
4.	A	11.	B	18.	E	25.	B
5.	A	12.	D	19.	C		
6.	D	13.	D	20.	B		
7.	E	14.	B	21.	A		

SECTION IV

1.	D	8.	C	15.	C	22.	C
2.	C	9.	A	16.	C	23.	D
3.	A	10.	E	17.	C		
4.	B	11.	D	18.	E		
5.	E	12.	B	19.	E		
6.	C	13.	D	20.	D		
7.	D	14.	B	21.	D		

The Official LSAT PrepTest

56

- December 2008
  PrepTest 56

- Form 8LSN78

1

SECTION I

Time—35 minutes

23 Questions

Directions: Each group of questions in this section is based on a set of conditions. In answering some of the questions, it may be useful to draw a rough diagram. Choose the response that most accurately and completely answers each question and blacken the corresponding space on your answer sheet.

Questions 1–6

Individual hour-long auditions will be scheduled for each of six saxophonists—Fujimura, Gabrieli, Herman, Jackson, King, and Lauder. The auditions will all take place on the same day. Each audition will begin on the hour, with the first beginning at 1 P.M. and the last at 6 P.M. The schedule of auditions must conform to the following conditions:

    Jackson auditions earlier than Herman does.
    Gabrieli auditions earlier than King does.
    Gabrieli auditions either immediately before or immediately after Lauder does.
    Exactly one audition separates the auditions of Jackson and Lauder.

1. Which one of the following is an acceptable schedule for the auditions, listed in order from 1 P.M. through 6 P.M.?

    (A)   Fujimura, Gabrieli, King, Jackson, Herman, Lauder
    (B)   Fujimura, King, Lauder, Gabrieli, Jackson, Herman
    (C)   Fujimura, Lauder, Gabrieli, King, Jackson, Herman
    (D)   Herman, Jackson, Gabrieli, Lauder, King, Fujimura
    (E)   Jackson, Gabrieli, Lauder, Herman, King, Fujimura

2. Which one of the following must be true?

    (A)   Lauder is scheduled to audition earlier than Herman.
    (B)   Lauder is scheduled to audition earlier than King.
    (C)   Jackson's audition is scheduled to begin at either 1 P.M. or 5 P.M.
    (D)   Fujimura and Jackson are not scheduled to audition in consecutive hours.
    (E)   Gabrieli and King are not scheduled to audition in consecutive hours.

3. The earliest King's audition could be scheduled to begin is

    (A)   5 P.M.
    (B)   4 P.M.
    (C)   3 P.M.
    (D)   2 P.M.
    (E)   1 P.M.

4. The order in which the saxophonists are scheduled to audition is completely determined if which one of the following is true?

    (A)   Herman's audition is scheduled to begin at 4 P.M.
    (B)   Jackson's audition is scheduled to begin at 1 P.M.
    (C)   Jackson's audition is scheduled to begin at 5 P.M.
    (D)   Lauder's audition is scheduled to begin at 1 P.M.
    (E)   Lauder's audition is scheduled to begin at 2 P.M.

5. If Fujimura's audition is not scheduled to begin at 1 P.M., which one of the following could be true?

    (A)   Herman's audition is scheduled to begin at 6 P.M.
    (B)   Gabrieli's audition is scheduled to begin at 5 P.M.
    (C)   Herman's audition is scheduled to begin at 3 P.M.
    (D)   Jackson's audition is scheduled to begin at 2 P.M.
    (E)   Jackson's audition is scheduled to begin at 5 P.M.

6. Which one of the following must be true?

    (A)   Gabrieli's audition is scheduled to begin before 5 P.M.
    (B)   Herman's audition is scheduled to begin after 2 P.M.
    (C)   Herman's audition is scheduled to begin before 6 P.M.
    (D)   King's audition is scheduled to begin before 6 P.M.
    (E)   Lauder's audition is scheduled to begin before 5 P.M.

GO ON TO THE NEXT PAGE.

Questions 7–11

Four people—Grace, Heather, Josh, and Maria—will help each other move exactly three pieces of furniture—a recliner, a sofa, and a table. Each piece of furniture will be moved by exactly two of the people, and each person will help move at least one of the pieces of furniture, subject to the following constraints:

Grace helps move the sofa if, but only if, Heather helps move the recliner.

If Josh helps move the table, then Maria helps move the recliner.

No piece of furniture is moved by Grace and Josh together.

7. Which one of the following could be an accurate matching of each piece of furniture to the two people who help each other move it?

(A) recliner: Grace and Maria; sofa: Heather and Josh; table: Grace and Heather

(B) recliner: Grace and Maria; sofa: Heather and Maria; table: Grace and Josh

(C) recliner: Heather and Josh; sofa: Grace and Heather; table: Josh and Maria

(D) recliner: Heather and Josh; sofa: Heather and Maria; table: Grace and Maria

(E) recliner: Josh and Maria; sofa: Grace and Heather; table: Grace and Maria

8. If Josh and Maria help each other move the recliner, then which one of the following must be true?

(A) Heather helps move the sofa.
(B) Josh helps move the sofa.
(C) Maria helps move the sofa.
(D) Grace helps move the table.
(E) Heather helps move the table.

9. If Heather helps move each of the pieces of furniture, then which one of the following could be true?

(A) Grace helps move the recliner.
(B) Maria helps move the recliner.
(C) Josh helps move the sofa.
(D) Maria helps move the sofa.
(E) Grace helps move the table.

10. Which one of the following could be a pair of people who help each other move both the recliner and the table?

(A) Grace and Josh
(B) Grace and Maria
(C) Heather and Josh
(D) Heather and Maria
(E) Josh and Maria

11. If Josh and Maria help each other move the sofa, then which one of the following could be true?

(A) Heather and Josh help each other move the recliner.

(B) Heather and Maria help each other move the recliner.

(C) Grace and Josh help each other move the table.

(D) Grace and Maria help each other move the table.

(E) Heather and Maria help each other move the table.

GO ON TO THE NEXT PAGE.

Questions 12–16

A town has exactly two public parks—Graystone Park and Landing Park—which are to be planted with North American trees. There are exactly four varieties of trees available— maples, oaks, sycamores, and tamaracks. The planting of the trees must be in accord with the following:

Each of the parks is planted with exactly three of the varieties.

At least one of the parks is planted with both maples and sycamores.

Any park that is planted with oaks will also be planted with tamaracks.

Graystone Park is planted with maples.

12. Which one of the following could be a complete and accurate list of the varieties of trees planted in each of the parks?

(A) Graystone Park: maples, oaks, sycamores
     Landing Park: maples, oaks, sycamores
(B) Graystone Park: maples, oaks, tamaracks
     Landing Park: maples, oaks, tamaracks
(C) Graystone Park: maples, sycamores, tamaracks
     Landing Park: maples, oaks, sycamores
(D) Graystone Park: maples, sycamores, tamaracks
     Landing Park: maples, oaks, tamaracks
(E) Graystone Park: oaks, sycamores, tamaracks
     Landing Park: maples, sycamores, tamaracks

13. Which one of the following must be true?

(A) Graystone Park is planted with sycamores.
(B) Landing Park is planted with maples.
(C) Landing Park is planted with tamaracks.
(D) The number of the parks planted with maples is equal to the number of the parks planted with sycamores.
(E) The number of the parks planted with maples is greater than the number of the parks planted with sycamores.

14. If both parks are planted with sycamores, which one of the following could be true?

(A) The number of the parks planted with maples is equal to the number of the parks planted with oaks.
(B) The number of the parks planted with maples is greater than the number of the parks planted with sycamores.
(C) The number of the parks planted with oaks is equal to the number of the parks planted with sycamores.
(D) Graystone Park is planted with both maples and oaks.
(E) Landing Park is planted with both maples and oaks.

15. Which one of the following must be false?

(A) Both parks are planted with oaks.
(B) Both parks are planted with sycamores.
(C) Both parks are planted with tamaracks.
(D) Exactly one of the parks is planted with maples.
(E) Exactly one of the parks is planted with sycamores.

16. Which one of the following could be true?

(A) The number of the parks planted with oaks is equal to the number of the parks planted with tamaracks.
(B) The number of the parks planted with oaks is greater than the number of the parks planted with sycamores.
(C) Exactly one of the parks is planted with tamaracks.
(D) Neither park is planted with tamaracks.
(E) Both parks contain exactly the same three varieties of trees as each other.

GO ON TO THE NEXT PAGE.

Questions 17–23

Five executives—Quinn, Rodriguez, Sasada, Taylor, and Vandercar—are being scheduled to make site visits to three of their company's manufacturing plants—Farmington, Homestead, and Morningside. Each site will be visited by at least one of the executives and each executive will visit just one site. Each of the three site visits will take place on a different day. The schedule of site visits must conform to the following requirements:

The Farmington visit must take place before the Homestead visit.

The Farmington visit will include only one of the executives.

The site visit that includes Quinn must take place before any site visit that includes either Rodriguez or Taylor.

The site visit that includes Sasada cannot take place after any site visit that includes Vandercar.

17. Which one of the following could be the executives included in each of the site visits, with the sites listed in the order in which they are visited?

(A) Farmington: Quinn
    Homestead: Rodriguez, Sasada
    Morningside: Taylor, Vandercar
(B) Farmington: Quinn
    Homestead: Rodriguez, Vandercar
    Morningside: Sasada, Taylor
(C) Farmington: Rodriguez
    Morningside: Quinn, Taylor
    Homestead: Sasada, Vandercar
(D) Homestead: Sasada
    Farmington: Quinn
    Morningside: Rodriguez, Taylor, Vandercar
(E) Morningside: Quinn
    Farmington: Rodriguez, Sasada
    Homestead: Taylor, Vandercar

18. If the second of the three site visits includes both Rodriguez and Taylor, which one of the following must be true?

(A) The Farmington visit includes Quinn.
(B) The Homestead visit includes Vandercar.
(C) The Morningside visit includes Sasada.
(D) The second of the three site visits includes Sasada.
(E) The second of the three site visits includes exactly three of the executives.

19. If one of the site visits includes both Quinn and Sasada, which one of the following could be true?

(A) The Farmington visit is the first of the three site visits.
(B) The Homestead visit is the second of the three site visits.
(C) One of the site visits includes only Vandercar.
(D) The second of the three site visits includes Sasada.
(E) The second of the three site visits includes exactly two of the executives.

20. The executives who visit Homestead CANNOT be

(A) Quinn and Vandercar only
(B) Rodriguez and Taylor only
(C) Sasada and Taylor only
(D) Quinn, Sasada, and Vandercar
(E) Rodriguez, Sasada, and Taylor

21. If the Morningside visit includes both Quinn and Vandercar, which one of the following could be true?

(A) One of the site visits includes both Rodriguez and Sasada.
(B) The second of the three site visits includes exactly three of the executives.
(C) The last of the three site visits includes exactly three of the executives.
(D) The Homestead visit takes place earlier than the Morningside visit.
(E) The Morningside visit takes place earlier than the Farmington visit.

22. Which one of the following must be true?

(A) The Farmington visit takes place earlier than the Morningside visit.
(B) The site visit that includes Vandercar takes place earlier than the site visit that includes Rodriguez.
(C) One of the first two site visits includes Sasada.
(D) The second of the three site visits includes at least two of the executives.
(E) At least one of the first two site visits includes only one of the executives.

23. If the Farmington visit includes Sasada, which one of the following must be true?

(A) One of the site visits includes exactly three of the executives.
(B) The last of the three site visits includes Rodriguez.
(C) The Homestead visit includes Quinn.
(D) The Morningside visit includes Taylor.
(E) The site visit that includes Vandercar also includes Quinn.

S T O P

IF YOU FINISH BEFORE TIME IS CALLED, YOU MAY CHECK YOUR WORK ON THIS SECTION ONLY.
DO NOT WORK ON ANY OTHER SECTION IN THE TEST.

SECTION II
Time—35 minutes
25 Questions

<u>Directions:</u> The questions in this section are based on the reasoning contained in brief statements or passages. For some questions, more than one of the choices could conceivably answer the question. However, you are to choose the <u>best</u> answer; that is, the response that most accurately and completely answers the question. You should not make assumptions that are by commonsense standards implausible, superfluous, or incompatible with the passage. After you have chosen the best answer, blacken the corresponding space on your answer sheet.

1. This region's swimmers generally swim during the day because they are too afraid of sharks to swim after dark but feel safe swimming during daylight hours. Yet all recent shark attacks on swimmers in the area have occurred during the day, indicating that, contrary to popular opinion, it is not more dangerous to swim here at night than during the day.

   The reasoning in the argument is most vulnerable to criticism on the grounds that it

   (A)   overlooks the possibility that some sharks are primarily nocturnal hunters
   (B)   bases its conclusion on evidence from an unreliable source
   (C)   overlooks the possibility that swimmers might feel anxiety caused by not being able to see one's surroundings in the dark
   (D)   presumes, without providing justification, that swimmers cannot be the most knowledgeable about which times of day are safest for swimming
   (E)   fails to take into account the possibility that the number of shark attacks at night would increase dramatically if more people swam at night

2. Denise: Crime will be reduced only when punishment is certain and is sufficiently severe to give anyone considering committing a crime reason to decide against doing so.

   Reshmi: No, crime will be most effectively reduced if educational opportunities are made readily available to everyone, so that those who once viewed criminal activity as the only means of securing a comfortable lifestyle will choose a different path.

   Their dialogue provides the most support for the claim that Denise and Reshmi agree that

   (A)   people are capable of choosing whether or not to commit crimes
   (B)   crime is the most important issue facing modern society
   (C)   reducing crime requires fair and consistent responses to criminal behavior
   (D)   crimes are committed in response to economic need
   (E)   reducing crime requires focusing on assured punishments

3. Acme Corporation offers unskilled workers excellent opportunities for advancement. As evidence, consider the fact that the president of the company, Ms. Garon, worked as an assembly line worker, an entry-level position requiring no special skills, when she first started at Acme.

   Which one of the following statements, if true, most weakens the reasoning above?

   (A)   Acme's vice president of operations also worked as an assembly line worker when he first started at Acme.
   (B)   Acme regularly hires top graduates of business schools and employs them briefly in each of a succession of entry-level positions before promoting them to management.
   (C)   Acme promotes its own employees to senior management positions much more frequently than it hires senior managers from other companies.
   (D)   Ms. Garon worked at Acme for more than 20 years before she was promoted to president.
   (E)   Acme pays entry-level employees slightly higher wages than most other businesses in the same industry.

GO ON TO THE NEXT PAGE.

4. The song of the yellow warbler signals to other yellow warblers that a particular area has been appropriated by the singer as its own feeding territory. Although the singing deters other yellow warblers from taking over the feeding territory of the singer, other yellow warblers may range for food within a portion of the singer's territory. However, a warbler sings a special song when it molts (sheds its feathers). Other yellow warblers will not enter the smaller core territory of a yellow warbler singing its molting song. Therefore yellow warblers, which can only fly short distances during molting, have no competition for the food supply within the range of their restricted flying.

The argument makes which one of the following assumptions?

(A) The core areas contain just enough food to sustain one yellow warbler while it molts.

(B) Warblers are the only molting birds that lay claim to core areas of feeding territories by singing.

(C) There are no birds other than yellow warblers that compete with yellow warblers for food.

(D) Warblers often share their feeding areas with other kinds of birds, which often do not eat the same insects or seeds as warblers do.

(E) The core areas of each feeding territory are the same size for each molting warbler.

5. Chinh: Television producers should not pay attention to the preferences of the viewing public when making creative decisions. Great painters do not consider what the museum-going public wants to see.

Lana: But television is expressly for the viewing public. So a producer is more like a CEO than like an artist. Just as a company would be foolhardy not to consider consumers' tastes when developing products, the TV producer must consider viewers' preferences.

According to Lana, Chinh's argument is flawed in that it

(A) is circular

(B) relies on a sample of consumers that is unrepresentative of consumers in general

(C) infers from the effect produced by an action that the action is intended to produce that effect

(D) fails to consider the possibility that painters may in fact try to please the museum-going public

(E) offers a faulty analogy

6. Dietitian: High consumption of sodium increases some people's chances of developing heart disease. To maintain cardiac health without lowering sodium consumption, therefore, these people should eat fresh, rather than canned or frozen, fruit and vegetables, since the potassium in plant foods helps to prevent sodium's malign effects.

Which one of the following is an assumption required by the dietitian's argument?

(A) Fresh fruits and vegetables contain more potassium than sodium.

(B) Food processing businesses often add sodium to foods being canned or frozen.

(C) Potassium is the only mineral that helps to prevent sodium's malign effects.

(D) Potassium in fruits and vegetables has few negative side effects.

(E) Fresh fruits and vegetables contain more potassium than do canned or frozen ones.

7. Dana intentionally watered the plant every other day. But since the plant was a succulent, and needed dry soil, the frequent watering killed the plant. Therefore Dana intentionally killed the plant.

Which one of the following arguments exhibits a flawed pattern of reasoning most similar to the flawed pattern of reasoning exhibited in the argument above?

(A) Jack stole $10 from Kelly and bet it on a race. The bet returned $100 to Jack. Therefore Jack really stole $100 from Kelly.

(B) Celeste knows that coffee is grown in the mountains in Peru and that Peru is in South America. Therefore Celeste should know that coffee is grown in South America.

(C) The restaurant owner decided to take an item off her restaurant's menu. This decision disappointed Jerry because that item was his favorite dish. Therefore the restaurant owner decided to disappoint Jerry.

(D) The heavy rain caused the dam to break, and the breaking of the dam caused the fields downstream to be flooded. Therefore the heavy rain caused the flooding of the fields.

(E) The power plant raised the water temperature, and whatever raised the water temperature is responsible for the decrease in fish. Therefore the power plant is responsible for the decrease in fish.

GO ON TO THE NEXT PAGE.

8. This boulder is volcanic in origin and yet the rest of the rock in this area is sedimentary. Since this area was covered by southward-moving glaciers during the last ice age, this boulder was probably deposited here, hundreds of miles from its geological birthplace, by a glacier.

Which one of the following, if true, most seriously undermines the conclusion drawn in the argument above?

(A) Most boulders that have been moved by glaciers have not been moved more than 100 miles.

(B) The closest geological source of volcanic rock is 50 miles south of this boulder.

(C) The closest geological source of volcanic rock is 50 miles north of this boulder.

(D) There are no geological sources of volcanic rock north of this boulder.

(E) No other boulders of volcanic origin exist within 50 miles of this boulder.

9. Rifka: We do not need to stop and ask for directions. We would not need to do that unless, of course, we were lost.

Craig: The fact that we are lost is precisely why we need to stop.

In the exchange above, the function of Craig's comment is to

(A) contradict the conclusion of Rifka's argument without offering any reason to reject any of Rifka's implicit premises

(B) deny one of Rifka's implicit premises and thereby arrive at a different conclusion

(C) imply that Rifka's argument is invalid by accepting the truth of its premises while rejecting its conclusion

(D) provide a counterexample to Rifka's generalization

(E) affirm the truth of the stated premise of Rifka's argument while remaining noncommittal about its conclusion

10. Critic: The idealized world portrayed in romance literature is diametrically opposed to the debased world portrayed in satirical literature. Nevertheless, the major characters in both types of works have moral qualities that reflect the worlds in which they are presented. Comedy and tragedy, meanwhile, require that the moral qualities of major characters change during the course of the action. Therefore, neither tragedy nor comedy can be classified as satirical literature or romance literature.

The critic's conclusion follows logically if which one of the following is assumed?

(A) Some characters in comedies and tragedies are neither debased nor idealized.

(B) The visions of the world portrayed in works of tragedy and works of comedy change during the course of the action.

(C) If a character in a tragedy is idealized at the beginning of the action depicted in the tragedy, he or she must be debased at the end.

(D) In romance literature and satirical literature, characters' moral qualities do not change during the course of the action.

(E) Both comedy and tragedy require that the moral qualities of minor characters change during the course of the action.

11. Lance: If experience teaches us nothing else, it teaches us that every general rule has at least one exception.

Frank: What you conclude is itself a general rule. If we assume that it is true, then there is at least one general rule that has no exceptions. Therefore, you must withdraw your conclusion.

Frank's argument is an attempt to counter Lance's conclusion by

(A) demonstrating that Lance assumes the very thing he sets out to prove

(B) showing that Lance's conclusion involves him in a contradiction

(C) showing that no general rule can have exceptions

(D) establishing that experience teaches us the opposite of what Lance concludes

(E) showing that it has no implications for any real cases

GO ON TO THE NEXT PAGE.

12. Throughout a certain nation, electricity has actually become increasingly available to people in urban areas while energy production has been subsidized to help residents of rural areas gain access to electricity. However, even with the subsidy, many of the most isolated rural populations still have no access to electricity. Thus, the energy subsidy has failed to achieve its intended purpose.

The reasoning in the argument is most vulnerable to criticism on the grounds that the argument

(A) takes for granted that the subsidy's intended purpose could have been achieved if the subsidy had not existed

(B) takes for granted that if a subsidy has any benefit for those whom it was not intended to benefit, then that subsidy has failed to achieve its intended purpose

(C) presumes, without providing justification, that the intended purpose of the subsidy was to benefit not only rural populations in the nation who have no electricity, but other people in the nation as well

(D) overlooks the possibility that even many of the people in the nation who live in urban areas would have difficulty gaining access to electricity without the subsidy

(E) fails to take into account that the subsidy could have helped many of the rural residents in the nation gain access to electricity even if many other rural residents in the nation were not helped in this way

13. Heart attacks are most likely to occur on Mondays. The accepted explanation is that because Monday is the first day of the workweek, people feel more stress on Mondays than on other days. However, research shows that even unemployed retired people are more likely to have heart attacks on Mondays than on other days.

Which one of the following, if true, most helps to explain the increased likelihood that an unemployed retiree will have a heart attack on a Monday?

(A) Because they associate Monday with work, retired people are more likely to begin large projects on Mondays.

(B) Many retired people take up part-time jobs after they retire from their careers.

(C) People seldom change their dietary and other health habits after retirement.

(D) Stress is the major factor influencing the risk of heart attack.

(E) Unemployed retired people are even more likely to have heart attacks than are people who have jobs.

14. Psychologist: We asked 100 entrepreneurs and 100 business managers to answer various questions and rate how confident they were that their responses were correct. While members of each group were overconfident, in general the entrepreneurs were much more so than the business managers. This indicates that people who are especially overconfident are more likely to attempt to start a business in spite of the enormous odds against success than people who are less confident.

Which one of the following, if true, lends the most support to the psychologist's conclusion?

(A) The questions asked of the entrepreneurs and business managers included personal, political, and business questions.

(B) At least some of the entrepreneurs surveyed had accurately determined before attempting to start their businesses what the odds were against their attempts being successful.

(C) Another survey showed that degree of confidence was highly correlated with success in business.

(D) The business managers who were most overconfident were found to have attempted to start businesses in the past.

(E) How confident each person surveyed was that his or her answers to the questions asked were correct corresponded closely to that person's confidence in his or her business acumen.

GO ON TO THE NEXT PAGE.

15. If Agnes's research proposal is approved, the fourth-floor lab must be cleaned out for her use. Immanuel's proposal, on the other hand, requires less space. So if his proposal is approved, he will continue to work in the second-floor lab. Only those proposals the director supports will be approved. So since the director will support both proposals, the fourth-floor lab must be cleaned out.

The argument's reasoning is flawed because the argument

(A) presumes, without providing justification, that the fourth-floor lab is bigger than the second-floor lab

(B) fails to consider the possibility that a proposal will be rejected even with the director's support

(C) presumes, without providing justification, that the director will support both proposals with equal enthusiasm

(D) fails to consider the possibility that Immanuel will want to move to a bigger lab once his proposal is approved

(E) presumes, without providing justification, that no lab other than the fourth-floor lab would be adequate for Agnes's research

16. In order to expand its mailing lists for e-mail advertising, the Outdoor Sports Company has been offering its customers financial incentives if they provide the e-mail addresses of their friends. However, offering such incentives is an unethical business practice, because it encourages people to exploit their personal relationships for profit, which risks damaging the integrity of those relationships.

Which one of the following principles, if valid, most helps to justify the reasoning in the argument?

(A) It is unethical for people to exploit their personal relationships for profit if in doing so they risk damaging the integrity of those relationships.

(B) If it would be unethical to use information that was gathered in a particular way, then it is unethical to gather that information in the first place.

(C) It is an unethical business practice for a company to deliberately damage the integrity of its customers' personal relationships in any way.

(D) It is unethical to encourage people to engage in behavior that could damage the integrity of their personal relationships.

(E) Providing a friend's personal information to a company in exchange for a financial reward will almost certainly damage the integrity of one's personal relationship with that friend.

17. Glen: An emphasis on law's purely procedural side produces a concern with personal rights that leads to the individual's indifference to society's welfare. Law's primary role should be to create virtuous citizens.

Sara: But such a role would encourage government to decide which modes of life are truly virtuous; that would be more dangerous than government's being overprotective of individuals' rights.

The dialogue provides the most support for the claim that Glen and Sara disagree about whether

(A) citizens can be assumed to be capable of making good choices without governmental interference

(B) virtuousness on the part of citizens is more important than the protection of citizens' rights

(C) there is an inherent danger in allowing government to decide what constitutes virtuous behavior among citizens

(D) an emphasis on law's purely procedural side results in government's being overprotective of citizens' rights

(E) the cultivation of virtue among citizens should be the primary role of law

GO ON TO THE NEXT PAGE.

18. Some credit card companies allow cardholders to skip payments for up to six months under certain circumstances, but it is almost never in a cardholder's interest to do so. Finance charges accumulate during the skipped-payment period, and the cost to the cardholder is much greater in the long run.

Which one of the following arguments illustrates a principle most similar to the principle underlying the argument above?

(A) Although insecticides are effective in ridding the environment of insect pests, they often kill beneficial insects at the same time. Since these beneficial insects are so important, we must find other ways to combat insect pests.

(B) Increasing the base salary of new employees is good for a company. Although the company's payroll will increase, it will be easier for the company to recruit new employees.

(C) It is unwise to use highway maintenance funds for construction of new roads. There is some immediate benefit from new roads, but if these funds are not used for maintenance, the total maintenance cost will be greater in the long run.

(D) It is better to invest in a used piece of equipment than to purchase a new one. Although used equipment requires more repairs and is sometimes more costly in the long run, buying a new machine requires a far greater initial outlay of capital.

(E) Sports cars are impractical for most drivers. While there is undoubtedly a certain thrill associated with driving these cars, their small size makes them incapable of transporting any but the smallest amounts of cargo.

19. None of the students taking literature are taking physics, but several of the students taking physics are taking art. In addition, none of the students taking rhetoric are taking physics.

Which one of the following statements follows logically from the statements above?

(A) There are students who are taking art but not literature.

(B) None of the students taking literature are taking art.

(C) There are students who are taking rhetoric but not literature.

(D) None of the students taking rhetoric are taking literature.

(E) There are students who are taking both art and literature.

20. Psychologist: Psychotherapists who attempt to provide psychotherapy on radio or television talk shows are expected to do so in ways that entertain a broad audience. However, satisfying this demand is nearly always incompatible with providing high-quality psychological help. For this reason, psychotherapists should never provide psychotherapy on talk shows.

Which one of the following principles must be assumed in order for the psychologist's conclusion to be properly drawn?

(A) It is never appropriate for psychotherapists to attempt to entertain a broad audience.

(B) The context in which psychological help is presented has a greater impact on its quality than the nature of the advice that is given.

(C) Psychotherapy should never be provided in a context in which there is any chance that the therapy might be of less than high quality.

(D) Most members of radio and television talk show audiences are seeking entertainment rather than high-quality psychological help.

(E) Psychotherapists should never attempt to provide psychological help in a manner that makes it unlikely to be of high quality.

GO ON TO THE NEXT PAGE.

21. Tania: A good art critic is not fair in the ordinary sense; it is only about things that do not interest one that one can give a truly unbiased opinion. Since art is a passion, good criticism of art cannot be separated from emotion.

Monique: Art is not simply a passion. The best art critics passionately engage with the artwork, but render their criticism only after shedding all of their biases and consulting general principles of aesthetics.

The dialogue most strongly supports the claim that Tania and Monique disagree about whether

(A) art is not simply a passion
(B) good art criticism is sometimes unbiased
(C) art critics should not feel emotion toward artworks
(D) fairness generally requires minimizing the influence of bias
(E) the passionate engagement of the art critic with the artwork is the most important aspect of art criticism

22. The writing styles in works of high literary quality are not well suited to the avoidance of misinterpretation. For this reason, the writing in judicial decisions, which are primarily intended as determinations of law, is rarely of high literary quality. However, it is not uncommon to find writing of high literary quality in dissenting opinions, which are sometimes included in written decisions in cases heard by a panel of judges.

Which one of the following, if true, most helps to resolve the apparent discrepancy in the statements above?

(A) It is not uncommon for more than one judge to have an influence on the way a dissenting opinion is written.
(B) Unlike literary works, legal opinions rely heavily on the use of technical terminology.
(C) The law is not to any great extent determined by dissenting opinions.
(D) Judges spend much more time reading judicial decisions than reading works of high literary quality.
(E) Judicial decisions issued by panels of judges are likely to be more widely read than are judicial decisions issued by a single judge who hears a case alone.

23. Ecologist: Without the intervention of conservationists, squirrel monkeys will become extinct. But they will survive if large tracts of second-growth forest habitat are preserved for them. Squirrel monkeys flourish in second-growth forest because of the plentiful supply of their favorite insects and fruit.

Which one of the following can be properly inferred from the ecologist's statements?

(A) No habitat other than second-growth forest contains plentiful supplies of squirrel monkeys' favorite insects and fruit.
(B) At least some of the conservationists who intervene to help the squirrel monkeys survive will do so by preserving second-growth forest habitat for the monkeys.
(C) Without plentiful supplies of their favorite insects and fruit, squirrel monkeys will become extinct.
(D) If conservationists intervene to help squirrel monkeys survive, then the squirrel monkeys will not become extinct.
(E) Without the intervention of conservationists, large tracts of second-growth forest habitat will not be preserved for squirrel monkeys.

GO ON TO THE NEXT PAGE.

24. Over 40,000 lead seals from the early Byzantine Empire remain today. Apart from the rare cases where the seal authenticated a document of special importance, most seals had served their purpose when the document was opened. Lead was not expensive, but it was not free: most lead seals would have been recast once they had served their purpose. Thus the number of early Byzantine documents sealed in such a fashion must have been many times the number of remaining lead seals.

Which one of the following statements, if true, most strengthens the argument?

(A) Most of the lead seals produced during the early Byzantine Empire were affixed to documents that were then opened during that period.

(B) Most of the lead seals produced during the early Byzantine Empire were affixed to documents that have since been destroyed.

(C) The amount of lead available for seals in the early Byzantine Empire was much greater than the amount of lead that remains in the seals today.

(D) During the time of the early Byzantine Empire there were at most 40,000 documents of enough importance to prevent the removing and recycling of the seal.

(E) During the time of the early Byzantine Empire there were fewer than 40,000 seals affixed to documents at any given time.

25. Farmer: In the long run, it is counterproductive for farmers to use insecticides. Because insects' resistance to insecticides increases with insecticide use, farmers have to use greater and greater amounts of costly insecticides to control insect pests.

Which one of the following most accurately describes the role played in the farmer's argument by the proposition that farmers have to use greater and greater amounts of costly insecticides to control insect pests?

(A) It is the argument's main conclusion, but not its only conclusion.

(B) It is a claim for which a causal explanation is provided and which itself is used as direct support for the argument's only conclusion.

(C) It is the argument's only conclusion.

(D) It is a claim that is used as direct support for an intermediary conclusion, which in turn is used as direct support for the argument's main conclusion.

(E) It identifies a phenomenon for which the argument's main conclusion offers a causal explanation.

S T O P

IF YOU FINISH BEFORE TIME IS CALLED, YOU MAY CHECK YOUR WORK ON THIS SECTION ONLY.
DO NOT WORK ON ANY OTHER SECTION IN THE TEST.

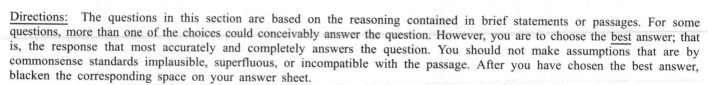

SECTION III
Time—35 minutes
25 Questions

Directions: The questions in this section are based on the reasoning contained in brief statements or passages. For some questions, more than one of the choices could conceivably answer the question. However, you are to choose the best answer; that is, the response that most accurately and completely answers the question. You should not make assumptions that are by commonsense standards implausible, superfluous, or incompatible with the passage. After you have chosen the best answer, blacken the corresponding space on your answer sheet.

1. Anna: Did you know that rainbows always occur opposite the sun, appearing high in the sky when the sun is low, and low in the sky when the sun is high? The Roman scholar Pliny the Elder claimed that this was so, in the first century A.D.

   William: His claim cannot be correct. After all, Pliny the Elder wrote that there are tribes of dog-headed people and beings with no heads or necks but with eyes on their shoulders, and said that smearing snails on your forehead cures headaches!

   William's argument against Anna's claims about rainbows is most vulnerable to criticism because it

   (A) inappropriately distorts Anna's conclusion, making it appear more extreme than it really is
   (B) takes for granted that Pliny the Elder was in bad faith when he reported about unheard-of creatures
   (C) illicitly infers that, because Pliny the Elder made some incorrect assertions, Pliny the Elder's assertions about rainbows are also incorrect
   (D) accepts the assertions of an ancient scholar without presenting contemporary verification of that scholar's views
   (E) implies that Pliny the Elder's writings are too outdated to be of any value

2. Shareholder: The company's current operations are time-proven successes. The move into food services may siphon off funds needed by these other operations. Also, the food service industry is volatile, with a higher inherent risk than with, for instance, pharmaceuticals, another area into which the company has considered expanding.

   If the shareholder's statements are true, which one of the following is most strongly supported by them?

   (A) The company's present operations require increased funding.
   (B) Investment into pharmaceuticals would not siphon off money from other operations.
   (C) The company will lose money as it expands into the food service industry.
   (D) Only if the company expands its operations into pharmaceuticals are increased profits possible.
   (E) The company has a greater chance of losing money in food services than in pharmaceuticals.

3. Mariah: Joanna has argued that Adam should not judge the essay contest because several of his classmates have entered the contest. However, the essays are not identified by author to the judge and, moreover, none of Adam's friends are classmates of his. Still, Adam has no experience in critiquing essays. Therefore, I agree with Joanna that Adam should not judge the contest.

   Which one of the following principles, if valid, most helps to justify Mariah's argument?

   (A) A suspicion of bias is insufficient grounds on which to disqualify someone from judging a contest.
   (B) Expertise should be the primary prerequisite for serving as a contest judge.
   (C) The ability of a judge to make objective decisions is more important than that judge's content expertise.
   (D) In selecting a contest judge, fairness concerns should override concern for the appropriate expertise.
   (E) A contest judge, no matter how well qualified, cannot judge properly if the possibility of bias exists.

GO ON TO THE NEXT PAGE.

4. The manufacturers of NoSmoke claim that their product reduces smokers' cravings for cigarettes. However, in a recent study, smokers given the main ingredient in NoSmoke reported no decrease in cravings for cigarettes. Thus, since NoSmoke has only two ingredients, if similar results are found for the second ingredient, we can conclude that NoSmoke does not reduce smokers' cravings.

The argument above is flawed in that it

(A) illicitly presumes that a whole must lack a certain quality if all of its parts lack that quality

(B) confuses a mere correlation with a cause

(C) relies on a sample that is likely to be unrepresentative

(D) overlooks the possibility that NoSmoke helps people to quit smoking in ways other than by reducing smokers' cravings for cigarettes

(E) illicitly presumes that a claim must be false because the people making the claim are biased

5. Gardener: Researchers encourage us to allow certain kinds of weeds to grow among garden vegetables because they can repel caterpillars from the garden. While it is wise to avoid unnecessary use of insecticides, the researchers' advice is premature. For all we know, those kinds of weeds can deplete the soil of nutrients and moisture that garden crops depend on, and might even attract other kinds of damaging pests.

Which one of the following most accurately expresses the main conclusion of the gardener's argument?

(A) To the extent that it is possible to do so, we should eliminate the use of insecticides in gardening.

(B) Allowing certain kinds of weeds to grow in vegetable gardens may contribute to a net increase in unwanted garden pests.

(C) Allowing the right kinds of weeds to grow in vegetable gardens can help toward controlling caterpillars without the use of insecticides.

(D) We should be cautious about the practice of allowing certain kinds of weeds to grow among garden vegetables.

(E) We should be skeptical about the extent to which certain kinds of weeds can reduce the presence of caterpillars in gardens.

6. Executive: We recently ran a set of advertisements in the print version of a travel magazine and on that magazine's website. We were unable to get any direct information about consumer response to the print ads. However, we found that consumer response to the ads on the website was much more limited than is typical for website ads. We concluded that consumer response to the print ads was probably below par as well.

The executive's reasoning does which one of the following?

(A) bases a prediction of the intensity of a phenomenon on information about the intensity of that phenomenon's cause

(B) uses information about the typical frequency of events of a general kind to draw a conclusion about the probability of a particular event of that kind

(C) infers a statistical generalization from claims about a large number of specific instances

(D) uses a case in which direct evidence is available to draw a conclusion about an analogous case in which direct evidence is unavailable

(E) bases a prediction about future events on facts about recent comparable events

7. Conservation officers justified their decision to remove a pack of ten coyotes from a small island by claiming that the coyotes, which preyed on wild cats and plover, were decimating the plover population and would soon wipe it out. After the coyotes were removed, however, the plover population plummeted dramatically, and within two years plover could no longer be found on the island.

Which one of the following would, if true, most help explain the phenomenon described above?

(A) Plover are ground-nesting birds, which makes them easy prey for coyotes.

(B) Wild cat and plover populations tend to fluctuate together.

(C) Coyotes are not susceptible to any of the diseases that commonly infect plover or wild cats.

(D) The wild cat population on the island was once significantly larger than it is currently.

(E) The coyotes preyed mainly on wild cats, and wild cats prey on plover.

GO ON TO THE NEXT PAGE.

8. Economist: During a recession, a company can cut personnel costs either by laying off some employees without reducing the wages of remaining employees or by reducing the wages of all employees without laying off anyone. Both damage morale, but layoffs damage it less, since the aggrieved have, after all, left. Thus, when companies must reduce personnel costs during recessions, they are likely to lay off employees.

Which one of the following, if true, most strengthens the economist's reasoning?

(A) Employee morale is usually the primary concern driving companies' decisions about whether to lay off employees or to reduce their wages.

(B) In general, companies increase wages only when they are unable to find enough qualified employees.

(C) Some companies will be unable to make a profit during recessions no matter how much they reduce personnel costs.

(D) When companies cut personnel costs during recessions by reducing wages, some employees usually resign.

(E) Some companies that have laid off employees during recessions have had difficulty finding enough qualified employees once economic growth resumed.

9. There are far fewer independent bookstores than there were 20 years ago, largely because chain bookstores prospered and multiplied during that time. Thus, chain bookstores' success has been to the detriment of book consumers, for the shortage of independent bookstores has prevented the variety of readily available books from growing as much as it otherwise would have.

Which one of the following is an assumption on which the argument relies?

(A) Book consumers would be better off if there were a greater variety of readily available books than there currently is.

(B) Independent bookstores typically do not sell the kinds of books that are available in chain bookstores.

(C) The average bookstore today is larger than the average bookstore of 20 years ago.

(D) The average bookstore today is smaller than the average bookstore of 20 years ago.

(E) Some book consumers value low prices more highly than wide selection.

10. Concert promoter: Some critics claim that our concert series lacks popular appeal. But our income from the sales of t-shirts and other memorabilia at the concerts is equal to or greater than that for similar sales at comparable series. So those critics are mistaken.

The concert promoter's argument is flawed in that it

(A) attacks the critics on the basis of emotional considerations rather than factual ones

(B) takes for granted that income from sales of memorabilia is the sole indicator of popular appeal

(C) takes for granted that the comparable series possess popular appeal

(D) draws a conclusion about the popularity of a series based on a comparison with other, dissimilar events

(E) fails to adequately distinguish the series as a whole from individual concerts in it

11. The sun emits two types of ultraviolet radiation that damage skin: UV-A, which causes premature wrinkles, and UV-B, which causes sunburn. Until about ten years ago, sunscreens protected against UV-B radiation but not against UV-A radiation.

Which one of the following is best supported by the information above?

(A) Since about ten years ago, the percentage of people who wear sunscreen every time they spend time in the sun has increased.

(B) Most people whose skin is prematurely wrinkled have spent a large amount of time in the sun without wearing sunscreen.

(C) The specific cause of premature skin wrinkling was not known until about ten years ago.

(D) People who wear sunscreen now are less likely to become sunburned than were people who spent the same amount of time in the sun wearing sunscreen ten years ago.

(E) Until about ten years ago, people who wore sunscreen were no less likely to have premature wrinkles than were people who spent the same amount of time in the sun without wearing sunscreen.

GO ON TO THE NEXT PAGE.

12. Advice columnist: Several scientific studies have shown that, when participating in competitive sports, those people who have recently been experiencing major stress in their lives are several times more likely to suffer serious injuries than are other participants in competitive sports. Since risking serious injury is unwise, no sports activity should be used as a method for coping with stress.

Which one of the following principles, if valid, most helps to justify the reasoning in the advice columnist's argument?

(A) If people recently under stress should avoid a subset of activities of a certain type, they should avoid all activities of that type.

(B) A method for coping with stress should be used only if it has been subjected to scientific study.

(C) People who have not been experiencing major stress in their lives should participate in competitive sports.

(D) When people have been under considerable stress, they should engage in competitive activities in order to relieve the stress.

(E) People with a history of sports injuries should not engage in sports activities if they have recently been under stress.

13. Tent caterpillars' routes between their nests and potential food sources are marked with chemical traces called pheromones that the caterpillars leave behind. Moreover, routes from food sources back to the nest are marked more heavily than are merely exploratory routes that have failed to turn up a food source. Thus, tent caterpillars are apparently among the insect species that engage in communal foraging, which consists in the conveying of information concerning the location of food to other members of the colony, nest, or hive.

Which one of the following, if true, adds the most support to the argument?

(A) A hungry tent caterpillar is more likely to follow heavily marked routes than lightly marked routes.

(B) Tent caterpillars can detect the presence but not the concentration of pheromones.

(C) Sometimes individual tent caterpillars will not return to the nest until a food source is located.

(D) The pheromones left by tent caterpillars are different from the pheromones left by other animals.

(E) The pheromones that tent caterpillars leave behind are detectable by certain other species of caterpillars.

14. Many movies starring top actors will do well at the box office because the actors are already well known and have a loyal following. Movies starring unknown actors are therefore unlikely to do well.

The flawed reasoning in the argument above is most similar to that in which one of the following?

(A) Many animals must devote most of their energy to locating food, or they will not get enough food to maintain optimal energy levels. Thus, if immediate survival requires such an animal to devote most of its energy to some other purpose, optimal energy levels generally will not be maintained.

(B) Often the presence of the flower bee balm in a garden will attract bumblebees that pollinate the plants and enable the garden to produce an abundant crop. So, gardens that lack bee balm usually do not produce abundant crops.

(C) A person's ability to keep confidences is a large part of being a friend, since frequently such an ability enables a high degree of openness in communication. Thus, a high degree of openness in communication is an essential feature of friendship.

(D) Visual aids can be very useful in effectively teaching math skills, because they generally allow vivid conceptualization of math principles. If such visual aids were never employed, therefore, teaching math skills might sometimes be more difficult.

(E) An understanding of the rules of perspective is necessary for achieving success as a painter, since it is the understanding of these most basic rules that allows the painter to paint realistically. Thus, painters with an understanding of the rules of perspective will achieve success.

GO ON TO THE NEXT PAGE.

15. As part of a new trend in the writing of history, an emphasis on the details of historical events and motivations has replaced the previous emphasis on overarching historical trends and movements, with the result that the latter are often overlooked. In consequence, the ominous parallels that may exist between historical trends and current trends are also overlooked, which lessens our ability to learn from history.

The statements above, if true, most strongly support which one of the following?

(A) Studying the details of historical events and motivations lessens our ability to learn from history.
(B) Overarching historical trends and movements can be discerned only when details of historical events and motivations are not emphasized.
(C) Those who attend to overall trends and movements in history and not to details are the best able to learn from history.
(D) A change in emphasis in the interpretation of history has lessened our ability to learn from history.
(E) History should be interpreted in a way that gives equal emphasis to overarching historical trends and movements and to the details of historical events and motivations.

16. Therapist: The ability to trust other people is essential to happiness, for without trust there can be no meaningful emotional connection to another human being, and without meaningful emotional connections to others we feel isolated.

Which one of the following, if assumed, allows the conclusion of the therapist's argument to be properly inferred?

(A) No one who is feeling isolated can feel happy.
(B) Anyone who has a meaningful emotional connection to another human being can be happy.
(C) To avoid feeling isolated, it is essential to trust other people.
(D) At least some people who do not feel isolated are happy.
(E) Anyone who is able to trust other people has a meaningful emotional connection to at least one other human being.

17. Of all the Arabic epic poems that have been popular at various times, only *Sirat Bani Hilal* is still publicly performed. Furthermore, while most other epics were only recited, *Sirat Bani Hilal* has usually been sung. The musical character of the performance, therefore, is the main reason for its longevity.

The argument is most vulnerable to criticism on the grounds that it

(A) relies on evidence that is in principle impossible to corroborate
(B) relies on a source of evidence that may be biased
(C) takes for granted that a particular correlation is causal
(D) takes what may be mere popular opinion to be an established fact
(E) takes a sufficient condition to be a necessary condition

18. Fund-raiser: A charitable organization rarely gives its donors the right to vote on its policies. The inability to directly influence how charities spend contributions makes potential donors feel less of an emotional connection to the charity. Thus, most charities could probably increase the amount of money they raise through donations by giving donors the right to vote.

Which one of the following is an assumption that the fund-raiser's argument depends on?

(A) The most effective way for a charity to give potential donors the ability to directly influence what that charity does is by giving donors the right to vote on the charity's policies.
(B) Most charities that have increased the amount of money they raise through donations have done so by making potential donors feel a greater emotional connection to the charity.
(C) Every charity that has given donors the right to vote on its policies has seen a marked increase in the emotional connection donors have to that charity.
(D) Most potential donors to a charity are unwilling to give that charity any money if there is no possible way for them to have any influence on that charity's policies.
(E) The emotional connection potential donors feel to a charity can affect the amount of money that charity raises through donations.

GO ON TO THE NEXT PAGE.

19. Leslie: I'll show you that your quest for the treasure is irrational. Suppose you found a tablet inscribed, "Whoever touches this tablet will lose a hand, yet will possess the world." Would you touch it?

Erich: Certainly not.

Leslie: Just as I expected! It is clear from your answer that your hands are more important to you than possessing the world. But your entire body is necessarily more important to you than your hands. Yet you are ruining your health and harming your body in your quest for a treasure that is much less valuable than the whole world. I rest my case.

Which one of the following most accurately expresses the main conclusion drawn in Leslie's argument?

(A) Erich would not sacrifice one of his hands in order to possess the world.

(B) Erich should not risk his physical well-being regardless of the possible gains that such risks might bring.

(C) Erich is irrationally risking something that is precious to him for something that is of no value.

(D) Erich can be convinced that his quest for the treasure is irrational.

(E) Erich is engaging in irrational behavior by pursuing his quest for the treasure.

20. Newspaper article: People who take vitamin C supplements tend to be healthier than average. This was shown by a study investigating the relationship between high doses of vitamin C and heart disease, which showed that people who regularly consume high doses of vitamin C supplements have a significantly lower than average risk of heart disease.

Which one of the following, if true, would most weaken the argument in the newspaper article?

(A) Vitamin C taken in the form of supplements has a different effect on the body than does vitamin C taken in food.

(B) The reduction in risk of heart disease due to the consumption of vitamin C is no greater than the reduction due to certain other dietary changes.

(C) Taking both vitamin C supplements and vitamin E supplements lowers one's risk of heart disease far more than does taking either one alone.

(D) High doses of vitamin C supplements tend to reduce slightly one's resistance to certain common infectious diseases.

(E) Taking vitamin C supplements has been found to lower one's risk of developing cancer.

GO ON TO THE NEXT PAGE.

21. George: Throughout the 1980s and early 1990s, hardly anyone learned ballroom dancing. Why is it that a large number of people now take ballroom dancing lessons?

    Boris: It's because, beginning in 1995, many people learned the merengue and several related ballroom dances. Because these dances are so popular, other ballroom dances are now catching on.

    Boris's response to George is most vulnerable to criticism because it fails to

    (A) show that the people who learned the merengue are the same people who are now interested in other ballroom dances

    (B) explain why ballroom dancing was so unpopular before 1995

    (C) relate the merengue to the forms of dancing that were more prevalent before 1995

    (D) account for the beginning of the revival of interest in ballroom dancing

    (E) demonstrate that all types of ballroom dancing are currently popular

22. On the basis of relatively minor morphological differences, some scientists suggest that Neanderthals should be considered a species distinct from Cro-Magnons, the forerunners of modern humans. Yet the fact that the tools used by these two groups of hominids living in different environments were of exactly the same type indicates uncanny behavioral similarities, for only if they faced the same daily challenges and met them in the same way would they have used such similar tools. This suggests that they were members of the same species, and that the morphological differences are due merely to their having lived in different environments.

    If the statements above are true, then each of the following could be true EXCEPT:

    (A) Morphological differences between the members of two populations do not guarantee that the two populations do not belong to the same species.

    (B) The daily challenges with which an environment confronts its inhabitants are unique to that environment.

    (C) There are greater morphological differences between Cro-Magnons and modern humans than there are between Cro-Magnons and Neanderthals.

    (D) Use of similar tools is required if members of two distinct groups of tool-making hominids are to be considered members of the same species.

    (E) Through much of their coexistence, Cro-Magnons and Neanderthals were geographically isolated from one another.

23. A summer day is "pleasant" if there are intermittent periods of wind and the temperature stays below 84°F (29°C) all afternoon. A summer day with high humidity levels is "oppressive" either if the temperature stays above 84°F (29°C) all afternoon or if there is no wind.

    Which one of the following summer weather reports most closely conforms to the principles stated above?

    (A) The temperature on Friday stayed below 82°F (28°C) all day, and there was no wind at all. It was a day of low humidity, and it was a pleasant day.

    (B) On Monday, the temperature ranged from 85°F to 90°F (30°C to 32°C) from early morning until night. It was an oppressive day even though the humidity levels were low.

    (C) On Tuesday, the temperature neither rose above nor fell below 84°F (29°C) throughout late morning and all afternoon. It was a pleasant day because there were occasional periods of wind.

    (D) On Wednesday, a refreshing breeze in the early morning became intermittent by late morning, and the day's humidity levels were constantly high. It was an oppressive day, even though the temperature did not rise above 84°F (29°C) all day.

    (E) On Thursday morning, the air was very still, and it remained windless for the whole day. Humidity levels for the day were high, and even though the temperature fell below 84°F (29°C) between early and late afternoon, it was an oppressive day.

GO ON TO THE NEXT PAGE.

24. The local radio station will not win the regional ratings race this year. In the past ten years the station has never finished better than fifth place in the ratings. The station's manager has not responded to its dismal ratings by changing its musical format or any key personnel, while the competition has often sought to respond to changing tastes in music and has aggressively recruited the region's top radio personalities.

The reasoning in which one of the following is most similar to that in the argument above?

(A) Every swan I have seen was white. Therefore all swans are probably white.

(B) A fair coin was fairly flipped six times and was heads every time. The next flip will probably be heads too.

(C) All lions are mammals. Therefore Leo, the local zoo's oldest lion, is a mammal too.

(D) Recently stock prices have always been lower on Mondays. Therefore they will be lower this coming Monday too.

(E) Only trained swimmers are lifeguards, so it follows that the next lifeguard at the local pool will be a trained swimmer.

25. Chef: This mussel recipe's first step is to sprinkle the live mussels with cornmeal. The cornmeal is used to clean them out: they take the cornmeal in and eject the sand that they contain. But I can skip this step, because the mussels available at seafood markets are farm raised and therefore do not contain sand.

Which one of the following is an assumption required by the chef's argument?

(A) Cornmeal is not used to clean out farm-raised mussels before they reach seafood markets.

(B) Mussels contain no contaminants other than sand.

(C) Sprinkling the mussels with cornmeal does not affect their taste.

(D) The chef's mussel recipe was written before farm-raised mussels became available.

(E) The mussels the chef is using for the mussel recipe came from a seafood market.

S T O P

IF YOU FINISH BEFORE TIME IS CALLED, YOU MAY CHECK YOUR WORK ON THIS SECTION ONLY.
DO NOT WORK ON ANY OTHER SECTION IN THE TEST.

SECTION IV

Time—35 minutes

27 Questions

<u>Directions</u>: Each set of questions in this section is based on a single passage or a pair of passages. The questions are to be answered on the basis of what is <u>stated</u> or <u>implied</u> in the passage or pair of passages. For some of the questions, more than one of the choices could conceivably answer the question. However, you are to choose the <u>best</u> answer; that is, the response that most accurately and completely answers the question, and blacken the corresponding space on your answer sheet.

With his first published works in the 1950s, Amos Tutuola became the first Nigerian writer to receive wide international recognition. Written in a mix of standard English, idiomatic Nigerian English, and
(5) literal translation of his native language, Yoruba, Tutuola's works were quick to be praised by many literary critics as fresh, inventive approaches to the form of the novel. Others, however, dismissed his works as simple retellings of local tales, full of
(10) unwelcome liberties taken with the details of the well-known story lines. However, to estimate properly Tutuola's rightful position in world literature, it is essential to be clear about the genre in which he wrote; literary critics have assumed too facilely that
(15) he wrote novels.

No matter how flexible a definition of the novel one uses, establishing a set of criteria that enable Tutuola's works to be described as such applies to his works a body of assumptions the works are not
(20) designed to satisfy. Tutuola is not a novelist but a teller of folktales. Many of his critics are right to suggest that Tutuola's subjects are not strikingly original, but it is important to bear in mind that whereas realism and originality are expected of the
(25) novel, the teller of folktales is expected to derive subjects and frameworks from the corpus of traditional lore. The most useful approach to Tutuola's works, then, is one that regards him as working within the African oral tradition.

(30) Within this tradition, a folktale is common property, an expression of a people's culture and social circumstances. The teller of folktales knows that the basic story is already known to most listeners and, equally, that the teller's reputation depends on
(35) the inventiveness with which the tale is modified and embellished, for what the audience anticipates is not an accurate retelling of the story but effective improvisation and delivery. Thus, within the framework of the basic story, the teller is allowed
(40) considerable room to maneuver—in fact, the most brilliant tellers of folktales transform them into unique works.

Tutuola's adherence to this tradition is clear: specific episodes, for example, are often repeated for
(45) emphasis, and he embellishes familiar tales with personal interpretations or by transferring them to modern settings. The blend of English with local idiom and Yoruba grammatical constructs, in which adjectives and verbs are often interchangeable,
(50) re-creates the folktales in singular ways. And, perhaps

most revealingly, in the majority of Tutuola's works, the traditional accents and techniques of the teller of folktales are clearly discernible, for example in the adoption of an omniscient, summarizing voice at the
(55) end of his narratives, a device that is generally recognized as being employed to conclude most folktales.

1. Which one of the following most accurately expresses the main point of the passage?

    (A) Amos Tutuola is an internationally acclaimed writer of folktales whose unique writing style blends together aspects of Yoruba, Nigerian English, and standard English.
    (B) Amos Tutuola's literary works should be evaluated not as novels but as unique and inventively crafted retellings of folktales.
    (C) Amos Tutuola is an important author because he is able to incorporate the traditions of an oral art form into his novels.
    (D) Critics are divided as to whether Amos Tutuola's literary works should be regarded as novels or folktales.
    (E) The folktale is a valuable African literary genre that finds singular expression in the works of Amos Tutuola.

2. Tutuola's approach to writing folktales would be most clearly exemplified by a modern-day Irish author who

    (A) applied conventions of the modern novel to the retelling of Irish folktales
    (B) re-created important elements of the Irish literary style within a purely oral art form
    (C) combined characters from English and Irish folktales to tell a story of modern life
    (D) transplanted traditional Irish folktales from their original setting to contemporary Irish life
    (E) utilized an omniscient narrator in telling original stories about contemporary Irish life

GO ON TO THE NEXT PAGE.

3. Which one of the following most accurately characterizes the author's attitude toward Tutuola's position in world literature?

   (A) convinced that Tutuola's works should be viewed within the context of the African oral tradition

   (B) certain that Tutuola's works will generate a renewed interest in the study of oral traditions

   (C) pleased at the reception that Tutuola's works have received from literary critics

   (D) confident that the original integrity of Tutuola's works will be preserved despite numerous translations

   (E) optimistic that Tutuola's works reflect what will become a growing new trend in literature

4. According to the passage, some critics have criticized Tutuola's work on the ground that

   (A) his literary works do not exhibit enough similarities to the African oral tradition from which they are drawn

   (B) his mixture of languages is not entirely effective as a vehicle for either traditional folktales or contemporary novels

   (C) his attempt to fuse elements of traditional storytelling style with the format of the novel is detrimental to his artistic purposes

   (D) his writing borrows substantially from well-known story lines and at the same time alters their details

   (E) his unique works are not actually novels, even though he characterizes them as such

5. The author attributes each of the following to Tutuola EXCEPT:

   (A) repetition of elements in his stories for emphasis

   (B) relocation of traditional stories to modern settings

   (C) attainment of international recognition

   (D) use of an omniscient narrator in his works

   (E) transformation of Yoruba folktales into modern novels

6. The author refers to the "corpus of traditional lore" (lines 26–27) as part of an attempt to

   (A) distinguish expectations that apply to one literary genre from those that apply to another literary genre

   (B) argue that two sharply differing literary genres are both equally valuable

   (C) challenge critics who ascribe little merit to innovative ways of blending two distinct literary genres

   (D) elucidate those characteristics of one literary genre that have direct counterparts in another, largely dissimilar genre

   (E) argue for a new, more precise analysis of two literary genres whose distinguishing characteristics are poorly understood

7. The primary purpose of the passage is to

   (A) illustrate the wide range of Tutuola's body of work

   (B) explain the significance of the literary genre of the folktale and to defend it as a valid art form

   (C) provide an account of Tutuola's body of work in order to help establish appropriate criteria for its evaluation

   (D) distinguish accurately between the genre of the novel and that of the folktale

   (E) summarize the disagreement among critics regarding Tutuola's place in world literature

GO ON TO THE NEXT PAGE.

Mechanisms for recognizing kin are found throughout the plant and animal kingdoms, regardless of an organism's social or mental complexity. Improvements in the general understanding of these

(5) mechanisms have turned some biologists' attention to the question of why kin recognition occurs at all. One response to this question is offered by the inclusive fitness theory, which was developed in the 1960s. The theory is based on the realization that an organism

(10) transmits its genetic attributes to succeeding generations not solely through its offspring, but more generally through all of its close relatives. Whereas the traditional view of evolution held that natural selection favors the continued genetic representation

(15) of individuals within a species that produce the greatest number of offspring, the inclusive fitness theory posits that natural selection similarly favors organisms that help their relatives, because doing so also increases their own total genetic representation.

(20) The theory has helped to explain previously mysterious phenomena, including the evolution of social insect species like the honeybee, most of whose members do not produce offspring and exist only to nurture relatives.

(25) Inclusive fitness theory has also been applied usefully to new findings concerning cannibalism within animal species. Based on the theory, cannibals should have evolved to avoid eating their own kin because of the obvious genetic costs of such a

(30) practice. Spadefoot toad tadpoles provide an illustration. Biologists have found that all tadpoles of that species begin life as omnivores, feeding mainly on organic debris in their soon-to-be-dry pool in the desert, but that occasionally one tadpole eats another

(35) or eats a freshwater shrimp. This event can trigger changes in the tadpole's physiology and dietary preference, causing the tadpole to become larger and exclusively carnivorous, feasting on other animals including members of its own species. Yet the

(40) cannibals have a procedure of discrimination whereby they nip at other tadpoles, eating nonsiblings but releasing siblings unharmed. This suggests that the inclusive fitness theory offers at least a partial answer to why kin recognition develops. Interestingly, a

(45) cannibal tadpole is less likely to avoid eating kin when it becomes very hungry, apparently putting its own unique genetic makeup ahead of its siblings'.

But there may be other reasons why organisms recognize kin. For example, it has recently been

(50) found that tiger salamander larvae, also either omnivorous or cannibalistic, are plagued in nature by a deadly bacterium. Furthermore, it was determined that cannibal larvae are especially likely to be infected by eating diseased species members. The fact

(55) that this bacterium is more deadly when it comes from a close relative with a similar immune system suggests that natural selection may favor cannibals that avoid such pathogens by not eating kin. For tiger salamanders then, kin recognition can be explained

(60) simply as a means by which an organism preserves its own life, not as a means to aid in relatives' survival.

8. Which one of the following most accurately expresses the main point of the passage?

(A) Some findings support the hypothesis that kin recognition emerged through natural selection because it increased organisms' total genetic representation, but this hypothesis may not explain all instances of kin recognition.

(B) Current research supports the view that the mechanisms enabling the members of a species to recognize close relatives are as various as the purposes served by that ability.

(C) Recent research involving tiger salamanders undermines the hypothesis concerning the purpose of kin recognition that is espoused by traditional evolutionary theorists.

(D) New research involving tiger salamanders indicates that the traditional theory of natural selection is more strongly supported by the evidence than is thought by those who consider only the case of the spadefoot toad tadpole.

(E) While traditional evolutionary theory was unable to account for the phenomenon of kin recognition, this phenomenon is fully explained by the inclusive fitness theory.

9. The passage states which one of the following about some spadefoot toad tadpoles?

(A) They develop the ability to recognize fellow carnivores.

(B) They feed only upon omnivorous tadpoles.

(C) They change in body size when they become carnivores.

(D) Their carnivorousness constitutes an important piece of evidence that calls into question the inclusive fitness theory.

(E) Their carnivorousness would not occur unless it contributed in some way to the evolutionary success of the spadefoot toad species.

10. Based on the passage, the author would be most likely to agree with which one of the following statements about evolutionary explanations of kin recognition?

(A) It is impossible to understand the mechanisms underlying kin recognition until an evolutionary explanation of such recognition has been attained.

(B) Such explanations require no modifications to traditional evolutionary theory.

(C) For any such explanation to be fully adequate it should ignore the differences of social or mental complexity of the organisms whose abilities it is intended to explain.

(D) Kin recognition may have different evolutionary explanations in different species.

(E) No other evolutionary explanation can account for the wide diversity of unusual phenomena with the same success as the inclusive fitness theory.

GO ON TO THE NEXT PAGE.

11. Which one of the following most accurately describes the function of the last sentence of the second paragraph?

(A) to draw attention to behavior that further complicates the set of facts to be explained by any theory of natural selection that accounts for kin recognition

(B) to explain why cannibals in most species eat their kin less often than do cannibal spadefoot toad tadpoles

(C) to describe behavior that lends support to the account of kin recognition presented in the second paragraph

(D) to offer evidence that the behavior of cannibal spadefoot toad tadpoles is unexplainable

(E) to imply that the described behavior is more relevant to the issue at hand than is the immediately preceding material

12. The passage most strongly supports which one of the following statements about the mechanism by which cannibal spadefoot toad tadpoles recognize their kin?

(A) It is not dependent solely on the use of visual cues.

(B) It is neither utilized nor possessed by those tadpoles that do not become cannibalistic.

(C) It does not always allow a tadpole to distinguish its siblings from tadpoles that are not siblings.

(D) It is rendered unnecessary by physiological changes accompanying the dietary shift from omnivorousness to carnivorousness.

(E) It could not have developed in a species in which all members are omnivorous.

13. The passage states which one of the following about the mechanisms that enable organisms to recognize their close genetic relatives?

(A) The mechanisms are most easily explained if we assume that they have a similar purpose in all species regardless of the species' social or mental complexities.

(B) The mechanisms have become more clearly understood, prompting interest in the purpose they serve.

(C) The mechanisms have become the focus of theoretical attention only since the 1960s.

(D) The detailed workings of these mechanisms must be better understood before their purpose can be fully explained.

(E) The mechanisms operate differently in different species even when they serve exactly the same function.

14. The information in the passage most strongly suggests that the fact that most honeybees exist only to nurture relatives

(A) was not known to be true before the 1960s

(B) can be explained only if we assume that these members are in turn nurtured by the relatives they nurture

(C) is what led most biologists to reject the traditional view of evolution

(D) calls into question the view that evolution proceeds by natural selection

(E) is difficult to explain without at least supplementing the traditional view of evolution with further explanatory hypotheses

15. Which one of the following would, if true, most help to undermine the author's evaluation in the last sentence of the passage?

(A) Many tiger salamander larvae infected by the deadly bacterium are not cannibalistic.

(B) The factor that determines which tiger salamander larvae are carnivorous and which are omnivorous is not contained in the genetic makeup of the larvae.

(C) Kin recognition helps tiger salamanders avoid inbreeding that may be life-threatening to their offspring.

(D) Noncannibalistic tiger salamanders tend to produce fewer offspring than cannibalistic tiger salamanders.

(E) Cannibalistic tiger salamanders are immune to certain diseases to which noncannibalistic salamanders are not.

GO ON TO THE NEXT PAGE.

Passage A

There is no universally accepted definition within international law for the term "national minority." It is most commonly applied to (1) groups of persons—not necessarily citizens—under the jurisdiction of one
(5) country who have ethnic ties to another "homeland" country, or (2) groups of citizens of a country who have lasting ties to that country and have no such ties to any other country, but are distinguished from the majority of the population by ethnicity, religion, or
(10) language. The terms "people" and "nation" are also vaguely defined in international agreements. Documents that refer to a "nation" generally link the term to the concept of "nationalism," which is often associated with ties to land. It also connotes sovereignty, for
(15) which reason, perhaps, "people" is often used instead of "nation" for groups subject to a colonial power.

While the lack of definition of the terms "minority," "people," and "nation" presents difficulties to numerous minority groups, this lack is particularly problematic
(20) for the Roma (Gypsies). The Roma are not a colonized people, they do not have a homeland, and many do not bear ties to any currently existing country. Some Roma are not even citizens of any country, in part because of their nomadic way of life, which developed in response
(25) to centuries of fleeing persecution. Instead, they have ethnic and linguistic ties to other groups of Roma that reside in other countries.

Passage B

Capotorti's definition of a minority includes four empirical criteria—a group's being numerically smaller
(30) than the rest of the population of the state; their being nondominant; their having distinctive ethnic, linguistic, or religious characteristics; and their desiring to preserve their own culture—and one legal criterion, that they be citizens of the state in question. This last
(35) element can be problematic, given the previous nomadic character of the Roma, that they still cross borders between European states to avoid persecution, and that some states have denied them citizenship, and thus minority status. Because this element essentially
(40) grants the state the arbitrary right to decide if the Roma constitute a minority without reference to empirical characteristics, it seems patently unfair that it should be included in the definition.

However, the Roma easily fulfill the four
(45) objective elements of Capotorti's definition and should, therefore, be considered a minority in all major European states. Numerically, they are nowhere near a majority, though they number in the hundreds of thousands, even millions, in some states. Their
(50) nondominant position is evident—they are not even acknowledged as a minority in some states. The Roma have a number of distinctive linguistic, ethnic, and religious characteristics. For example, most speak Romani, an Indo-European language descended from

(55) Sanskrit. Roma groups also have their own distinctive legal and court systems, which are group oriented rather than individual-rights oriented. That they have preserved their language, customs, and identity through centuries of persecution is evidence enough
(60) of their desire to preserve their culture.

16. Which one of the following most accurately expresses the main point of passage A?

(A) Different definitions of certain key terms in international law conflict with one another in their application to the Roma.

(B) In at least some countries in which they live, the Roma are not generally considered a minority group.

(C) The lack of agreement regarding the definitions of such terms as "minority," "people," and "nation" is partly due to the unclear application of the terms to groups such as the Roma.

(D) Any attempt to define such concepts as people, nation, or minority group will probably fail to apply to certain borderline cases such as the Roma.

(E) The absence of a clear, generally agreed-upon understanding of what constitutes a people, nation, or minority group is a problem, especially in relation to the Roma.

17. The term "problematic" has which one of the following meanings in both passage A (line 19) and passage B (line 35)?

(A) giving rise to intense debate
(B) confusing and unclear
(C) resulting in difficulties
(D) difficult to solve
(E) theoretically incoherent

GO ON TO THE NEXT PAGE.

18. Which one of the following claims about the Roma is NOT made in passage A?

(A) Those living in one country have ethnic ties to Roma in other countries.
(B) Some of them practice a nomadic way of life.
(C) They, as a people, have no recognizable homeland.
(D) In some countries, their population exceeds one million.
(E) The lack of a completely satisfactory definition of "minority" is a greater problem for them than for most.

19. The authors' views regarding the status of the Roma can most accurately be described in which one of the following ways?

(A) The author of passage A, but not the author of passage B, disapproves of the latitude that international law allows individual states in determining their relations to nomadic Roma populations.
(B) The author of passage B, but not the author of passage A, considers the problems of the Roma to be a noteworthy example of how international law can be ineffective.
(C) The author of passage B, but not the author of passage A, considers the Roma to be a paradigmatic example of a people who do not constitute a nation.
(D) Both authors would prefer that the political issues involving the Roma be resolved on a case-by-case basis within each individual country rather than through international law.
(E) Both authors consider the problems that the Roma face in relation to international law to be anomalous and special.

20. The relationship between which one of the following pairs of documents is most analogous to the relationship between passage A and passage B?

(A) "The Lack of Clear-Cut Criteria for Classifying Jobs as Technical Causes Problems for Welders" and "A Point-by-Point Argument That Welding Fulfills the Union's Criteria for Classification of Jobs as 'Technical'"
(B) "Why the Current Criteria for Professional Competence in Welding Have Not Been Effectively Applied" and "A Review of the Essential Elements of Any Formal Statement of Professional Standards"
(C) "The Need for a Revised Definition of the Concept of Welding in Relation to Other Technical Jobs" and "An Enumeration and Description of the Essential Job Duties Usually Carried Out by Union Welders"
(D) "The Lack of Competent Welders in Our Company Can Be Attributed to a General Disregard for Professional and Technical Staff Recruitment" and "A Discussion of the Factors That Companies Should Consider in Recruiting Employees"
(E) "The Conceptual Links Between Professionalism and Technical Expertise" and "A Refutation of the Union's Position Regarding Which Types of Jobs Should Be Classified as Neither Professional nor Technical"

21. Which one of the following is a principle that can be most reasonably considered to underlie the reasoning in both of the passages?

(A) A definition that is vaguely formulated cannot serve as the basis for the provisions contained in a document of international law.
(B) A minority group's not being officially recognized as such by the government that has jurisdiction over it can be detrimental to the group's interests.
(C) Provisions in international law that apply only to minority groups should not be considered valid.
(D) Governments should recognize the legal and court systems used by minority populations within their jurisdictions.
(E) A group that often moves back and forth across a boundary between two countries can be legitimately considered citizens of both countries.

GO ON TO THE NEXT PAGE.

During most of the nineteenth century, many French women continued to be educated according to models long established by custom and religious tradition. One recent observer has termed the failure
(5) to institute real and lasting educational reform at the end of the eighteenth century a "missed opportunity"—for in spite of the egalitarian and secular aims of the French Revolution in 1789, a truly nondiscriminatory education system for both
(10) women and men would not be established in the country until the 1880s. However, legislators had put forth many proposals for educational reform in the years just after the revolution; two in particular attempted to institute educational systems for women
(15) that were, to a great extent, egalitarian.

The first of these proposals endeavored to replace the predominantly religious education that women originally received in convents and at home with reformed curricula. More importantly, the proposal
(20) insisted that, because education was a common good that should be offered to both sexes, instruction should be available to everyone. By the same token, teachers would be drawn from both sexes. Thus the proposal held it essential that schools for both men
(25) and women be established promptly throughout the country and that these schools be public, a tangible sign of the state's interest in all of its citizens. One limitation of this proposal, however, was that girls, unlike boys, were to leave school at age eight in
(30) order to be educated at home in the skills necessary for domestic life and for the raising of families. The second proposal took a more comprehensive approach. It advocated equal education for women and men on the grounds that women and men enjoy
(35) the same rights, and it was the only proposal of the time that called for coeducational schools, which were presented as a bulwark against the traditional gender roles enforced by religious tradition. In other respects, however, this proposal also continued to
(40) define women in terms of their roles in the domestic sphere and as mothers.

That neither proposal was able to envision a system of education that was fully equal for women, and that neither was adopted into law even as such,
(45) bespeaks the immensity of the cultural and political obstacles to egalitarian education for women at the time. Nevertheless, the vision of egalitarian educational reform was not entirely lost. Nearly a century later, in the early 1880s, French legislators
(50) recalled the earlier proposals in their justification of new laws that founded public secondary schools for women, abolished fees for education, and established compulsory attendance for all students. In order to pass these reforms, the government needed to
(55) demonstrate that its new standards were rooted in a long philosophical, political, and pedagogical tradition. Various of the resulting institutions also made claim to revolutionary origin, as doing so allowed them to appropriate the legitimacy conferred
(60) by tradition and historical continuity.

22. It can be inferred from the passage that the French legislators who passed new educational laws in the early 1880s were

(A) committed to removing education in the skills necessary for domestic life from the public school curriculum

(B) unaware of the difficulties that the earlier legislators faced when advocating similar legislation

(C) concerned with improving educational equality across economic strata as well as between the sexes

(D) more open to political compromise than were the legislators who introduced the previous proposals for reform

(E) more inclined to give religious authorities a role in education than were the legislators who introduced the previous proposals for reform

23. Which one of the following most accurately describes the organization of the passage?

(A) Education in France during one historical period is described; two proposals that attempted to reform the educational system are presented; inconsistencies within each proposal are identified and lamented.

(B) The movement toward gender equality in France during one historical period is discussed; two proposals for educational reform are presented; the differences between the proposals and the educational system of that era are outlined.

(C) The traditional nature of French education for women is described; proposed breaks with tradition are discussed, followed by a discussion of why eventual change required less of a break with tradition.

(D) The egalitarian aims in France during one historical period are presented; proposals that foreshadowed eventual reform are described; the initial characterization of the aims is modified.

(E) The nature of education for women in France during one historical period is described; proposals for educational reform are presented; the relationship between the proposals and eventual reform is indicated.

GO ON TO THE NEXT PAGE.

24. Suppose that two proposals were put forward by lawmakers concerning housing reform today. Which one of the following pairs of proposals is most closely analogous to the pair of proposals discussed in the second paragraph of the passage?

 (A) "Housing should be made available to all" and "Real estate practices should be nondiscriminatory"
 (B) "Housing should be made available to all" and "The quality of housing should be improved"
 (C) "There should be housing for all who can pay" and "Housing should be of uniform quality"
 (D) "The quality of housing should be improved" and "Real estate practices should be nondiscriminatory"
 (E) "Low-cost housing should be constructed" and "Housing should be of uniform quality"

25. According to the passage, the second of the two proposals discussed was distinctive because it asserted that

 (A) everyone should both learn and teach
 (B) males and females should go to the same schools
 (C) education should involve lifelong learning
 (D) religious schools should be abolished
 (E) education for girls should be both public and secular

26. Based on the passage, the fact that the proposed reforms were introduced shortly after the French Revolution most clearly suggests that the proposals

 (A) were a reaction to the excesses of the new government
 (B) had their roots in a belief in the power of education
 (C) had vast popular support within French society
 (D) treated education for women as a prerequisite to the implementation of other reforms
 (E) were influenced by egalitarian ideals

27. The author would most likely describe the proposals mentioned in the passage with which one of the following statements?

 (A) They espoused reforms that were very modest by the standards of the day.
 (B) They were fundamentally unethical due to their incomplete view of equality.
 (C) They were well-meaning attempts to do as much as was feasible at the time.
 (D) They were reasonable, and it is difficult to understand why they failed.
 (E) They were not adopted because their aims were not fully comprehensive.

S T O P

IF YOU FINISH BEFORE TIME IS CALLED, YOU MAY CHECK YOUR WORK ON THIS SECTION ONLY. DO NOT WORK ON ANY OTHER SECTION IN THE TEST.

LSAC

Topic Code
078395

Print Your Full Name Here		
Last	First	M.I.

Date
/ /

Sign Your Name Here

Scratch Paper
Do not write your essay in this space.

LSAT® Writing Sample Topic

> Directions: The scenario presented below describes two choices, either one of which can be supported on the basis of the information given. Your essay should consider both choices and argue for one over the other, based on the two specified criteria and the facts provided. There is no "right" or "wrong" choice: a reasonable argument can be made for either.

An online business named It's Yours (IY) is a custom designer and seller of jewelry. IY plans to expand its offerings to include a line of customized watches and must decide how to incorporate the new products into the business—either by adding the customizations itself or by having the watch manufacturer do it. Using the facts below, write an essay in which you argue for one option over the other based on the following two criteria:

- IY wants to maintain control over the quality of the products and service it provides.
- IY wants to be adequately prepared for an anticipated increase in sales volume.

One option is for IY to bring the watch customization in house, adding the watches to its work with the other jewelry lines. IY would need to make substantial investments in specialized equipment and training for its design and assembly staff. In producing its personalized jewelry, IY frequently receives novel, unexpected requests and then works one-on-one with customers to design items. Bringing the watch personalization on board would double its in-house production. Keeping up with demand might require IY to decline orders or delay production.

Alternatively, IY could have the watch manufacturer implement the requested personalizations. The watch manufacturer is a large company that currently has excess production capacity. It has an existing customization capacity. Customization is not the core of its business. Based on its experience with the jewelry production, IY believes that the manufacturer will be able to respond to a substantial range of typical customer requests. IY would have to decline any unusual requests that present a design challenge.

WP-P078A

Scratch Paper
Do not write your essay in this space.

Writing Sample Response Sheet

DO NOT WRITE IN THIS SPACE

Begin your essay in the lined area below.
Continue on the back if you need more space.

COMPUTING YOUR SCORE

Directions:

1. Use the Answer Key on the next page to check your answers.

2. Use the Scoring Worksheet below to compute your raw score.

3. Use the Score Conversion Chart to convert your raw score into the 120–180 scale.

Scoring Worksheet

1. Enter the number of questions you answered correctly in each section.

	Number Correct
SECTION I.................	_____
SECTION II................	_____
SECTION III..............	_____
SECTION IV	_____

2. Enter the sum here: _____

   This is your Raw Score.

Conversion Chart
For Converting Raw Score to the 120–180 LSAT Scaled Score
LSAT Form 8LSN78

Reported Score	Raw Score Lowest	Raw Score Highest
180	98	100
179	97	97
178	96	96
177	—*	—*
176	95	95
175	94	94
174	93	93
173	92	92
172	91	91
171	90	90
170	89	89
169	88	88
168	87	87
167	85	86
166	84	84
165	82	83
164	81	81
163	79	80
162	78	78
161	76	77
160	74	75
159	73	73
158	71	72
157	69	70
156	67	68
155	66	66
154	64	65
153	62	63
152	60	61
151	58	59
150	57	57
149	55	56
148	53	54
147	51	52
146	50	50
145	48	49
144	46	47
143	45	45
142	43	44
141	41	42
140	40	40
139	38	39
138	37	37
137	35	36
136	34	34
135	32	33
134	31	31
133	29	30
132	28	28
131	27	27
130	25	26
129	24	24
128	23	23
127	21	22
126	20	20
125	19	19
124	18	18
123	17	17
122	15	16
121	—*	—*
120	0	14

*There is no raw score that will produce this scaled score for this form.

ANSWER KEY

SECTION I

1.	E	8.	D	15.	A	22.	E
2.	B	9.	B	16.	E	23.	B
3.	C	10.	B	17.	A		
4.	C	11.	E	18.	A		
5.	A	12.	D	19.	C		
6.	E	13.	C	20.	D		
7.	A	14.	A	21.	E		

SECTION II

1.	E	8.	D	15.	B	22.	C
2.	A	9.	B	16.	D	23.	E
3.	B	10.	D	17.	E	24.	A
4.	C	11.	B	18.	C	25.	B
5.	E	12.	E	19.	A		
6.	E	13.	A	20.	E		
7.	C	14.	D	21.	B		

SECTION III

1.	C	8.	A	15.	D	22.	B
2.	E	9.	A	16.	A	23.	E
3.	B	10.	C	17.	C	24.	D
4.	A	11.	E	18.	E	25.	E
5.	D	12.	A	19.	E		
6.	D	13.	A	20.	D		
7.	E	14.	B	21.	D		

SECTION IV

1.	B	8.	A	15.	C	22.	C
2.	D	9.	C	16.	E	23.	E
3.	A	10.	D	17.	C	24.	A
4.	D	11.	A	18.	D	25.	B
5.	E	12.	A	19.	E	26.	E
6.	A	13.	B	20.	A	27.	C
7.	C	14.	E	21.	B		

The Official LSAT PrepTest

57

- June 2009
  PrepTest 57

- Form 0LSN87

1

SECTION I
Time—35 minutes
23 Questions

Directions: Each group of questions in this section is based on a set of conditions. In answering some of the questions, it may be useful to draw a rough diagram. Choose the response that most accurately and completely answers each question and blacken the corresponding space on your answer sheet.

Questions 1–5

On a particular Saturday, a student will perform six activities—grocery shopping, hedge trimming, jogging, kitchen cleaning, laundry, and motorbike servicing. Each activity will be performed once, one at a time. The order in which the activities are performed is subject to the following conditions:

Grocery shopping has to be immediately after hedge trimming.
Kitchen cleaning has to be earlier than grocery shopping.
Motorbike servicing has to be earlier than laundry.
Motorbike servicing has to be either immediately before or immediately after jogging.

1. Which one of the following could be the order, from first to last, of the student's activities?

   (A) jogging, kitchen cleaning, hedge trimming, grocery shopping, motorbike servicing, laundry
   (B) jogging, motorbike servicing, laundry, hedge trimming, grocery shopping, kitchen cleaning
   (C) kitchen cleaning, hedge trimming, grocery shopping, laundry, motorbike servicing, jogging
   (D) kitchen cleaning, jogging, motorbike servicing, laundry, hedge trimming, grocery shopping
   (E) motorbike servicing, jogging, laundry, hedge trimming, kitchen cleaning, grocery shopping

2. Which one of the following activities CANNOT be third?

   (A) grocery shopping
   (B) hedge trimming
   (C) jogging
   (D) kitchen cleaning
   (E) motorbike servicing

3. Which one of the following CANNOT be true?

   (A) Hedge trimming is fourth.
   (B) Jogging is fourth.
   (C) Kitchen cleaning is second.
   (D) Laundry is third.
   (E) Motorbike servicing is second.

4. Which one of the following activities CANNOT be fifth?

   (A) grocery shopping
   (B) hedge trimming
   (C) jogging
   (D) laundry
   (E) motorbike servicing

5. Which one of the following, if substituted for the condition that motorbike servicing has to be earlier than laundry, would have the same effect in determining the order of the student's activities?

   (A) Laundry has to be one of the last three activities.
   (B) Laundry has to be either immediately before or immediately after jogging.
   (C) Jogging has to be earlier than laundry.
   (D) Laundry has to be earlier than hedge trimming.
   (E) Laundry has to be earlier than jogging.

GO ON TO THE NEXT PAGE.

Questions 6–11

Each of exactly three actors—Gombrich, Otto, and Raines—auditions for parts on exactly two of the following days of a particular week: Wednesday, Thursday, Friday, and Saturday. On each of these days at least one of the actors auditions for parts. The order of that week's auditions must meet the following conditions:

The first day on which Otto auditions is some day before the first day on which Raines auditions.

There is at least one day on which both Gombrich and Raines audition.

At least one of the actors auditions on both Thursday and Saturday.

6. Which one of the following could be an accurate matching of the actors to the days on which they audition?

(A) Gombrich: Thursday, Friday
Otto: Wednesday, Saturday
Raines: Friday, Saturday

(B) Gombrich: Thursday, Saturday
Otto: Wednesday, Friday
Raines: Friday, Saturday

(C) Gombrich: Friday, Saturday
Otto: Thursday, Saturday
Raines: Wednesday, Friday

(D) Gombrich: Wednesday, Thursday
Otto: Wednesday, Saturday
Raines: Thursday, Saturday

(E) Gombrich: Wednesday, Friday
Otto: Wednesday, Thursday
Raines: Thursday, Saturday

7. If Otto auditions on both Thursday and Saturday, then Gombrich could audition on both

(A) Wednesday and Thursday
(B) Wednesday and Friday
(C) Thursday and Friday
(D) Thursday and Saturday
(E) Friday and Saturday

8. Which one of the following CANNOT be true of the week's auditions?

(A) Gombrich's last audition is on Thursday.
(B) Gombrich's last audition is on Friday.
(C) Otto's last audition is on Saturday.
(D) Raines's last audition is on Friday.
(E) Raines's last audition is on Thursday.

9. Which one of the following pairs of days CANNOT be the two days on which Otto auditions?

(A) Wednesday and Thursday
(B) Wednesday and Friday
(C) Wednesday and Saturday
(D) Thursday and Friday
(E) Thursday and Saturday

10. Which one of the following could be true?

(A) All three actors audition on Wednesday.
(B) All three actors audition on Friday.
(C) All three actors audition on Saturday.
(D) Otto auditions on Friday and on Saturday.
(E) Raines auditions on Wednesday and on Friday.

11. If Gombrich auditions on both Wednesday and Saturday, then which one of the following could be true?

(A) Otto auditions on both Wednesday and Thursday.
(B) Otto auditions on both Wednesday and Friday.
(C) Otto auditions on both Wednesday and Saturday.
(D) Raines auditions on both Wednesday and Saturday.
(E) Raines auditions on both Thursday and Friday.

GO ON TO THE NEXT PAGE.

Questions 12–17

Each of seven toy dinosaurs—an iguanadon, a lambeosaur, a plateosaur, a stegosaur, a tyrannosaur, an ultrasaur, and a velociraptor—is completely colored either green, mauve, red, or yellow. A display is to consist entirely of exactly five of these toys. The display must meet the following specifications:

Exactly two mauve toys are included.

The stegosaur is red and is included.

The iguanadon is included only if it is green.

The plateosaur is included only if it is yellow.

The velociraptor is included only if the ultrasaur is not.

If both the lambeosaur and the ultrasaur are included, at least one of them is not mauve.

12. Which one of the following could be the toys included in the display?

(A) the lambeosaur, the plateosaur, the stegosaur, the ultrasaur, the velociraptor

(B) the lambeosaur, the plateosaur, the stegosaur, the tyrannosaur, the ultrasaur

(C) the iguanadon, the lambeosaur, the plateosaur, the stegosaur, the ultrasaur

(D) the iguanadon, the lambeosaur, the plateosaur, the tyrannosaur, the velociraptor

(E) the iguanadon, the lambeosaur, the stegosaur, the ultrasaur, the velociraptor

13. If the tyrannosaur is not included in the display, then the display must contain each of the following EXCEPT:

(A) a green iguanadon
(B) a mauve velociraptor
(C) a mauve lambeosaur
(D) a mauve ultrasaur
(E) a yellow plateosaur

14. Which one of the following is a pair of toys that could be included in the display together?

(A) a green lambeosaur and a mauve velociraptor
(B) a green lambeosaur and a yellow tyrannosaur
(C) a green lambeosaur and a yellow ultrasaur
(D) a yellow tyrannosaur and a green ultrasaur
(E) a yellow tyrannosaur and a red velociraptor

15. If the display includes a yellow tyrannosaur, then which one of the following must be true?

(A) The iguanadon is included in the display.
(B) The plateosaur is not included in the display.
(C) The display includes two yellow toy dinosaurs.
(D) The display contains a green lambeosaur.
(E) The display contains a mauve velociraptor.

16. If both the iguanadon and the ultrasaur are included in the display, then the display must contain which one of the following?

(A) a mauve tyrannosaur
(B) a mauve ultrasaur
(C) a yellow lambeosaur
(D) a yellow plateosaur
(E) a yellow ultrasaur

17. If the display includes two green toys, then which one of the following could be true?

(A) There is exactly one yellow toy included in the display.
(B) The tyrannosaur is included in the display and it is green.
(C) Neither the lambeosaur nor the velociraptor is included in the display.
(D) Neither the tyrannosaur nor the velociraptor is included in the display.
(E) Neither the ultrasaur nor the velociraptor is included in the display.

GO ON TO THE NEXT PAGE.

Questions 18–23

A charitable foundation awards grants in exactly four areas—medical services, theater arts, wildlife preservation, and youth services—each grant being in one of these areas. One or more grants are awarded in each of the four quarters of a calendar year. Additionally, over the course of a calendar year, the following must obtain:

Grants are awarded in all four areas.
No more than six grants are awarded.
No grants in the same area are awarded in the same quarter or in consecutive quarters.
Exactly two medical services grants are awarded.
A wildlife preservation grant is awarded in the second quarter.

18. Which one of the following is a possible allocation of grants in a particular calendar year?

(A) first quarter: theater arts
      second quarter: wildlife preservation
      third quarter: medical services, youth services
      fourth quarter: theater arts
(B) first quarter: wildlife preservation
      second quarter: medical services
      third quarter: theater arts
      fourth quarter: medical services, youth services
(C) first quarter: youth services
      second quarter: wildlife preservation, medical services
      third quarter: theater arts
      fourth quarter: medical services, youth services
(D) first quarter: medical services, theater arts
      second quarter: theater arts, wildlife preservation
      third quarter: youth services
      fourth quarter: medical services
(E) first quarter: medical services, theater arts
      second quarter: wildlife preservation, youth services
      third quarter: theater arts
      fourth quarter: medical services, youth services

19. Which one of the following CANNOT be true in a particular calendar year?

(A) In each of the two quarters in which a medical services grant is awarded, no other grant is awarded.
(B) Exactly two theater arts grants are awarded, one in the second quarter and one in the fourth quarter.
(C) Exactly two youth services grants are awarded, one in the first quarter and one in the third quarter.
(D) Two wildlife preservation grants and two youth services grants are awarded.
(E) Three grants are awarded in the fourth quarter.

20. If a wildlife preservation grant and a youth services grant are awarded in the same quarter of a particular calendar year, then any of the following could be true that year EXCEPT:

(A) A medical services grant is awarded in the second quarter.
(B) A theater arts grant is awarded in the first quarter.
(C) A theater arts grant is awarded in the second quarter.
(D) A wildlife preservation grant is awarded in the fourth quarter.
(E) A youth services grant is awarded in the third quarter.

21. If exactly two grants are awarded in just one of the four quarters of a particular calendar year, then which one of the following could be true that year?

(A) Two youth services grants are awarded.
(B) Neither a medical services grant nor a youth services grant is awarded in the first quarter.
(C) A wildlife preservation grant is awarded in the fourth quarter.
(D) Both a youth services grant and a theater arts grant are awarded in the first quarter.
(E) A youth services grant is awarded in the first quarter and a theater arts grant is awarded in the second quarter.

22. Which one of the following CANNOT be true in a particular calendar year?

(A) Three grants are awarded in a quarter, none of which is a medical services grant.
(B) Exactly two grants are awarded in the first quarter and exactly two in the third quarter.
(C) Exactly two grants are awarded in the first quarter and exactly two in the fourth quarter.
(D) Theater arts grants are awarded in the first and fourth quarters, and no other grants are awarded in those two quarters.
(E) Wildlife preservation grants are awarded in the second and fourth quarters, and no other grants are awarded in those two quarters.

23. It is fully determined which grants are awarded for each quarter of a particular calendar year if which one of the following is true that year?

(A) Two theater arts grants are awarded.
(B) Two youth services grants are awarded.
(C) Three grants are awarded in the first quarter.
(D) Three grants are awarded in the second quarter.
(E) Three grants are awarded in the third quarter.

S T O P

IF YOU FINISH BEFORE TIME IS CALLED, YOU MAY CHECK YOUR WORK ON THIS SECTION ONLY.
DO NOT WORK ON ANY OTHER SECTION IN THE TEST.

SECTION II
Time—35 minutes

26 Questions

<u>Directions:</u> The questions in this section are based on the reasoning contained in brief statements or passages. For some questions, more than one of the choices could conceivably answer the question. However, you are to choose the <u>best</u> answer; that is, the response that most accurately and completely answers the question. You should not make assumptions that are by commonsense standards implausible, superfluous, or incompatible with the passage. After you have chosen the best answer, blacken the corresponding space on your answer sheet.

1. Many doctors cater to patients' demands that they be prescribed antibiotics for their colds. However, colds are caused by viruses, and antibiotics have no effect on viruses, and so antibiotics have no effect on colds. Such treatments are also problematic because antibiotics can have dangerous side effects. So doctors should never prescribe antibiotics to treat colds.

   The reasoning above most closely conforms to which one of the following principles?

   (A) A doctor should not prescribe a drug for a condition if it cannot improve that condition and if the drug potentially has adverse side effects.

   (B) A doctor should not prescribe any drug that might have harmful effects on the patient even if the drug might have a positive effect on the patient.

   (C) A doctor should attempt to prescribe every drug that is likely to affect the patient's health positively.

   (D) A doctor should withhold treatment from a patient if the doctor is uncertain whether the treatment will benefit the patient.

   (E) A doctor should never base the decision to prescribe a certain medication for a patient on the patient's claims about the effectiveness of that medication.

2. Long-distance runners use two different kinds of cognitive strategies: "associative" and "dissociative." Associative strategies involve attending closely to physical sensations, while dissociative strategies involve mostly ignoring physical sensations. Associative strategies, unlike dissociative ones, require so much concentration that they result in mental exhaustion lasting more than a day. Since it is important for long-distance runners to enter a race mentally refreshed, _____.

   Which one of the following most logically completes the argument?

   (A) long-distance runners should not rely heavily on associative strategies during training the day before they run in a race

   (B) unless they regularly train using associative strategies, long-distance runners should use dissociative strategies during races

   (C) maximizing the benefits of training for long-distance running involves frequently alternating associative and dissociative strategies

   (D) long-distance runners are about evenly divided between those who use dissociative strategies during races and those who use associative strategies during races

   (E) in long-distance running, dissociative strategies are generally more effective for a day's training run than are associative strategies

GO ON TO THE NEXT PAGE.

3. MetroBank made loans to ten small companies, in amounts ranging from $1,000 to $100,000. These ten loans all had graduated payment plans, i.e., the scheduled monthly loan payment increased slightly each month over the five-year term of the loan. Nonetheless, the average payment received by MetroBank for these ten loans had decreased by the end of the five-year term.

Which one of the following, if true, most helps to resolve the apparent discrepancy in the statements above?

(A)   The number of small companies receiving new loans from MetroBank increased over the five-year term.

(B)   Several of the ten small companies also borrowed money from other banks.

(C)   Most banks offer a greater number of loans for under $100,000 than for over $100,000.

(D)   Of the ten small companies, the three that had borrowed the largest amounts paid off their loans within three years.

(E)   For some loans made by MetroBank, the monthly payment decreases slightly over the term of the loan.

4. Professor: A guest speaker recently delivered a talk entitled "The Functions of Democratic Governments" to a Political Ideologies class at this university. The talk was carefully researched and theoretical in nature. But two students who disagreed with the theory hurled vicious taunts at the speaker. Several others applauded their attempt to humiliate the speaker. This incident shows that universities these days do not foster fair-minded and tolerant intellectual debate.

The professor's reasoning is flawed in that it

(A)   draws a conclusion based on the professor's own opinion rather than on that of the majority of the students present at the talk

(B)   is inconsistent in advocating tolerance while showing intolerance of the dissenting students' views

(C)   relies primarily on an emotional appeal

(D)   draws a general conclusion based on too small a sample

(E)   incorrectly focuses on the behavior of the dissenting students rather than relating the reasons for that behavior

5. Studies reveal that most people select the foods they eat primarily on the basis of flavor, and that nutrition is usually a secondary concern at best. This suggests that health experts would have more success in encouraging people to eat wholesome foods if they emphasized how flavorful those foods truly are rather than how nutritious they are.

Which one of the following, if true, most strengthens the argument above?

(A)   Most people currently believe that wholesome foods are more flavorful, on average, than unwholesome foods are.

(B)   Few people, when given a choice between foods that are flavorful but not nutritious and foods that are nutritious but not flavorful, will choose the foods that are nutritious but not flavorful.

(C)   Health experts' attempts to encourage people to eat wholesome foods by emphasizing how nutritious those foods are have been moderately successful.

(D)   The studies that revealed that people choose the foods they eat primarily on the basis of flavor also revealed that people rated as most flavorful those foods that were least nutritious.

(E)   In a study, subjects who were told that a given food was very flavorful were more willing to try the food and more likely to enjoy it than were subjects who were told that the food was nutritious.

GO ON TO THE NEXT PAGE.

6. Studies show that individuals with a high propensity for taking risks tend to have fewer ethical principles to which they consciously adhere in their business interactions than do most people. On the other hand, individuals with a strong desire to be accepted socially tend to have more such principles than do most people. And, in general, the more ethical principles to which someone consciously adheres, the more ethical is that person's behavior. Therefore, business schools can promote more ethical behavior among future businesspeople by promoting among their students the desire to be accepted socially and discouraging the propensity for taking risks.

The reasoning in the argument is flawed because the argument

(A) infers from the fact that something is usually true that it is always true
(B) takes for granted that promoting ethical behavior is more important than any other goal
(C) concludes merely from the fact that two things are correlated that one causes the other
(D) takes for granted that certain actions are morally wrong simply because most people believe that they are morally wrong
(E) draws a conclusion that simply restates a claim presented in support of that conclusion

7. Essayist: Lessing contended that an art form's medium dictates the kind of representation the art form must employ in order to be legitimate; painting, for example, must represent simultaneous arrays of colored shapes, while literature, consisting of words read in succession, must represent events or actions occurring in sequence. The claim about literature must be rejected, however, if one regards as legitimate the imagists' poems, which consist solely of amalgams of disparate images.

Which one of the following, if assumed, enables the essayist's conclusion to be properly drawn?

(A) An amalgam of disparate images cannot represent a sequence of events or actions.
(B) Poems whose subject matter is not appropriate to their medium are illegitimate.
(C) Lessing was not aware that the imagists' poetry consists of an amalgam of disparate images.
(D) All art, even the imagists' poetry, depicts or represents some subject matter.
(E) All art represents something either as simultaneous or as successive.

8. A psychiatrist argued that there is no such thing as a multiple personality disorder on the grounds that in all her years of clinical practice, she had never encountered one case of this type.

Which one of the following most closely parallels the questionable reasoning cited above?

(A) Anton concluded that colds are seldom fatal on the grounds that in all his years of clinical practice, he never had a patient who died of a cold.
(B) Lyla said that no one in the area has seen a groundhog and so there are probably no groundhogs in the area.
(C) Sauda argued that because therapy rarely had an effect on her patient's type of disorder, therapy was not warranted.
(D) Thomas argued that because Natasha has driven her car to work every day since she bought it, she would probably continue to drive her car to work.
(E) Jerod had never spotted a deer in his area and concluded from this that there are no deer in the area.

9. Even if many more people in the world excluded meat from their diet, world hunger would not thereby be significantly reduced.

Which one of the following, if true, most calls into question the claim above?

(A) Hunger often results from natural disasters like typhoons or hurricanes, which sweep away everything in their path.
(B) Both herds and crops are susceptible to devastating viral and other diseases.
(C) The amount of land needed to produce enough meat to feed one person for a week can grow enough grain to feed more than ten people for a week.
(D) Often people go hungry because they live in remote barren areas where there is no efficient distribution for emergency food relief.
(E) Most historical cases of famine have been due to bad social and economic policies or catastrophes such as massive crop failure.

GO ON TO THE NEXT PAGE.

10. Dairy farmer: On our farm, we have great concern for our cows' environmental conditions. We have recently made improvements that increase their comfort, such as providing them with special sleeping mattresses. These changes are intended to increase blood flow to the udder. This increased blood flow would boost milk output and thus increase profits.

Of the following propositions, which one is best illustrated by the dairy farmer's statements?

(A) Dairy cows cannot have comfortable living conditions unless farmers have some knowledge about the physiology of milk production.

(B) Farming practices introduced for the sake of maximizing profits can improve the living conditions of farm animals.

(C) More than other farm animals, dairy cows respond favorably to improvements in their living environments.

(D) The productivity of dairy farms should be increased only if the quality of the product is not compromised.

(E) The key to maximizing profits on a dairy farm is having a concern for dairy cows' environment.

11. Pat: E-mail fosters anonymity, which removes barriers to self-revelation. This promotes a degree of intimacy with strangers that would otherwise take years of direct personal contact to attain.

Amar: Frankness is not intimacy. Intimacy requires a real social bond, and social bonds cannot be formed without direct personal contact.

The dialogue most strongly supports the claim that Pat and Amar disagree with each other about whether

(A) barriers to self-revelation hinder the initial growth of intimacy

(B) E-mail can increase intimacy between friends

(C) intimacy between those who communicate with each other solely by e-mail is possible

(D) real social bonds always lead to intimacy

(E) the use of e-mail removes barriers to self-revelation

12. Criminologist: The main purpose of most criminal organizations is to generate profits. The ongoing revolutions in biotechnology and information technology promise to generate enormous profits. Therefore, criminal organizations will undoubtedly try to become increasingly involved in these areas.

The conclusion of the criminologist's argument is properly inferred if which one of the following is assumed?

(A) If an organization tries to become increasingly involved in areas that promise to generate enormous profits, then the main purpose of that organization is to generate profits.

(B) At least some criminal organizations are or will at some point become aware that the ongoing revolutions in biotechnology and information technology promise to generate enormous profits.

(C) Criminal organizations are already heavily involved in every activity that promises to generate enormous profits.

(D) Any organization whose main purpose is to generate profits will try to become increasingly involved in any technological revolution that promises to generate enormous profits.

(E) Most criminal organizations are willing to become involved in legal activities if those activities are sufficiently profitable.

13. Administrators of educational institutions are enthusiastic about the educational use of computers because they believe that it will enable schools to teach far more courses with far fewer teachers than traditional methods allow. Many teachers fear computers for the same reason. But this reason is mistaken. Computerized instruction requires more, not less, time of instructors, which indicates that any reduction in the number of teachers would require an accompanying reduction in courses offered.

The statement that the educational use of computers enables schools to teach far more courses with far fewer teachers figures in the argument in which one of the following ways?

(A) It is presented as a possible explanation for an observation that follows it.

(B) It is a statement of the problem the argument sets out to solve.

(C) It is a statement that the argument is designed to refute.

(D) It is a statement offered in support of the argument's main conclusion.

(E) It is the argument's main conclusion.

GO ON TO THE NEXT PAGE.

14. Scientists have shown that older bees, which usually forage outside the hive for food, tend to have larger brains than do younger bees, which usually do not forage but instead remain in the hive to tend to newly hatched bees. Since foraging requires greater cognitive ability than does tending to newly hatched bees, it appears that foraging leads to the increased brain size of older bees.

Which one of the following, if true, most seriously weakens the argument above?

(A) Bees that have foraged for a long time do not have significantly larger brains than do bees that have foraged for a shorter time.

(B) The brains of older bees that stop foraging to take on other responsibilities do not become smaller after they stop foraging.

(C) Those bees that travel a long distance to find food do not have significantly larger brains than do bees that locate food nearer the hive.

(D) In some species of bees, the brains of older bees are only marginally larger than those of younger bees.

(E) The brains of older bees that never learn to forage are the same size as those of their foraging counterparts of the same age.

15. Carla: Professors at public universities should receive paid leaves of absence to allow them to engage in research. Research not only advances human knowledge, but also improves professors' teaching by keeping them abreast of the latest information in their fields.

David: But even if you are right about the beneficial effects of research, why should our limited resources be devoted to supporting professors taking time off from teaching?

David's response to Carla is most vulnerable to criticism on the grounds that it

(A) ignores the part of Carla's remarks that could provide an answer to David's question

(B) takes for granted that the only function of a university professor is teaching

(C) incorrectly takes Carla's remarks as claiming that all funding for professors comes from tax money

(D) takes for granted that providing the opportunity for research is the only function of paid leaves of absence

(E) presumes, without providing justification, that professors do not need vacations

16. Software reviewer: Dictation software allows a computer to produce a written version of sentences that are spoken to it. Although dictation software has been promoted as a labor-saving invention, it fails to live up to its billing. The laborious part of writing is in the thinking and the editing, not in the typing. And proofreading the software's error-filled output generally squanders any time saved in typing.

Which one of the following most accurately describes the role played in the software reviewer's argument by the claim that dictation software fails to live up to its billing?

(A) It is the argument's main conclusion but not its only conclusion.

(B) It is the argument's only conclusion.

(C) It is an intermediate conclusion that is offered as direct support for the argument's main conclusion.

(D) It is a premise offered in support of the argument's conclusion.

(E) It is a premise offered as direct support for an intermediate conclusion of the argument.

17. Poetry journal patron: Everybody who publishes in
The Brick Wall Review has to agree in advance
that if a poem is printed in one of its regular
issues, the magazine also has the right to reprint
it, without monetary compensation, in its annual
anthology. *The Brick Wall Review* makes enough
money from sales of its anthologies to cover most
operating expenses. So, if your magazine also
published an anthology of poems first printed in
your magazine, you could depend less on
donations. After all, most poems published in
your magazine are very similar to those published
in *The Brick Wall Review.*

Which one of the following, if true, most weakens the
patron's argument?

(A) Neither *The Brick Wall Review* nor the other
magazine under discussion depends on
donations to cover most operating expenses.

(B) Many of the poets whose work appears in
The Brick Wall Review have had several poems
rejected for publication by the other magazine
under discussion.

(C) The only compensation poets receive for
publishing in the regular issues of the
magazines under discussion are free copies
of the issues in which their poems appear.

(D) *The Brick Wall Review* depends on donations to
cover most operating expenses not covered by
income from anthology sales.

(E) *The Brick Wall Review*'s annual poetry
anthology always contains a number of poems
by famous poets not published in the regular
issues of the magazine.

18. No one with a serious medical problem would rely on
the average person to prescribe treatment. Similarly,
since a good public servant has the interest of the public
at heart, _____.

Which one of the following statements would most
reasonably complete the argument?

(A) public servants should not be concerned about
the outcomes of public opinion surveys

(B) the average public servant knows more about
what is best for society than the average
person does

(C) public servants should be more knowledgeable
about the public good than they are

(D) public servants should base decisions on
something other than the average person's
recommendations

(E) one is a good public servant if one is more
knowledgeable about the public good than is
the average person

19. Team captain: Winning requires the willingness to
cooperate, which in turn requires motivation.
So you will not win if you are not motivated.

The pattern of reasoning in which one of the following
is most similar to that in the argument above?

(A) Being healthy requires exercise. But exercising
involves risk of injury. So, paradoxically,
anyone who wants to be healthy will not
exercise.

(B) Learning requires making some mistakes. And
you must learn if you are to improve. So you
will not make mistakes without there being a
noticeable improvement.

(C) Our political party will retain its status only if
it raises more money. But raising more money
requires increased campaigning. So our party
will not retain its status unless it increases
its campaigning.

(D) You can repair your own bicycle only if you are
enthusiastic. And if you are enthusiastic, you
will also have mechanical aptitude. So if you
are not able to repair your own bicycle, you
lack mechanical aptitude.

(E) Getting a ticket requires waiting in line. Waiting
in line requires patience. So if you do not wait
in line, you lack patience.

GO ON TO THE NEXT PAGE.

20. In the past, when there was no highway speed limit, the highway accident rate increased yearly, peaking a decade ago. At that time, the speed limit on highways was set at 90 kilometers per hour (kph) (55 miles per hour). Every year since the introduction of the highway speed limit, the highway accident rate has been at least 15 percent lower than that of its peak rate. Thus, setting the highway speed limit at 90 kph (55 mph) has reduced the highway accident rate by at least 15 percent.

Which one of the following, if true, most seriously weakens the argument?

(A) In the years prior to the introduction of the highway speed limit, many cars could go faster than 90 kph (55 mph).

(B) Ten years ago, at least 95 percent of all automobile accidents in the area occurred on roads with a speed limit of under 80 kph (50 mph).

(C) Although the speed limit on many highways is officially set at 90 kph (55 mph), most people typically drive faster than the speed limit.

(D) Thanks to changes in automobile design in the past ten years, drivers are better able to maintain control of their cars in dangerous situations.

(E) It was not until shortly after the introduction of the highway speed limit that most cars were equipped with features such as seat belts and airbags designed to prevent harm to passengers.

21. Editorial: It is a travesty of justice, social critics say, that we can launch rockets into outer space but cannot solve social problems that have plagued humanity. The assumption underlying this assertion is that there are greater difficulties involved in a space launch than are involved in ending long-standing social problems, which in turn suggests that a government's failure to achieve the latter is simply a case of misplaced priorities. The criticism is misplaced, however, for rocket technology is much simpler than the human psyche, and until we adequately understand the human psyche we cannot solve the great social problems.

The statement that rocket technology is much simpler than the human psyche plays which one of the following roles in the editorial's argument?

(A) It is cited as a possible objection to the argument's conclusion.

(B) According to the argument, it is a fact that has misled some social critics.

(C) It is the argument's conclusion.

(D) It is claimed to be a false assumption on which the reasoning that the argument seeks to undermine rests.

(E) It is used by the argument to attempt to undermine the reasoning behind a viewpoint.

22. Archaeologist: After the last ice age, groups of paleohumans left Siberia and crossed the Bering land bridge, which no longer exists, into North America. Archaeologists have discovered in Siberia a cache of Clovis points—the distinctive stone spear points made by paleohumans. This shows that, contrary to previous belief, the Clovis point was not invented in North America.

Which one of the following, if true, would most strengthen the archaeologist's argument?

(A) The Clovis points found in Siberia are older than any of those that have been found in North America.

(B) The Bering land bridge disappeared before any of the Clovis points found to date were made.

(C) Clovis points were more effective hunting weapons than earlier spear points had been.

(D) Archaeologists have discovered in Siberia artifacts that date from after the time paleohumans left Siberia.

(E) Some paleohuman groups that migrated from Siberia to North America via the Bering land bridge eventually returned to Siberia.

GO ON TO THE NEXT PAGE.

23. Taxi drivers, whose income is based on the fares they receive, usually decide when to finish work each day by setting a daily income target; they stop when they reach that target. This means that they typically work fewer hours on a busy day than on a slow day.

The facts described above provide the strongest evidence against which one of the following?

(A) The number of hours per day that a person is willing to work depends on that person's financial needs.

(B) People work longer when their effective hourly wage is high than when it is low.

(C) Workers will accept a lower hourly wage in exchange for the freedom to set their own schedules.

(D) People are willing to work many hours a day in order to avoid a reduction in their standard of living.

(E) People who are paid based on their production work more efficiently than those who are paid a fixed hourly wage.

24. Sometimes one reads a poem and believes that the poem expresses contradictory ideas, even if it is a great poem. So it is wrong to think that the meaning of a poem is whatever the author intends to communicate to the reader by means of the poem. No one who is writing a great poem intends it to communicate contradictory ideas.

Which one of the following is an assumption on which the argument depends?

(A) Different readers will usually disagree about what the author of a particular poem intends to communicate by means of that poem.

(B) If someone writes a great poem, he or she intends the poem to express one primary idea.

(C) Readers will not agree about the meaning of a poem if they do not agree about what the author of the poem intended the poem to mean.

(D) Anyone reading a great poem can discern every idea that the author intended to express in the poem.

(E) If a reader believes that a poem expresses a particular idea, then that idea is part of the meaning of the poem.

25. The law of the city of Weston regarding contributions to mayoral campaigns is as follows: all contributions to these campaigns in excess of $100 made by nonresidents of Weston who are not former residents of Weston must be registered with the city council. Brimley's mayoral campaign clearly complied with this law since it accepted contributions only from residents and former residents of Weston.

If all the statements above are true, which one of the following statements must be true?

(A) No nonresident of Weston contributed in excess of $100 to Brimley's campaign.

(B) Some contributions to Brimley's campaign in excess of $100 were registered with the city council.

(C) No contributions to Brimley's campaign needed to be registered with the city council.

(D) All contributions to Brimley's campaign that were registered with the city council were in excess of $100.

(E) Brimley's campaign did not register any contributions with the city council.

26. Historian: Flavius, an ancient Roman governor who believed deeply in the virtues of manual labor and moral temperance, actively sought to discourage the arts by removing state financial support for them. Also, Flavius was widely unpopular among his subjects, as we can conclude from the large number of satirical plays that were written about him during his administration.

The historian's argumentation is most vulnerable to criticism on the grounds that it

(A) fails to consider the percentage of plays written during Flavius's administration that were not explicitly about Flavius

(B) treats the satirical plays as a reliable indicator of Flavius's popularity despite potential bias on the part of the playwrights

(C) presumes, without providing evidence, that Flavius was unfavorably disposed toward the arts

(D) takes for granted that Flavius's attempt to discourage the arts was successful

(E) fails to consider whether manual labor and moral temperance were widely regarded as virtues in ancient Rome

S T O P

IF YOU FINISH BEFORE TIME IS CALLED, YOU MAY CHECK YOUR WORK ON THIS SECTION ONLY.
DO NOT WORK ON ANY OTHER SECTION IN THE TEST.

SECTION III

Time—35 minutes

25 Questions

<u>Directions</u>: The questions in this section are based on the reasoning contained in brief statements or passages. For some questions, more than one of the choices could conceivably answer the question. However, you are to choose the <u>best</u> answer; that is, the response that most accurately and completely answers the question. You should not make assumptions that are by commonsense standards implausible, superfluous, or incompatible with the passage. After you have chosen the best answer, blacken the corresponding space on your answer sheet.

1. Educators studied the performance of 200 students in a university's history classes. They found that those students who performed the best had either part-time jobs or full-time jobs, had their history classes early in the morning, and had a very limited social life, whereas those students who performed the worst had no jobs, had their history classes early in the morning, and had a very active social life.

   Which one of the following, if true, most helps to explain the educators' findings?

   (A) The students compensated for any study time lost due to their jobs but they did not compensate for any study time lost due to their social lives.

   (B) The students who had full-time jobs typically worked late-night hours at those jobs.

   (C) Better students tend to choose classes that are scheduled to meet early in the morning.

   (D) A larger percentage of those students interested in majoring in history had part-time jobs than had full-time jobs.

   (E) Although having a job tends to provide a release from stress, thus increasing academic performance, having a full-time job, like having an active social life, can distract a student from studying.

2. Politician: Most of those at the meeting were not persuaded by Kuyler's argument, nor should they have been, for Kuyler's argument implied that it would be improper to enter into a contract with the government; and yet—as many people know—Kuyler's company has had numerous lucrative contracts with the government.

   Which one of the following describes a flaw in the politician's argument?

   (A) It concludes that an argument is defective merely on the grounds that the argument has failed to persuade anyone of the truth of its conclusion.

   (B) It relies on testimony that is likely to be biased.

   (C) It rejects an argument merely on the grounds that the arguer has not behaved in a way that is consistent with the argument.

   (D) It rejects a position merely on the grounds that an inadequate argument has been given for it.

   (E) It rejects an argument on the basis of an appeal to popular opinion.

3. Although free international trade allows countries to specialize, which in turn increases productivity, such specialization carries risks. After all, small countries often rely on one or two products for the bulk of their exports. If those products are raw materials, the supply is finite and can be used up. If they are foodstuffs, a natural disaster can wipe out a season's production overnight.

   Which one of the following most accurately expresses the conclusion of the argument as a whole?

   (A) Specialization within international trade comes with risks.

   (B) A natural disaster can destroy a whole season's production overnight, devastating a small country's economy.

   (C) A small country's supply of raw materials can be used up in a short period.

   (D) Some countries rely on a small number of products for the export-based sectors of their economies.

   (E) When international trade is free, countries can specialize in what they export.

GO ON TO THE NEXT PAGE.

4. Two randomly selected groups of 30 adults each were asked to write short stories on a particular topic. One group was told that the best stories would be awarded cash prizes, while the other group was not told of any prizes. Each story was evaluated by a team of judges who were given no indication of the group from which the story came. The stories submitted by those who thought they were competing for prizes were ranked on average significantly lower than the stories from the other group.

Which one of the following, if true, most helps to explain the difference in average ranking between the two groups' stories?

(A) The cash prizes were too small to motivate an average adult to make a significant effort to produce stories of high quality.

(B) People writing to win prizes show a greater than usual tendency to produce stereotypical stories that show little creativity.

(C) Most adults show little originality in writing stories on a topic suggested by someone else.

(D) The team of judges was biased in favor of stories that they judged to be more realistic.

(E) No one explained clearly to either group what standards would be used in judging their stories.

5. Hernandez: I recommend that staff cars be replaced every four years instead of every three years. Three-year-old cars are still in good condition and this would result in big savings.

Green: I disagree. Some of our salespeople with big territories wear out their cars in three years.

Hernandez: I meant three-year-old cars subjected to normal use.

In the conversation, Hernandez responds to Green's objection in which one of the following ways?

(A) by explicitly qualifying a premise used earlier

(B) by criticizing salespeople who wear out their cars in three years

(C) by disputing the accuracy of Green's evidence

(D) by changing the subject to the size of sales territories

(E) by indicating that Green used a phrase ambiguously

6. Economist: As should be obvious, raising the minimum wage significantly would make it more expensive for businesses to pay workers for minimum-wage jobs. Therefore, businesses could not afford to continue to employ as many workers for such jobs. So raising the minimum wage significantly will cause an increase in unemployment.

Which one of the following, if true, most weakens the economist's argument?

(A) Businesses typically pass the cost of increased wages on to consumers without adversely affecting profits.

(B) When the difference between minimum wage and a skilled worker's wage is small, a greater percentage of a business's employees will be skilled workers.

(C) A modest increase in unemployment is acceptable because the current minimum wage is not a livable wage.

(D) Most workers are earning more than the current minimum wage.

(E) The unemployment rate has been declining steadily in recent years.

7. Scientists removed all viruses from a seawater sample and then measured the growth rate of the plankton population in the water. They expected the rate to increase dramatically, but the population actually got smaller.

Which one of the following, if true, most helps to explain the unexpected result described above?

(A) Viruses in seawater help to keep the plankton population below the maximum level that the resources in the water will support.

(B) Plankton and viruses in seawater compete for some of the same nutrients.

(C) Plankton utilize the nutrients released by the death of organisms killed by viruses.

(D) The absence of viruses can facilitate the flourishing of bacteria that sometimes damage other organisms.

(E) At any given time, a considerable portion of the plankton in seawater are already infected by viruses.

GO ON TO THE NEXT PAGE.

8. City council member: The Senior Guild has asked for a temporary exception to the ordinance prohibiting automobiles in municipal parks. Their case does appear to deserve the exception. However, if we grant this exception, we will find ourselves granting many other exceptions to this ordinance, some of which will be undeserved. Before long, we will be granting exceptions to all manner of other city ordinances. If we are to prevent anarchy in our city, we must deny the Senior Guild's request.

The city council member's argument is most vulnerable to criticism on the grounds that it

(A) distorts an argument and then attacks this distorted argument
(B) dismisses a claim because of its source rather than because of its content
(C) presumes, without sufficient warrant, that one event will lead to a particular causal sequence of events
(D) contains premises that contradict one another
(E) fails to make a needed distinction between deserved exceptions and undeserved ones

9. Physician: In comparing our country with two other countries of roughly the same population size, I found that even though we face the same dietary, bacterial, and stress-related causes of ulcers as they do, prescriptions for ulcer medicines in all socioeconomic strata are much rarer here than in those two countries. It's clear that we suffer significantly fewer ulcers, per capita, than they do.

Which one of the following, if true, most strengthens the physician's argument?

(A) The two countries that were compared with the physician's country had approximately the same ulcer rates as each other.
(B) The people of the physician's country have a cultural tradition of stoicism that encourages them to ignore physical ailments rather than to seek remedies for them.
(C) Several other countries not covered in the physician's comparisons have more prescriptions for ulcer medication than does the physician's country.
(D) A person in the physician's country who is suffering from ulcers is just as likely to obtain a prescription for the ailment as is a person suffering from ulcers in one of the other two countries.
(E) The physician's country has a much better system for reporting the number of prescriptions of a given type that are obtained each year than is present in either of the other two countries.

10. Columnist: The failure of bicyclists to obey traffic regulations is a causal factor in more than one quarter of the traffic accidents involving bicycles. Since inadequate bicycle safety equipment is also a factor in more than a quarter of such accidents, bicyclists are at least partially responsible for more than half of the traffic accidents involving bicycles.

The columnist's reasoning is flawed in that it

(A) presumes, without providing justification, that motorists are a factor in less than half of the traffic accidents involving bicycles
(B) improperly infers the presence of a causal connection on the basis of a correlation
(C) fails to consider the possibility that more than one factor may contribute to a given accident
(D) fails to provide the source of the figures it cites
(E) fails to consider that the severity of injuries to bicyclists from traffic accidents can vary widely

11. Many vaccines create immunity to viral diseases by introducing a certain portion of the disease-causing virus's outer coating into the body. Exposure to that part of a virus is as effective as exposure to the whole virus in stimulating production of antibodies that will subsequently recognize and kill the whole virus. To create a successful vaccine of this type, doctors must first isolate in the disease-causing virus a portion that stimulates antibody production. Now that a suitable portion of the virus that causes hepatitis E has been isolated, doctors claim they can produce a vaccine that will produce permanent immunity to that disease.

Which one of the following, if true, most strongly counters the doctors' claim?

(A) Most of the people who contract hepatitis E are young adults who were probably exposed to the virus in childhood also.
(B) Some laboratory animals exposed to one strain of the hepatitis virus developed immunity to all strains of the virus.
(C) Researchers developed a successful vaccine for another strain of hepatitis, hepatitis B, after first isolating the virus that causes it.
(D) The virus that causes hepatitis E is very common in some areas, so the number of people exposed to that virus is likely to be quite high in those areas.
(E) Many children who are exposed to viruses that cause childhood diseases such as chicken pox never develop those diseases.

GO ON TO THE NEXT PAGE.

12. Editorial: To qualify as an effective law, as opposed to merely an impressive declaration, a command must be backed up by an effective enforcement mechanism. That is why societies have police. The power of the police to enforce a society's laws makes those laws effective. But there is currently no international police force. Hence, what is called "international law" is not effective law.

Which one of the following is an assumption required by the editorial's argument?

(A) No one obeys a command unless mechanisms exist to compel obedience.

(B) If an international police force were established, then so-called international law would become effective law.

(C) The only difference between international law and the law of an individual society is the former's lack of an effective enforcement mechanism.

(D) The primary purpose of a police force is to enforce the laws of the society.

(E) Only an international police force could effectively enforce international law.

13. Art historian: More than any other genre of representational painting, still-life painting lends itself naturally to art whose goal is the artist's self-expression, rather than merely the reflection of a preexisting external reality. This is because in still-life painting, the artist invariably chooses, modifies, and arranges the objects to be painted. Thus, the artist has considerably more control over the composition and subject of a still-life painting than over those of a landscape painting or portrait, for example.

Which one of the following is most strongly supported by the art historian's statements?

(A) Landscape painting and portraiture are the artistic genres that lend themselves most naturally to the mere reflection of a preexisting external reality.

(B) The only way in which artists control the composition and subject of a painting is by choosing, modifying, and arranging the objects to be represented in that painting.

(C) Nonrepresentational painting does not lend itself as naturally as still-life painting does to the goal of the artist's self-expression.

(D) In genres of representational painting other than still-life painting, the artist does not always choose, modify, and arrange the objects to be painted.

(E) When painting a portrait, artists rarely attempt to express themselves through the choice, modification, or arrangement of the background elements against which the subject of the portrait is painted.

14. Food labeling regulation: Food of a type that does not ordinarily contain fat cannot be labeled "nonfat" unless most people mistakenly believe the food ordinarily contains fat. If most people mistakenly believe that a food ordinarily contains fat, the food may be labeled "nonfat" if the label also states that the food ordinarily contains no fat.

Which one of the following situations violates the food labeling regulation?

(A) Although most people know that bran flakes do not normally contain fat, Lester's Bran Flakes are not labeled "nonfat."

(B) Although most people are aware that lasagna ordinarily contains fat, Lester's Lasagna, which contains no fat, is not labeled "nonfat."

(C) Although most garlic baguettes contain fat, Lester's Garlic Baguettes are labeled "nonfat."

(D) Although most people are aware that applesauce does not ordinarily contain fat, Lester's Applesauce is labeled "nonfat."

(E) Although most people mistakenly believe that salsa ordinarily contains fat, the label on Lester's Zesty Salsa says "This product, like all salsas, is nonfat."

GO ON TO THE NEXT PAGE.

15. Medical ethicist: Assuming there is a reasonable chance for a cure, it is acceptable to offer experimental treatments for a disease to patients who suffer from extreme symptoms of that disease. Such patients are best able to weigh a treatment's risks against the benefits of a cure. Therefore, it is never acceptable to offer experimental treatments to patients who experience no extreme symptoms of the relevant disease.

The flawed reasoning in which one of the following is most similar to the flawed reasoning in the medical ethicist's argument?

(A) Even a geological engineer with a background in economics can lose money investing in mineral extraction. So, those who are less knowledgeable about geology or economics should not expect to make money in every investment in mineral extraction.

(B) One is always in a better position to judge whether an automobile would be worth its cost if one has test-driven that automobile. Therefore, if an automobile proves to be not worth its cost, it is likely that it was not test-driven.

(C) Someone born and raised in a country, who has lived abroad and then returned, is exceptionally qualified to judge the merits of living in that country. That is why someone who has not lived in that country should not form judgments about the merits of living there.

(D) One can never eliminate all of the risks of daily life, and even trying to avoid every risk in life is costly. Therefore, anyone who is reasonable will accept some of the risks of daily life.

(E) Almost any industrial development will have unwelcome environmental side effects. Therefore, it is not worthwhile to weigh the costs of potential environmental side effects since such side effects are unavoidable.

16. Critic: As modern methods of communication and transportation have continued to improve, the pace of life today has become faster than ever before. This speed has created feelings of impermanence and instability, making us feel as if we never have enough time to achieve what we want—or at least what we think we want.

The critic's statements most closely conform to which one of the following assessments?

(A) The fast pace of modern life has made it difficult for people to achieve their goals.

(B) The disadvantages of technological progress often outweigh the advantages.

(C) Changes in people's feelings about life can result from technological changes.

(D) The perception of impermanence in contemporary life makes it more difficult for people to know what they want.

(E) Changes in people's feelings fuel the need for technological advancement.

17. Consumer: If you buy a watch at a department store and use it only in the way it was intended to be used, but the watch stops working the next day, then the department store will refund your money. So by this very reasonable standard, Bingham's Jewelry Store should give me a refund even though they themselves are not a department store, since the watch I bought from them stopped working the very next day.

The consumer's argument relies on the assumption that

(A) one should not sell something unless one expects that it will function in the way it was originally designed to function

(B) a watch bought at a department store and a watch bought at Bingham's Jewelry Store can both be expected to keep working for about the same length of time if each is used only as it was intended to be used

(C) a seller should refund the money that was paid for a product if the product does not perform as the purchaser expected it to perform

(D) the consumer did not use the watch in a way contrary to the way it was intended to be used

(E) the watch that was purchased from Bingham's Jewelry Store was not a new watch

GO ON TO THE NEXT PAGE.

18. A study found that patients referred by their doctors to psychotherapists practicing a new experimental form of therapy made more progress with respect to their problems than those referred to psychotherapists practicing traditional forms of therapy. Therapists practicing the new form of therapy, therefore, are more effective than therapists practicing traditional forms.

Which one of the following most accurately describes a flaw in the argument?

(A) It ignores the possibility that therapists trained in traditional forms of therapy use the same techniques in treating their patients as therapists trained in the new form of therapy do.

(B) It ignores the possibility that the patients referred to therapists practicing the new form of therapy had problems more amenable to treatment than did those referred to therapists practicing traditional forms.

(C) It presumes, without providing justification, that any psychotherapist trained in traditional forms of therapy is untrained in the new form of therapy.

(D) It ignores the possibility that therapists practicing the new form of therapy systematically differ from therapists practicing traditional forms of therapy with regard to some personality attribute relevant to effective treatment.

(E) It presumes, without providing justification, that the personal rapport between therapist and patient has no influence on the effectiveness of the treatment the patient receives.

19. Essayist: One of the drawbacks of extreme personal and political freedom is that free choices are often made for the worst. To expect people to thrive when they are given the freedom to make unwise decisions is frequently unrealistic. Once people see the destructive consequences of extreme freedom, they may prefer to establish totalitarian political regimes that allow virtually no freedom. Thus, one should not support political systems that allow extreme freedom.

Which one of the following principles, if valid, most helps to justify the essayist's reasoning?

(A) One should not support any political system that will inevitably lead to the establishment of a totalitarian political regime.

(B) One should not expect everyone to thrive even in a political system that maximizes people's freedom in the long run.

(C) One should support only those political systems that give people the freedom to make wise choices.

(D) One should not support any political system whose destructive consequences could lead people to prefer totalitarian political regimes.

(E) One should not support any political system that is based on unrealistic expectations about people's behavior under that system.

GO ON TO THE NEXT PAGE.

20. Ethicist: Every moral action is the keeping of an agreement, and keeping an agreement is nothing more than an act of securing mutual benefit. Clearly, however, not all instances of agreement-keeping are moral actions. Therefore, some acts of securing mutual benefit are not moral actions.

The pattern of reasoning in which one of the following arguments is most similar to that in the ethicist's argument?

(A) All calculators are kinds of computers, and all computers are devices for automated reasoning. However, not all devices for automated reasoning are calculators. Therefore, some devices for automated reasoning are not computers.

(B) All exercise is beneficial, and all things that are beneficial promote health. However, not all things that are beneficial are forms of exercise. Therefore, some exercise does not promote health.

(C) All metaphors are comparisons, and not all comparisons are surprising. However, all metaphors are surprising. Therefore, some comparisons are not metaphors.

(D) All architecture is design and all design is art. However, not all design is architecture. Therefore, some art is not design.

(E) All books are texts, and all texts are documents. However, not all texts are books. Therefore, some documents are not books.

21. Sociologist: The more technologically advanced a society is, the more marked its members' resistance to technological innovations. This is not surprising, because the more technologically advanced a society is, the more aware its members are of technology's drawbacks. Specifically, people realize that sophisticated technologies deeply affect the quality of human relations.

The claim that the more technologically advanced a society is, the more aware its members are of technology's drawbacks plays which one of the following roles in the sociologist's argument?

(A) It is a conclusion supported by the claim that people realize that sophisticated technologies deeply affect the quality of human relations.

(B) It is offered as an explanation of why people's resistance to technological innovations is more marked the more technologically advanced the society in which they live is.

(C) It is a premise in support of the claim that the quality of human relations in technologically advanced societies is extremely poor.

(D) It is a generalization based on the claim that the more people resist technological innovations, the more difficult it is for them to adjust to those innovations.

(E) It is an example presented to illustrate the claim that resistance to technological innovations deeply affects the quality of human relations.

GO ON TO THE NEXT PAGE.

22. To win democratic elections that are not fully subsidized by the government, nonwealthy candidates must be supported by wealthy patrons. This makes plausible the belief that these candidates will compromise their views to win that support. But since the wealthy are dispersed among the various political parties in roughly equal proportion to their percentage in the overall population, this belief is false.

The argument is vulnerable to criticism on the grounds that it fails to consider that

(A) the primary function of political parties in democracies whose governments do not subsidize elections might not be to provide a means of negating the influence of wealth on elections

(B) in democracies in which elections are not fully subsidized by the government, positions endorsed by political parties might be much less varied than the positions taken by candidates

(C) in democracies, government-subsidized elections ensure that the views expressed by the people who run for office might not be overly influenced by the opinions of the wealthiest people in those countries

(D) in democracies in which elections are not fully subsidized by the government, it might be no easier for a wealthy person to win an election than it is for a nonwealthy person to win an election

(E) a democracy in which candidates do not compromise their views in order to be elected to office might have other flaws

23. In modern "brushless" car washes, cloth strips called mitters have replaced brushes. Mitters are easier on most cars' finishes than brushes are. This is especially important with the new clear-coat finishes found on many cars today, which are more easily scratched than older finishes are.

Which one of the following is most strongly supported by the statements above, if those statements are true?

(A) When car washes all used brushes rather than mitters, there were more cars on the road with scratched finishes than there are today.

(B) Modern "brushless" car washes were introduced as a direct response to the use of clear-coat finishes on cars.

(C) Modern "brushless" car washes usually do not produce visible scratches on cars with older finishes.

(D) Brushes are more effective than mitters and are preferred for cleaning cars with older finishes.

(E) More cars in use today have clear-coat finishes rather than older finishes.

24. It is widely believed that lancelets—small, primitive sea animals—do not have hearts. Each lancelet has a contracting vessel, but this vessel is considered an artery rather than a heart. However, this vessel is indeed a heart. After all, it strongly resembles the structure of the heart of certain other sea animals. Moreover, the muscular contractions in the lancelet's vessel closely resemble the muscular contractions of other animals' hearts.

The argument's conclusion follows logically if which one of the following is assumed?

(A) Only animals that have contracting vessels have hearts.

(B) Some primitive animals other than lancelets have what is widely held to be a heart.

(C) A vessel whose structure and actions closely resemble those of other animal hearts is a heart.

(D) For a vessel in an animal to be properly considered a heart, that vessel must undergo muscular contractions.

(E) No animal that has a heart lacks an artery.

25. Manager: I recommend that our company reconsider the decision to completely abandon our allegedly difficult-to-use computer software and replace it companywide with a new software package advertised as more flexible and easier to use. Several other companies in our region officially replaced the software we currently use with the new package, and while their employees can all use the new software, unofficially many continue to use their former software as much as possible.

Which one of the following is most strongly supported by the manager's statements?

(A) The current company software is as flexible as the proposed new software package.

(B) The familiarity that employees have with a computer software package is a more important consideration in selecting software than flexibility or initial ease of use.

(C) The employees of the manager's company would find that the new software package lacks some of the capabilities of the present software.

(D) Adopting the new software package would create two classes of employees, those who can use it and those who cannot.

(E) Many of the employees in the manager's company would not prefer the new software package to the software currently in use.

S T O P

IF YOU FINISH BEFORE TIME IS CALLED, YOU MAY CHECK YOUR WORK ON THIS SECTION ONLY.
DO NOT WORK ON ANY OTHER SECTION IN THE TEST.

SECTION IV

Time—35 minutes

27 Questions

<u>Directions</u>: Each set of questions in this section is based on a single passage or a pair of passages. The questions are to be answered on the basis of what is <u>stated</u> or <u>implied</u> in the passage or pair of passages. For some of the questions, more than one of the choices could conceivably answer the question. However, you are to choose the <u>best</u> answer; that is, the response that most accurately and completely answers the question, and blacken the corresponding space on your answer sheet.

The United States government agency responsible for overseeing television and radio broadcasting, the Federal Communications Commission (FCC), had an early history of addressing only the concerns of parties
(5) with an economic interest in broadcasting—chiefly broadcasting companies. The rights of viewers and listeners were not recognized by the FCC, which regarded them merely as members of the public. Unless citizens' groups were applying for broadcasting
(10) licenses, citizens did not have the standing necessary to voice their views at an FCC hearing. Consequently, the FCC appeared to be exclusively at the service of the broadcasting industry.

A landmark case changed the course of that
(15) history. In 1964, a local television station in Jackson, Mississippi was applying for a renewal of its broadcasting license. The United Church of Christ, representing Jackson's African American population, petitioned the FCC for a hearing about the broadcasting
(20) policies of that station. The church charged that the station advocated racial segregation to the point of excluding news and programs supporting integration. Arguing that the church lacked the level of economic interest required for a hearing, the FCC rejected the
(25) petition, though it attempted to mollify the church by granting only a short-term, probationary renewal to the station. Further, the FCC claimed that since it accepted the church's contentions with regard to misconduct on the part of the broadcasters, no hearing was necessary.
(30) However, that decision raised a question: If the contentions concerning the station were accepted, why was its license renewed at all? The real reason for denying the church a hearing was more likely the prospect that citizens' groups representing community
(35) preferences would begin to enter the closed worlds of government and industry.

The church appealed the FCC's decision in court, and in 1967 was granted the right to a public hearing on the station's request for a long-term license. The
(40) hearing was to little avail: the FCC dismissed much of the public input and granted a full renewal to the station. The church appealed again, and this time the judge took the unprecedented step of revoking the station's license without remand to the FCC, ruling that the
(45) church members were performing a public service in voicing the legitimate concerns of the community and, as such, should be accorded the right to challenge the renewal of the station's broadcasting license.

The case established a formidable precedent for
(50) opening up to the public the world of broadcasting.

Subsequent rulings have supported the right of the public to question the performance of radio and television licensees before the FCC at renewal time every three years. Along with racial issues, a range of
(55) other matters—from the quality of children's programming and the portrayal of violence to equal time for opposing political viewpoints—are now discussed at licensing proceedings because of the church's intervention.

1. Which one of the following most accurately expresses the main point of the passage?

(A) Because of the efforts of a church group in challenging an FCC decision, public input is now considered in broadcast licensing proceedings.

(B) Court rulings have forced the FCC to abandon policies that appeared to encourage biased coverage of public issues.

(C) The history of the FCC is important because it explains why government agencies are now forced to respond to public input.

(D) Because it has begun to serve the interests of the public, the FCC is less responsive to the broadcasting industry.

(E) In response to pressure from citizens' groups, the FCC has decided to open its license renewal hearings to the public.

GO ON TO THE NEXT PAGE.

2. The author mentions some additional topics now discussed at FCC hearings (lines 54–59) primarily in order to

(A) support the author's claim that the case helped to open up to the public the world of broadcasting

(B) suggest the level of vigilance that citizens' groups must maintain with regard to broadcasters

(C) provide an explanation of why the public is allowed to question the performance of broadcasters on such a frequent basis

(D) illustrate other areas of misconduct with which the station discussed in the passage was charged

(E) demonstrate that the station discussed in the passage was not the only one to fall short of its obligation to the public

3. Which one of the following statements is affirmed by the passage?

(A) The broadcasting industry's economic goals can be met most easily by minimizing the attention given to the interests of viewers and listeners.

(B) The FCC was advised by broadcasters to bar groups with no economic interest in broadcasting from hearings concerning the broadcasting industry.

(C) The court ruled in the case brought by the United Church of Christ that the FCC had the ultimate authority to decide whether to renew a broadcaster's license.

(D) Before the United Church of Christ won its case, the FCC would not allow citizens' groups to speak as members of the public at FCC hearings.

(E) The case brought by the United Church of Christ represents the first time a citizens' group was successful in getting its concerns about government agencies addressed to its satisfaction.

4. Based on information presented in the passage, with which one of the following statements would the author be most likely to agree?

(A) If the United Church of Christ had not pursued its case, the FCC would not have been aware of the television station's broadcasting policies.

(B) By their very nature, industrial and business interests are opposed to public interests.

(C) The recourse of a citizens' group to the courts represents an effective means of protecting public interests.

(D) Governmental regulation cannot safeguard against individual businesses acting contrary to public interests.

(E) The government cannot be trusted to favor the rights of the public over broadcasters' economic interests.

5. The passage suggests that which one of the following has been established by the case discussed in the third paragraph?

(A) Broadcasters are legally obligated to hold regular meetings at which the public can voice its concerns about broadcasting policies.

(B) Broadcasters are now required by the FCC to consult citizens' groups when making programming decisions.

(C) Except in cases involving clear misconduct by a broadcaster, the FCC need not seek public input in licensing hearings.

(D) When evaluating the performance of a broadcaster applying for a license renewal, the FCC must obtain information about the preferences of the public.

(E) In FCC licensing proceedings, parties representing community preferences should be granted standing along with those with an economic interest in broadcasting.

GO ON TO THE NEXT PAGE.

An effort should be made to dispel the misunderstandings that still prevent the much-needed synthesis and mutual supplementation of science and the humanities. This reconciliation should not be too
(5) difficult once it is recognized that the separation is primarily the result of a basic misunderstanding of the philosophical foundations of both science and the humanities.

Some humanists still identify science with an
(10) absurd mechanistic reductionism. There are many who feel that the scientist is interested in nothing more than "bodies in motion," in the strictly mathematical, physical, and chemical laws that govern the material world. This is the caricature of science drawn by
(15) representatives of the humanities who are ignorant of the nature of modern science and also of the scientific outlook in philosophy. For example, it is claimed that science either ignores or explains away the most essential human values. Those who believe this also
(20) assert that there are aspects of the human mind, manifest especially in the domains of morality, religion, and the arts, that contain an irreducible spiritual element and for that reason can never be adequately explained by science.
(25) Some scientists, on the other hand, claim that the humanist is interested in nothing more than emotion and sentiment, exhibiting the vagrant fancies of an undisciplined mind. To such men and women the humanities are useless because they serve no immediate
(30) and technological function for the practical survival of human society in the material world. Such pragmatists believe that the areas of morality, religion, and the arts should have only a secondary importance in people's lives.
(35) Thus there are misconceptions among humanists and scientists alike that are in need of correction. This correction leads to a much more acceptable position that could be called "scientific humanism," attempting as it does to combine the common elements of both
(40) disciplines. Both science and the humanities attempt to describe and explain. It is true that they begin their descriptions and explanations at widely separated points, but the objectives remain the same: a clearer understanding of people and their world. In achieving
(45) this understanding, science in fact does not depend exclusively on measurable data, and the humanities in fact profit from attempts at controlled evaluation. Scientific humanism can combine the scientific attitude with an active interest in the whole scale of
(50) human values. If uninformed persons insist on viewing science as only materialistic and the humanities as only idealistic, a fruitful collaboration of both fields is unlikely. The combination of science and the humanities is, however, possible, even probable, if we
(55) begin by noting their common objectives, rather than seeing only their different means.

6. Which one of the following best describes the main idea of the passage?

(A) Scientists' failure to understand humanists hinders collaborations between the two groups.
(B) The materialism of science and the idealism of the humanities have both been beneficial to modern society.
(C) Technological development will cease if science and the humanities remain at odds with each other.
(D) The current relationship between science and the humanities is less cooperative than their relationship once was.
(E) A synthesis of science and the humanities is possible and much-needed.

7. Which one of the following would the author be most likely to characterize as an example of a misunderstanding of science by a humanist?

(A) Science encourages the view that emotions are inexplicable.
(B) Science arises out of practical needs but serves other needs as well.
(C) Science depends exclusively on measurable data to support its claims.
(D) Science recognizes an irreducible spiritual element that makes the arts inexplicable.
(E) Science encourages the use of description in the study of human values.

8. It can be inferred from the passage that the author would be most likely to agree with which one of the following statements?

(A) Scientific humanism is characterized by the extension of description and explanation from science to the humanities.
(B) A clearer understanding of people is an objective of humanists that scientists have not yet come to share.
(C) Controlled measures of aesthetic experience are of little use in the study of the humanities.
(D) Humanists have profited from using methods generally considered useful primarily to scientists.
(E) Fruitful collaboration between scientists and humanists is unlikely to become more common.

GO ON TO THE NEXT PAGE.

9. According to the author, which one of the following is the primary cause of the existing separation between science and the humanities?

(A) inflammatory claims by scientists regarding the pragmatic value of the work of humanists
(B) misunderstandings of the philosophical foundations of each by the other
(C) the excessive influence of reductionism on both
(D) the predominance of a concern with mechanics in science
(E) the failure of humanists to develop rigorous methods

10. Which one of the following best describes one of the functions of the last paragraph in the passage?

(A) to show that a proposal introduced in the first paragraph is implausible because of information presented in the second and third paragraphs
(B) to show that the views presented in the second and third paragraphs are correct but capable of reconciliation
(C) to present information supporting one of two opposing views presented in the second and third paragraphs
(D) to present an alternative to views presented in the second and third paragraphs
(E) to offer specific examples of the distinct views presented in the second and third paragraphs

11. The passage suggests that the author would recommend that humanists accept which one of the following modifications of their point of view?

(A) a realization that the scientist is less interested in describing "bodies in motion" than in constructing mathematical models of the material world
(B) an acknowledgement that there is a spiritual element in the arts that science does not account for
(C) an acceptance of the application of controlled evaluation to the examination of human values
(D) a less strident insistence on the primary importance of the arts in people's lives
(E) an emphasis on developing ways for showing how the humanities support the practical survival of mankind

12. In using the phrase "vagrant fancies of an undisciplined mind" (lines 27–28), the author suggests that humanists are sometimes considered to be

(A) wildly emotional
(B) excessively impractical
(C) unnecessarily intransigent
(D) justifiably optimistic
(E) logically inconsistent

GO ON TO THE NEXT PAGE.

The following passages are adapted from critical essays on the American writer Willa Cather (1873–1947).

Passage A

When Cather gave examples of high quality in fiction, she invariably cited Russian writers Ivan Turgenev or Leo Tolstoy or both. Indeed, Edmund Wilson noted in 1922 that Cather followed
(5) the manner of Turgenev, not depicting her characters' emotions directly but telling us how they behave and letting their "inner blaze of glory shine through the simple recital." Turgenev's method was to select details that described a character's appearance and
(10) actions without trying to explain them. A writer, he said, "must be a psychologist—but a secret one; he must know and feel the roots of phenomena, but only present the phenomena themselves." Similarly, he argued that a writer must have complete knowledge
(15) of a character so as to avoid overloading the work with unnecessary detail, concentrating instead on what is characteristic and typical.

Here we have an impressionistic aesthetic that anticipates Cather's: what Turgenev referred to as
(20) secret knowledge Cather called "the thing not named." In one essay she writes that "whatever is felt upon the page without being specifically named there—that, one might say, is created." For both writers, there is the absolute importance of selection and simplification;
(25) for both, art is the fusing of the physical world of setting and actions with the emotional reality of the characters. What synthesizes all the elements of narrative for these writers is the establishment of a prevailing mood.

Passage B

(30) In a famous 1927 letter, Cather writes of her novel *Death Comes for the Archbishop*, "Many [reviewers] assert vehemently that it is not a novel. Myself, I prefer to call it a narrative." Cather's preference anticipated an important reformulation of
(35) the criticism of fiction: the body of literary theory, called "narratology," articulated by French literary theorists in the 1960s. This approach broadens and simplifies the fundamental paradigms according to which we view fiction: they ask of narrative only that
(40) it be narrative, that it tell a story. Narratologists tend *not* to focus on the characteristics of narrative's dominant modern Western form, the "realistic novel": direct psychological characterization, realistic treatment of time, causal plotting, logical closure.
(45) Such a model of criticism, which takes as its object "narrative" rather than the "novel," seems exactly appropriate to Cather's work.

Indeed, her severest critics have always questioned precisely her capabilities as a *novelist*. Morton Zabel
(50) argued that "[Cather's] themes...could readily fail to find the structure and substance that might have given them life or redeemed them from the tenuity of a sketch"; Leon Edel called one of her novels "two inconclusive fragments." These critics and others like
(55) them treat as failures some of the central features of

Cather's impressionistic technique: unusual treatment of narrative time, unexpected focus, ambiguous conclusions, a preference for the bold, simple, and stylized in character as well as in landscape. These
(60) "non-novelistic" structures indirectly articulate the essential and conflicting forces of desire at work throughout Cather's fiction.

13. If the author of passage A were to read passage B, he or she would be most likely to agree with which one of the following?

(A) Though Cather preferred to call *Death Comes for the Archbishop* a narrative rather than a novel, she would be unlikely to view most of her other novels in the same way.

(B) The critics who questioned Cather's abilities as a novelist focused mostly on her failed experiments and ignored her more aesthetically successful novels.

(C) A model of criticism that takes narrative rather than the novel as its object is likely to result in flawed interpretations of Cather's work.

(D) Critics who questioned Cather's abilities as a novelist fail to perceive the extent to which Cather actually embraced the conventions of the realistic novel.

(E) Cather's goal of representing the "thing not named" explains her preference for the bold, simple, and stylized in the presentation of character.

14. Passage B indicates which one of the following?

(A) Narratologists point to Cather's works as prime examples of pure narrative.

(B) Cather disliked the work of many of the novelists who preceded her.

(C) Cather regarded at least one of her works as not fitting straightforwardly into the category of the novel.

(D) Cather's unusual treatment of narrative time was influenced by the Russian writers Turgenev and Tolstoy.

(E) Cather's work was regarded as flawed by most contemporary critics.

GO ON TO THE NEXT PAGE.

15. It can be inferred that both authors would be most likely to regard which one of the following as exemplifying Cather's narrative technique?

(A) A meticulous inventory of the elegant furniture and décor in a character's living room is used to indicate that the character is wealthy.

(B) An account of a character's emotional scars is used to explain the negative effects the character has on his family.

(C) A description of a slightly quivering drink in the hand of a character at a dinner party is used to suggest that the character is timid.

(D) A chronological summary of the events that spark a family conflict is used to supply the context for an in-depth narration of that conflict.

(E) A detailed narration of an unprovoked act of violence and the reprisals it triggers is used to portray the theme that violence begets violence.

16. Which one of the following most accurately states the main point of passage B?

(A) Cather's fiction is best approached by focusing purely on narrative, rather than on the formal characteristics of the novel.

(B) Most commentators on Cather's novels have mistakenly treated her distinctive narrative techniques as aesthetic flaws.

(C) Cather intentionally avoided the realistic psychological characterization that is the central feature of the modern Western novel.

(D) Cather's impressionistic narratives served as an important impetus for the development of narratology in the 1960s.

(E) Cather rejected the narrative constraints of the realistic novel and instead concentrated on portraying her characters by sketching their inner lives.

17. It is most likely that the authors of the two passages would both agree with which one of the following statements?

(A) More than her contemporaries, Cather used stream-of-consciousness narration to portray her characters.

(B) Cather's works were not intended as novels, but rather as narratives.

(C) Narratology is the most appropriate critical approach to Cather's work.

(D) Cather's technique of evoking the "thing not named" had a marked influence on later novelists.

(E) Cather used impressionistic narrative techniques to portray the psychology of her characters.

18. Both authors would be likely to agree that which one of the following, though typical of many novels, would NOT be found in Cather's work?

(A) Description of the salient features of the setting, such as a chair in which a character often sits.

(B) A plot that does not follow chronological time, but rather moves frequently between the novel's past and present.

(C) Description of a character's physical appearance, dress, and facial expressions.

(D) Direct representation of dialogue between the novel's characters, using quotation marks to set off characters' words.

(E) A narration of a character's inner thoughts, including an account of the character's anxieties and wishes.

19. A central purpose of each passage is to

(A) describe the primary influences on Cather's work

(B) identify some of the distinctive characteristics of Cather's work

(C) explain the critical reception Cather's work received in her lifetime

(D) compare Cather's novels to the archetypal form of the realistic novel

(E) examine the impact of European literature and literary theory on Cather's work

GO ON TO THE NEXT PAGE.

Fractal geometry is a mathematical theory devoted to the study of complex shapes called fractals. Although an exact definition of fractals has not been established, fractals commonly exhibit the property of self-similarity:
(5) the reiteration of irregular details or patterns at progressively smaller scales so that each part, when magnified, looks basically like the object as a whole. The Koch curve is a significant fractal in mathematics and examining it provides some insight into fractal
(10) geometry. To generate the Koch curve, one begins with a straight line. The middle third of the line is removed and replaced with two line segments, each as long as the removed piece, which are positioned so as to meet and form the top of a triangle. At this stage,
(15) the curve consists of four connected segments of equal length that form a pointed protrusion in the middle. This process is repeated on the four segments so that all the protrusions are on the same side of the curve, and then the process is repeated indefinitely on the
(20) segments at each stage of the construction.

Self-similarity is built into the construction process by treating segments at each stage the same way as the original segment was treated. Since the rules for getting from one stage to another are fully
(25) explicit and always the same, images of successive stages of the process can be generated by computer. Theoretically, the Koch curve is the result of infinitely many steps in the construction process, but the finest image approximating the Koch curve will be limited
(30) by the fact that eventually the segments will get too short to be drawn or displayed. However, using computer graphics to produce images of successive stages of the construction process dramatically illustrates a major attraction of fractal geometry:
(35) simple processes can be responsible for incredibly complex patterns.

A worldwide public has become captivated by fractal geometry after viewing astonishing computer-generated images of fractals; enthusiastic practitioners
(40) in the field of fractal geometry consider it a new language for describing complex natural and mathematical forms. They anticipate that fractal geometry's significance will rival that of calculus and expect that proficiency in fractal geometry will allow
(45) mathematicians to describe the form of a cloud as easily and precisely as an architect can describe a house using the language of traditional geometry. Other mathematicians have reservations about the fractal geometers' preoccupation with computer-generated
(50) graphic images and their lack of interest in theory. These mathematicians point out that traditional mathematics consists of proving theorems, and while many theorems about fractals have already been proven using the notions of pre-fractal mathematics,
(55) fractal geometers have proven only a handful of theorems that could not have been proven with pre-fractal mathematics. According to these mathematicians, fractal geometry can attain a lasting role in mathematics only if it becomes a precise
(60) language supporting a system of theorems and proofs.

20. Which one of the following most accurately expresses the main point of the passage?

(A) Because of its unique forms, fractal geometry is especially adaptable to computer technology and is therefore likely to grow in importance and render pre-fractal mathematics obsolete.

(B) Though its use in the generation of extremely complex forms makes fractal geometry an intriguing new mathematical theory, it is not yet universally regarded as having attained the theoretical rigor of traditional mathematics.

(C) Fractal geometry is significant because of its use of self-similarity, a concept that has enabled geometers to generate extremely detailed computer images of natural forms.

(D) Using the Koch curve as a model, fractal geometers have developed a new mathematical language that is especially useful in technological contexts because it does not rely on theorems.

(E) Though fractal geometry has thus far been of great value for its capacity to define abstract mathematical shapes, it is not expected to be useful for the description of ordinary natural shapes.

21. Which one of the following is closest to the meaning of the phrase "fully explicit" as used in lines 24–25?

(A) illustrated by an example
(B) uncomplicated
(C) expressed unambiguously
(D) in need of lengthy computation
(E) agreed on by all

22. According to the description in the passage, each one of the following illustrates the concept of self-similarity EXCEPT:

(A) Any branch broken off a tree looks like the tree itself.
(B) Each portion of the intricately patterned frost on a window looks like the pattern as a whole.
(C) The pattern of blood vessels in each part of the human body is similar to the pattern of blood vessels in the entire body.
(D) The seeds of several subspecies of maple tree resemble one another in shape despite differences in size.
(E) The florets composing a cauliflower head resemble the entire cauliflower head.

GO ON TO THE NEXT PAGE.

23. The explanation of how a Koch curve is generated (lines 10–20) serves primarily to

(A) show how fractal geometry can be reduced to traditional geometry
(B) give an example of a natural form that can be described by fractal geometry
(C) anticipate the objection that fractal geometry is not a precise language
(D) illustrate the concept of self-similarity
(E) provide an exact definition of fractals

24. Which one of the following does the author present as a characteristic of fractal geometry?

(A) It is potentially much more important than calculus.
(B) Its role in traditional mathematics will expand as computers become faster.
(C) It is the fastest-growing field of mathematics.
(D) It encourages the use of computer programs to prove mathematical theorems.
(E) It enables geometers to generate complex forms using simple processes.

25. Each of the following statements about the Koch curve can be properly deduced from the information given in the passage EXCEPT:

(A) The total number of protrusions in the Koch curve at any stage of the construction depends on the length of the initial line chosen for the construction.
(B) The line segments at each successive stage of the construction of the Koch curve are shorter than the segments at the previous stage.
(C) Theoretically, as the Koch curve is constructed its line segments become infinitely small.
(D) At every stage of constructing the Koch curve, all the line segments composing it are of equal length.
(E) The length of the line segments in the Koch curve at any stage of its construction depends on the length of the initial line chosen for the construction.

26. The enthusiastic practitioners of fractal geometry mentioned in lines 39–40 would be most likely to agree with which one of the following statements?

(A) The Koch curve is the most easily generated, and therefore the most important, of the forms studied by fractal geometers.
(B) Fractal geometry will eventually be able to be used in the same applications for which traditional geometry is now used.
(C) The greatest importance of computer images of fractals is their ability to bring fractal geometry to the attention of a wider public.
(D) Studying self-similarity was impossible before the development of sophisticated computer technologies.
(E) Certain complex natural forms exhibit a type of self-similarity like that exhibited by fractals.

27. The information in the passage best supports which one of the following assertions?

(A) The appeal of a mathematical theory is limited to those individuals who can grasp the theorems and proofs produced in that theory.
(B) Most of the important recent breakthroughs in mathematical theory would not have been possible without the ability of computers to graphically represent complex shapes.
(C) Fractal geometry holds the potential to replace traditional geometry in most of its engineering applications.
(D) A mathematical theory can be developed and find applications even before it establishes a precise definition of its subject matter.
(E) Only a mathematical theory that supports a system of theorems and proofs will gain enthusiastic support among a significant number of mathematicians.

S T O P

IF YOU FINISH BEFORE TIME IS CALLED, YOU MAY CHECK YOUR WORK ON THIS SECTION ONLY.
DO NOT WORK ON ANY OTHER SECTION IN THE TEST.

Acknowledgment is made to the following sources from which material has been adapted for use in this test booklet:

Jerome Barron, *Freedom of the Press for Whom? The Right of Access to Mass Media.* ©1973 by Indiana University Press.

Huw Jones, "Fractals Before Mandelbrot: A Selective History." ©1993 by Springer-Verlag New York Inc.

Wait for the supervisor's instructions before you open the page to the topic.
Please print and sign your name and write the date in the designated spaces below.

Time: 35 Minutes

General Directions

You will have 35 minutes in which to plan and write an essay on the topic inside. Read the topic and the accompanying directions carefully. You will probably find it best to spend a few minutes considering the topic and organizing your thoughts before you begin writing. In your essay, be sure to develop your ideas fully, leaving time, if possible, to review what you have written. **Do not write on a topic other than the one specified. Writing on a topic of your own choice is not acceptable.**

No special knowledge is required or expected for this writing exercise. Law schools are interested in the reasoning, clarity, organization, language usage, and writing mechanics displayed in your essay. How well you write is more important than how much you write.

Confine your essay to the blocked, lined area on the front and back of the separate Writing Sample Response Sheet. Only that area will be reproduced for law schools. Be sure that your writing is legible.

Both this topic sheet and your response sheet must be turned over to the testing staff before you leave the room.

LSAC®

Topic Code
080102

Date
/   /

Print Your Full Name Here		
Last	First	M.I.

Sign Your Name Here

Scratch Paper
Do not write your essay in this space.

LSAT® Writing Sample Topic

Directions: The scenario presented below describes two choices, either one of which can be supported on the basis of the information given. Your essay should consider both choices and argue for one over the other, based on the two specified criteria and the facts provided. There is no "right" or "wrong" choice: a reasonable argument can be made for either.

Linda intends to spend her vacation walking part of a national trail. Over the course of one week, she will walk the trail while her luggage is taken on ahead of her each day. At this point, she must choose between either making all the arrangements herself or hiring a company that organizes walking tours to do this for her. Using the facts below, write an essay in which you argue for one approach over the other, based on the following two criteria:

- Linda wants to minimize the effort she puts into managing the vacation, both prior to and during the walk.
- She wants to have as much control over each day's experience as possible.

If Linda chooses to design her own walk and make the arrangements herself, she will research the trail and the available accommodations to estimate the distance she can comfortably cover each day and determine appropriate nightly stopover points. She will arrange for the luggage transportation and lodging. During her walk, it will be easy for her to add rest days as needed and otherwise change her itinerary from day to day.

If she hires a company that organizes walking tours, the company will plan the length of each day's walk based on its knowledge of the terrain. Linda will designate any planned rest days ahead of time. The walking company typically chooses among a limited set of nightly accommodations that it has selected based on customer feedback, honoring specific requests when possible. She will walk on her own. Complete lodging and route details will be provided to her the evening before her first day out. The company will oversee day-to-day luggage transportation.

WP-Q080A

Scratch Paper
Do not write your essay in this space.

COMPUTING YOUR SCORE

Directions:

1. Use the Answer Key on the next page to check your answers.

2. Use the Scoring Worksheet below to compute your raw score.

3. Use the Score Conversion Chart to convert your raw score into the 120–180 scale.

Scoring Worksheet

1. Enter the number of questions you answered correctly in each section.

	Number Correct
SECTION I.................	_____
SECTION II................	_____
SECTION III..............	_____
SECTION IV	_____

2. Enter the sum here: _____
   This is your Raw Score.

Conversion Chart
For Converting Raw Score to the 120–180 LSAT Scaled Score
LSAT Form 0LSN87

Reported Score	Raw Score Lowest	Raw Score Highest
180	99	101
179	98	98
178	—*	—*
177	97	97
176	96	96
175	95	95
174	94	94
173	93	93
172	92	92
171	91	91
170	90	90
169	89	89
168	87	88
167	86	86
166	84	85
165	83	83
164	81	82
163	80	80
162	78	79
161	76	77
160	75	75
159	73	74
158	71	72
157	69	70
156	68	68
155	66	67
154	64	65
153	62	63
152	61	61
151	59	60
150	57	58
149	55	56
148	54	54
147	52	53
146	50	51
145	49	49
144	47	48
143	45	46
142	44	44
141	42	43
140	41	41
139	39	40
138	37	38
137	36	36
136	34	35
135	33	33
134	32	32
133	30	31
132	29	29
131	27	28
130	26	26
129	25	25
128	23	24
127	22	22
126	21	21
125	20	20
124	18	19
123	17	17
122	15	16
121	—*	—*
120	0	14

*There is no raw score that will produce this scaled score for this form.

ANSWER KEY

SECTION I

1.	D	8.	E	15.	E	22.	D
2.	B	9.	D	16.	A	23.	E
3.	C	10.	C	17.	B		
4.	D	11.	B	18.	C		
5.	C	12.	B	19.	D		
6.	B	13.	D	20.	E		
7.	B	14.	A	21.	B		

SECTION II

1.	A	8.	E	15.	A	22.	A
2.	A	9.	C	16.	B	23.	B
3.	D	10.	B	17.	E	24.	E
4.	D	11.	C	18.	D	25.	C
5.	E	12.	D	19.	C	26.	B
6.	C	13.	C	20.	D		
7.	A	14.	E	21.	E		

SECTION III

1.	A	8.	C	15.	C	22.	B
2.	C	9.	D	16.	C	23.	C
3.	A	10.	C	17.	D	24.	C
4.	B	11.	A	18.	B	25.	E
5.	A	12.	E	19.	D		
6.	A	13.	D	20.	E		
7.	C	14.	D	21.	B		

SECTION IV

1.	A	8.	D	15.	C	22.	D
2.	A	9.	B	16.	A	23.	D
3.	D	10.	D	17.	E	24.	E
4.	C	11.	C	18.	E	25.	A
5.	E	12.	B	19.	B	26.	E
6.	E	13.	E	20.	B	27.	D
7.	C	14.	C	21.	C		

The Official LSAT PrepTest

58

- September 2009
  PrepTest 58

- Form 9LSN81

SECTION I

Time—35 minutes

26 Questions

Directions: The questions in this section are based on the reasoning contained in brief statements or passages. For some questions, more than one of the choices could conceivably answer the question. However, you are to choose the <u>best</u> answer; that is, the response that most accurately and completely answers the question. You should not make assumptions that are by commonsense standards implausible, superfluous, or incompatible with the passage. After you have chosen the best answer, blacken the corresponding space on your answer sheet.

1. Commentator: Although the present freshwater supply is adequate for today's patterns of water use, the human population will increase substantially over the next few decades, drastically increasing the need for freshwater. Hence, restrictions on water use will be necessary to meet the freshwater needs of humankind in the not-too-distant future.

   Which one of the following is an assumption required by the argument?

   (A)   Humans will adapt to restrictions on the use of water without resorting to wasteful use of other natural resources.
   (B)   The total supply of freshwater has not diminished in recent years.
   (C)   The freshwater supply will not increase sufficiently to meet the increased needs of humankind.
   (D)   No attempt to synthesize water will have an appreciable effect on the quantity of freshwater available.
   (E)   No water conservation measure previously attempted yielded an increase in the supply of freshwater available for human use.

2. Psychologist: The best way to recall a certain word or name that one is having trouble remembering is to occupy one's mind with other things, since often the more we strive to remember a certain word or name that we can't think of, the less likely it becomes that the word will come to mind.

   The principle that underlies the psychologist's argument underlies which one of the following arguments?

   (A)   Often, the best way to achieve happiness is to pursue other things besides wealth and fame, for there are wealthy and famous people who are not particularly happy, which suggests that true happiness does not consist in wealth and fame.
   (B)   The best way to succeed in writing a long document is not to think about how much is left to write but only about the current paragraph, since on many occasions thinking about what remains to be done will be so discouraging that the writer will be tempted to abandon the project.
   (C)   The best way to overcome a serious mistake is to continue on confidently as though all is well. After all, one can overcome a serious mistake by succeeding in new challenges, and dwelling on one's errors usually distracts one's mind from new challenges.
   (D)   The best way to fall asleep quickly is to engage in some mental diversion like counting sheep, because frequently the more one concentrates on falling asleep the lower the chance of falling asleep quickly.
   (E)   The best way to cope with sorrow or grief is to turn one's attention to those who are experiencing even greater hardship, for in many circumstances this will make our own troubles seem bearable by comparison.

GO ON TO THE NEXT PAGE.

3. Letter to the editor: The Planning Department budget increased from $100,000 in 2001 to $524,000 for this year. However, this does not justify your conclusion in yesterday's editorial that the department now spends five times as much money as it did in 2001 to perform the same duties.

Which one of the following, if true, most helps to support the claim made in the letter regarding the justification of the editorial's conclusion?

(A) Departments other than the Planning Department have had much larger budget increases since 2001.

(B) Since 2001, the Planning Department has dramatically reduced its spending on overtime pay.

(C) In some years between 2001 and this year, the Planning Department budget did not increase.

(D) The budget figures used in the original editorial were adjusted for inflation.

(E) A restructuring act, passed in 2003, broadened the duties of the Planning Department.

4. At mock trials in which jury instructions were given in technical legal jargon, jury verdicts tended to mirror the judge's own opinions. Jurors had become aware of the judge's nonverbal behavior: facial expressions, body movements, tone of voice. Jurors who viewed the same case but were given instruction in clear, nontechnical language, however, were comparatively more likely to return verdicts at odds with the judge's opinion.

Which one of the following is best illustrated by the example described above?

(A) Technical language tends to be more precise than nontechnical language.

(B) A person's influence is proportional to that person's perceived status.

(C) Nonverbal behavior is not an effective means of communication.

(D) Real trials are better suited for experimentation than are mock trials.

(E) The way in which a judge instructs a jury can influence the jury's verdict.

5. Doctor: While a few alternative medicines have dangerous side effects, some, such as many herbs, have been proven safe to consume. Thus, though there is little firm evidence of medicinal effect, advocates of these herbs as remedies for serious illnesses should always be allowed to prescribe them, since their patients will not be harmed, and might be helped, by the use of these products.

Which one of the following, if true, most seriously weakens the doctor's argument?

(A) Many practitioners and patients neglect more effective conventional medicines in favor of herbal remedies.

(B) Many herbal remedies are marketed with claims of proven effectiveness when in fact their effectiveness is unproven.

(C) Some patients may have allergic reactions to certain medicines that have been tolerated by other patients.

(D) The vast majority of purveyors of alternative medicines are driven as much by the profit motive as by a regard for their patients' health.

(E) Any pain relief or other benefits of many herbs have been proven to derive entirely from patients' belief in the remedy, rather than from its biochemical properties.

6. When a nation is on the brink of financial crisis, its government does not violate free-market principles if, in order to prevent economic collapse, it limits the extent to which foreign investors and lenders can withdraw their money. After all, the right to free speech does not include the right to shout "Fire!" in a crowded theatre, and the harm done as investors and lenders rush madly to get their money out before everyone else does can be just as real as the harm resulting from a stampede in a theatre.

The argument does which one of the following?

(A) tries to show that a set of principles is limited in a specific way by using an analogy to a similar principle that is limited in a similar way

(B) infers a claim by arguing that the truth of that claim would best explain observed facts

(C) presents numerous experimental results as evidence for a general principle

(D) attempts to demonstrate that an explanation of a phenomenon is flawed by showing that it fails to explain a particular instance of that phenomenon

(E) applies an empirical generalization to reach a conclusion about a particular case

GO ON TO THE NEXT PAGE.

7. Although many political candidates object to being made the target of advertising designed to cast them in an adverse light, such advertising actually benefits its targets because most elections have been won by candidates who were the targets of that kind of advertising.

The pattern of flawed reasoning in the argument most closely parallels that in which one of the following?

(A) Although many people dislike physical exercise, they should exercise because it is a good way to improve their overall health.

(B) Although many actors dislike harsh reviews of their work, such reviews actually help their careers because most of the really prestigious acting awards have gone to actors who have had performances of theirs reviewed harshly.

(C) Although many students dislike studying, it must be a good way to achieve academic success because most students who study pass their courses.

(D) Although many film critics dislike horror films, such films are bound to be successful because a large number of people are eager to attend them.

(E) Although many people dislike feeling sleepy as a result of staying up late the previous night, such sleepiness must be acceptable to those who experience it because most people who stay up late enjoy doing so.

8. Working residents of Springfield live, on average, farther from their workplaces than do working residents of Rorchester. Thus, one would expect that the demand for public transportation would be greater in Springfield than in Rorchester. However, Springfield has only half as many bus routes as Rorchester.

Each of the following, if true, contributes to a resolution of the apparent discrepancy described above EXCEPT:

(A) Three-fourths of the Springfield workforce is employed at the same factory outside the city limits.

(B) The average number of cars per household is higher in Springfield than in Rorchester.

(C) Rorchester has fewer railway lines than Springfield.

(D) Buses in Springfield run more frequently and on longer routes than in Rorchester.

(E) Springfield has a larger population than Rorchester does.

9. People who need to reduce their intake of fat and to consume fewer calories often turn to fat substitutes, especially those with zero calories such as N5. But studies indicate that N5 is of no use to such people. Subjects who ate foods prepared with N5 almost invariably reported feeling hungrier afterwards than after eating foods prepared with real fat and consequently they ate more, quickly making up for the calories initially saved by using N5.

The reasoning in the argument is most vulnerable to criticism on the grounds that the argument fails to consider the possibility that

(A) many foods cannot be prepared with N5

(B) N5 has mild but unpleasant side effects

(C) not everyone who eats foods prepared with N5 pays attention to caloric intake

(D) people who know N5 contains zero calories tend to eat more foods prepared with N5 than do people who are unaware that N5 is calorie-free

(E) the total fat intake of people who eat foods prepared with N5 tends to decrease even if their caloric intake does not

10. Music historian: Some critics lament the fact that impoverished postwar recording studios forced early bebop musicians to record extremely short solos, thus leaving a misleading record of their music. But these musicians' beautifully concise playing makes the recordings superb artistic works instead of mere representations of their live solos. Furthermore, the conciseness characteristic of early bebop musicians' recordings fostered a compactness in their subsequent live playing, which the playing of the next generation lacks.

The music historian's statements, if true, most strongly support which one of the following?

(A) Representations of live solos generally are not valuable artistic works.

(B) The difficult postwar recording conditions had some beneficial consequences for bebop.

(C) Short bebop recordings are always superior to longer ones.

(D) The music of the generation immediately following early bebop is of lower overall quality than early bebop.

(E) Musicians will not record extremely short solos unless difficult recording conditions force them to do so.

GO ON TO THE NEXT PAGE.

11. Recent studies indicate a correlation between damage to human chromosome number six and adult schizophrenia. We know, however, that there are people without damage to this chromosome who develop adult schizophrenia and that some people with damage to chromosome number six do not develop adult schizophrenia. So there is no causal connection between damage to human chromosome number six and adult schizophrenia.

Which one of the following most accurately describes a reasoning flaw in the argument above?

(A) The argument ignores the possibility that some but not all types of damage to chromosome number six lead to schizophrenia.

(B) The argument presumes, without providing evidence, that schizophrenia is caused solely by chromosomal damage.

(C) The argument makes a generalization based on an unrepresentative sample population.

(D) The argument mistakes a cause for an effect.

(E) The argument presumes, without providing warrant, that correlation implies causation.

12. City councilperson: Many city residents oppose the city art commission's proposed purchase of an unusual stone edifice, on the grounds that art critics are divided over whether the edifice really qualifies as art. But I argue that the purpose of art is to cause experts to debate ideas, including ideas about what constitutes art itself. Since the edifice has caused experts to debate what constitutes art itself, it does qualify as art.

Which one of the following, if assumed, enables the conclusion of the city councilperson's argument to be properly inferred?

(A) Nothing qualifies as art unless it causes debate among experts.

(B) If an object causes debate among experts, no expert can be certain whether that object qualifies as art.

(C) The purchase of an object that fulfills the purpose of art should not be opposed.

(D) Any object that fulfills the purpose of art qualifies as art.

(E) The city art commission should purchase the edifice if it qualifies as art.

13. It is a given that to be an intriguing person, one must be able to inspire the perpetual curiosity of others. Constantly broadening one's abilities and extending one's intellectual reach will enable one to inspire that curiosity. For such a perpetual expansion of one's mind makes it impossible to be fully comprehended, making one a constant mystery to others.

Which one of the following most accurately expresses the conclusion drawn in the argument above?

(A) To be an intriguing person, one must be able to inspire the perpetual curiosity of others.

(B) If one constantly broadens one's abilities and extends one's intellectual reach, one will be able to inspire the perpetual curiosity of others.

(C) If one's mind becomes impossible to fully comprehend, one will always be a mystery to others.

(D) To inspire the perpetual curiosity of others, one must constantly broaden one's abilities and extend one's intellectual reach.

(E) If one constantly broadens one's abilities and extends one's intellectual reach, one will always have curiosity.

14. Theater managers will not rent a film if they do not believe it will generate enough total revenue—including food-and-beverage concession revenue—to yield a profit. Therefore, since film producers want their films to be shown as widely as possible, they tend to make films that theater managers consider attractive to younger audiences.

Which one of the following is an assumption required by the argument?

(A) Adults consume less of the sort of foods and beverages sold at movie concession stands than do either children or adolescents.

(B) Movies of the kinds that appeal to younger audiences almost never also appeal to older audiences.

(C) Food-and-beverage concession stands in movie theaters are usually more profitable than the movies that are shown.

(D) Theater managers generally believe that a film that is attractive to younger audiences is more likely to be profitable than other films.

(E) Films that have an appeal to older audiences almost never generate a profit for theaters that show them.

GO ON TO THE NEXT PAGE.

15. Almost all advances in genetic research give rise to ethical dilemmas. Government is the exclusive source of funding for most genetic research; those projects not funded by government are funded solely by corporations. One or the other of these sources of funding is necessary for any genetic research.

If all the statements above are true, then which one of the following must be true?

(A)   Most advances in genetic research occur in projects funded by government rather than by corporations.

(B)   Most genetic research funded by government results in advances that give rise to ethical dilemmas.

(C)   At least some advances in genetic research occur in projects funded by corporations.

(D)   No ethical dilemmas resulting from advances in genetic research arise without government or corporate funding.

(E)   As long as government continues to fund genetic research, that research will give rise to ethical dilemmas.

16. Corporate businesses, like species, must adapt to survive. Businesses that are no longer efficient will become extinct. But sometimes a business cannot adapt without changing its core corporate philosophy. Hence, sometimes a business can survive only by becoming a different corporation.

Which one of the following is an assumption required by the argument?

(A)   No business can survive without changing its core corporate philosophy.

(B)   As a business becomes less efficient, it invariably surrenders its core corporate philosophy.

(C)   Different corporations have different core corporate philosophies.

(D)   If a business keeps its core corporate philosophy intact, it will continue to exist.

(E)   A business cannot change its core corporate philosophy without becoming a different corporation.

17. A survey taken ten years ago of residents of area L showed that although living conditions were slightly below their country's average, most residents of L reported general satisfaction with their living conditions. However, this year the same survey found that while living conditions are now about the same as the national average, most residents of L report general dissatisfaction with their living conditions.

Which one of the following, if true, would most help to resolve the apparent conflict between the results of the surveys described above?

(A)   Residents of area L typically value aspects of living conditions different from the aspects of living conditions that are valued by residents of adjacent areas.

(B)   Between the times that the two surveys were conducted, the average living conditions in L's country had substantially declined.

(C)   Optimal living conditions were established in the survey by taking into account governmental policies and public demands on three continents.

(D)   Living conditions in an area generally improve only if residents perceive their situation as somehow in need of improvement.

(E)   Ten years ago the residents of area L were not aware that their living conditions were below the national average.

GO ON TO THE NEXT PAGE.

18. Travel agent: Although most low-fare airlines have had few, if any, accidents, very few such airlines have been in existence long enough for their safety records to be reliably established. Major airlines, on the other hand, usually have long-standing records reliably indicating their degree of safety. Hence, passengers are safer on a major airline than on one of the newer low-fare airlines.

Of the following, which one is the criticism to which the reasoning in the travel agent's argument is most vulnerable?

(A) The argument fails to address adequately the possibility that the average major airline has had a total number of accidents as great as the average low-fare airline has had.

(B) The argument draws a general conclusion about how safe passengers are on different airlines on the basis of safety records that are each from too brief a period to adequately justify such a conclusion.

(C) The argument fails to consider the possibility that long-standing and reliable records documenting an airline's degree of safety may indicate that the airline is unsafe.

(D) The argument takes for granted that airlines that are the safest are also the most reliable in documenting their safety.

(E) The argument fails to address adequately the possibility that even airlines with long-standing, reliable records indicating their degree of safety are still likely to have one or more accidents.

19. Economist: Our economy's weakness is the direct result of consumers' continued reluctance to spend, which in turn is caused by factors such as high-priced goods and services. This reluctance is exacerbated by the fact that the average income is significantly lower than it was five years ago. Thus, even though it is not a perfect solution, if the government were to lower income taxes, the economy would improve.

Which one of the following is an assumption required by the economist's argument?

(A) Increasing consumer spending will cause prices for goods and services to decrease.

(B) If consumer spending increases, the average income will increase.

(C) If income taxes are not lowered, consumers' wages will decline even further.

(D) Consumers will be less reluctant to spend money if income taxes are lowered.

(E) Lowering income taxes will have no effect on government spending.

20. A person with a type B lipid profile is at much greater risk of heart disease than a person with a type A lipid profile. In an experiment, both type A volunteers and type B volunteers were put on a low-fat diet. The cholesterol levels of the type B volunteers soon dropped substantially, although their lipid profiles were unchanged. The type A volunteers, however, showed no benefit from the diet, and 40 percent of them actually shifted to type B profiles.

If the information above is true, which one of the following must also be true?

(A) In the experiment, most of the volunteers had their risk of heart disease reduced at least marginally as a result of having been put on the diet.

(B) People with type B lipid profiles have higher cholesterol levels, on average, than do people with type A lipid profiles.

(C) Apart from adopting the low-fat diet, most of the volunteers did not substantially change any aspect of their lifestyle that would have affected their cholesterol levels or lipid profiles.

(D) The reduction in cholesterol levels in the volunteers is solely responsible for the change in their lipid profiles.

(E) For at least some of the volunteers in the experiment, the risk of heart disease increased after having been put on the low-fat diet.

GO ON TO THE NEXT PAGE.

21. Columnist: Although there is and should be complete freedom of thought and expression, that does not mean that there is nothing wrong with exploiting depraved popular tastes for the sake of financial gain.

Which one of the following judgments conforms most closely to the principle cited by the columnist?

(A) The government should grant artists the right to create whatever works of art they want to create so long as no one considers those works to be depraved.

(B) People who produce depraved movies have the freedom to do so, but that means that they also have the freedom to refrain from doing so.

(C) There should be no laws restricting what books are published, but publishing books that pander to people with depraved tastes is not thereby morally acceptable.

(D) The public has the freedom to purchase whatever recordings are produced, but that does not mean that the government may not limit the production of recordings deemed to be depraved.

(E) One who advocates complete freedom of speech should not criticize others for saying things that he or she believes to exhibit depraved tastes.

22. When a society undergoes slow change, its younger members find great value in the advice of its older members. But when a society undergoes rapid change, young people think that little in the experience of their elders is relevant to them, and so do not value their advice. Thus, we may measure the rate at which a society is changing by measuring the amount of deference its younger members show to their elders.

Which one of the following is an assumption on which the argument depends?

(A) A society's younger members can often accurately discern whether that society is changing rapidly.

(B) How much deference young people show to their elders depends on how much of the elders' experience is practically useful to them.

(C) The deference young people show to their elders varies according to how much the young value their elders' advice.

(D) The faster a society changes, the less relevant the experience of older members of the society is to younger members.

(E) Young people value their elders' advice just insofar as the elders' experience is practically useful to them.

23. Politician: We should impose a tariff on imported fruit to make it cost consumers more than domestic fruit. Otherwise, growers from other countries who can grow better fruit more cheaply will put domestic fruit growers out of business. This will result in farmland's being converted to more lucrative industrial uses and the consequent vanishing of a unique way of life.

The politician's recommendation most closely conforms to which one of the following principles?

(A) A country should put its own economic interest over that of other countries.

(B) The interests of producers should always take precedence over those of consumers.

(C) Social concerns should sometimes take precedence over economic efficiency.

(D) A country should put the interests of its own citizens ahead of those of citizens of other countries.

(E) Government intervention sometimes creates more economic efficiency than free markets.

24. The Kiffer Forest Preserve, in the northernmost part of the Abbimac Valley, is where most of the bears in the valley reside. During the eight years that the main road through the preserve has been closed the preserve's bear population has nearly doubled. Thus, the valley's bear population will increase if the road is kept closed.

Which one of the following, if true, most undermines the argument?

(A) Most of the increase in the preserve's bear population over the past eight years is due to migration.

(B) Only some of the increase in the preserve's bear population over the past eight years is due to migration of bears from other parts of the Abbimac Valley.

(C) Only some of the increase in the preserve's bear population over the past eight years is due to migration of bears from outside the Abbimac Valley.

(D) The bear population in areas of the Abbimac Valley outside the Kiffer Forest Preserve has decreased over the past eight years.

(E) The bear population in the Abbimac Valley has remained about the same over the past eight years.

GO ON TO THE NEXT PAGE.

25. If a wig has any handmade components, it is more expensive than one with none. Similarly, a made-to-measure wig ranges from medium-priced to expensive. Handmade foundations are never found on wigs that do not use human hair. Furthermore, any wig that contains human hair should be dry-cleaned. So all made-to-measure wigs should be dry-cleaned.

The conclusion of the argument follows logically if which one of the following is assumed?

(A) Any wig whose price falls in the medium-priced to expensive range has a handmade foundation.
(B) If a wig's foundation is handmade, then it is more expensive than one whose foundation is not handmade.
(C) A wig that has any handmade components should be dry-cleaned.
(D) If a wig's foundation is handmade, then its price is at least in the medium range.
(E) Any wig that should be dry-cleaned has a foundation that is handmade.

26. Philosopher: Wolves do not tolerate an attack by one wolf on another if the latter wolf demonstrates submission by baring its throat. The same is true of foxes and domesticated dogs. So it would be erroneous to deny that animals have rights on the grounds that only human beings are capable of obeying moral rules.

The philosopher's argument proceeds by attempting to

(A) provide counterexamples to refute a premise on which a particular conclusion is based
(B) establish inductively that all animals possess some form of morality
(C) cast doubt on the principle that being capable of obeying moral rules is a necessary condition for having rights
(D) establish a claim by showing that the denial of that claim entails a logical contradiction
(E) provide evidence suggesting that the concept of morality is often applied too broadly

S T O P

IF YOU FINISH BEFORE TIME IS CALLED, YOU MAY CHECK YOUR WORK ON THIS SECTION ONLY.
DO NOT WORK ON ANY OTHER SECTION IN THE TEST.

SECTION II

Time—35 minutes

27 Questions

Directions: Each set of questions in this section is based on a single passage or a pair of passages. The questions are to be answered on the basis of what is <u>stated</u> or <u>implied</u> in the passage or pair of passages. For some of the questions, more than one of the choices could conceivably answer the question. However, you are to choose the <u>best</u> answer; that is, the response that most accurately and completely answers the question, and blacken the corresponding space on your answer sheet.

Traditional sources of evidence about ancient history are archaeological remains and surviving texts. Those investigating the crafts practiced by women in ancient times, however, often derive little information
(5) from these sources, and the archaeological record is particularly unavailing for the study of ancient textile production, as researchers are thwarted by the perishable nature of cloth. What shreds persisted through millennia were, until recently, often discarded
(10) by excavators as useless, as were loom weights, which appeared to be nothing more than blobs of clay. Ancient texts, meanwhile, rarely mention the creation of textiles; moreover, those references that do exist use archaic, unrevealing terminology. Yet despite these
(15) obstacles, researchers have learned a great deal about ancient textiles and those who made them, and also about how to piece together a whole picture from many disparate sources of evidence.
    Technological advances in the analysis of
(20) archaeological remains provide much more information than was previously available, especially about minute remains. Successful modern methods include radiocarbon dating, infrared photography for seeing through dirt without removing it, isotope
(25) "fingerprinting" for tracing sources of raw materials, and thin-layer chromatography for analyzing dyes. As if in preparation for such advances, the field of archaeology has also undergone an important philosophical revolution in the past century. Once little
(30) more than a self-serving quest for artifacts to stock museums and private collections, the field has transformed itself into a scientific pursuit of knowledge about past cultures. As part of this process, archaeologists adopted the fundamental precept of
(35) preserving all objects, even those that have no immediately discernible value. Thus in the 1970s two researchers found the oldest known complete garment, a 5,000-year-old linen shirt, among a tumbled heap of dirty linens that had been preserved as part of the well-
(40) known Petrie collection decades before anyone began to study the history of textiles.
    The history of textiles and of the craftswomen who produced them has also advanced on a different front: recreating the actual production of cloth.
(45) Reconstructing and implementing ancient production methods provides a valuable way of generating and checking hypotheses. For example, these techniques made it possible to confirm that the excavated pieces of clay once considered useless in fact functioned as loom
(50) weights. Similarly, scholars have until recently been

obliged to speculate as to which one of two statues of Athena, one large and one small, was adorned with a dress created by a group of Athenian women for a festival, as described in surviving texts. Because
(55) records show that it took nine months to produce the dress, scholars assumed it must have adorned the large statue. But by investigating the methods of production and the size of the looms used, researchers have ascertained that in fact a dress for the small statue
(60) would have taken nine months to produce.

1. Which one of the following most accurately expresses the main point of the passage?

(A) Archaeology is an expanding discipline that has transformed itself in response both to scientific advances and to changing cultural demands such as a recently increasing interest in women's history.

(B) A diversity of new approaches to the study of ancient textiles has enabled researchers to infer much about the history of textiles and their creators in the ancient world from the scant evidence that remains.

(C) Despite many obstacles, research into the textile production methods used by women in the ancient world has advanced over the past century to the point that archaeologists can now replicate ancient equipment and production techniques.

(D) Research into the history of textiles has spurred sweeping changes in the field of archaeology, from the application of advanced technology to the revaluation of ancient artifacts that were once deemed useless.

(E) Though researchers have verified certain theories about the history of textiles by using technological developments such as radiocarbon dating, most significant findings in this field have grown out of the reconstruction of ancient production techniques.

GO ON TO THE NEXT PAGE.

2. The author's attitude concerning the history of ancient textile production can most accurately be described as

(A) skeptical regarding the validity of some of the new hypotheses proposed by researchers

(B) doubtful that any additional useful knowledge can be generated given the nature of the evidence available

(C) impatient about the pace of research in light of the resources available

(D) optimistic that recent scholarly advances will attract increasing numbers of researchers

(E) satisfied that considerable progress is being made in this field

3. The passage indicates that the re-creation of ancient techniques was used in which one of the following?

(A) investigating the meanings of certain previously unintelligible technical terms in ancient texts

(B) tracing the sources of raw materials used in the production of certain fabrics

(C) constructing certain public museum displays concerning cloth-making

(D) verifying that a particular 5,000-year-old cloth was indeed a shirt

(E) exploring the issue of which of two statues of Athena was clothed with a particular garment

4. The author intends the term "traditional sources" (line 1) to exclude which one of the following?

(A) ancient clay objects that cannot be identified as pieces of pottery by the researchers who unearth them

(B) historically significant pieces of cloth discovered in the course of an excavation

(C) the oldest known complete garment, which was found among other pieces of cloth in a collection

(D) re-creations of looms from which inferences about ancient weaving techniques can be made

(E) ancient accounts of the adornment of a statue of Athena with a dress made by Athenian women

5. The passage as a whole functions primarily as

(A) a defense of the controversial methods adopted by certain researchers in a particular discipline

(B) a set of recommendations to guide future activities in a particular field of inquiry

(C) an account of how a particular branch of research has successfully coped with certain difficulties

(D) a rejection of some commonly held views about the methodologies of a certain discipline

(E) a summary of the hypotheses advanced by researchers who have used innovative methods of investigation

6. According to the passage, which one of the following was an element in the transformation of archaeology in the past century?

(A) an increased interest in the crafts practiced in the ancient world

(B) some archaeologists' adoption of textile conservation experts' preservation techniques

(C) innovative methods of restoring damaged artifacts

(D) the discovery of the oldest known complete garment

(E) archaeologists' policy of not discarding ancient objects that have no readily identifiable value

7. Which one of the following most accurately describes the function of the first paragraph in relation to the rest of the passage?

(A) A particularly difficult archaeological problem is described in order to underscore the significance of new methods used to resolve that problem, which are described in the following paragraphs.

(B) A previously neglected body of archaeological evidence is described in order to cast doubt on received views regarding ancient cultures developed from conventional sources of evidence, as described in the following paragraphs.

(C) The fruitfulness of new technologically based methods of analysis is described in order to support the subsequent argument that apparently insignificant archaeological remains ought to be preserved for possible future research.

(D) The findings of recent archaeological research are outlined as the foundation for a claim advanced in the following paragraphs that the role of women in ancient cultures has been underestimated by archaeologists.

(E) A recently developed branch of archaeological research is described as evidence for the subsequent argument that other, more established branches of archaeology should take advantage of new technologies in their research.

GO ON TO THE NEXT PAGE.

This passage was adapted from articles published in the 1990s.

The success that Nigerian-born computer scientist Philip Emeagwali (b. 1954) has had in designing computers that solve real-world problems has been fueled by his willingness to reach beyond established
(5) paradigms and draw inspiration for his designs from nature. In the 1980s, Emeagwali achieved breakthroughs in the design of parallel computer systems. Whereas single computers work sequentially, making one calculation at a time, computers
(10) connected in parallel can process calculations simultaneously. In 1989, Emeagwali pioneered the use of massively parallel computers that used a network of thousands of smaller computers to solve what is considered one of the most computationally difficult
(15) problems: predicting the flow of oil through the subterranean geologic formations that make up oil fields. Until that time, supercomputers had been used for oil field calculations, but because these supercomputers worked sequentially, they were too
(20) slow and inefficient to accurately predict such extremely complex movements.

To model oil field flow using a computer requires the simulation of the distribution of the oil at tens of thousands of locations throughout the field. At each
(25) location, hundreds of simultaneous calculations must be made at regular time intervals relating to such variables as temperature, direction of oil flow, viscosity, and pressure, as well as geologic properties of the basin holding the oil. In order to solve this
(30) problem, Emeagwali designed a massively parallel computer by using the Internet to connect to more than 65,000 smaller computers. One of the great difficulties of parallel computing is dividing up the tasks among the separate smaller computers so that
(35) they do not interfere with each other, and it was here that Emeagwali turned to natural processes for ideas, noting that tree species that survive today are those that, over the course of hundreds of millions of years, have developed branching patterns that have
(40) maximized the amount of sunlight gathered and the quantity of water and sap delivered. Emeagwali demonstrated that, for modeling certain phenomena such as subterranean oil flow, a network design based on the mathematical principle that underlies the
(45) branching structures of trees will enable a massively parallel computer to gather and broadcast the largest quantity of messages to its processing points in the shortest time.

In 1996 Emeagwali had another breakthrough
(50) when he presented the design for a massively parallel computer that he claims will be powerful enough to predict global weather patterns a century in advance. The computer's design is based on the geometry of bees' honeycombs, which use an extremely efficient

(55) three-dimensional spacing. Emeagwali believes that computer scientists in the future will increasingly look to nature for elegant solutions to complex technical problems. This paradigm shift, he asserts, will enable us to better understand the systems
(60) evolved by nature and, thereby, to facilitate the evolution of human technology.

8. Which one of the following most accurately expresses the main point of the passage?

(A) Emeagwali's establishment of new computational paradigms has enabled parallel computer systems to solve a wide array of real-world problems that supercomputers cannot solve.

(B) Emeagwali has shown that scientists' allegiance to established paradigms has until now prevented the solution of many real-world computational problems that could otherwise have been solved with little difficulty.

(C) Emeagwali's discovery of the basic mathematical principles underlying natural systems has led to a growing use of parallel computer systems to solve complex real-world computational problems.

(D) Emeagwali has designed parallel computer systems that are modeled on natural systems and that are aimed at solving real-world computational problems that would be difficult to solve with more traditional designs.

(E) The paradigm shift initiated by Emeagwali's computer designs has made it more likely that scientists will in the future look to systems evolved by nature to facilitate the evolution of human technology.

GO ON TO THE NEXT PAGE.

9. According to the passage, which one of the following is true?

(A) Emeagwali's breakthroughs in computer design have begun to make computers that work sequentially obsolete.

(B) Emeagwali's first breakthrough in computer design came in response to a request by an oil company.

(C) Emeagwali was the first to use a massively parallel computer to predict the flow of oil in oil fields.

(D) Emeagwali was the first computer scientist to use nature as a model for human technology.

(E) Emeagwali was the first to apply parallel processing to solving real-world problems.

10. The passage most strongly suggests that Emeagwali holds which one of the following views?

(A) Some natural systems have arrived at efficient solutions to problems that are analogous in significant ways to technical problems faced by computer scientists.

(B) Global weather is likely too complicated to be accurately predictable more than a few decades in advance.

(C) Most computer designs will in the future be inspired by natural systems.

(D) Massively parallel computers will eventually be practical enough to warrant their use even in relatively mundane computing tasks.

(E) The mathematical structure of branching trees is useful primarily for designing computer systems to predict the flow of oil through oil fields.

11. Which one of the following most accurately describes the function of the first two sentences of the second paragraph?

(A) They provide an example of an established paradigm that Emeagwali's work has challenged.

(B) They help explain why supercomputers are unable to accurately predict the movements of oil through underground geologic formations.

(C) They provide examples of a network design based on the mathematical principles underlying the branching structures of trees.

(D) They describe a mathematical model that Emeagwali used in order to understand a natural system.

(E) They provide specific examples of a paradigm shift that will help scientists understand certain systems evolved by nature.

12. Which one of the following, if true, would provide the most support for Emeagwali's prediction mentioned in lines 55–58?

(A) Until recently, computer scientists have had very limited awareness of many of the mathematical principles that have been shown to underlie a wide variety of natural processes.

(B) Some of the variables affecting global weather patterns have yet to be discovered by scientists who study these patterns.

(C) Computer designs for the prediction of natural phenomena tend to be more successful when those phenomena are not affected by human activities.

(D) Some of the mathematical principles underlying Emeagwali's model of oil field flow also underlie his designs for other massively parallel computer systems.

(E) Underlying the designs for many traditional technologies are mathematical principles of which the designers of those technologies were not explicitly aware.

13. It can be inferred from the passage that one of the reasons massively parallel computers had not been used to model oil field flow prior to 1989 is that

(A) supercomputers are sufficiently powerful to handle most computational problems, including most problems arising from oil production

(B) the possibility of using a network of smaller computers to solve computationally difficult problems had not yet been considered

(C) the general public was not yet aware of the existence or vast capabilities of the Internet

(D) oil companies had not yet perceived the need for modeling the flow of oil in subterranean fields

(E) smaller computers can interfere with one another when they are connected together in parallel to solve a computationally difficult problem

GO ON TO THE NEXT PAGE.

Proponents of the tangible-object theory of copyright argue that copyright and similar intellectual-property rights can be explained as logical extensions of the right to own concrete, tangible objects. This
(5) view depends on the claim that every copyrightable work can be manifested in some physical form, such as a manuscript or a videotape. It also accepts the premise that ownership of an object confers a number of rights on the owner, who may essentially do whatever he or
(10) she pleases with the object to the extent that this does not violate other people's rights. One may, for example, hide or display the object, copy it, or destroy it. One may also transfer ownership of it to another.

In creating a new and original object from
(15) materials that one owns, one becomes the owner of that object and thereby acquires all of the rights that ownership entails. But if the owner transfers ownership of the object, the full complement of rights is not necessarily transferred to the new owner; instead, the
(20) original owner may retain one or more of these rights. This notion of retained rights is common in many areas of law; for example, the seller of a piece of land may retain certain rights to the land in the form of easements or building restrictions. Applying the notion
(25) of retained rights to the domain of intellectual property, theorists argue that copyrighting a work secures official recognition of one's intention to retain certain rights to that work. Among the rights typically retained by the original producer of an object such as a literary
(30) manuscript or a musical score would be the right to copy the object for profit and the right to use it as a guide for the production of similar or analogous things—for example, a public performance of a musical score.

(35) According to proponents of the tangible-object theory, its chief advantage is that it justifies intellectual property rights without recourse to the widely accepted but problematic supposition that one can own abstract, intangible things such as ideas. But while this account
(40) seems plausible for copyrightable entities that do, in fact, have enduring tangible forms, it cannot accommodate the standard assumption that such evanescent things as live broadcasts of sporting events can be copyrighted. More importantly, it does not
(45) acknowledge that in many cases the work of conceiving ideas is more crucial and more valuable than that of putting them into tangible form. Suppose that a poet dictates a new poem to a friend, who writes it down on paper that the friend has supplied. The
(50) creator of the tangible object in this case is not the poet but the friend, and there would seem to be no ground for the poet's claiming copyright unless the poet can be said to already own the ideas expressed in the work.

14. Which one of the following most accurately expresses the main point of the passage?

(A)   Copyright and other intellectual-property rights can be explained as logical extensions of the right to own concrete objects.
(B)   Attempts to explain copyright and similar intellectual-property rights purely in terms of rights to ownership of physical objects are ultimately misguided.
(C)   Copyrighting a work amounts to securing official recognition of one's intention to retain certain rights to that work.
(D)   Explanations of copyright and other intellectual-property rights in terms of rights to ownership of tangible objects fail to consider the argument that ideas should be allowed to circulate freely.
(E)   Under the tangible-object theory of intellectual property, rights of ownership are straightforwardly applicable to both ideas and physical objects.

15. According to the passage, the theory that copyright and other intellectual-property rights can be construed as logical extensions of the right to own concrete, tangible objects depends on the claim that

(A)   any work entitled to intellectual-property protection can be expressed in physical form
(B)   only the original creator of an intellectual work can hold the copyright for that work
(C)   the work of putting ideas into tangible form is more crucial and more valuable than the work of conceiving those ideas
(D)   in a few cases, it is necessary to recognize the right to own abstract, intangible things
(E)   the owner of an item of intellectual property may legally destroy it

16. The passage most directly answers which one of the following questions?

(A)   Do proponents of the tangible-object theory of intellectual property advocate any changes in existing laws relating to copyright?
(B)   Do proponents of the tangible-object theory of intellectual property hold that ownership of anything besides real estate can involve retained rights?
(C)   Has the tangible-object theory of intellectual property influenced the ways in which copyright cases or other cases involving issues of intellectual property are decided in the courts?
(D)   Does existing copyright law provide protection against unauthorized copying of manuscripts and musical scores in cases in which their creators have not officially applied for copyright protection?
(E)   Are there standard procedures governing the transfer of intellectual property that are common to most legal systems?

GO ON TO THE NEXT PAGE.

17. Suppose an inventor describes an innovative idea for an invention to an engineer, who volunteers to draft specifications for a prototype and then produces the prototype using the engineer's own materials. Which one of the following statements would apply to this case under the tangible-object theory of intellectual property, as the author describes that theory?

(A) Only the engineer is entitled to claim the invention as intellectual property.

(B) Only the inventor is entitled to claim the invention as intellectual property.

(C) The inventor and the engineer are equally entitled to claim the invention as intellectual property.

(D) The engineer is entitled to claim the invention as intellectual property, but only if the inventor retains the right to all profits generated by the invention.

(E) The inventor is entitled to claim the invention as intellectual property, but only if the engineer retains the right to all profits generated by the invention.

18. Legal theorists supporting the tangible-object theory of intellectual property are most likely to believe which one of the following?

(A) A literary work cannot receive copyright protection unless it exists in an edition produced by an established publisher.

(B) Most legal systems explicitly rely on the tangible-object theory of intellectual property in order to avoid asserting that one can own abstract things.

(C) Copyright protects the right to copy for profit, but not the right to copy for other reasons.

(D) Some works deserving of copyright protection simply cannot be manifested as concrete, tangible objects.

(E) To afford patent protection for inventions, the law need not invoke the notion of inventors' ownership of abstract ideas.

19. The passage provides the most support for inferring which one of the following statements?

(A) In most transactions involving the transfer of non-intellectual property, at least some rights of ownership are retained by the seller.

(B) The notion of retained rights of ownership is currently applied to only those areas of law that do not involve intellectual property.

(C) The idea that ownership of the right to copy an item for profit can be transferred is compatible with a tangible-object theory of intellectual property.

(D) Ownership of intellectual property is sufficiently protected by the provisions that, under many legal systems, apply to ownership of material things such as land.

(E) Protection of computer programs under intellectual-property law is justifiable only if the programs are likely to be used as a guide for the production of similar or analogous programs.

20. It can be inferred that the author of the passage is most likely to believe which one of the following?

(A) Theorists who suggest that the notion of retained rights is applicable to intellectual property do not fully understand what it means to transfer ownership of property.

(B) If a work does not exist in a concrete, tangible form, there is no valid theoretical basis for claiming that it should have copyright protection.

(C) Under existing statutes, creators of original tangible works that have intellectual or artistic significance generally do not have the legal right to own the abstract ideas embodied in those works.

(D) An adequate theoretical justification of copyright would likely presuppose that a work's creator originally owns the ideas embodied in that work.

(E) It is common, but incorrect, to assume that such evanescent things as live broadcasts of sporting events can be copyrighted.

GO ON TO THE NEXT PAGE.

Passage A

In music, a certain complexity of sounds can be expected to have a positive effect on the listener. A single, pure tone is not that interesting to explore; a measure of intricacy is required to excite human
(5) curiosity. Sounds that are too complex or disorganized, however, tend to be overwhelming. We prefer some sort of coherence, a principle that connects the various sounds and makes them comprehensible.

In this respect, music is like human language.
(10) Single sounds are in most cases not sufficient to convey meaning in speech, whereas when put together in a sequence they form words and sentences. Likewise, if the tones in music are not perceived to be tied together sequentially or rhythmically—for
(15) example, in what is commonly called melody— listeners are less likely to feel any emotional connection or to show appreciation.

Certain music can also have a relaxing effect. The fact that such music tends to be continuous and
(20) rhythmical suggests a possible explanation for this effect. In a natural environment, danger tends to be accompanied by sudden, unexpected sounds. Thus, a background of constant noise suggests peaceful conditions; discontinuous sounds demand more
(25) attention. Even soft discontinuous sounds that we consciously realize do not signal danger can be disturbing—for example, the erratic dripping of a leaky tap. A continuous sound, particularly one that is judged to be safe, relaxes the brain.

Passage B

(30) There are certain elements within music, such as a change of melodic line or rhythm, that create expectations about the future development of the music. The expectation the listener has about the further course of musical events is a key determinant
(35) for the experience of "musical emotions." Music creates expectations that, if not immediately satisfied, create tension. Emotion is experienced in relation to the buildup and release of tension. The more elaborate the buildup of tension, the more intense the emotions
(40) that will be experienced. When resolution occurs, relaxation follows.

The interruption of the expected musical course, depending on one's personal involvement, causes the search for an explanation. This results from a
(45) "mismatch" between one's musical expectation and the actual course of the music. Negative emotions will be the result of an extreme mismatch between expectations and experience. Positive emotions result if the converse happens.
(50) When we listen to music, we take into account factors such as the complexity and novelty of the music. The degree to which the music sounds familiar determines whether the music is experienced as pleasurable or uncomfortable. The pleasure
(55) experienced is minimal when the music is entirely new to the listener, increases with increasing familiarity, and decreases again when the music is totally known.

Musical preference is based on one's desire to maintain a constant level of certain preferable
(60) emotions. As such, a trained listener will have a greater preference for complex melodies than will a naive listener, as the threshold for experiencing emotion is higher.

21. Which one of the following concepts is linked to positive musical experiences in both passages?

  (A) continuous sound
  (B) tension
  (C) language
  (D) improvisation
  (E) complexity

22. The passages most strongly suggest that both are targeting an audience that is interested in which one of the following?

  (A) the theoretical underpinnings of how music is composed
  (B) the nature of the conceptual difference between music and discontinuous sound
  (C) the impact music can have on human emotional states
  (D) the most effective techniques for teaching novices to appreciate complex music
  (E) the influence music has had on the development of spoken language

23. Which one of the following describes a preference that is most analogous to the preference mentioned in the first paragraph of passage A?

  (A) the preference of some people for falling asleep to white noise, such as the sound of an electric fan
  (B) the preference of many moviegoers for movies with plots that are clear and easy to follow
  (C) the preference of many diners for restaurants that serve large portions
  (D) the preference of many young listeners for fast music over slower music
  (E) the preference of most children for sweet foods over bitter foods

GO ON TO THE NEXT PAGE.

24. Which one of the following most accurately expresses the main point of passage B?

(A) The type of musical emotion experienced by a listener is determined by the level to which the listener's expectations are satisfied.

(B) Trained listeners are more able to consciously manipulate their own emotional experiences of complex music than are naive listeners.

(C) If the development of a piece of music is greatly at odds with the listener's musical expectations, then the listener will experience negative emotions.

(D) Listeners can learn to appreciate changes in melodic line and other musical complexities.

(E) Music that is experienced by listeners as relaxing usually produces a buildup and release of tension in those listeners.

25. Which one of the following most undermines the explanation provided in passage A for the relaxing effect that some music has on listeners?

(A) The musical traditions of different cultures vary greatly in terms of the complexity of the rhythms they employ.

(B) The rhythmic structure of a language is determined in part by the pattern of stressed syllables in the words and sentences of the language.

(C) Many people find the steady and rhythmic sound of a rocking chair to be very unnerving.

(D) The sudden interruption of the expected development of a melody tends to interfere with listeners' perception of the melody as coherent.

(E) Some of the most admired contemporary composers write music that is notably simpler than is most of the music written in previous centuries.

26. Which one of the following would be most appropriate as a title for each of the passages?

(A) "The Biological Underpinnings of Musical Emotions"

(B) "The Psychology of Listener Response to Music"

(C) "How Music Differs from Other Art Forms"

(D) "Cultural Patterns in Listeners' Responses to Music"

(E) "How Composers Convey Meaning Through Music"

27. It can be inferred that both authors would be likely to agree with which one of the following statements?

(A) The more complex a piece of music, the more it is likely to be enjoyed by most listeners.

(B) More knowledgeable listeners tend to prefer music that is discontinuous and unpredictable.

(C) The capacity of music to elicit strong emotional responses from listeners is the central determinant of its artistic value.

(D) Music that lacks a predictable course is unlikely to cause a listener to feel relaxed.

(E) Music that changes from soft to loud is perceived as disturbing and unpleasant by most listeners.

S T O P

IF YOU FINISH BEFORE TIME IS CALLED, YOU MAY CHECK YOUR WORK ON THIS SECTION ONLY.
DO NOT WORK ON ANY OTHER SECTION IN THE TEST.

SECTION III

Time—35 minutes

23 Questions

Directions: Each group of questions in this section is based on a set of conditions. In answering some of the questions, it may be useful to draw a rough diagram. Choose the response that most accurately and completely answers each question and blacken the corresponding space on your answer sheet.

Questions 1–6

Historical records show that over the course of five consecutive years—601, 602, 603, 604, and 605—a certain emperor began construction of six monuments: F, G, H, L, M, and S. A historian is trying to determine the years in which the individual monuments were begun. The following facts have been established:

L was begun in a later year than G, but in an earlier year than F.
H was begun no earlier than 604.
M was begun earlier than 604.
Two of the monuments were begun in 601, and no other monument was begun in the same year as any of the other monuments.

1. Which one of the following could be an accurate matching of monuments to the years in which they were begun?

   (A) 601: G;   602: L, S;   603: M;   604: H;   605: F
   (B) 601: G, M;   602: L;   603: H;   604: S;   605: F
   (C) 601: G, M;   602: S;   603: F;   604: L;   605: H
   (D) 601: G, S;   602: L;   603: F;   604: M;   605: H
   (E) 601: G, S;   602: L;   603: M;   604: H;   605: F

2. What is the latest year in which L could have been begun?

   (A) 601
   (B) 602
   (C) 603
   (D) 604
   (E) 605

3. The years in which each of the monuments were begun can be completely determined if which one of the following is discovered to be true?

   (A) F was begun in 603.
   (B) G was begun in 602.
   (C) H was begun in 605.
   (D) M was begun in 602.
   (E) S was begun in 604.

4. Which one of the following must be true?

   (A) F was begun in a later year than M.
   (B) F was begun in a later year than S.
   (C) H was begun in a later year than F.
   (D) H was begun in a later year than S.
   (E) M was begun in a later year than G.

5. L must be the monument that was begun in 602 if which one of the following is true?

   (A) F was begun in 605.
   (B) G was begun in 601.
   (C) H was begun in 604.
   (D) M was begun in 601.
   (E) S was begun in 603.

6. If M was begun in a later year than L, then which one of the following could be true?

   (A) F was begun in 603.
   (B) G was begun in 602.
   (C) H was begun in 605.
   (D) L was begun in 603.
   (E) S was begun in 604.

GO ON TO THE NEXT PAGE.

Questions 7–12

A company organizing on-site day care consults with a group of parents composed exclusively of volunteers from among the seven employees—Felicia, Leah, Masatomo, Rochelle, Salman, Terry, and Veena—who have become parents this year. The composition of the volunteer group must be consistent with the following:

If Rochelle volunteers, then so does Masatomo.
If Masatomo volunteers, then so does Terry.
If Salman does not volunteer, then Veena volunteers.
If Rochelle does not volunteer, then Leah volunteers.
If Terry volunteers, then neither Felicia nor Veena volunteers.

7. Which one of the following could be a complete and accurate list of the volunteers?

(A) Felicia, Salman
(B) Masatomo, Rochelle
(C) Leah, Salman, Terry
(D) Salman, Rochelle, Veena
(E) Leah, Salman, Terry, Veena

8. If Veena volunteers, then which one of the following could be true?

(A) Felicia and Rochelle also volunteer.
(B) Felicia and Salman also volunteer.
(C) Leah and Masatomo also volunteer.
(D) Leah and Terry also volunteer.
(E) Salman and Terry also volunteer.

9. If Terry does not volunteer, then which one of the following CANNOT be true?

(A) Felicia volunteers.
(B) Leah volunteers.
(C) Rochelle volunteers.
(D) Salman volunteers.
(E) Veena volunteers.

10. If Masatomo volunteers, then which one of the following could be true?

(A) Felicia volunteers.
(B) Leah volunteers.
(C) Veena volunteers.
(D) Salman does not volunteer.
(E) Terry does not volunteer.

11. If Felicia volunteers, then which one of the following must be true?

(A) Leah volunteers.
(B) Salman volunteers.
(C) Veena does not volunteer.
(D) Exactly three of the employees volunteer.
(E) Exactly four of the employees volunteer.

12. Which one of the following pairs of employees is such that at least one member of the pair volunteers?

(A) Felicia and Terry
(B) Leah and Masatomo
(C) Leah and Veena
(D) Rochelle and Salman
(E) Salman and Terry

GO ON TO THE NEXT PAGE.

Flyhigh Airlines owns exactly two planes: P and Q. Getaway Airlines owns exactly three planes: R, S, T. On Sunday, each plane makes exactly one flight, according to the following conditions:

Only one plane departs at a time.

Each plane makes either a domestic or an international flight, but not both.

Plane P makes an international flight.

Planes Q and R make domestic flights.

All international flights depart before any domestic flight.

Any Getaway domestic flight departs before Flyhigh's domestic flight.

13. Which one of the following could be the order, from first to last, in which the five planes depart?

(A)   P, Q, R, S, T
(B)   P, Q, T, S, R
(C)   P, S, T, Q, R
(D)   P, S, T, R, Q
(E)   T, S, R, P, Q

14. The plane that departs second could be any one of exactly how many of the planes?

(A)   one
(B)   two
(C)   three
(D)   four
(E)   five

15. If plane S departs sometime before plane P, then which one of the following must be false?

(A)   Plane S departs first.
(B)   Plane S departs third.
(C)   Plane T departs second.
(D)   Plane T departs third.
(E)   Plane T departs fourth.

16. Which one of the following must be true?

(A)   Plane P departs first.
(B)   Plane Q departs last.
(C)   Plane R departs second.
(D)   Plane S departs first.
(E)   Plane T departs fourth.

17. If plane S departs third, then each of the following can be true EXCEPT:

(A)   Plane R departs sometime before plane S and sometime before plane T.
(B)   Plane S departs sometime before plane Q and sometime before plane T.
(C)   Plane S departs sometime before plane R and sometime before plane T.
(D)   Plane T departs sometime before plane P and sometime before plane S.
(E)   Plane T departs sometime before plane R and sometime before plane S.

GO ON TO THE NEXT PAGE.

Questions 18–23

A student is choosing courses to take during a summer school session. Each summer school student must take at least three courses from among the following seven: history, linguistics, music, physics, statistics, theater, and writing. The summer school schedule restricts the courses a student can take in the following ways:

If history is taken, then neither statistics nor music can be taken.

If music is taken, then neither physics nor theater can be taken.

If writing is taken, then neither physics nor statistics can be taken.

18. The student could take which one of the following groups of courses during the summer school session?

   (A)   history, linguistics, and statistics
   (B)   history, music, and physics
   (C)   history, physics, and theater
   (D)   linguistics, physics, theater, and writing
   (E)   music, theater, and writing

19. What is the maximum number of courses the student could take during the summer school session?

   (A)   seven
   (B)   six
   (C)   five
   (D)   four
   (E)   three

20. If the student takes neither physics nor writing, then it could be true that the student also takes neither

   (A)   history nor linguistics
   (B)   history nor music
   (C)   history nor statistics
   (D)   linguistics nor music
   (E)   statistics nor theater

21. If the student takes music, then which one of the following must the student also take?

   (A)   writing
   (B)   theater
   (C)   statistics
   (D)   physics
   (E)   linguistics

22. The student must take one or the other or both of

   (A)   history or statistics
   (B)   linguistics or theater
   (C)   linguistics or writing
   (D)   music or physics
   (E)   theater or writing

23. Which one of the following, if substituted for the restriction that if music is taken, then neither physics nor theater can be taken, would have the same effect in determining which courses the student can take?

   (A)   If music is taken, then either statistics or writing must also be taken.
   (B)   The only courses that are eligible to be taken together with music are linguistics, statistics, and writing.
   (C)   The only courses that are eligible to be taken together with physics are history and linguistics.
   (D)   The only courses that are eligible to be taken together with theater are history, linguistics, and writing.
   (E)   If both physics and theater are taken, then music cannot be taken.

S T O P

IF YOU FINISH BEFORE TIME IS CALLED, YOU MAY CHECK YOUR WORK ON THIS SECTION ONLY.
DO NOT WORK ON ANY OTHER SECTION IN THE TEST.

SECTION IV

Time—35 minutes

25 Questions

<u>Directions</u>: The questions in this section are based on the reasoning contained in brief statements or passages. For some questions, more than one of the choices could conceivably answer the question. However, you are to choose the <u>best</u> answer; that is, the response that most accurately and completely answers the question. You should not make assumptions that are by commonsense standards implausible, superfluous, or incompatible with the passage. After you have chosen the best answer, blacken the corresponding space on your answer sheet.

1. Automated flight technology can guide an aircraft very reliably, from navigation to landing. Yet this technology, even when functioning correctly, is not a perfect safeguard against human error.

   Which one of the following, if true, most helps to explain the situation described above?

   (A) Automated flight technology does not always function correctly.
   (B) Smaller aircraft do not always have their automated flight technology updated regularly.
   (C) If a plane's automated flight technology malfunctions, crew members have to operate the plane manually.
   (D) Some airplane crashes are due neither to human error nor to malfunction of automated flight technology.
   (E) Automated flight technology invariably executes exactly the commands that humans give it.

2. To keep one's hands warm during the winter, one never needs gloves or mittens. One can always keep one's hands warm simply by putting on an extra layer of clothing, such as a thermal undershirt or a sweater. After all, keeping one's vital organs warm can keep one's hands warm as well.

   Which one of the following, if true, most weakens the argument?

   (A) Maintaining the temperature of your hands is far less important, physiologically, than maintaining the temperature of your torso.
   (B) Several layers of light garments will keep one's vital organs warmer than will one or two heavy garments.
   (C) Wearing an extra layer of clothing will not keep one's hands warm at temperatures low enough to cause frostbite.
   (D) Keeping one's hands warm by putting on an extra layer of clothing is less effective than turning up the heat.
   (E) The physical effort required to put on an extra layer of clothing does not stimulate circulation enough to warm your hands.

3. The reason music with a simple recurring rhythm exerts a strong primordial appeal is that it reminds us of the womb environment. After all, the first sound heard within the womb is the comforting sound of the mother's regular heartbeat. So in taking away from us the warmth and security of the womb, birth also takes away a primal and constant source of comfort. Thus it is extremely natural that in seeking sensations of warmth and security throughout life, people would be strongly drawn toward simple recurring rhythmic sounds.

   Which one of the following most accurately expresses the main conclusion drawn in the reasoning above?

   (A) The explanation of the strong primordial appeal of music with a simple recurring rhythm is that it reminds us of the womb environment.
   (B) The comforting sound of the mother's regular heartbeat is the first sound that is heard inside the womb.
   (C) Birth deprives us of a primal and constant source of comfort when it takes away the warmth and security of the womb.
   (D) People seek sensations of warmth and security throughout life because birth takes away the warmth and security of the womb.
   (E) The comforting sound of the mother's regular heartbeat is a simple recurring rhythmic sound.

GO ON TO THE NEXT PAGE.

4. Linguist: Most people can tell whether a sequence of words in their own dialect is grammatical. Yet few people who can do so are able to specify the relevant grammatical rules.

Which one of the following best illustrates the principle underlying the linguist's statements?

(A)   Some people are able to write cogent and accurate narrative descriptions of events. But these people are not necessarily also capable of composing emotionally moving and satisfying poems.

(B)   Engineers who apply the principles of physics to design buildings and bridges must know a great deal more than do the physicists who discover these principles.

(C)   Some people are able to tell whether any given piece of music is a waltz. But the majority of these people cannot state the defining characteristics of a waltz.

(D)   Those travelers who most enjoy their journeys are not always those most capable of vividly describing the details of those journeys to others.

(E)   Quite a few people know the rules of chess, but only a small number of them can play chess very well.

5. Company president: For the management consultant position, we shall interview only those applicants who have worked for management consulting firms generally recognized as in the top 1 percent of firms worldwide. When we finally select somebody, then, we can be sure to have selected one of the best management consultants available.

The company president's reasoning is most vulnerable to criticism on the grounds that it

(A)   takes for granted that only the best management consultants have worked for the top management consulting firms

(B)   generalizes from too small a sample of management consulting firms worldwide

(C)   takes for granted that if something is true of each member of a collection, then it is also true of the collection as a whole

(D)   presumes, without providing warrant, that persons who have worked for the top companies will accept a job offer

(E)   presumes, without providing justification, that highly competent management consultants are highly competent at every task

6. Beginners typically decide each chess move by considering the consequences. Expert players, in contrast, primarily use pattern-recognition techniques. That is, such a player recognizes having been in a similar position before and makes a decision based on information recalled about the consequences of moves chosen on that prior occasion.

Which one of the following is most strongly supported by the information above?

(A)   Beginning chess players are better at thinking through the consequences of chess moves than experts are.

(B)   A beginning chess player should use pattern-recognition techniques when deciding what move to make.

(C)   One's chess skills will improve only if one learns to use pattern-recognition techniques.

(D)   In playing chess, an expert player relies crucially on his or her memory.

(E)   Any chess player who played other games that require pattern-recognition skills would thereby improve his or her chess skills.

7. Farmer: Because water content is what makes popcorn pop, the kernels must dry at just the right speed to trap the correct amount of water. The best way to achieve this effect is to have the sun dry the corn while the corn is still in the field, but I always dry the ears on a screen in a warm, dry room.

Which one of the following, if true, most helps to resolve the apparent discrepancy between the farmer's theory and practice?

(A)   The region in which the farmer grows popcorn experiences a long, cloudy season that begins shortly before the popcorn in fields would begin to dry.

(B)   Leaving popcorn to dry on its stalks in the field is the least expensive method of drying it.

(C)   Drying popcorn on its stalks in the field is only one of several methods that allow the kernels' water content to reach acceptable levels.

(D)   When popcorn does not dry sufficiently, it will still pop, but it will take several minutes to do so, even under optimal popping conditions.

(E)   If popcorn is allowed to dry too much, it will not pop.

GO ON TO THE NEXT PAGE.

8. Factory manager: One reason the automobile parts this factory produces are expensive is that our manufacturing equipment is outdated and inefficient. Our products would be more competitively priced if we were to refurbish the factory completely with new, more efficient equipment. Therefore, since to survive in today's market we have to make our products more competitively priced, we must completely refurbish the factory in order to survive.

The reasoning in the factory manager's argument is flawed because this argument

(A) fails to recognize that the price of a particular commodity can change over time

(B) shifts without justification from treating something as one way of achieving a goal to treating it as the only way of achieving that goal

(C) argues that one thing is the cause of another when the evidence given indicates that the second thing may in fact be the cause of the first

(D) recommends a solution to a problem without first considering any possible causes of that problem

(E) fails to make a definite recommendation and instead merely suggests that some possible course of action might be effective

9. Two months ago a major shipment of pythons arrived from Africa, resulting in a great number of inexpensive pythons in pet stores. Anyone interested in buying a python, however, should beware: many pythons hatched in Africa are afflicted with a deadly liver disease. Although a few pythons recently hatched in North America have this disease, a much greater proportion of African-hatched pythons have it. The disease is difficult to detect in its early stages, and all pythons die within six months of contracting the disease.

Which one of the following statements can be properly inferred from the statements above?

(A) Some pythons hatched in North America may appear fine but will die within six months as a result of the liver disease.

(B) Pythons that hatch in Africa are more susceptible to the liver disease than are pythons that hatch in North America.

(C) Any python that has not died by the age of six months does not have the liver disease.

(D) The pythons are inexpensively priced because many of them suffer from the liver disease.

(E) Pythons hatched in neither Africa nor North America are not afflicted with the liver disease.

10. Nutritionists believe that a person's daily requirement for vitamins can readily be met by eating five servings of fruits and vegetables daily. However, most people eat far less than this. Thus, most people need to take vitamin pills.

Which one of the following statements, if true, most seriously weakens the argument?

(A) Even five servings of fruits and vegetables a day is insufficient unless the intake is varied to ensure that different vitamins are consumed.

(B) Certain commonly available fruits and vegetables contain considerably more nutrients than others.

(C) Nutritionists sometimes disagree on how much of a fruit or vegetable constitutes a complete serving.

(D) Many commonly consumed foods that are neither fruits nor vegetables are fortified by manufacturers with the vitamins found in fruits and vegetables.

(E) Fruits and vegetables are also important sources of fiber, in forms not found in vitamin pills.

11. Researcher: This fall I returned to a research site to recover the armadillos I had tagged there the previous spring. Since a large majority of the armadillos I recaptured were found within a few hundred yards of the location of their tagging last spring, I concluded that armadillos do not move rapidly into new territories.

Which one of the following is an assumption required by the researcher's argument?

(A) Of the armadillos living in the area of the tagging site last spring, few were able to avoid being tagged by the researcher.

(B) Most of the armadillos tagged the previous spring were not recaptured during the subsequent fall.

(C) Predators did not kill any of the armadillos that had been tagged the previous spring.

(D) The tags identifying the armadillos cannot be removed by the armadillos, either by accident or deliberately.

(E) A large majority of the recaptured armadillos did not move to a new territory in the intervening summer and then move back to the old territory by the fall.

GO ON TO THE NEXT PAGE.

12. Sahira: To make a living from their art, artists of great potential would have to produce work that would gain widespread popular acclaim, instead of their best work. That is why governments are justified in subsidizing artists.

Rahima: Your argument for subsidizing art depends on claiming that to gain widespread popular acclaim, artists must produce something other than their best work; but this need not be true.

In her argument, Rahima

(A) disputes an implicit assumption of Sahira's
(B) presents independent support for Sahira's argument
(C) accepts Sahira's conclusion, but for reasons different from those given by Sahira
(D) uses Sahira's premises to reach a conclusion different from that reached by Sahira
(E) argues that a standard that she claims Sahira uses is self-contradictory

13. Adult frogs are vulnerable to dehydration because of their highly permeable skins. Unlike large adult frogs, small adult frogs have such a low ratio of body weight to skin surface area that they cannot survive in arid climates. The animals' moisture requirements constitute the most important factor determining where frogs can live in the Yucatán peninsula, which has an arid climate in the north and a wet climate in the south.

The information above most strongly supports which one of the following conclusions about frogs in the Yucatán peninsula?

(A) Large adult frogs cannot coexist with small adult frogs in the wet areas.
(B) Frogs living in wet areas weigh more on average than frogs in the arid areas.
(C) Large adult frogs can live in more of the area than small adult frogs can.
(D) Fewer small adult frogs live in the south than do large adult frogs.
(E) Small adult frogs in the south have less permeable skins than small adult frogs in the north.

14. Editorial: A recent survey shows that 77 percent of people feel that crime is increasing and that 87 percent feel the judicial system should be handing out tougher sentences. Therefore, the government must firmly address the rising crime rate.

The reasoning in the editorial's argument is most vulnerable to criticism on the grounds that the argument

(A) appeals to survey results that are inconsistent because they suggest that more people are concerned about the sentencing of criminals than are concerned about crime itself
(B) presumes, without providing justification, that there is a correlation between criminal offenders being treated leniently and a high crime rate
(C) fails to consider whether other surveys showing different results have been conducted over the years
(D) fails to distinguish between the crime rate's actually rising and people's believing that the crime rate is rising
(E) presumes, without providing justification, that tougher sentences are the most effective means of alleviating the crime problem

15. Proofs relying crucially on computers provide less certainty than do proofs not requiring computers. Human cognition alone cannot verify computer-dependent proofs; such proofs can never provide the degree of certainty that attends our judgments concerning, for instance, simple arithmetical facts, which can be verified by human calculation. Of course, in these cases one often uses electronic calculators, but here the computer is a convenience rather than a supplement to human cognition.

The statements above, if true, most strongly support which one of the following?

(A) Only if a proof's result is arrived at without the help of a computer can one judge with any degree of certainty that the proof is correct.
(B) We can never be completely sure that proofs relying crucially on computers do not contain errors that humans do not detect.
(C) Whenever a computer replaces human calculation in a proof, the degree of certainty provided by the proof is reduced.
(D) If one can corroborate something by human calculation, one can be completely certain of it.
(E) It is impossible to supplement the cognitive abilities of humans by means of artificial devices such as computers.

GO ON TO THE NEXT PAGE.

16. Madden: Industrialists address problems by simplifying them, but in farming that strategy usually leads to oversimplification. For example, industrialists see water retention and drainage as different and opposite functions—that good topsoil both drains and retains water is a fact alien to industrial logic. To facilitate water retention, they use a terrace or a dam; to facilitate drainage, they use drain tile, a ditch, or a subsoiler. More farming problems are created than solved when agriculture is the domain of the industrialist, not of the farmer.

The situation as Madden describes it best illustrates which one of the following propositions?

(A) The handling of water drainage and retention is the most important part of good farming.
(B) The problems of farming should be viewed in all their complexity.
(C) Farmers are better than anyone else at solving farming problems.
(D) Industrial solutions for problems in farming should never be sought.
(E) The approach to problem solving typical of industrialists is fundamentally flawed.

17. Critic: Works of modern literature cannot be tragedies as those of ancient playwrights and storytellers were unless their protagonists are seen as possessing nobility, which endures through the calamities that befall one. In an age that no longer takes seriously the belief that human endeavors are governed by fate, it is therefore impossible for a contemporary work of literature to be a tragedy.

Which one of the following is an assumption required by the critic's argument?

(A) Whether or not a work of literature is a tragedy should not depend on characteristics of its audience.
(B) The belief that human endeavors are governed by fate is false.
(C) Most plays that were once classified as tragedies were misclassified.
(D) Those whose endeavors are not regarded as governed by fate will not be seen as possessing nobility.
(E) If an ignoble character in a work of literature endures through a series of misfortunes, that work of literature is not a tragedy.

18. Despite the efforts of a small minority of graduate students at one university to unionize, the majority of graduate students there remain unaware of the attempt. Most of those who are aware believe that a union would not represent their interests or that, if it did, it would not effectively pursue them. Thus, the graduate students at the university should not unionize, since the majority of them obviously disapprove of the attempt.

The reasoning in the argument is most vulnerable to criticism on the grounds that the argument

(A) tries to establish a conclusion simply on the premise that the conclusion agrees with a long-standing practice
(B) fails to exclude alternative explanations for why some graduate students disapprove of unionizing
(C) presumes that simply because a majority of a population is unaware of something, it must not be a good idea
(D) ignores the possibility that although a union might not effectively pursue graduate student interests, there are other reasons for unionizing
(E) blurs the distinction between active disapproval and mere lack of approval

19. Anyone who believes in democracy has a high regard for the wisdom of the masses. Griley, however, is an elitist who believes that any artwork that is popular is unlikely to be good. Thus, Griley does not believe in democracy.

The conclusion follows logically if which one of the following is assumed?

(A) Anyone who believes that an artwork is unlikely to be good if it is popular is an elitist.
(B) Anyone who believes that if an artwork is popular it is unlikely to be good does not have a high regard for the wisdom of the masses.
(C) If Griley is not an elitist, then he has a high regard for the wisdom of the masses.
(D) Anyone who does not have a high regard for the wisdom of the masses is an elitist who believes that if an artwork is popular it is unlikely to be good.
(E) Unless Griley believes in democracy, Griley does not have a high regard for the wisdom of the masses.

GO ON TO THE NEXT PAGE.

20. A recent study confirmed that salt intake tends to increase blood pressure and found that, as a result, people with high blood pressure who significantly cut their salt intake during the study had lower blood pressure by the end of the study. However, it was also found that some people who had very high salt intake both before and throughout the study maintained very low blood pressure.

Which one of the following, if true, contributes the most to an explanation of the results of the study?

(A) Study participants with high blood pressure who cut their salt intake only slightly during the study did not have significantly lower blood pressure by the end of the study.

(B) Salt intake is only one of several dietary factors associated with high blood pressure.

(C) For most people who have high blood pressure, reducing salt intake is not the most effective dietary change they can make to reduce their blood pressure.

(D) At the beginning of the study, some people who had very low salt intake also had very high blood pressure.

(E) Persons suffering from abnormally low blood pressure have heightened salt cravings, which ensure that their blood pressure does not drop too low.

21. The odds of winning any major lottery jackpot are extremely slight. However, the very few people who do win major jackpots receive a great deal of attention from the media. Thus, since most people come to have at least some awareness of events that receive extensive media coverage, it is likely that many people greatly overestimate the odds of their winning a major jackpot.

Which one of the following is an assumption on which the argument depends?

(A) Most people who overestimate the likelihood of winning a major jackpot do so at least in part because media coverage of other people who have won major jackpots downplays the odds against winning such a jackpot.

(B) Very few people other than those who win major jackpots receive a great deal of attention from the media.

(C) If it were not for media attention, most people who purchase lottery tickets would not overestimate their chances of winning a jackpot.

(D) Becoming aware of individuals who have won a major jackpot leads at least some people to incorrectly estimate their own chances of winning such a jackpot.

(E) At least some people who are heavily influenced by the media do not believe that the odds of their winning a major jackpot are significant.

GO ON TO THE NEXT PAGE.

22. A book tour will be successful if it is well publicized and the author is an established writer. Julia is an established writer, and her book tour was successful. So her book tour must have been well publicized.

Which one of the following exhibits a pattern of flawed reasoning most closely parallel to the pattern of flawed reasoning exhibited by the argument above?

(A) This recipe will turn out only if one follows it exactly and uses high-quality ingredients. Arthur followed the recipe exactly and it turned out. Thus, Arthur must have used high-quality ingredients.

(B) If a computer has the fastest microprocessor and the most memory available, it will meet Aletha's needs this year. This computer met Aletha's needs last year. So it must have had the fastest microprocessor and the most memory available last year.

(C) If cacti are kept in the shade and watered more than twice weekly, they will die. This cactus was kept in the shade, and it is now dead. Therefore, it must have been watered more than twice weekly.

(D) A house will suffer from dry rot and poor drainage only if it is built near a high water table. This house suffers from dry rot and has poor drainage. Thus, it must have been built near a high water table.

(E) If one wears a suit that has double vents and narrow lapels, one will be fashionably dressed. The suit that Joseph wore to dinner last night had double vents and narrow lapels, so Joseph must have been fashionably dressed.

23. Eight large craters run in a long straight line across a geographical region. Although some of the craters contain rocks that have undergone high-pressure shocks characteristic of meteorites slamming into Earth, these shocks could also have been caused by extreme volcanic events. Because of the linearity of the craters, it is very unlikely that some of them were caused by volcanoes and others were caused by meteorites. Thus, since the craters are all different ages, they were probably caused by volcanic events rather than meteorites.

Which one of the following statements, if true, would most strengthen the argument?

(A) A similar but shorter line of craters that are all the same age is known to have been caused by volcanic activity.

(B) No known natural cause would likely account for eight meteorite craters of different ages forming a straight line.

(C) There is no independent evidence of either meteorites or volcanic activity in the region where the craters are located.

(D) There is no independent evidence of a volcanic event strong enough to have created the high-pressure shocks that are characteristic of meteorites slamming into Earth.

(E) No known single meteor shower has created exactly eight impact craters that form a straight line.

GO ON TO THE NEXT PAGE.

24. The genuine creative genius is someone who is dissatisfied with merely habitual assent to widely held beliefs; thus these rare innovators tend to anger the majority. Those who are dissatisfied with merely habitual assent to widely held beliefs tend to seek out controversy, and controversy seekers enjoy demonstrating the falsehood of popular viewpoints.

The conclusion of the argument follows logically if which one of the following is assumed?

(A) People become angry when they are dissatisfied with merely habitual assent to widely held beliefs.

(B) People who enjoy demonstrating the falsehood of popular viewpoints anger the majority.

(C) People tend to get angry with individuals who hold beliefs not held by a majority of people.

(D) People who anger the majority enjoy demonstrating the falsehood of popular viewpoints.

(E) People who anger the majority are dissatisfied with merely habitual assent to widely held beliefs.

25. Claude: When I'm having lunch with job candidates, I watch to see if they salt their food without first tasting it. If they do, I count that against them, because they're making decisions based on inadequate information.

Larissa: That's silly. It's perfectly reasonable for me to wear a sweater whenever I go into a supermarket, because I already know supermarkets are always too cool inside to suit me. And I never open a credit card offer that comes in the mail, because I already know that no matter how low its interest rate may be, it will never be worthwhile for me.

The two analogies that Larissa offers can most reasonably be interpreted as invoking which one of the following principles to criticize Claude's policy?

(A) In matters involving personal preference, performing an action without first ascertaining whether it is appropriate in the specific circumstances should not be taken as good evidence of faulty decision making, because the action may be based on a reasoned policy relating to knowledge of a general fact about the circumstances.

(B) In professional decision-making contexts, those who have the responsibility of judging other people's suitability for a job should not use observations of job-related behavior as a basis for inferring general conclusions about those people's character.

(C) General conclusions regarding a job candidate's suitability for a position should not be based exclusively on observations of the candidate's behavior in situations that are neither directly job related nor likely to be indicative of a pattern of behavior that the candidate engages in.

(D) Individuals whose behavior in specific circumstances does not conform to generally expected norms should not automatically be considered unconcerned with meeting social expectations, because such individuals may be acting in accordance with reasoned policies that they believe should be generally adopted by people in similar circumstances.

(E) Evidence that a particular individual uses bad decision-making strategies in matters of personal taste should not be considered sufficient to warrant a negative assessment of his or her suitability for a job, because any good decision maker can have occasional lapses of rationality with regard to such matters.

S T O P

IF YOU FINISH BEFORE TIME IS CALLED, YOU MAY CHECK YOUR WORK ON THIS SECTION ONLY.
DO NOT WORK ON ANY OTHER SECTION IN THE TEST.

Acknowledgment is made to the following sources from which material has been adapted for use in this test booklet:

Elizabeth Wayland Barber, *Women's Work: The First 20,000 Years: Women, Cloth, and Society in Early Times.* ©1994 by Elizabeth Wayland Barber.

LSAC

Topic Code	Print Your Full Name Here		
087205	Last	First	M.I.

Date	Sign Your Name Here
/ /	

Scratch Paper
Do not write your essay in this space.

LSAT® Writing Sample Topic

Directions: The scenario presented below describes two choices, either one of which can be supported on the basis of the information given. Your essay should consider both choices and argue for one over the other, based on the two specified criteria and the facts provided. There is no "right" or "wrong" choice: a reasonable argument can be made for either.

A local amateur astronomical association is going to build a new observatory that will house a medium-sized telescope near the association's home town of Brenton. The association has narrowed the possible building sites down to two. Using the facts below, write an essay in which you argue for one site over the other based on the following two criteria:

- The site should provide seeing conditions for the use of the telescope that minimize atmospheric haze and sources of light pollution.
- The site should facilitate holding public observing sessions and lectures on astronomy for people from Brenton.

The first site is on top of a 2,000 foot (600 meter) ridge within a small forest park. This height is above some of the atmosphere's haze. To reach the summit, visitors must drive up a gravel road that is narrow and winding. Light pollution from a relatively distant megalopolis seriously affects about a quarter of the night sky. Currently, the land surrounding the park is mostly undeveloped farmland. How much will be developed is unpredictable.

The second site is almost at sea level in the middle of a large forest park. Some of the land near the site is swampy. City lights cause some light pollution across about a quarter of the night sky. The roads from Brenton to the site are all paved and in good condition. The travel time to this site from Brenton is about a third less than that to the first site. Unscheduled visitors are more likely at this site than at the first site. They could disturb the work of the amateur astronomers.

WP-Q087A

Scratch Paper
Do not write your essay in this space.

LAST NAME (Print)

FIRST NAME (Print)

SSN/ SIN

L

MI

TEST CENTER NO.

SIGNATURE

M M D D Y Y
TEST DATE

LSAC ACCOUNT NO.

TOPIC CODE

Writing Sample Response Sheet

DO NOT WRITE IN THIS SPACE

**Begin your essay in the lined area below.
Continue on the back if you need more space.**

COMPUTING YOUR SCORE

Directions:

1. Use the Answer Key on the next page to check your answers.

2. Use the Scoring Worksheet below to compute your raw score.

3. Use the Score Conversion Chart to convert your raw score into the 120–180 scale.

Scoring Worksheet

1. Enter the number of questions you answered correctly in each section.

	Number Correct
SECTION I................	_____
SECTION II...............	_____
SECTION III..............	_____
SECTION IV	_____

2. Enter the sum here: _____
   This is your Raw Score.

Conversion Chart
For Converting Raw Score to the 120–180 LSAT Scaled Score
LSAT Form 9LSN81

Reported Score	Raw Score Lowest	Raw Score Highest
180	99	101
179	—*	—*
178	98	98
177	97	97
176	96	96
175	95	95
174	—*	—*
173	94	94
172	93	93
171	91	92
170	90	90
169	89	89
168	88	88
167	86	87
166	85	85
165	84	84
164	82	83
163	80	81
162	79	79
161	77	78
160	75	76
159	74	74
158	72	73
157	70	71
156	69	69
155	67	68
154	65	66
153	63	64
152	61	62
151	60	60
150	58	59
149	56	57
148	54	55
147	53	53
146	51	52
145	49	50
144	47	48
143	46	46
142	44	45
141	42	43
140	41	41
139	39	40
138	38	38
137	36	37
136	34	35
135	33	33
134	31	32
133	30	30
132	29	29
131	27	28
130	26	26
129	25	25
128	23	24
127	22	22
126	21	21
125	20	20
124	18	19
123	17	17
122	16	16
121	15	15
120	0	14

*There is no raw score that will produce this scaled score for this form.

SECTION I

1.	C	8.	E	15.	D	22.	C
2.	D	9.	E	16.	E	23.	C
3.	E	10.	B	17.	B	24.	E
4.	E	11.	A	18.	C	25.	A
5.	A	12.	D	19.	D	26.	A
6.	A	13.	B	20.	E		
7.	B	14.	D	21.	C		

SECTION II

1.	B	8.	D	15.	A	22.	C
2.	E	9.	C	16.	B	23.	B
3.	E	10.	A	17.	A	24.	A
4.	D	11.	B	18.	E	25.	C
5.	C	12.	A	19.	C	26.	B
6.	E	13.	E	20.	D	27.	D
7.	A	14.	B	21.	E		

SECTION III

1.	E	8.	B	15.	B	22.	B
2.	C	9.	C	16.	B	23.	B
3.	E	10.	B	17.	C		
4.	A	11.	A	18.	C		
5.	E	12.	B	19.	D		
6.	C	13.	D	20.	B		
7.	C	14.	D	21.	E		

SECTION IV

1.	E	8.	B	15.	B	22.	C
2.	C	9.	A	16.	B	23.	B
3.	A	10.	D	17.	D	24.	B
4.	C	11.	E	18.	E	25.	A
5.	A	12.	A	19.	B		
6.	D	13.	C	20.	E		
7.	A	14.	D	21.	D		

The Official LSAT PrepTest

59

- December 2009
  PrepTest 59

- Form 9LSN82

SECTION I

Time—35 minutes

23 Questions

Directions: Each group of questions in this section is based on a set of conditions. In answering some of the questions, it may be useful to draw a rough diagram. Choose the response that most accurately and completely answers each question and blacken the corresponding space on your answer sheet.

Questions 1–5

A law firm has seven departments—family law, health law, injury law, labor law, probate, securities, and tax law. The firm is to occupy a building with three floors—the bottom floor, the middle floor, and the top floor. Each floor can accommodate up to four departments, and no department is to be on more than one floor. Assignment of departments to floors is subject to the following constraints:

Probate must be on the same floor as tax law.

Health law must be on the floor immediately above injury law.

Labor law must occupy an entire floor by itself.

1. Which one of the following could be the assignment of departments to floors?

   (A)   top floor: labor law
           middle floor: injury law, probate, tax law
           bottom floor: family law, health law, securities
   (B)   top floor: family law, health law, probate
           middle floor: injury law, securities, tax law
           bottom floor: labor law
   (C)   top floor: health law, probate, tax law
           middle floor: family law, injury law, securities
           bottom floor: labor law
   (D)   top floor: health law, probate, tax law
           middle floor: injury law, securities
           bottom floor: family law, labor law
   (E)   top floor: family law, health law, probate, tax law
           middle floor: labor law
           bottom floor: injury law, securities

2. If injury law and probate are both assigned to the middle floor, which one of the following could be true?

   (A)   Family law is assigned to the middle floor.
   (B)   Health law is assigned to the middle floor.
   (C)   Labor law is assigned to the top floor.
   (D)   Securities is assigned to the bottom floor.
   (E)   Tax law is assigned to the top floor.

3. Which one of the following CANNOT be the assignment for any of the floors?

   (A)   family law, health law, probate, and tax law
   (B)   family law, injury law, probate, and tax law
   (C)   family law, probate, securities, and tax law
   (D)   health law, probate, securities, and tax law
   (E)   injury law, probate, securities, and tax law

4. If family law is assigned to the same floor as securities, which one of the following could be true?

   (A)   Exactly one department is assigned to the middle floor.
   (B)   Exactly four departments are assigned to the middle floor.
   (C)   Exactly two departments are assigned to the bottom floor.
   (D)   Exactly three departments are assigned to the bottom floor.
   (E)   Exactly four departments are assigned to the bottom floor.

5. If probate is assigned to the middle floor along with exactly two other departments, then which one of the following must be true?

   (A)   Family law is assigned to the floor immediately above health law.
   (B)   Family law is assigned to the floor immediately below labor law.
   (C)   Family law is assigned to the same floor as securities.
   (D)   Probate is assigned to the same floor as health law.
   (E)   Probate is assigned to the same floor as injury law.

GO ON TO THE NEXT PAGE.

Questions 6–10

A museum curator is arranging seven photographs—*Fence, Gardenias, Hibiscus, Irises, Katydid, Lotus,* and *Magnolia*—on a gallery wall in accordance with the photographer's requirements. The photographs are to be hung along the wall in a row, in seven positions sequentially numbered from first to seventh. The photographer's requirements are as follows:

> *Gardenias* must be immediately before *Katydid*.
> *Hibiscus* must be somewhere before *Katydid* but cannot be the first photograph.
> *Irises* and *Lotus* must be next to one another.
> *Magnolia* must be one of the first three photographs.
> *Fence* must be either first or seventh.

6. Which one of the following could be the positions, from first to seventh, in which the photographs are hung?

   (A)   *Fence, Hibiscus, Gardenias, Magnolia, Katydid, Irises, Lotus*
   (B)   *Hibiscus, Magnolia, Gardenias, Katydid, Irises, Lotus, Fence*
   (C)   *Irises, Lotus, Magnolia, Hibiscus, Gardenias, Katydid, Fence*
   (D)   *Lotus, Magnolia, Irises, Hibiscus, Gardenias, Katydid, Fence*
   (E)   *Magnolia, Fence, Hibiscus, Gardenias, Katydid, Lotus, Irises*

7. If *Irises* is immediately before *Gardenias*, which one of the following could be true?

   (A)   *Gardenias* is fourth.
   (B)   *Hibiscus* is fourth.
   (C)   *Irises* is third.
   (D)   *Lotus* is second.
   (E)   *Magnolia* is third.

8. Where each photograph is hung is fully determined if which one of the following is true?

   (A)   *Gardenias* is fourth.
   (B)   *Hibiscus* is second.
   (C)   *Irises* is second.
   (D)   *Lotus* is first.
   (E)   *Magnolia* is third.

9. If *Magnolia* is second, which one of the following CANNOT be true?

   (A)   *Hibiscus* is third.
   (B)   *Hibiscus* is fourth.
   (C)   *Hibiscus* is fifth.
   (D)   *Gardenias* is fourth.
   (E)   *Gardenias* is sixth.

10. Which one of the following, if substituted for the condition that *Hibiscus* must be hung somewhere before *Katydid* but cannot be the first photograph, would have the same effect in determining the arrangement of the photographs?

   (A)   If *Fence* is seventh, *Hibiscus* is second.
   (B)   *Gardenias* is somewhere after *Hibiscus*, and either *Fence* or *Magnolia* is first.
   (C)   *Hibiscus* must be somewhere between the first and sixth photographs.
   (D)   Unless *Hibiscus* is second, it must be somewhere between *Magnolia* and *Gardenias*.
   (E)   *Katydid* is somewhere after *Hibiscus*, which must be somewhere after *Fence*.

GO ON TO THE NEXT PAGE.

Questions 11–16

Alicia will take exactly four courses this semester. She must choose from the following seven courses—Geography, Japanese, Macroeconomics, Psychology, Russian, Statistics (which is offered twice, once each on Tuesdays at 9 A.M. and 3 P.M.), and World History. No one is allowed to take any course more than once per semester. Because of university requirements and time conflicts, the following restrictions apply to Alicia's choices:

> She must take Japanese if she does not take Russian.
> She cannot take Japanese if she takes Macroeconomics.
> She cannot take World History if she takes Statistics at 9 A.M.
> She must take Statistics at 9 A.M. if she takes Psychology.
> She must take either Geography or World History but cannot take both.

11. Which one of the following could be the list of the four courses Alicia takes?

    (A)   Geography, Japanese, Psychology, Russian
    (B)   Geography, Macroeconomics, Psychology, Statistics
    (C)   Geography, Japanese, Macroeconomics, Russian
    (D)   Geography, Psychology, Russian, Statistics
    (E)   Macroeconomics, Psychology, Russian, Statistics

12. Which one of the following could be an accurate list of three of the courses Alicia takes?

    (A)   Geography, Statistics, World History
    (B)   Japanese, Macroeconomics, Statistics
    (C)   Japanese, Psychology, World History
    (D)   Psychology, Russian, World History
    (E)   Russian, Statistics, World History

13. Which courses Alicia takes is fully determined if she takes Russian and which one of the following?

    (A)   World History
    (B)   Statistics
    (C)   Psychology
    (D)   Macroeconomics
    (E)   Japanese

14. Alicia could take Statistics at either of the available times if she takes which one of the following pairs of courses?

    (A)   Geography and Japanese
    (B)   Geography and Psychology
    (C)   Japanese and World History
    (D)   Psychology and Russian
    (E)   Russian and World History

15. If Alicia takes Statistics at 3 P.M. and Geography, then which one of the following courses must she also take?

    (A)   Japanese
    (B)   Macroeconomics
    (C)   Psychology
    (D)   Russian
    (E)   World History

16. Suppose that Alicia must take Statistics if she takes Psychology, but rather than being restricted to taking Statistics at 9 A.M. she can take it at either 9 A.M. or at 3 P.M. If all the other restrictions remain the same, then which one of the following could be the list of the four courses Alicia takes?

    (A)   Psychology, Russian, Statistics, World History
    (B)   Macroeconomics, Psychology, Statistics, World History
    (C)   Macroeconomics, Psychology, Russian, World History
    (D)   Geography, Psychology, Russian, World History
    (E)   Geography, Macroeconomics, Russian, World History

GO ON TO THE NEXT PAGE.

Questions 17–23

An organization will hold its first six annual meetings in exactly six cities—Los Angeles, Montreal, New York, Toronto, Vancouver, and Washington—using each city only once. The following conditions govern the order in which the cities are used:

Los Angeles must be used in some year after the year in which Toronto is used.

Vancouver must be used either immediately before or immediately after Washington.

The meeting in Toronto must be separated from the meeting in Montreal by meetings in exactly two other cities.

The meeting in Vancouver must be separated from the meeting in Los Angeles by meetings in exactly two other cities.

17. Which one of the following lists the cities in an order in which they could be used for the meetings, from the first year through the sixth?

(A) Toronto, Vancouver, Washington, Montreal, Los Angeles, New York

(B) Vancouver, Washington, Montreal, Los Angeles, New York, Toronto

(C) Vancouver, Washington, Toronto, New York, Los Angeles, Montreal

(D) Washington, Montreal, Vancouver, New York, Toronto, Los Angeles

(E) Washington, Vancouver, New York, Toronto, Los Angeles, Montreal

18. Which one of the following must be true?

(A) Toronto is used in the first year.

(B) Montreal is used in the fourth year.

(C) Toronto is used at some time before Montreal is used.

(D) New York is used either immediately before or immediately after Vancouver.

(E) The meeting in New York is separated from the meeting in Washington by meetings in exactly two other cities.

19. There is exactly one possible order in which the cities are used if which one of the following is true?

(A) Los Angeles is used in the fifth year.

(B) Montreal is used in the sixth year.

(C) New York is used in the fifth year.

(D) Vancouver is used in the first year.

(E) Washington is used in the second year.

20. Which one of the following is a complete and accurate list of the years in which Washington could be used?

(A) 1, 3, 5

(B) 2, 3, 4, 5

(C) 2, 3, 4, 6

(D) 1, 2, 4, 6

(E) 1, 2, 3, 4, 5, 6

21. If Montreal is used in the first year, which one of the following CANNOT be true?

(A) Washington is used in the third year.

(B) Vancouver is used in the third year.

(C) Toronto is used in the fourth year.

(D) New York is used in the fifth year.

(E) Los Angeles is used in the third year.

22. Which one of the following could be true?

(A) Los Angeles is used in the first year.

(B) New York is used in the second year.

(C) Montreal is used in the third year.

(D) Vancouver is used in the fourth year.

(E) Toronto is used in the sixth year.

23. Which one of the following must be false?

(A) Los Angeles is used either immediately before or immediately after New York.

(B) Los Angeles is used either immediately before or immediately after Washington.

(C) New York is used either immediately before or immediately after Toronto.

(D) Toronto is used either immediately before or immediately after Vancouver.

(E) Toronto is used either immediately before or immediately after Washington.

S T O P

IF YOU FINISH BEFORE TIME IS CALLED, YOU MAY CHECK YOUR WORK ON THIS SECTION ONLY.
DO NOT WORK ON ANY OTHER SECTION IN THE TEST.

SECTION II

Time—35 minutes

26 Questions

<u>Directions:</u> The questions in this section are based on the reasoning contained in brief statements or passages. For some questions, more than one of the choices could conceivably answer the question. However, you are to choose the <u>best</u> answer; that is, the response that most accurately and completely answers the question. You should not make assumptions that are by commonsense standards implausible, superfluous, or incompatible with the passage. After you have chosen the best answer, blacken the corresponding space on your answer sheet.

1. On the Caribbean island of Guadeloupe, a researcher examined 35 patients with atypical Parkinson's disease and compared their eating habits to those of 65 healthy adults. She found that all of the patients with atypical Parkinson's regularly ate the tropical fruits soursop, custard apple, and pomme cannelle, whereas only 10 of the healthy adults regularly ate these fruits. From this, she concluded that eating these fruits causes atypical Parkinson's.

   Which one of the following, if true, most strengthens the researcher's reasoning?

   (A)   For many of the atypical Parkinson's patients, their symptoms stopped getting worse, and in some cases actually abated, when they stopped eating soursop, custard apple, and pomme cannelle.

   (B)   Of the healthy adults who did not regularly eat soursop, custard apple, and pomme cannelle, most had eaten each of these fruits on at least one occasion.

   (C)   In areas other than Guadeloupe, many people who have never eaten soursop, custard apple, and pomme cannelle have contracted atypical Parkinson's.

   (D)   The 10 healthy adults who regularly ate soursop, custard apple, and pomme cannelle ate significantly greater quantities of these fruits, on average, than did the 35 atypical Parkinson's patients.

   (E)   Soursop, custard apple, and pomme cannelle contain essential vitamins not contained in any other food that is commonly eaten by residents of Guadeloupe.

2. Price: A corporation's primary responsibility is to its shareholders. They are its most important constituency because they take the greatest risks. If the corporation goes bankrupt, they lose their investment.

   Albrecht: Shareholders typically have diversified investment portfolios. For employees, however, the well-being of the corporation for which they have chosen to work represents their very livelihood. The corporation's primary responsibility should be to them.

   On the basis of their statements, Price and Albrecht are committed to disagreeing about whether

   (A)   corporations have a responsibility to their shareholders

   (B)   corporations are responsible for the welfare of their employees

   (C)   means should be provided for a corporation's investors to recoup their losses if the corporation goes bankrupt

   (D)   a corporation's shareholders have more at stake than anyone else does in the corporation's success or failure

   (E)   the livelihood of some of the shareholders depends on the corporation's success

GO ON TO THE NEXT PAGE.

3. Despite the enormous number of transactions processed daily by banks nowadays, if a customer's bank account is accidentally credited with a large sum of money, it is extremely unlikely that the error will not be detected by the bank's internal audit procedures.

Which one of the following, if true, most strongly supports the claim above?

(A) Banks initially process all transactions using one set of computer programs, but then use a different set of programs to double-check large transactions.

(B) Recent changes in banking standards require that customers present identification both when making deposits into their accounts and when making withdrawals from their accounts.

(C) Banks are required by law to send each customer a monthly statement detailing every transaction of the previous month.

(D) The average ratio of bank auditors to customer accounts has slowly increased over the past 100 years.

(E) The development of sophisticated security software has rendered bank computers nearly impervious to tampering by computer hackers.

4. Scientist: While studying centuries-old Antarctic ice deposits, I found that several years of relatively severe atmospheric pollution in the 1500s coincided with a period of relatively high global temperatures. So it is clear in this case that atmospheric pollution did cause global temperatures to rise.

The reasoning in the scientist's argument is most vulnerable to criticism on the grounds that the argument

(A) presumes, without providing justification, that a rise in global temperatures is harmful

(B) draws a general conclusion based on a sample that is likely to be unrepresentative

(C) inappropriately generalizes from facts about a specific period of time to a universal claim

(D) takes for granted that the method used for gathering data was reliable

(E) infers, merely from a claim that two phenomena are associated, that one phenomenon causes the other

5. Gilbert: This food label is mistaken. It says that these cookies contain only natural ingredients, but they contain alphahydroxy acids that are chemically synthesized by the cookie company at their plant.

Sabina: The label is not mistaken. After all, alphahydroxy acids also are found occurring naturally in sugarcane.

Which one of the following, if true, would most strengthen Sabina's argument?

(A) The cookie company has recently dropped alphahydroxy acids from its cookie ingredients.

(B) Not all chemicals that are part of the manufacturing process are ingredients of the cookies.

(C) The label was printed before the cookie company decided to switch from sugarcane alphahydroxy acids to synthesized ones.

(D) Many other foods advertising all natural ingredients also contain some ingredients that are chemically synthesized.

(E) All substances except those that do not occur naturally in any source are considered natural.

6. Although Jaaks is a respected historian, her negative review of Yancey's new book on the history of coastal fisheries in the region rests on a mistake. Jaaks's review argues that the book inaccurately portrays the lives of fishery workers. However, Yancey used the same research methods in this book as in her other histories, which have been very popular. This book is also very popular in local bookstores.

The reasoning above is flawed in that it

(A) relies on the word of a scholar who is unqualified in the area in question

(B) attacks the person making the claim at issue rather than addressing the claim

(C) takes for granted that the popularity of a book is evidence of its accuracy

(D) bases a general conclusion on a sample that is likely to be unrepresentative

(E) presumes, without providing justification, that the methods used by Yancey are the only methods that would produce accurate results

GO ON TO THE NEXT PAGE.

7. Columnist: It has been noted that attending a live
   musical performance is a richer experience than is
   listening to recorded music. Some say that this is
   merely because we do not see the performers
   when we listen to recorded music. However, there
   must be some other reason, for there is relatively
   little difference between listening to someone
   read a story over the radio and listening to
   someone in the same room read a story.

   Which one of the following most accurately expresses
   the role played in the argument by the observation that
   attending a live musical performance is a richer
   experience than is listening to recorded music?

   (A)   It is what the columnist's argument purports to
         show.
   (B)   It is the reason given for the claim that the
         columnist's argument is attempting to
         undermine.
   (C)   It is what the columnist's argument purports to
         explain.
   (D)   It is what the columnist's argument purports to
         refute.
   (E)   It is what the position that the columnist tries to
         undermine is purported to explain.

8. Though ice cream is an excellent source of calcium,
   dairy farmers report that during the past ten years there
   has been a sharp decline in ice cream sales. And during
   the same period, sales of cheddar cheese have nearly
   doubled. Therefore, more and more people must be
   choosing to increase their intake of calcium by eating
   cheddar cheese rather than ice cream.

   The reasoning above is most vulnerable to criticism on
   the grounds that it

   (A)   fails to produce statistical evidence supporting
         the dairy farmers' claims
   (B)   fails to consider alternative explanations of the
         decline in sales of ice cream
   (C)   relies solely on the testimony of individuals
         who are likely to be biased
   (D)   presumes, without providing justification, that
         ice cream is a better source of calcium than is
         cheddar cheese
   (E)   presumes, without providing justification, that
         people who eat cheddar cheese never eat ice
         cream

9. No member of the Richardson Theater Group is both a
   performer and an administrator. Since Leon and Marta
   are both members of the Richardson Theater Group but
   neither is an administrator, it follows that both are
   performers.

   Which one of the following arguments displays a flawed
   pattern of reasoning most similar to that in the argument
   above?

   (A)   Not all of the employees of the Tedenco
         Company are salaried employees of that
         company. Since Mr. López and Ms. Allen are
         both salaried employees of the Tedenco
         Company, it follows that they are not the only
         employees of the Tedenco Company.
   (B)   No employee of the Tedenco Company is both
         an accountant and a corporate attorney. Since
         Ms. Walsh is both an accountant and a
         corporate attorney, it follows that she is not an
         employee of the Tedenco Company.
   (C)   No company can have its headquarters in both
         Canada and Mexico. Since neither the Dumone
         Company nor the Tedenco Company has its
         headquarters in Mexico, it follows that both
         have their headquarters in Canada.
   (D)   No corporate attorney represents both the
         Dumone Company and the Tedenco Company.
         Since Ms. Tseung is a corporate attorney who
         represents the Dumone Company, it follows
         that she does not also represent the Tedenco
         Company.
   (E)   No member of the board of directors of the
         Dumone Company is also a member of the
         board of directors of the Tedenco Company.
         Since neither company has fewer than five
         board members, it follows that both boards
         together include at least ten members.

10. Chemical fertilizers not only create potential health
    hazards, they also destroy earthworms, which are highly
    beneficial to soil. For this reason alone the use of
    chemical fertilizers should be avoided. The castings
    earthworms leave behind are much richer than the soil
    they ingest, thus making a garden rich in earthworms
    much more fertile than a garden without them.

    Which one of the following most accurately expresses
    the main conclusion of the argument?

    (A)   Earthworms are highly beneficial to soil.
    (B)   Chemical fertilizers destroy earthworms.
    (C)   The castings that earthworms leave behind are
          much richer than the soil they ingest.
    (D)   The use of chemical fertilizers should be
          avoided.
    (E)   A garden rich in earthworms is much more
          fertile than a garden that is devoid of
          earthworms.

GO ON TO THE NEXT PAGE.

11. Medical research has established that the Beta Diet is healthier than a more conventional diet. But on average, people who have followed the Beta Diet for several decades are much more likely to be in poor health than are people whose diet is more conventional.

Which one of the following, if true, most helps to resolve the apparent conflict between the two statements above?

(A) On average, people who have followed the Beta Diet for their entire lives are much more likely to have a variety of healthful habits than are people whose diet is more conventional.

(B) The Beta Diet is used primarily as a treatment for a condition that adversely affects overall health.

(C) People of average health who switch from a conventional diet to the Beta Diet generally find that their health improves substantially as a result.

(D) The Beta Diet provides dramatic health benefits for some people but only minor benefits for others.

(E) Recent research has shown that a diet high in fruits, vegetables, and skim milk is even healthier than the Beta Diet.

12. A theoretical framework facilitates conceptual organization of material and fruitful expansions of research. Many historians argue that historical analysis is therefore done best within a theoretical framework. But the past is too complex for all of its main trends to be captured within a theoretical framework. Therefore, _____.

Which one of the following most logically completes the argument?

(A) there is no benefit ever to be gained in recommending to historians that they place their work within a theoretical framework

(B) theoretical frameworks are less useful in history than they are in any other discipline

(C) even the best historical analysis done within a theoretical framework fails to capture all of history's main trends

(D) the value of theoretical work in extending research has been emphasized by historians who recommend doing historical analysis within a theoretical framework

(E) there is no difference between historical analysis that is placed within a theoretical framework and historical analysis that is not

13. Bethany: Psychologists have discovered a technique for replacing one's nightmares with pleasant dreams, and have successfully taught it to adults suffering from chronic nightmares. Studies have found that nightmare-prone children are especially likely to suffer from nightmares as adults. Thus, psychologists should direct efforts toward identifying nightmare-prone children so that these children can be taught the technique for replacing their nightmares with pleasant dreams.

Which one of the following principles, if valid, most helps to justify drawing the conclusion in Bethany's argument?

(A) Psychologists should make an effort to determine why certain children are especially prone to nightmares while other children are not.

(B) Any psychological technique that can be successfully taught to a child can also be successfully taught to an adult.

(C) Psychologists should do everything they can to minimize the number of adults troubled by chronic nightmares.

(D) Identifying nightmare-prone children is generally more difficult than teaching adults the technique for replacing nightmares with pleasant dreams.

(E) Psychologists should not teach the technique for replacing nightmares with pleasant dreams to children who are unlikely to suffer from nightmares as adults.

14. At one sitting, a typical doughnut eater consumes 4 doughnuts containing a total of 680 calories and 40 grams of fat. The typical bagel eater consumes exactly one bagel, at 500 calories and one or two grams of fat per sitting, though the addition of spreads can raise calorie and fat content to the four-doughnut range. Thus, as far as total calorie content is concerned, there is very little difference between what a typical doughnut eater and a typical bagel eater each consumes at one sitting.

The argument depends on assuming which one of the following?

(A) The calories and fat in bagels have the same health impact on bagel eaters as the calories and fat in doughnuts have on doughnut eaters.

(B) Most bagel eaters are not fully aware of the calorie and fat content of a bagel.

(C) Eating bagels instead of eating doughnuts provides no real health benefit.

(D) The typical doughnut eater does not add to doughnuts any substances that increase the total caloric intake.

(E) Most typical doughnut eaters are not also bagel eaters.

GO ON TO THE NEXT PAGE.

15. Bowers: A few theorists hold the extreme view that society could flourish in a condition of anarchy, the absence of government. Some of these theorists have even produced interesting arguments to support that position. One writer, for example, contends that anarchy is laissez-faire capitalism taken to its logical extreme. But these theorists' views ignore the fundamental principle of social philosophy—that an acceptable social philosophy must promote peace and order. Any social philosophy that countenances chaos, i.e., anarchy, accordingly deserves no further attention.

The reasoning in Bowers's argument is most vulnerable to criticism on the grounds that

(A) the meaning of a key term shifts illicitly during the course of the argument

(B) the argument fails to show that laissez-faire capitalism deserves to be rejected as a social philosophy

(C) the truth or falsity of a view is not determined by the number of people who accept it as true

(D) the argument presumes, without providing justification, that any peaceful society will flourish

(E) it is unreasonable to reject a view merely because it can be described as extreme

16. All poets, aside from those who write only epigrams, have wit. All lyrical composers are poets. Azriel does not write epigrams, though he is a lyrical composer. So Azriel has wit.

The pattern of reasoning in which one of the following is most similar to that in the argument above?

(A) All squeeze toys, except those designed for cats, are safe for infants. All squeeze toys are sold prewrapped. This item is not designed for cats, and it is sold prewrapped. So it must be safe for infants.

(B) Aside from the dogcatcher and the police chief, all of the politicians in town are lawyers. All of the politicians in town have websites. Sal is a politician in town, but is neither the dogcatcher nor the police chief. Since Sal is a politician in town he must have a website.

(C) All visas are assigned by this office, except for those that are issued through diplomatic channels. All visit permits are visas. Thus, the visit permit in Will's passport was assigned through diplomatic channels.

(D) All of this store's winter garments are on sale, except for the designer clothes. None of the shirts in this store are designer clothes. This shirt, therefore, since it is on sale, is a winter garment.

(E) All residential buildings are subject to the original fire code, except for those built last year. All townhouses are residential buildings. Bloom House was not built last year, and it is a townhouse, so it is subject to the original fire code.

17. Teachers should not do anything to cause their students to lose respect for them. And students can sense when someone is trying to hide his or her ignorance. Therefore, a teacher who does not know the answer to a question a student has asked should not pretend to know the answer.

The conclusion is properly drawn if which one of the following is assumed?

(A) A teacher cannot be effective unless he or she retains the respect of students.

(B) Students respect honesty above all else.

(C) Students' respect for a teacher is independent of the amount of knowledge they attribute to that teacher.

(D) Teachers are able to tell when students respect them.

(E) Students lose respect for teachers whenever they sense that the teachers are trying to hide their ignorance.

18. Contrary to Malthus's arguments, human food-producing capacity has increased more rapidly than human population. Yet, agricultural advances often compromise biological diversity. Therefore, Malthus's prediction that insufficient food will doom humanity to war, pestilence, and famine will likely be proven correct in the future, because a lack of biodiversity will eventually erode our capacity to produce food.

The statement that human food-producing capacity has increased more rapidly than human population plays which one of the following roles in the argument?

(A) It is a hypothesis the argument provides reasons for believing to be presently false.

(B) It is a part of the evidence used in the argument to support the conclusion that a well-known view is misguided.

(C) It is an observation that the argument suggests actually supports Malthus's position.

(D) It is a general fact that the argument offers reason to believe will eventually change.

(E) It is a hypothesis that, according to the argument, is accepted on the basis of inadequate evidence.

GO ON TO THE NEXT PAGE.

19. At a gathering at which bankers, athletes, and lawyers are present, all of the bankers are athletes and none of the lawyers are bankers.

If the statements above are true, which one of the following statements must also be true?

(A) All of the athletes are bankers.
(B) Some of the lawyers are not athletes.
(C) Some of the athletes are not lawyers.
(D) All of the bankers are lawyers.
(E) None of the lawyers are athletes.

20. Quality control investigator: Upon testing samples of products from our supplier that were sent by our field inspectors from various manufacturing locations, our laboratory discovered that over 20 percent of the samples were defective. Since our supplier is contractually required to limit the rate of defects among items it manufactures for us to below 5 percent, it has violated its contract with us.

The reasoning in the quality control investigator's argument is flawed in that the argument

(A) bases its conclusion on too small a sample of items tested by the laboratory
(B) presumes, without providing justification, that the field inspectors were just as likely to choose a defective item for testing as they were to choose a nondefective item
(C) overlooks the possibility that a few of the manufacturing sites are responsible for most of the defective items
(D) overlooks the possibility that the field inspectors tend to choose items for testing that they suspect are defective
(E) presumes, without providing justification, that the field inspectors made an equal number of visits to each of the various manufacturing sites of the supplier

21. Essayist: When the first prehistoric migrations of humans from Asia to North America took place, the small bands of new arrivals encountered many species of animals that would be extinct only 2,000 years later. Since it is implausible that hunting by these small bands of humans could have had such an effect, and since disease-causing microorganisms not native to North America were undoubtedly borne by the new arrivals as well as by the animals that followed them, these microorganisms were probably the crucial factor that accounts for the extinctions.

Which one of the following, if true, most weakens the essayist's argument?

(A) Animals weakened by disease are not only less able to avoid hunters but are also less able to avoid their other predators.
(B) Human beings generally have a substantial degree of biological immunity to the diseases carried by other species.
(C) Very few species of North American animals not hunted by the new arrivals from Asia were extinct 2,000 years after the first migrations.
(D) Individual humans and animals can carry a disease-causing microorganism without themselves suffering from the disease.
(E) Some species of North American animals became extinct more than 2,000 years after the arrival in North America of the first prehistoric human migrants from Asia.

22. A recent study confirms that nutritious breakfasts make workers more productive. For one month, workers at Plant A received free nutritious breakfasts every day before work, while workers in Plant B did not. The productivity of Plant A's workers increased, while that of Plant B's workers did not.

Which one of the following, if true, most strengthens the argument?

(A) Few workers in Plant B consumed nutritious breakfasts during the month of the study.
(B) Workers in the study from Plant A and Plant B started work at the same time of day.
(C) During the month before the study, workers at Plant A and Plant B were equally productive.
(D) Workers from Plant A took fewer vacation days per capita during the month than did workers from Plant B.
(E) Workers in Plant B were more productive during the month of the study than were workers from Plant A.

GO ON TO THE NEXT PAGE.

23. This year a flood devastated a small river town. Hollyville, also a river town, responded with an outpouring of aid in which a majority of its residents participated, a proportion that far surpassed that of a few years ago when Hollyville sent aid to victims of a highly publicized earthquake. This year's circumstances were a reversal of last year's, when Hollyville itself was the scene of a deadly tornado and so the recipient rather than the supplier of emergency aid.

The situation described above most closely conforms to which one of the following generalizations?

(A) People are more likely to aid people they know than they are to aid strangers.

(B) Those who have received aid are more likely to be in favor of government relief programs than are those who have not.

(C) The amount of aid that victims of a disaster receive is unrelated to the extent to which the disaster is publicized.

(D) Once a disaster has struck them, people are more likely to aid others in need than they were before the disaster.

(E) People are more likely to aid those who have experienced a hardship similar to one they themselves have experienced than to aid those who have experienced a dissimilar hardship.

24. Market analyst: According to my research, 59 percent of consumers anticipate paying off their credit card balances in full before interest charges start to accrue, intending to use the cards only to avoid carrying cash and writing checks. This research also suggests that in trying to win business from their competitors, credit card companies tend to concentrate on improving the services their customers are the most interested in. Therefore, my research would lead us to expect that _____.

Which one of the following most logically completes the market analyst's argument?

(A) most consumers would be indifferent about which company's credit card they use

(B) credit card companies would not make the interest rates they charge on cards the main selling point

(C) most consumers would prefer paying interest on credit card debts over borrowing money from banks

(D) most consumers would ignore the length of time a credit card company allows to pay the balance due before interest accrues

(E) the most intense competition among credit card companies would be over the number of places that they can get to accept their credit card

GO ON TO THE NEXT PAGE.

25. About 3 billion years ago, the Sun was only 80 percent as luminous as it is currently. Such conditions today would result in the freezing of Earth's oceans, but geological evidence shows that water rather than ice filled the oceans at that time. Heat is trapped within Earth's atmosphere through the presence of carbon dioxide, which, like methane, is a "greenhouse gas." Only if the level of greenhouse gases were higher 3 billion years ago than it is today would Earth have retained enough heat to keep the oceans from freezing. It is likely, therefore, that the level of carbon dioxide in the atmosphere was significantly higher then than it is today.

Which one of the following, if true, weakens the argument?

(A) Sufficient heat to keep the oceans liquid 3 billion years ago could not have been generated through geological processes such as volcanic activity.

(B) Geological studies indicate that there is much less methane in Earth's atmosphere today than there was 3 billion years ago.

(C) Geological evidence indicates that the oceans contained greater amounts of dissolved minerals 3 billion years ago, but not enough to alter their freezing points significantly.

(D) The increase in the Sun's luminosity over the past 3 billion years roughly coincided with an increasing complexity of life forms on Earth.

(E) Because the distance from Earth to the Sun has not changed significantly over the last 3 billion years, the increase in the Sun's luminosity has resulted in more radiation reaching Earth.

26. Commentator: For a free market to function properly, each prospective buyer of an item must be able to contact a large number of independent prospective sellers and compare the prices charged for the item to what the item is worth. Thus, despite advertised prices and written estimates available from many of its individual businesses, the auto repair industry does not constitute a properly functioning free market.

The conclusion of the commentator's argument follows logically if which one of the following is assumed?

(A) People do not usually shop for auto repairs but instead take their autos to their regular repair shop out of habit.

(B) Some persons who are shopping for auto repairs cannot determine what these repairs are worth.

(C) Not all auto repair shops give customers written estimates.

(D) Many auto repair shops charge more for auto repairs than these repairs are worth.

(E) Because it is not regulated, the auto repair industry does not have standardized prices.

S T O P

**IF YOU FINISH BEFORE TIME IS CALLED, YOU MAY CHECK YOUR WORK ON THIS SECTION ONLY.
DO NOT WORK ON ANY OTHER SECTION IN THE TEST.**

SECTION III

Time—35 minutes

25 Questions

Directions: The questions in this section are based on the reasoning contained in brief statements or passages. For some questions, more than one of the choices could conceivably answer the question. However, you are to choose the <u>best</u> answer; that is, the response that most accurately and completely answers the question. You should not make assumptions that are by commonsense standards implausible, superfluous, or incompatible with the passage. After you have chosen the best answer, blacken the corresponding space on your answer sheet.

1. New technologies that promise to extend life and decrease pain involve innovations that require extensive scientific research. Therefore, investment in such technologies is very risky, because innovations requiring extensive scientific research also require large amounts of capital but are unlikely to provide any financial return. Nonetheless, some people are willing to invest in these new technologies.

Which one of the following, if true, most helps to explain why some people are willing to invest in new technologies that promise to extend life and decrease pain?

(A) When investments in new technologies that promise to extend life and decrease pain do provide financial return, they generally return many times the original investment, which is much more than the return on safer investments.

(B) A large variety of new technologies that promise to extend life and decrease pain have been developed in the last decade.

(C) The development of certain new technologies other than those that promise to extend life and decrease pain is also very risky, because these technologies require large amounts of capital but are unlikely to provide any financial return.

(D) Some investments that initially seem likely to provide reasonably large financial return ultimately provide no financial return.

(E) The scientific research necessary to develop new technologies that promise to extend life and decrease pain sometimes leads to no greater understanding of the natural world.

2. A university psychology department received a large donation from a textbook company after agreeing to use one of the company's books for a large introductory course. The department chair admitted that the department would not have received the donation if it used another company's textbook, but insisted that the book was chosen solely for academic reasons. As proof, she noted that the department's textbook committee had given that textbook its highest rating.

Which one of the following, if true, most weakens the case for the department chair's position?

(A) The members of the textbook committee were favorably influenced toward the textbook by the prospect of their department receiving a large donation.

(B) The department has a long-standing policy of using only textbooks that receive the committee's highest rating.

(C) In the previous year, a different textbook from the same company was used in the introductory course.

(D) The department chair is one of the members of the textbook committee.

(E) The textbook company does not routinely make donations to academic departments that use its books.

GO ON TO THE NEXT PAGE.

3. Hemoglobin, a substance in human blood, transports oxygen from the lungs to the rest of the body. With each oxygen molecule it picks up, a hemoglobin molecule becomes more effective at picking up additional oxygen molecules until its maximum capacity of four oxygen molecules is reached. Grabbing an oxygen molecule changes the shape of the hemoglobin molecule, each time causing it literally to open itself to receive more oxygen.

Which one of the following is most strongly supported by the information above?

(A)   A hemoglobin molecule that has picked up three oxygen molecules will probably acquire a fourth oxygen molecule.

(B)   The only factor determining how effective a hemoglobin molecule is at picking up oxygen molecules is how open the shape of that hemoglobin molecule is.

(C)   A hemoglobin molecule that has picked up three oxygen molecules will be more effective at picking up another oxygen molecule than will a hemoglobin molecule that has picked up only one oxygen molecule.

(D)   A hemoglobin molecule that has picked up four oxygen molecules will have the same shape as a hemoglobin molecule that has not picked up any oxygen molecules.

(E)   Each hemoglobin molecule in human blood picks up between one and four oxygen molecules in or near the lungs and transports them to some other part of the body.

4. On a short trip a driver is more likely to have an accident if there is a passenger in the car, presumably because passengers distract drivers. However, on a long trip a driver is more likely to have an accident if the driver is alone.

Which one of the following, if true, most helps to explain the facts described above?

(A)   People are much more likely to drive alone on short trips than on long trips.

(B)   Good drivers tend to take more long trips than bad drivers.

(C)   The longer a car trip is, the more likely a passenger is to help the driver maintain alertness.

(D)   On a long trip the likelihood of an accident does not increase with each additional passenger.

(E)   Most drivers take far more short trips than long trips.

5. Challenger: The mayor claims she has vindicated those who supported her in the last election by fulfilling her promise to increase employment opportunities in our city, citing the 8 percent increase in the number of jobs in the city since she took office. But during her administration, the national government relocated an office to our city, bringing along nearly the entire staff from the outside. The 8 percent increase merely represents the jobs held by these newcomers.

Mayor: Clearly my opponent does not dispute the employment statistics. The unemployed voters in this city want jobs. The 8 percent increase in the number of jobs during my term exceeds that of any of my predecessors.

As a response to the challenger, the mayor's answer is flawed in that it

(A)   takes for granted that those who supported the mayor in the last election believed job availability to be a significant city issue

(B)   does not consider whether the number of unemployed persons within the city represents more than 8 percent of the eligible voters

(C)   fails to address the challenger's objection that the 8 percent increase did not result in an increase in job availability for those who lived in the city at the time of the last election

(D)   ignores the challenger's contention that the influx of newcomers during the mayor's administration has increased the size of the voting public and altered its priorities

(E)   explicitly attributes to the challenger beliefs that the challenger has neither asserted nor implied

GO ON TO THE NEXT PAGE.

6. A recent magazine editorial criticizes psychologists for not attempting to establish the order in which different areas of the brain are activated during a cognitive task such as imagining the face of a friend. However, the editorial is unfair because there is currently no technology that can detect the order of activation of brain areas.

Which one of the following most closely conforms to the principle to which the reasoning in the passage conforms?

(A) Construction companies have been unfairly criticized for using fewer layers of heating insulation in new houses than the number of layers used in previous years. Recent technology has made insulation more efficient, so fewer layers are required.

(B) Utility companies have been unfairly criticized for not using nuclear fusion to meet the nation's electricity needs. There is no way to harness fusion that could produce enough electricity to supply even one small town.

(C) The food industry has been unfairly criticized for attempting to preserve food longer by treating it with radiation. If food remained edible for longer, the cost of food would decrease substantially.

(D) The school system has been unfairly criticized for not making familiarity with computer technology a requirement. Computer studies could not be added to the curriculum without sacrificing some other subject.

(E) CEOs of large companies have been unfairly criticized for not always using their knowledge of economic theory to run their companies. Economic theory is sometimes irrelevant to making wise corporate decisions.

7. Although most people know what their bad habits are and want to rid themselves of them, a majority of these people find it very difficult to do so. This is because cessation of habitual behavior is immediately and vividly painful, while whatever benefit is to be gained by the absence of the habit is perceived only dimly because it is remote.

The information above most strongly supports the statement that the people who are most successful at ending their bad habits are those who

(A) can vividly imagine remote but attainable benefit

(B) can vividly imagine their present pain being felt in the future

(C) have succeeded in the past at modifying their behavior

(D) are relatively unaware of their own behavioral characteristics

(E) can vividly remember the pain caused them in the past by their bad habits

8. The more modern archaeologists learn about Mayan civilization, the better they understand its intellectual achievements. Not only were numerous scientific observations and predictions made by Mayan astronomers, but the people in general seem to have had a strong grasp of sophisticated mathematical concepts. We know this from the fact that the writings of the Mayan religious scribes exhibit a high degree of mathematical competence.

The argument's reasoning is most vulnerable to criticism on the grounds that the argument

(A) fails to provide an adequate definition of the term "intellectual achievement"

(B) bases a generalization on a sample that is likely to be unrepresentative

(C) overlooks the impressive achievements of other past civilizations

(D) relies on two different senses of the term "scientific"

(E) takes a mere correlation to be evidence of a causal relationship

9. Manager: There is no good reason to suppose that promoting creativity is a proper goal of an employee training program. Many jobs require little or no creativity and, in those positions, using creativity is more likely to be disruptive than innovative. Furthermore, even if creativity were in demand, there is no evidence that it can be taught.

Which one of the following most accurately expresses the main conclusion drawn in the manager's argument?

(A) Using creativity in jobs that require little or no creativity can be disruptive.

(B) Employee training programs are not able to teach employees creativity.

(C) Many jobs require little or no creativity.

(D) There is no good reason to suppose that employee training programs should promote creativity.

(E) Creativity is in demand, but there is no evidence that it can be taught.

GO ON TO THE NEXT PAGE.

10. Producer: It has been argued that, while the government should not censor television shows, the public should boycott the advertisers of shows that promote violence and erode our country's values. But this would be censorship nonetheless, for if the public boycotted the advertisers, then they would cancel their advertisements, causing some shows to go off the air; the result would be a restriction of the shows that the public can watch.

The producer's conclusion is properly inferred if which one of the following is assumed?

(A) If there is neither government censorship nor boycotting of advertisers, there will be no restriction of the television shows that the public can watch.

(B) Public boycotts could force some shows off the air even though the shows neither promote violence nor erode values.

(C) For any television show that promotes violence and erodes values, there will be an audience.

(D) There is widespread public agreement about which television shows promote violence and erode values.

(E) Any action that leads to a restriction of what the public can view is censorship.

11. Predictions that printed books will soon be replaced by books in electronic formats such as CD-ROM are exaggerated. While research libraries may find an electronic format more convenient for scholars and scientists, bookstores and public libraries will stock books in the format desired by the general public, which will be something other than an electronic format.

Which one of the following, if true, most strengthens the argument?

(A) Scholars and scientists find an electronic format for books the most convenient one for quick searching and cross-referencing.

(B) Publishers will continue to print books in the format stocked by bookstores and public libraries.

(C) Scholars and scientists do not usually conduct their research in public libraries.

(D) At some bookstores and libraries, the popularity of books on tape and of videos is beginning to rival that of printed books.

(E) Some members of the general public prefer to purchase books in an electronic format rather than borrow them from the library.

12. To cut costs, a high school modified its air-conditioning system to increase its efficiency. The modified system, however, caused the humidity in the school air to decrease by 18 percent. Twenty-four hours after the decrease in air humidity, a 25 percent increase in the number of visits to the school nurse was reported. This shows that a decrease in humidity can make people ill.

The argument depends on assuming which one of the following?

(A) At least some of the visits to the school nurse after the system was modified were due to illness.

(B) Most of the students at the high school suffered from the decrease in air humidity.

(C) It takes 24 hours after a person is infected with a virus for that person to exhibit symptoms.

(D) A decrease of 18 percent in air humidity causes an increase of 25 percent in one's probability of becoming ill.

(E) Modifying the air-conditioning system proved to be an ineffective way to cut costs.

13. A recent study of 10,000 people who were involved in automobile accidents found that a low percentage of those driving large automobiles at the time of their accidents were injured, but a high percentage of those who were driving small automobiles at the time of their accidents were injured. Thus, one is less likely to be injured in an automobile accident if one drives a large car rather than a small car.

Which one of the following, if true, most seriously weakens the argument?

(A) Most of the accidents analyzed in the study occurred in areas with very high speed limits.

(B) Most people who own small cars also drive large cars on occasion.

(C) Half of the study participants drove medium-sized cars at the time of their accidents.

(D) A large automobile is far more likely to be involved in an accident than is a small automobile.

(E) Only a small percentage of those people involved in an automobile accident are injured as a result.

GO ON TO THE NEXT PAGE.

14. Economist: A country's trade deficit may indicate weakness in its economy, but it does not in itself weaken that economy. So restricting imports to reduce a trade deficit would be like sticking a thermometer into a glass of cold water in the hope of bringing down a patient's feverish temperature.

The economist's argument employs which one of the following techniques?

(A) claiming that a crucial assumption entails a falsehood

(B) demonstrating that an analogy explicitly used to establish a certain conclusion is faulty

(C) appealing to an analogy in order to indicate the futility of a course of action

(D) calling into question the authority on the basis of which a claim is made

(E) showing that a recommended course of action would have disastrous consequences

15. There are circumstances in which it is not immoral to make certain threats, and there are circumstances in which it is not immoral to ask for money or some other favor. Therefore, there are circumstances in which it is not immoral to ask for money or a favor while making a threat.

Which one of the following exhibits a flawed pattern of reasoning most similar to that in the argument above?

(A) There are many business events for which casual dress is appropriate, and there are many social events for which casual dress is appropriate; therefore, if an occasion is neither a business event nor a social event, casual dress is not likely to be appropriate.

(B) It is usually easy to move a piano after you have convinced five people to help you, provided that you do not need to take it up or down stairs. Therefore, it is usually easy to move a piano.

(C) It is healthful to take drug A for a headache, and it is healthful to take drug B for a headache; therefore, it is healthful to take drug A together with drug B for a headache.

(D) Heavy trucks are generally operated in a safe manner, but the ability to drive a truck safely can be impaired by certain prescription drugs. Therefore, heavy trucks cannot be operated safely while the driver is under the effect of a prescription drug.

(E) The mountain roads are treacherous after it rains, and the mountain streams are full after a rain. So, if the roads in the mountains are treacherous, and the mountain streams are full, it surely has rained recently.

16. A common genetic mutation that lowers levels of the enzyme cathepsin C severely reduces a person's ability to ward off periodontitis, or gum disease. The enzyme triggers immunological reactions that destroy diseased cells and eliminate infections in the mouth. But researchers are developing ways to restore the enzyme to normal levels. Once that happens, we will be able to eliminate periodontitis.

Which one of the following is an assumption on which the argument depends?

(A) Restoring cathepsin C to normal levels is the only way to eliminate periodontitis.

(B) Genetic mutation is the only cause of lowered levels of cathepsin C.

(C) Researchers will soon succeed in finding means of restoring cathepsin C to normal levels.

(D) Persons who do not have the genetic mutation that lowers levels of cathepsin C do not get gum disease.

(E) A person whose cathepsin C level has been restored to normal will not suffer from periodontitis.

17. A recent study of major motion pictures revealed that the vast majority of their plots were simply variations on plots that had been used many times before. Despite this fact, many people enjoy seeing several new movies each year.

Each of the following, if true, would contribute to an explanation of the apparent discrepancy in the information above EXCEPT:

(A) Movies based on standard plots are more likely to be financially successful than are ones based on original plots.

(B) If the details of their stories are sufficiently different, two movies with the same basic plot will be perceived by moviegoers as having different plots.

(C) Because of the large number of movies produced each year, the odds of a person seeing two movies with the same general plot structure in a five-year period are fairly low.

(D) A certain aesthetic pleasure is derived from seeing several movies that develop the same plot in slightly different ways.

(E) Although most modern movie plots have been used before, most of those previous uses occurred during the 1940s and 1950s.

GO ON TO THE NEXT PAGE.

18. Those who claim that governments should not continue to devote resources to space exploration are wrong. Although most people's lives are relatively unaffected by the direct consequences of space exploration, many modern technologies that have a tremendous impact on daily life—e.g., fiber optics, computers, and lasers—are unexpected consequences of it. Society might have missed the benefits of these technologies if governments had not devoted resources to space exploration.

Which one of the following most accurately expresses the principle underlying the argument above?

(A) Governments should not be prevented from allocating resources to projects whose intended consequences do not directly benefit most people.

(B) One can never underestimate the beneficial consequences of government support of ambitious technological undertakings.

(C) The less practical the goal of a government-supported project, the more unexpected the consequences of that project.

(D) Governments should continue to support those projects that have, in the past, produced unintended benefits.

(E) In attempting to advance the welfare of society, governments should continue to dedicate resources to ambitious technological undertakings.

19. If understanding a word always involves knowing its dictionary definition, then understanding a word requires understanding the words that occur in that definition. But clearly there are people—for example, all babies—who do not know the dictionary definitions of some of the words they utter.

Which one of the following statements follows logically from the statements above?

(A) Some babies utter individual words that they do not understand.

(B) Any number of people can understand some words without knowing their dictionary definitions.

(C) If some words can be understood without knowing their dictionary definitions, then babies understand some words.

(D) If it is possible to understand a word without knowing its dictionary definition, then it is possible to understand a word without having to understand any other word.

(E) If some babies understand all the words they utter, then understanding a word does not always involve knowing its dictionary definition.

20. The peppered moth avoids predators by blending into its background, typically the bark of trees. In the late nineteenth century, those peppered moths with the lightest pigmentation had the greatest contrast with their backgrounds, and therefore were the most likely to be seen and eaten by predators. It follows, then, that the darkest peppered moths were the least likely to be seen and eaten.

Which one of the following most accurately describes a flaw in the reasoning of the argument?

(A) The argument overlooks the possibility that light peppered moths had more predators than dark peppered moths.

(B) The argument takes for granted that peppered moths are able to control the degree to which they blend into their backgrounds.

(C) The argument presumes, without providing justification, that all peppered moths with the same coloring had the same likelihood of being seen and eaten by a predator.

(D) The argument overlooks the possibility that there were peppered moths of intermediate color that contrasted less with their backgrounds than the darkest peppered moths did.

(E) The argument presumes, without providing justification, that the only defense mechanism available to peppered moths was to blend into their backgrounds.

GO ON TO THE NEXT PAGE.

21. Historian: The standard "QWERTY" configuration of the keys on typewriters and computer keyboards was originally designed to be awkward and limit typing speed. This was because early typewriters would jam frequently if adjacent keys were struck in quick succession. Experiments have shown that keyboard configurations more efficient than QWERTY can double typing speed while tremendously reducing typing effort. However, the expense and inconvenience of switching to a new keyboard configuration prevent any configuration other than QWERTY from attaining widespread use.

Which one of the following is most strongly supported by the historian's statements?

(A) Most people who have tried typing with non-QWERTY keyboards have typed significantly more quickly using those keyboards than they usually have done using QWERTY keyboards.

(B) Early QWERTY typewriters were less likely to jam than were at least some more recent typewriters if adjacent keys were struck in quick succession.

(C) If the designers of early typewriters had foreseen the possibility that technology would make it possible for adjacent keyboard keys to be struck in rapid succession without jamming, then they would not have proposed the QWERTY configuration.

(D) The benefit to society that would result from switching to a keyboard configuration other than QWERTY is significantly greater than the overall cost of such a switch.

(E) If the keyboard had been designed for computers, then it would not have been designed to limit typing speed.

22. Since anyone who makes an agreement has an obligation to fulfill the terms of that agreement, it follows that anyone who is obligated to perform an action has agreed to perform that action. Hence, saying that one has a legal obligation to perform a given action is the same as saying that one is required to fulfill one's agreement to perform that action.

Which one of the following statements most accurately characterizes the argument's reasoning flaws?

(A) The argument fails to make a crucial distinction between an action one is legally obligated to perform and an action with good consequences, and it takes for granted that everything true of legal obligations is true of obligations generally.

(B) The argument takes for granted that there are obligations other than those resulting from agreements made, and it fails to consider the possibility that actions that uphold agreements made are sometimes performed for reasons other than to uphold those agreements.

(C) The argument contains a premise that is logically equivalent to its conclusion, and it takes for granted that there are only certain actions that one should agree to perform.

(D) The argument treats a condition that is sufficient to make something an obligation as also a requirement for something to be an obligation, and it takes for granted that any obligation to perform an action is a legal obligation.

(E) The argument rests on an ambiguous use of the term "action," and it fails to consider the possibility that people are sometimes unwilling to perform actions that they have agreed to perform.

23. To predict that a device will be invented, one must develop a conception of the device that includes some details at least about how it will function and the consequences of its use. But clearly, then, the notion of predicting an invention is self-contradictory, for inventing means developing a detailed conception, and one cannot predict what has already taken place.

Which one of the following most accurately describes the technique of reasoning employed by the argument?

(A) constructing a counterexample to a general hypothesis about the future

(B) appealing to definitions to infer the impossibility of a kind of occurrence

(C) countering a hypothesis by indicating the falsehood of the implications of that hypothesis

(D) pointing out how a problem is widely thought to be scientific yet is really conceptual

(E) attempting to show that predicting any event implies that it has in fact already taken place

GO ON TO THE NEXT PAGE.

24. Eighteenth-century European aesthetics was reasonably successful in providing an understanding of all art, including early abstract art, until the 1960s, when artists self-consciously rebelled against earlier notions of art. Since the work of these rebellious artists is quite beautiful but outside the bounds of the aesthetic theory then current, there can be no complete theory of aesthetics.

The reasoning above is most vulnerable to criticism in that it

(A) takes for granted that it is more important for a complete aesthetic theory to account for the beauty of traditional art than for it to account for the beauty of self-consciously rebellious art

(B) presumes, without providing justification, that artists' rebellion in the 1960s against earlier notions of art was not guided by their knowledge of eighteenth-century European aesthetic theory

(C) presumes, without providing justification, that an aesthetic theory developed in one part of the world cannot be applied in another

(D) presumes, without providing justification, that art from the 1960s is the only art that cannot be adequately addressed by eighteenth-century European aesthetics

(E) presumes, without providing justification, that eighteenth-century European aesthetics is as encompassing as an aesthetic theory can be

25. Science writer: All scientists have beliefs and values that might slant their interpretations of the data from which they draw their conclusions. However, serious scientific papers are carefully reviewed by many other scientists before publication. These reviewers are likely to notice and object to biases that they do not share. Thus, any slanted interpretations of scientific data will generally have been removed before publication.

Which one of the following is an assumption required by the science writer's argument?

(A) The scientists reviewing serious scientific papers for publication do not always have biases likely to slant their interpretations of the data in those papers.

(B) In general, biases that slant interpretations of data in serious scientific papers being reviewed for publication are not shared among all scientists.

(C) Biases that are present in published scientific papers and shared by most scientists, including those who review the papers, are unlikely to impair the scientific value of those papers.

(D) The interpretation of data is the only part of a serious scientific paper that is sometimes slanted by the beliefs and values of scientists.

(E) Slanted interpretations of data in a scientific paper can be removed only through careful review by scientists who do not share the biases of the author or authors of the paper.

S T O P

IF YOU FINISH BEFORE TIME IS CALLED, YOU MAY CHECK YOUR WORK ON THIS SECTION ONLY.
DO NOT WORK ON ANY OTHER SECTION IN THE TEST.

SECTION IV
Time—35 minutes
27 Questions

Directions: Each set of questions in this section is based on a single passage or a pair of passages. The questions are to be answered on the basis of what is stated or implied in the passage or pair of passages. For some of the questions, more than one of the choices could conceivably answer the question. However, you are to choose the best answer; that is, the response that most accurately and completely answers the question, and blacken the corresponding space on your answer sheet.

Passage A

Recent studies have shown that sophisticated computer models of the oceans and atmosphere are capable of simulating large-scale climate trends with remarkable accuracy. But these models make use of
(5) large numbers of variables, many of which have wide ranges of possible values. Because even small differences in those values can have a significant impact on what the simulations predict, it is important to determine the impact when values differ even
(10) slightly.

Since the interactions between the many variables in climate simulations are highly complex, there is no alternative to a "brute force" exploration of all possible combinations of their values if predictions
(15) are to be reliable. This method requires very large numbers of calculations and simulation runs. For example, exhaustive examination of five values for each of only nine variables would require 2 million calculation-intensive simulation runs. Currently
(20) available individual computers are completely inadequate for such a task.

However, the continuing increase in computing capacity of the average desktop computer means that climate simulations can now be run on privately
(25) owned desktop machines connected to one another via the Internet. The calculations are divided among the individual desktop computers, which work simultaneously on their share of the overall problem. Some public resource computing projects of this kind
(30) have already been successful, although only when they captured the public's interest sufficiently to secure widespread participation.

Passage B

Researchers are now learning that many problems in nature, human society, science, and engineering are
(35) naturally "parallel"; that is, that they can be effectively solved by using methods that work simultaneously in parallel. These problems share the common characteristic of involving a large number of similar elements such as molecules, animals, even
(40) people, whose individual actions are governed by simple rules but, taken collectively, function as a highly complex system.

An example is the method used by ants to forage for food. As Lewis Thomas observed, a solitary ant is
(45) little more than a few neurons strung together by fibers. Its behavior follows a few simple rules. But when one sees a dense mass of thousands of ants, crowded together around their anthill retrieving food or repelling an intruder, a more complex picture

(50) emerges; it is as if the whole is thinking, planning, calculating. It is an intelligence, a kind of live computer, with crawling bits for wits.

We are now living through a great paradigm shift in the field of computing, a shift from sequential
(55) computing (performing one calculation at a time) to massive parallel computing, which employs thousands of computers working simultaneously to solve one computation-intensive problem. Since many computation-intensive problems are inherently
(60) parallel, it only makes sense to use a computing model that exploits that parallelism. A computing model that resembles the inherently parallel problem it is trying to solve will perform best. The old paradigm, in contrast, is subject to the speed limits
(65) imposed by purely sequential computing.

1. Which one of the following most accurately expresses the main point of passage B?

   (A) Many difficult problems in computing are naturally parallel.
   (B) Sequential computing is no longer useful because of the speed limits it imposes.
   (C) There is currently a paradigm shift occurring in the field of computing toward parallel computing.
   (D) Complex biological and social systems are the next frontier in the field of computer simulation.
   (E) Inherently parallel computing problems are best solved by means of computers modeled on the human mind.

2. The large-scale climate trends discussed in passage A are most analogous to which one of the following elements in passage B?

   (A) the thousands of computers working simultaneously to solve a calculation-intensive problem
   (B) the simple rules that shape the behavior of a single ant
   (C) the highly complex behavior of a dense mass of thousands of ants
   (D) the paradigm shift from sequential to parallel computing
   (E) the speed limits imposed by computing purely sequentially

GO ON TO THE NEXT PAGE.

3. It can be inferred that the authors of the two passages would be most likely to agree on which one of the following statements concerning computing systems?

(A) Massive, parallel computing systems are able to solve complex computation-intensive problems without having to resort to "brute force."

(B) Computer models are not capable of simulating the behavior of very large biological populations such as insect colonies.

(C) Parallel computing systems that link privately owned desktop computers via the Internet are not feasible because they rely too heavily on public participation.

(D) Currently available computers are not well-suited to running simulations, even if the simulated problems are relatively simple.

(E) Parallel computing systems employing multiple computers are the best means for simulating large-scale climate trends.

4. The author of passage A mentions public participation (lines 30–32) primarily in order to

(A) encourage public engagement in the sort of computing model discussed in the passage

(B) identify a factor affecting the feasibility of the computing model advocated in the passage

(C) indicate that government support of large-scale computing efforts is needed

(D) demonstrate that adequate support for the type of approach described in the passage already exists

(E) suggest that a computing model like that proposed in the passage is infeasible because of forces beyond the designers' control

5. Passage B relates to passage A in which one of the following ways?

(A) The argument in passage B has little bearing on the issues discussed in passage A.

(B) The explanation offered in passage B shows why the plan proposed in passage A is unlikely to be implemented.

(C) The ideas advanced in passage B provide a rationale for the solution proposed in passage A.

(D) The example given in passage B illustrates the need for the "brute force" exploration mentioned in passage A.

(E) The discussion in passage B conflicts with the assumptions about individual computers made in passage A.

6. The passages share which one of the following as their primary purpose?

(A) to show that the traditional paradigm in computing is ineffective for many common computing tasks

(B) to argue that a new approach to computing is an effective way to solve a difficult type of problem

(C) to convince skeptics of the usefulness of desktop computers for calculation-intensive problems

(D) to demonstrate that a new computing paradigm has supplanted the traditional paradigm for most large-scale computing problems

(E) to describe complex and as yet unsolved problems that have recently arisen in computing

7. In calling a population of ants "an intelligence, a kind of live computer" (lines 51–52) the author of passage B most likely means that

(A) the behavior of the colony of ants functions as a complex, organized whole

(B) the paradigm shift taking place in computing was inspired by observations of living systems

(C) computers are agglomerations of elements that can be viewed as being alive in a metaphorical sense

(D) computer simulations can simulate the behavior of large biological populations with great accuracy

(E) the simple rules that govern the behavior of individual ants have been adapted for use in computer simulations

8. The author of passage B would be most likely to agree with which one of the following statements regarding the computing system proposed in the last paragraph of passage A?

(A) It would be a kind of live computer.
(B) It would be completely inadequate for simulating large-scale climate trends.
(C) It would impose strict limitations on the number of variables that could be used in any simulation it runs.
(D) It would be likely to secure widespread public participation.
(E) It would solve calculation-intensive problems faster than a traditional sequential computer would.

GO ON TO THE NEXT PAGE.

A proficiency in understanding, applying, and even formulating statutes—the actual texts of laws enacted by legislative bodies—is a vital aspect of the practice of law, but statutory law is often given too little
(5) attention by law schools. Much of legal education, with its focus on judicial decisions and analysis of cases, can give a law student the impression that the practice of law consists mainly in analyzing past cases to determine their relevance to a client's situation and
(10) arriving at a speculative interpretation of the law relevant to the client's legal problem.

Lawyers discover fairly soon, however, that much of their practice does not depend on the kind of painstaking analysis of cases that is performed in law
(15) school. For example, a lawyer representing the owner of a business can often find an explicit answer as to what the client should do about a certain tax-related issue by consulting the relevant statutes. In such a case the facts are clear and the statutes' relation to them
(20) transparent, so that the client's question can be answered by direct reference to the wording of the statutes. But statutes' meanings and their applicability to relevant situations are not always so obvious, and that is one reason that the ability to interpret them
(25) accurately is an essential skill for law students to learn.

Another skill that teaching statutory law would improve is synthesis. Law professors work hard at developing their students' ability to analyze individual cases, but in so doing they favor the ability to apply the
(30) law in particular cases over the ability to understand the interrelations among laws. In contrast, the study of all the statutes of a legal system in a certain small area of the law would enable the student to see how these laws form a coherent whole. Students would then be
(35) able to apply this ability to synthesize in other areas of statutory law that they encounter in their study or practice. This is especially important because most students intend to specialize in a chosen area, or areas, of the law.
(40) One possible argument against including training in statutory law as a standard part of law school curricula is that many statutes vary from region to region within a nation, so that the mastery of a set of statutes would usually not be generally applicable. There is some truth
(45) to this objection; law schools that currently provide some training in statutes generally intend it as a preparation for practice in their particular region, but for schools that are nationally oriented, this could seem to be an inappropriate investment of time and
(50) resources. But while the knowledge of a particular region's statutory law is not generally transferable to other regions, the skills acquired in mastering a particular set of statutes are, making the study of statutory law an important undertaking even for law
(55) schools with a national orientation.

9. Which one of the following most accurately expresses the main point of the passage?

(A) In spite of the reservations that nationally oriented law schools can be expected to have, law schools can serve the overall needs of law students better by implementing a standard national curriculum in statutory law.

(B) Since the skills promoted by the study of statutory law are ultimately more important than those promoted by case analysis, the relative emphasis that law schools place on these two areas should be reversed.

(C) Although statutes typically vary from region to region, law schools should provide training in statutory law in order to develop students' ability to synthesize legal information and interpret individual statutes.

(D) In the theoretical world of law school training, as opposed to the actual practice of law, a proficiency in case law is often one of the most important assets that students can have.

(E) Law schools generally are deficient in their attention to statutory law training and therefore fail to impart the skills necessary for the analysis of legal information.

10. Which one of the following is cited in the passage as a reason that might be given for not including statutory law training in law school curricula?

(A) Such training would divert resources away from the far more important development of the ability to analyze cases.

(B) Such training is not essentially different from what is already provided in the core areas of law school education.

(C) The goals of such training can better be achieved by other means, most of which are more directly related to the actual practice of law.

(D) Such training would be irrelevant for those students who do not plan to specialize.

(E) The lack of geographic uniformity among statutory laws makes expertise in the statutes of any particular region generally nontransferable.

GO ON TO THE NEXT PAGE.

11. Which one of the following would, if true, most weaken the author's argument as expressed in the passage?

(A) Many law school administrators recommend the inclusion of statutory law training in the curricula of their schools.

(B) Most lawyers easily and quickly develop proficiency in statutory law through their work experiences after law school.

(C) Most lawyers do not practice law in the same geographic area in which they attended law school.

(D) The curricula of many regionally oriented law schools rely primarily on analysis of cases.

(E) Most lawyers who have undergone training in statutory law are thoroughly familiar with only a narrow range of statutes.

12. The author discusses the skill of synthesis in the third paragraph primarily in order to

(A) identify and describe one of the benefits that the author says would result from the change that is advocated in the passage

(B) indicate that law schools currently value certain other skills over this skill and explain why this is so

(C) argue for the greater importance of this skill as compared with certain others that are discussed earlier in the passage

(D) explain why this skill is necessary for the study of statutory law

(E) provide an example of the type of problem typically encountered in the practice of law

13. Which one of the following questions can be most clearly and directly answered by reference to information in the passage?

(A) What are some ways in which synthetic skills are strengthened or encouraged through the analysis of cases and judicial decisions?

(B) In which areas of legal practice is a proficiency in case analysis more valuable than a proficiency in statutory law?

(C) What skills are common to the study of both statutory law and judicial decisions?

(D) What are some objections that have been raised against including the study of statutes in regionally oriented law schools?

(E) What is the primary focus of the curriculum currently offered in most law schools?

14. The information in the passage suggests that the author would most likely agree with which one of the following statements regarding training in statutory law?

(A) While nationally oriented law schools have been deficient in statutory law training, most regionally oriented law schools have been equally deficient in the teaching of case law.

(B) Training in statutory law would help lawyers resolve legal questions for which the answers are not immediately apparent in the relevant statutes.

(C) Lawyers who are trained in statutory law typically also develop a higher level of efficiency in manipulating details of past cases as compared with lawyers who are not trained in this way.

(D) Courses in statutory law are less effective if they focus specifically on the statutes of a particular region or in a particular area of the law.

(E) Lawyers who do not specialize probably have little need for training in statutory law beyond a brief introduction to the subject.

15. Each of the following conforms to the kinds of educational results that the author would expect from the course of action proposed in the passage EXCEPT:

(A) skill in locating references to court decisions on an issue involving a particular statute regarding taxation

(B) an understanding of the ways in which certain underlying purposes are served by an interrelated group of environmental laws

(C) a knowledge of how maritime statutes are formulated

(D) familiarity with the specific wordings of a group of laws applying to businesses in a particular region or locality

(E) an appreciation of the problems of wording involved in drafting antiterrorism laws

GO ON TO THE NEXT PAGE.

The Japanese American sculptor Isamu Noguchi (1904–1988) was an artist who intuitively asked—and responded to—deeply original questions. He might well have become a scientist within a standard
(5) scientific discipline, but he instead became an artist who repeatedly veered off at wide angles from the well-known courses followed by conventionally talented artists of both the traditional and modern schools. The story behind one particular sculpture
(10) typifies this aspect of his creativeness.

By his early twenties, Noguchi's sculptures showed such exquisite comprehension of human anatomy and deft conceptual realization that he won a Guggenheim Fellowship for travel in Europe. After
(15) arriving in Paris in 1927, Noguchi asked the Romanian-born sculptor Constantin Brancusi if he might become his student. When Brancusi said no, that he never took students, Noguchi asked if he needed a stonecutter. Brancusi did. Noguchi cut and
(20) polished stone for Brancusi in his studio, frequently also polishing Brancusi's brass and bronze sculptures. Noguchi, with his scientist's mind, pondered the fact that sculptors through the ages had relied exclusively upon negative light—that is, shadows—for their
(25) conceptual communication, precisely because no metals, other than the expensive, nonoxidizing gold, could be relied upon to give off positive-light reflections.

Noguchi wanted to create a sculpture that was purely reflective. In 1929, after returning to the
(30) United States, he met the architect and philosopher R. Buckminster Fuller, offering to sculpt a portrait of him. When Fuller heard of Noguchi's ideas regarding positive-light sculpture, he suggested using chrome-nickel steel, which Henry Ford, through automotive
(35) research and development, had just made commercially available for the first time in history. Here, finally, was a permanently reflective surface, economically available in massive quantities.

In sculpting his portrait of Fuller, Noguchi did not
(40) think of it as merely a shiny alternate model of traditional, negative-light sculptures. What he saw was that completely reflective surfaces provided a fundamental invisibility of surface like that of utterly still waters, whose presence can be apprehended only
(45) when objects—a ship's mast, a tree, or sky—are reflected in them. Seaplane pilots making offshore landings in dead calm cannot tell where the water is and must glide in, waiting for the unpredictable touchdown. Noguchi conceived a similarly invisible sculpture,
(50) hidden in and communicating through the reflections of images surrounding it. Then only the distortion of familiar shapes in the surrounding environment could be seen by the viewer. The viewer's awareness of the "invisible" sculpture's presence and dimensional
(55) relationships would be derived only secondarily.

Even after this stunning discovery, Noguchi remained faithful to his inquisitive nature. At the moment when his explorations had won critical recognition of the genius of his original and
(60) fundamental conception, Noguchi proceeded to the next phase of his evolution.

16. In saying that "no metals, other than the expensive, nonoxidizing gold, could be relied upon to give off positive-light reflections" (lines 25–27), the author draws a distinction between

(A) a metal that can be made moderately reflective in any sculptural application and metals that can be made highly reflective but only in certain applications

(B) a naturally highly reflective metal that was technically suited for sculpture and other highly reflective metals that were not so suited

(C) metals that can be made highly reflective but lose their reflective properties over time and a metal that does not similarly lose its reflective properties

(D) a highly reflective sculptural material that, because it is a metal, is long lasting and nonmetallic materials that are highly reflective but impermanent

(E) a highly reflective metal that was acceptable to both traditional and modern sculptors and highly reflective metals whose use in sculpture was purely experimental

17. The passage provides information sufficient to answer which one of the following questions?

(A) In what way did Noguchi first begin to acquire experience in the cutting and polishing of stone for use in sculpture?

(B) In the course of his career, did Noguchi ever work in any art form other than sculpture?

(C) What are some materials other than metal that Noguchi used in his sculptures after ending his association with Brancusi?

(D) During Noguchi's lifetime, was there any favorable critical response to his creation of a positive-light sculpture?

(E) Did Noguchi at any time in his career consider creating a transparent or translucent sculpture lighted from within?

GO ON TO THE NEXT PAGE.

18. The passage offers the strongest evidence that the author would agree with which one of the following statements?

(A) Noguchi's work in Paris contributed significantly to the art of sculpture in that it embodied solutions to problems that other sculptors, including Brancusi, had sought unsuccessfully to overcome.

(B) Noguchi's scientific approach to designing sculptures and to selecting materials for sculptures is especially remarkable in that he had no formal scientific training.

(C) Despite the fact that Brancusi was a sculptor and Fuller was not, Fuller played a more pivotal role than did Brancusi in Noguchi's realization of the importance of negative light to the work of previous sculptors.

(D) Noguchi was more interested in addressing fundamental aesthetic questions than in maintaining a consistent artistic style.

(E) Noguchi's work is of special interest for what it reveals not only about the value of scientific thinking in the arts but also about the value of aesthetic approaches to scientific inquiry.

19. In which one of the following is the relation between the two people most analogous to the relation between Ford and Noguchi as indicated by the passage?

(A) A building-materials dealer decides to market a new type of especially durable simulated-wood flooring material after learning that a famous architect has praised the material.

(B) An expert skier begins experimenting with the use of a new type of material in the soles of ski boots after a shoe manufacturer suggests that that material might be appropriate for that use.

(C) A producer of shipping containers begins using a new type of strapping material, which a rock-climbing expert soon finds useful as an especially strong and reliable component of safety ropes for climbing.

(D) A consultant to a book editor suggests the use of a new type of software for typesetting, and after researching the software the editor decides not to adopt it but finds a better alternative as a result of the research.

(E) A friend of a landscaping expert advises the use of a certain material for the creation of retaining walls and, as a result, the landscaper explores the use of several similar materials.

20. The passage most strongly supports which one of the following inferences?

(A) Prior to suggesting the sculptural use of chrome-nickel steel to Noguchi, Fuller himself had made architectural designs that called for the use of this material.

(B) Noguchi believed that the use of industrial materials to create sculptures would make the sculptures more commercially viable.

(C) Noguchi's "invisible" sculpture appears to have no shape or dimensions of its own, but rather those of surrounding objects.

(D) If a positive-light sculpture depicting a person in a realistic manner were coated with a metal subject to oxidation, it would eventually cease to be recognizable as a realistic likeness.

(E) The perception of the shape and dimensions of a negative-light sculpture does not depend on its reflection of objects from the environment around it.

21. Which one of the following inferences about the portrait of Fuller does the passage most strongly support?

(A) The material that Noguchi used in it had been tentatively investigated by other sculptors but not in direct connection with its reflective properties.

(B) It was similar to at least some of the sculptures that Noguchi produced prior to 1927 in that it represented a human form.

(C) Noguchi did not initially think of it as especially innovative or revolutionary and thus was surprised by Fuller's reaction to it.

(D) It was produced as a personal favor to Fuller and thus was not initially intended to be noticed and commented on by art critics.

(E) It was unlike the sculptures that Noguchi had helped Brancusi to produce in that the latter's aesthetic effects did not depend on contrasts of light and shadow.

22. Which one of the following would, if true, most weaken the author's position in the passage?

(A) Between 1927 and 1929, Brancusi experimented with the use of highly reflective material for the creation of positive-light sculptures.

(B) After completing the portrait of Fuller, Noguchi produced only a few positive-light sculptures and in fact changed his style of sculpture repeatedly throughout his career.

(C) When Noguchi arrived in Paris, he was already well aware of the international acclaim that Brancusi's sculptures were receiving at the time.

(D) Many of Noguchi's sculptures were, unlike the portrait of Fuller, entirely abstract.

(E) Despite his inquisitive and scientific approach to the art of sculpture, Noguchi neither thought of himself as a scientist nor had extensive scientific training.

GO ON TO THE NEXT PAGE.

In an experiment, two strangers are given the opportunity to share $100, subject to the following constraints: One person—the "proposer"—is to suggest how to divide the money and can make only
(5) one such proposal. The other person—the "responder"—must either accept or reject the offer without qualification. Both parties know that if the offer is accepted, the money will be split as agreed, but if the offer is rejected, neither will receive
(10) anything.

This scenario is called the Ultimatum Game. Researchers have conducted it numerous times with a wide variety of volunteers. Many participants in the role of the proposer seem instinctively to feel that
(15) they should offer 50 percent to the responder, because such a division is "fair" and therefore likely to be accepted. Two-thirds of proposers offer responders between 40 and 50 percent. Only 4 in 100 offer less than 20 percent. Offering such a small amount is
(20) quite risky; most responders reject such offers. This is a puzzle: Why would anyone reject an offer as too small? Responders who reject an offer receive nothing, so if one assumes—as theoretical economics traditionally has—that people make economic
(25) decisions primarily out of rational self-interest, one would expect that an individual would accept any offer.

Some theorists explain the insistence on fair divisions in the Ultimatum Game by citing our
(30) prehistoric ancestors' need for the support of a strong group. Small groups of hunter-gatherers depended for survival on their members' strengths. It is counterproductive to outcompete rivals within one's group to the point where one can no longer depend
(35) on them in contests with other groups. But this hypothesis at best explains why proposers offer large amounts, not why responders reject low offers.

A more compelling explanation is that our emotional apparatus has been shaped by millions of
(40) years of living in small groups, where it is hard to keep secrets. Our emotions are therefore not finely tuned to one-time, strictly anonymous interactions. In real life we expect our friends and neighbors to notice our decisions. If people know that someone is
(45) content with a small share, they are likely to make that person low offers. But if someone is known to angrily reject low offers, others have an incentive to make that person high offers. Consequently, evolution should have favored angry responses to low offers; if
(50) one regularly receives fair offers when food is divided, one is more likely to survive. Because one-shot interactions were rare during human evolution, our emotions do not discriminate between one-shot and repeated interactions. Therefore, we respond
(55) emotionally to low offers in the Ultimatum Game because we instinctively feel the need to reject dismal offers in order to keep our self-esteem. This self-esteem helps us to acquire a reputation that is beneficial in future encounters.

23. Which one of the following most accurately summarizes the main idea of the passage?

(A) Contrary to a traditional assumption of theoretical economics, the behavior of participants in the Ultimatum Game demonstrates that people do not make economic decisions out of rational self-interest.

(B) Although the reactions most commonly displayed by participants in the Ultimatum Game appear to conflict with rational self-interest, they probably result from a predisposition that had evolutionary value.

(C) Because our emotional apparatus has been shaped by millions of years of living in small groups in which it is hard to keep secrets, our emotions are not finely tuned to one-shot, anonymous interactions.

(D) People respond emotionally to low offers in the Ultimatum Game because they instinctively feel the need to maintain the strength of the social group to which they belong.

(E) When certain social and evolutionary factors are taken into account, it can be seen that the behavior of participants in the Ultimatum Game is motivated primarily by the need to outcompete rivals.

24. The passage implies that the Ultimatum Game is

(A) one that requires two strangers to develop trust in each other

(B) responsible for overturning a basic assumption of theoretical economics

(C) a situation that elicits unpredictable results

(D) a type of one-shot, anonymous interaction

(E) proof that our emotional apparatus has been shaped by millions of years of living in small groups

25. The author's primary purpose in the passage is to

(A) survey existing interpretations of the puzzling results of an experiment

(B) show how two theories that attempt to explain the puzzling results of an experiment complement each other

(C) argue that the results of an experiment, while puzzling, are valid

(D) offer a plausible explanation for the puzzling results of an experiment

(E) defend an experiment against criticism that methodological flaws caused its puzzling results

GO ON TO THE NEXT PAGE.

26. Which one of the following sentences would most logically conclude the final paragraph of the passage?

(A) Contrary to the assumptions of theoretical economics, human beings do not act primarily out of self-interest.

(B) Unfortunately, one-time, anonymous interactions are becoming increasingly common in contemporary society.

(C) The instinctive urge to acquire a favorable reputation may also help to explain the desire of many proposers in the Ultimatum Game to make "fair" offers.

(D) High self-esteem and a positive reputation offer individuals living in small groups many other benefits as well.

(E) The behavior of participants in the Ultimatum Game sheds light on the question of what constitutes a "fair" division.

27. In the context of the passage, the author would be most likely to consider the explanation in the third paragraph more favorably if it were shown that

(A) our prehistoric ancestors often belonged to large groups of more than a hundred people

(B) in many prehistoric cultures, there were hierarchies within groups that dictated which allocations of goods were to be considered fair and which were not

(C) it is just as difficult to keep secrets in relatively large social groups as it is in small social groups

(D) it is just as counterproductive to a small social group to allow oneself to be outcompeted by one's rivals within the group as it is to outcompete those rivals

(E) in many social groups, there is a mutual understanding among the group's members that allocations of goods will be based on individual needs as opposed to equal shares

S T O P

IF YOU FINISH BEFORE TIME IS CALLED, YOU MAY CHECK YOUR WORK ON THIS SECTION ONLY.
DO NOT WORK ON ANY OTHER SECTION IN THE TEST.

LSAC®

Topic Code	Print Your Full Name Here		
088304	Last	First	M.I.

Date	Sign Your Name Here
/ /	

Scratch Paper
Do not write your essay in this space.

LSAT® Writing Sample Topic

Directions: The scenario presented below describes two choices, either one of which can be supported on the basis of the information given. Your essay should consider both choices and argue for one over the other, based on the two specified criteria and the facts provided. There is no "right" or "wrong" choice: a reasonable argument can be made for either.

A new theater group has received an arts grant to produce an inaugural play. Its members are split over whether to use the money to commission and stage a new play, or to produce an existing play that is likely to attract a larger audience. Using the facts below, write an essay in which you argue for one option over the other based on the following two criteria:

- The theater group wants to serve as an ongoing education and entertainment resource for the people of its city.
- The theater group wants to serve as a creative outlet for the writers and actors residing in its city.

The existing play would be a complex production. It features a large cast and elaborate sets. The play was originally produced six years earlier and was popular enough to justify an extended run. The popularity of a theater group's first production affects the amount of corporate sponsorship that could be expected for future productions, and could determine whether the theater group survives into a full season. The first production by a theater group usually creates the expectation for the public as to what future productions will be like. The play has several challenging major parts that are difficult to cast effectively.

A new play would likely involve a smaller cast with simpler sets. It would give the actors a greater creative role in shaping their characters. It would showcase the work of a local playwright. There are currently no theater groups in the city dedicated to producing locally created material. Productions of original plays are more likely to be restaged in other cities. They result in scripts that could possibly be sold to other theater companies. Plays by local writers have drawn small audiences in the past.

WP-R088A

Scratch Paper
Do not write your essay in this space.

Writing Sample Response Sheet

LAST
NAME
(Print)

FIRST
NAME
(Print)

SSN/
SIN

L

MI

TEST
CENTER NO.

SIGNATURE

M   M   D   D   Y   Y
TEST DATE

LSAC ACCOUNT NO.

TOPIC CODE

Writing Sample Response Sheet

DO NOT WRITE
IN THIS SPACE

Begin your essay in the lined area below.
Continue on the back if you need more space.

EliteView™ forms by NCS Pearson EM-252259-6:654321   Printed in U.S.A.

COMPUTING YOUR SCORE

Directions:

1. Use the Answer Key on the next page to check your answers.

2. Use the Scoring Worksheet below to compute your raw score.

3. Use the Score Conversion Chart to convert your raw score into the 120–180 scale.

Scoring Worksheet

1. Enter the number of questions you answered correctly in each section.

	Number Correct
SECTION I..................	_____
SECTION II...............	_____
SECTION III..............	_____
SECTION IV	_____

2. Enter the sum here: _____

   This is your Raw Score.

Conversion Chart
For Converting Raw Score to the 120–180 LSAT Scaled Score
LSAT Form 9LSN82

Reported Score	Raw Score Lowest	Raw Score Highest
180	98	101
179	97	97
178	96	96
177	95	95
176	94	94
175	93	93
174	92	92
173	91	91
172	90	90
171	89	89
170	87	88
169	86	86
168	85	85
167	83	84
166	82	82
165	81	81
164	79	80
163	78	78
162	76	77
161	74	75
160	73	73
159	71	72
158	70	70
157	68	69
156	66	67
155	65	65
154	63	64
153	61	62
152	60	60
151	58	59
150	57	57
149	55	56
148	53	54
147	52	52
146	50	51
145	49	49
144	47	48
143	45	46
142	44	44
141	42	43
140	41	41
139	39	40
138	38	38
137	36	37
136	35	35
135	33	34
134	32	32
133	30	31
132	29	29
131	28	28
130	26	27
129	25	25
128	24	24
127	23	23
126	21	22
125	20	20
124	19	19
123	17	18
122	15	16
121	—*	—*
120	0	14

*There is no raw score that will produce this scaled score for this form.

ANSWER KEY

SECTION I

1.	C	8.	D	15.	D	22.	B
2.	A	9.	B	16.	A	23.	B
3.	C	10.	D	17.	A		
4.	D	11.	D	18.	E		
5.	C	12.	E	19.	D		
6.	C	13.	C	20.	E		
7.	E	14.	A	21.	E		

SECTION II

1.	A	8.	B	15.	A	22.	A
2.	D	9.	C	16.	E	23.	D
3.	A	10.	D	17.	E	24.	B
4.	E	11.	B	18.	D	25.	B
5.	E	12.	C	19.	C	26.	B
6.	C	13.	C	20.	D		
7.	E	14.	D	21.	C		

SECTION III

1.	A	8.	B	15.	C	22.	D
2.	A	9.	D	16.	E	23.	B
3.	C	10.	E	17.	A	24.	E
4.	C	11.	B	18.	D	25.	B
5.	C	12.	A	19.	E		
6.	B	13.	D	20.	D		
7.	A	14.	C	21.	E		

SECTION IV

1.	C	8.	E	15.	A	22.	A
2.	C	9.	C	16.	C	23.	B
3.	E	10.	E	17.	D	24.	D
4.	B	11.	B	18.	D	25.	D
5.	C	12.	A	19.	C	26.	C
6.	B	13.	E	20.	E	27.	D
7.	A	14.	B	21.	B		

THE OFFICIAL LSAT
PREPTEST®

60

- PrepTest 60
- Form 1LSN84

JUNE 2010

SECTION I

Time—35 minutes

25 Questions

<u>Directions</u>: The questions in this section are based on the reasoning contained in brief statements or passages. For some questions, more than one of the choices could conceivably answer the question. However, you are to choose the <u>best</u> answer; that is, the response that most accurately and completely answers the question. You should not make assumptions that are by commonsense standards implausible, superfluous, or incompatible with the passage. After you have chosen the best answer, blacken the corresponding space on your answer sheet.

1. Jim's teacher asked him to determine whether a sample of a substance contained iron. Jim knew that magnets attract iron, so he placed a magnet near the substance. Jim concluded that the substance did contain iron, because the substance became attached to the magnet.

   Jim's reasoning is questionable in that it fails to consider the possibility that

   (A) iron sometimes fails to be attracted to magnets
   (B) iron is attracted to other objects besides magnets
   (C) the magnet needed to be oriented in a certain way
   (D) magnets attract substances other than iron
   (E) some magnets attract iron more strongly than others

2. All the books in the library have their proper shelf locations recorded in the catalog. The book Horatio wants is missing from its place on the library shelves, and no one in the library is using it. Since it is not checked out to a borrower nor awaiting shelving nor part of a special display, it must have been either misplaced or stolen.

   Which one of the following most accurately describes the method of reasoning used in the argument?

   (A) An observation about one object is used as a basis for a general conclusion regarding the status of similar objects.
   (B) A deficiency in a system is isolated by arguing that the system failed to control one of the objects that it was intended to control.
   (C) A conclusion about a particular object is rebutted by observing that a generalization that applies to most such objects does not apply to the object in question.
   (D) A generalization is rejected by showing that it fails to hold in one particular instance.
   (E) The conclusion is supported by ruling out other possible explanations of an observed fact.

3. The level of sulfur dioxide in the atmosphere is slightly higher than it was ten years ago. This increase is troubling because ten years ago the Interior Ministry imposed new, stricter regulations on emissions from coal-burning power plants. If these regulations had been followed, then the level of sulfur dioxide in the atmosphere would have decreased.

   Which one of the following can be properly inferred from the statements above?

   (A) If current regulations on emissions from coal-burning power plants are not followed from now on, then the level of sulfur dioxide in the atmosphere will continue to increase.
   (B) There have been violations of the regulations on emissions from coal-burning power plants that were imposed ten years ago.
   (C) If the regulations on emissions from coal-burning power plants are made even stronger, the level of sulfur dioxide in the atmosphere still will not decrease.
   (D) Emissions from coal-burning power plants are one of the main sources of air pollution.
   (E) Government regulations will never reduce the level of sulfur dioxide in the atmosphere.

GO ON TO THE NEXT PAGE.

4. Ecologist: Landfills are generally designed to hold ten years' worth of waste. Some people maintain that as the number of active landfills consequently dwindles over the coming decade, there will inevitably be a crisis in landfill availability. However, their prediction obviously relies on the unlikely assumption that no new landfills will open as currently active ones close and is therefore unsound.

The claim that there will be a crisis in landfill availability plays which one of the following roles in the ecologist's argument?

(A) It follows from the claim stated in the argument's first sentence.
(B) It is the main conclusion of the argument.
(C) It establishes the truth of the argument's conclusion.
(D) It is a claim on which the argument as a whole is designed to cast doubt.
(E) It is an intermediate conclusion of the argument.

5. Recent epidemiological studies report that Country X has the lowest incidence of disease P of any country. Nevertheless, residents of Country X who are reported to have contracted disease P are much more likely to die from it than are residents of any other country.

Which one of the following, if true, most helps to resolve the apparent discrepancy described above?

(A) There are several forms of disease P, some of which are more contagious than others.
(B) Most of the fatal cases of disease P found in Country X involve people who do not reside in Country X.
(C) In Country X, diagnosis of disease P seldom occurs except in the most severe cases of the disease.
(D) The number of cases of disease P that occur in any country fluctuates widely from year to year.
(E) Because of its climate, more potentially fatal illnesses occur in Country X than in many other countries.

6. After an oil spill, rehabilitation centers were set up to save sea otters by removing oil from them. The effort was not worthwhile, however, since 357 affected live otters and 900 that had died were counted, but only 222 affected otters, or 18 percent of those counted, were successfully rehabilitated and survived. Further, the percentage of all those affected that were successfully rehabilitated was much lower still, because only a fifth of the otters that died immediately were ever found.

Which one of the following, as potential challenges, most seriously calls into question evidence offered in support of the conclusion above?

(A) Do sea otters of species other than those represented among the otters counted exist in areas that were not affected by the oil spill?
(B) How is it possible to estimate, of the sea otters that died, how many were not found?
(C) Did the process of capturing sea otters unavoidably involve trapping and releasing some otters that were not affected by the spill?
(D) Were other species of wildlife besides sea otters negatively affected by the oil spill?
(E) What was the eventual cost, per otter rehabilitated, of the rehabilitation operation?

7. Psychologist: Research has shown that a weakened immune system increases vulnerability to cancer. So, cancer-patient support groups, though derided by those who believe that disease is a purely biochemical phenomenon, may indeed have genuine therapeutic value, as it is clear that participation in such groups reduces participants' stress levels.

Which one of the following is an assumption required by the psychologist's argument?

(A) Cancer patients can learn to function well under extreme stress.
(B) Disease is not a biochemical phenomenon at all.
(C) Stress can weaken the immune system.
(D) Discussing one's condition eliminates the stress of being in that condition.
(E) Stress is a symptom of a weakened immune system.

GO ON TO THE NEXT PAGE.

8. Adobe is an ideal material for building in desert environments. It conducts heat very slowly. As a result, a house built of adobe retains the warmth of the desert sun during the cool evenings and then remains cool during the heat of the day, thereby helping to maintain a pleasant temperature. In contrast, houses built of other commonly used building materials, which conduct heat more rapidly, grow hot during the day and cold at night.

Which one of the following most accurately expresses the main conclusion drawn in the argument above?

(A) Adobe is a suitable substitute for other building materials where the heat-conduction properties of the structure are especially important.

(B) In the desert, adobe buildings remain cool during the heat of the day but retain the warmth of the sun during the cool evenings.

(C) Because adobe conducts heat very slowly, adobe houses maintain a pleasant, constant temperature.

(D) Ideally, a material used for building houses in desert environments should enable those houses to maintain a pleasant, constant temperature.

(E) Adobe is an especially suitable material to use for building houses in desert environments.

9. In one study of a particular plant species, 70 percent of the plants studied were reported as having patterned stems. In a second study, which covered approximately the same geographical area, only 40 percent of the plants of that species were reported as having patterned stems.

Which one of the following, if true, most helps to resolve the apparent discrepancy described above?

(A) The first study was carried out at the time of year when plants of the species are at their most populous.

(B) The first study, but not the second study, also collected information about patterned stems in other plant species.

(C) The second study included approximately 15 percent more individual plants than the first study did.

(D) The first study used a broader definition of "patterned."

(E) The focus of the second study was patterned stems, while the first study collected information about patterned stems only as a secondary goal.

10. Letter to the editor: Sites are needed for disposal of contaminated dredge spoils from the local harbor. However, the approach you propose would damage commercial fishing operations. One indication of this is that over 20,000 people have signed petitions opposing your approach and favoring instead the use of sand-capped pits in another area.

Which one of the following most accurately describes a reasoning flaw in the letter's argument?

(A) The argument distorts the editor's view in a manner that makes that view seem more vulnerable to criticism.

(B) The argument fails to establish that the alternative approach referred to is a viable one.

(C) The argument attempts to establish a particular conclusion because doing so is in the letter writer's self-interest rather than because of any genuine concern for the truth of the matter.

(D) The argument's conclusion is based on the testimony of people who have not been shown to have appropriate expertise.

(E) The argument takes for granted that no third option is available that will satisfy all the interested parties.

GO ON TO THE NEXT PAGE.

11. Most universities today offer students a more in-depth and cosmopolitan education than ever before. Until recently, for example, most university history courses required only the reading of textbooks that hardly mentioned the history of Africa or Asia after the ancient periods, or the history of the Americas' indigenous cultures. The history courses at most universities no longer display such limitations.

Which one of the following, if true, most strengthens the argument above?

(A) The history courses that university students find most interesting are comprehensive in their coverage of various periods and cultures.

(B) Many students at universities whose history courses require the reading of books covering all periods and world cultures participate in innovative study-abroad programs.

(C) The extent to which the textbooks of university history courses are culturally inclusive is a strong indication of the extent to which students at those universities get an in-depth and cosmopolitan education.

(D) Universities at which the history courses are quite culturally inclusive do not always have courses in other subject areas that show the same inclusiveness.

(E) University students who in their history courses are required only to read textbooks covering the history of a single culture will not get an in-depth and cosmopolitan education from these courses alone.

12. The government has recently adopted a policy of publishing airline statistics, including statistics about each airline's number of near collisions and its fines for safety violations. However, such disclosure actually undermines the government's goal of making the public more informed about airline safety, because airlines will be much less likely to give complete reports if such information will be made available to the public.

The reasoning in the argument is most vulnerable to criticism on the grounds that it

(A) fails to consider that, even if the reports are incomplete, they may nevertheless provide the public with important information about airline safety

(B) presumes, without providing justification, that the public has a right to all information about matters of public safety

(C) presumes, without providing justification, that information about airline safety is impossible to find in the absence of government disclosures

(D) presumes, without providing justification, that airlines, rather than the government, should be held responsible for accurate reporting of safety information

(E) fails to consider whether the publication of airline safety statistics will have an effect on the revenues of airlines

13. Many economists claim that financial rewards provide the strongest incentive for people to choose one job over another. But in many surveys, most people do not name high salary as the most desirable feature of a job. This shows that these economists overestimate the degree to which people are motivated by money in their job choices.

Which one of the following, if true, most weakens the argument?

(A) Even high wages do not enable people to obtain all the goods they desire.

(B) In many surveys, people say that they would prefer a high-wage job to an otherwise identical job with lower wages.

(C) Jobs that pay the same salary often vary considerably in their other financial benefits.

(D) Many people enjoy the challenge of a difficult job, as long as they feel that their efforts are appreciated.

(E) Some people are not aware that jobs with high salaries typically leave very little time for recreation.

14. Editorial: A proposed new law would limit elementary school class sizes to a maximum of 20 students. Most parents support this measure and argue that making classes smaller allows teachers to devote more time to each student, with the result that students become more engaged in the learning process. However, researchers who conducted a recent study conclude from their results that this reasoning is questionable. The researchers studied schools that had undergone recent reductions in class size, and found that despite an increase in the amount of time teachers spent individually with students, the students' average grades were unchanged.

Which one of the following is an assumption required by the researchers' argument?

(A) The only schools appropriate for study are large elementary schools.

(B) Teachers generally devote the same amount of individualized attention to each student in a class.

(C) Reductions in class size would also involve a decrease in the number of teachers.

(D) Degree of student engagement in the learning process correlates well with students' average grades.

(E) Parental support for the proposed law rests solely on expectations of increased student engagement in the learning process.

GO ON TO THE NEXT PAGE.

15. Camille: Manufacturers of water-saving faucets exaggerate the amount of money such faucets can save. Because the faucets handle such a low volume of water, people using them often let the water run longer than they would otherwise.

Rebecca: It is true that showering now takes longer. Nevertheless, I have had lower water bills since I installed a water-saving faucet. Thus, it is not true that the manufacturers' claims are exaggerated.

The reasoning in Rebecca's argument is questionable in that she takes for granted that

(A) the cost of installing her water-saving faucet was less than her overall savings on her water bill

(B) she saved as much on her water bills as the manufacturers' claims suggested she would

(C) the manufacturers' claims about the savings expected from the installation of water-saving faucets are consistent with one another

(D) people who use water-saving faucets are satisfied with the low volume of water handled by such faucets

(E) installing more water-saving faucets in her house would increase her savings

16. Company spokesperson: In lieu of redesigning our plants, our company recently launched an environmental protection campaign to buy and dispose of old cars, which are generally highly pollutive. Our plants account for just 4 percent of the local air pollution, while automobiles that predate 1980 account for 30 percent. Clearly, we will reduce air pollution more by buying old cars than we would by redesigning our plants.

Which one of the following, if true, most seriously weakens the company spokesperson's argument?

(A) Only 1 percent of the automobiles driven in the local area predate 1980.

(B) It would cost the company over $3 million to reduce its plants' toxic emissions, while its car-buying campaign will save the company money by providing it with reusable scrap metal.

(C) Because the company pays only scrap metal prices for used cars, almost none of the cars sold to the company still run.

(D) Automobiles made after 1980 account for over 30 percent of local air pollution.

(E) Since the company launched its car-buying campaign, the number of citizen groups filing complaints about pollution from the company's plants has decreased.

17. Humankind would not have survived, as it clearly has, if our ancestors had not been motivated by the desire to sacrifice themselves when doing so would ensure the survival of their children or other close relatives. But since even this kind of sacrifice is a form of altruism, it follows that our ancestors were at least partially altruistic.

Which one of the following arguments is most similar in its reasoning to the argument above?

(A) Students do not raise their grades if they do not increase the amount of time they spend studying. Increased study time requires good time management. However, some students do raise their grades. So some students manage their time well.

(B) Organisms are capable of manufacturing their own carbohydrate supply if they do not consume other organisms to obtain it. So plants that consume insects must be incapable of photosynthesis, the means by which most plants produce their carbohydrate supplies.

(C) If fragile ecosystems are not protected by government action their endemic species will perish, for endemic species are by definition those that exist nowhere else but in those ecosystems.

(D) The natural resources used by human beings will be depleted if they are not replaced by alternative materials. But since such replacement generally requires more power, the resources used to create that power will become depleted.

(E) Public buildings do not harmonize with their surroundings if they are not well designed. But any well-designed building is expensive to construct. Thus, either public buildings are expensive to construct or else they do not harmonize with their surroundings.

GO ON TO THE NEXT PAGE.

18. Bus driver: Had the garbage truck not been exceeding the speed limit, it would not have collided with the bus I was driving. I, on the other hand, was abiding by all traffic regulations—as the police report confirms. Therefore, although I might have been able to avoid the collision had I reacted more quickly, the bus company should not reprimand me for the accident.

Which one of the following principles, if valid, most helps to justify the reasoning in the bus driver's argument?

(A) If a vehicle whose driver is violating a traffic regulation collides with a vehicle whose driver is not, the driver of the first vehicle is solely responsible for the accident.

(B) A bus company should not reprimand one of its drivers whose bus is involved in a collision if a police report confirms that the collision was completely the fault of the driver of another vehicle.

(C) Whenever a bus driver causes a collision to occur by violating a traffic regulation, the bus company should reprimand that driver.

(D) A company that employs bus drivers should reprimand those drivers only when they become involved in collisions that they reasonably could have been expected to avoid.

(E) When a bus is involved in a collision, the bus driver should not be reprimanded by the bus company if the collision did not result from the bus driver's violating a traffic regulation.

19. Item Removed From Scoring.

20. Historian: Radio drama requires its listeners to think about what they hear, picturing for themselves such dramatic elements as characters' physical appearances and spatial relationships. Hence, while earlier generations, for whom radio drama was the dominant form of popular entertainment, regularly exercised their imaginations, today's generation of television viewers do so less frequently.

Which one of the following is an assumption required by the historian's argument?

(A) People spend as much time watching television today as people spent listening to radio in radio's heyday.

(B) The more familiar a form of popular entertainment becomes, the less likely its consumers are to exercise their imaginations.

(C) Because it inhibits the development of creativity, television is a particularly undesirable form of popular entertainment.

(D) For today's generation of television viewers, nothing fills the gap left by radio as a medium for exercising the imagination.

(E) Television drama does not require its viewers to think about what they see.

GO ON TO THE NEXT PAGE.

21. Each of the candidates in this year's mayoral election is a small-business owner. Most small-business owners are competent managers. Moreover, no competent manager lacks the skills necessary to be a good mayor. So, most of the candidates in this year's mayoral election have the skills necessary to be a good mayor.

The pattern of flawed reasoning in which one of the following is most similar to that in the argument above?

(A) Anyone who has worked in sales at this company has done so for at least a year. Most of this company's management has worked in its sales department. So, since no one who has worked in the sales department for more than a year fails to understand marketing, most of this company's upper management understands marketing.

(B) Everything on the menu at Maddy's Shake Shop is fat-free. Most fat-free foods and drinks are sugar-free. And all sugar-free foods and drinks are low in calories. Hence, most items on the menu at Maddy's are low in calories.

(C) All the books in Ed's apartment are hardcover books. Most hardcover books are more than 100 pages long. Ed has never read a book longer than 100 pages in its entirety in less than 3 hours. So, Ed has never read any of his books in its entirety in less than 3 hours.

(D) Each of the avant-garde films at this year's film festival is less than an hour long. Most films less than an hour long do not become commercially successful. So, since no movie less than an hour long has an intermission, it follows that most of the movies at this year's film festival do not have an intermission.

(E) All of the bicycle helmets sold in this store have some plastic in them. Most of the bicycle helmets sold in this store have some rubber in them. So, since no helmets that have rubber in them do not also have plastic in them, it follows that most of the helmets in this store that have plastic in them have rubber in them.

22. One of the most useful social conventions is money, whose universality across societies is matched only by language. Unlike language, which is rooted in an innate ability, money is an artificial, human invention. Hence, it seems probable that the invention of money occurred independently in more than one society.

The argument's conclusion is properly drawn if which one of the following is assumed?

(A) Some societies have been geographically isolated enough not to have been influenced by any other society.

(B) Language emerged independently in different societies at different times in human history.

(C) Universal features of human society that are not inventions are rooted in innate abilities.

(D) If money were not useful, it would not be so widespread.

(E) No human society that adopted the convention of money has since abandoned it.

23. Libel is defined as damaging the reputation of someone by making false statements. Ironically, strong laws against libel can make it impossible for anyone in the public eye to have a good reputation. For the result of strong libel laws is that, for fear of lawsuits, no one will say anything bad about public figures.

Which one of the following principles, if valid, most helps to justify the reasoning in the argument?

(A) The absence of laws against libel makes it possible for everyone in the public eye to have a good reputation.

(B) Even if laws against libel are extremely strong and rigorously enforced, some public figures will acquire bad reputations.

(C) If one makes statements that one sincerely believes, then those statements should not be considered libelous even if they are in fact false and damaging to the reputation of a public figure.

(D) In countries with strong libel laws, people make negative statements about public figures only when such statements can be proved.

(E) Public figures can have good reputations only if there are other public figures who have bad reputations.

GO ON TO THE NEXT PAGE.

24. Mammals cannot digest cellulose and therefore cannot directly obtain glucose from wood. Mushrooms can, however; and some mushrooms use cellulose to make highly branched polymers, the branches of which are a form of glucose called beta-glucans. Beta-glucan extracts from various types of mushrooms slow, reverse, or prevent the growth of cancerous tumors in mammals, and the antitumor activity of beta-glucans increases as the degree of branching increases. These extracts prevent tumor growth not by killing cancer cells directly but by increasing immune-cell activity.

Which one of the following is most strongly supported by the information above?

(A) Mammals obtain no beneficial health effects from eating cellulose.

(B) If extracts from a type of mushroom slow, reverse, or prevent the growth of cancerous tumors in mammals, then the mushroom is capable of using cellulose to make beta-glucans.

(C) The greater the degree of branching of beta-glucans, the greater the degree of immune-cell activity it triggers in mammals.

(D) Immune-cell activity in mammals does not prevent tumor growth by killing cancer cells.

(E) Any organism capable of obtaining glucose from wood can use cellulose to make beta-glucans.

25. A law is successful primarily because the behavior it prescribes has attained the status of custom. Just as manners are observed not because of sanctions attached to them but because, through repetition, contrary behavior becomes unthinkable, so societal laws are obeyed not because the behavior is ethically required or because penalties await those who act otherwise, but because to act otherwise would be uncustomary.

Which one of the following comparisons is utilized by the argument?

(A) As with manners and other customs, laws vary from society to society.

(B) As with manners, the primary basis for a society to consider when adopting a law is custom.

(C) As with manners, the main factor accounting for compliance with laws is custom.

(D) As with manners, most laws do not prescribe behavior that is ethically required.

(E) As with manners, most laws do not have strict penalties awaiting those who transgress them.

S T O P

IF YOU FINISH BEFORE TIME IS CALLED, YOU MAY CHECK YOUR WORK ON THIS SECTION ONLY.
DO NOT WORK ON ANY OTHER SECTION IN THE TEST.

SECTION II

Time—35 minutes

23 Questions

Directions: Each group of questions in this section is based on a set of conditions. In answering some of the questions, it may be useful to draw a rough diagram. Choose the response that most accurately and completely answers each question and blacken the corresponding space on your answer sheet.

Questions 1–6

A community center will host six arts-and-crafts workshops—Jewelry, Kite-making, Needlepoint, Quilting, Rug-making, and Scrapbooking. The workshops will be given on three consecutive days: Wednesday, Thursday, and Friday. Each workshop will be given once, and exactly two workshops will be given per day, one in the morning and one in the afternoon. The schedule for the workshops is subject to the following constraints:

> Jewelry must be given in the morning, on the same day as either Kite-making or Quilting.
>
> Rug-making must be given in the afternoon, on the same day as either Needlepoint or Scrapbooking.
>
> Quilting must be given on an earlier day than both Kite-making and Needlepoint.

1. Which one of the following is an acceptable schedule for the workshops, with each day's workshops listed in the order in which they are to be given?

    (A) Wednesday: Jewelry, Kite-making
         Thursday: Quilting, Scrapbooking
         Friday: Needlepoint, Rug-making
    (B) Wednesday: Jewelry, Quilting
         Thursday: Kite-making, Needlepoint
         Friday: Scrapbooking, Rug-making
    (C) Wednesday: Quilting, Needlepoint
         Thursday: Scrapbooking, Rug-making
         Friday: Jewelry, Kite-making
    (D) Wednesday: Quilting, Scrapbooking
         Thursday: Jewelry, Kite-making
         Friday: Rug-making, Needlepoint
    (E) Wednesday: Scrapbooking, Rug-making
         Thursday: Quilting, Jewelry
         Friday: Kite-making, Needlepoint

2. Which one of the following workshops CANNOT be given on Thursday morning?

    (A) Jewelry
    (B) Kite-making
    (C) Needlepoint
    (D) Quilting
    (E) Scrapbooking

3. Which one of the following pairs of workshops CANNOT be the ones given on Wednesday morning and Wednesday afternoon, respectively?

    (A) Jewelry, Kite-making
    (B) Jewelry, Quilting
    (C) Quilting, Scrapbooking
    (D) Scrapbooking, Quilting
    (E) Scrapbooking, Rug-making

4. If Kite-making is given on Friday morning, then which one of the following could be true?

    (A) Jewelry is given on Thursday morning.
    (B) Needlepoint is given on Thursday afternoon.
    (C) Quilting is given on Wednesday morning.
    (D) Rug-making is given on Friday afternoon.
    (E) Scrapbooking is given on Wednesday afternoon.

5. If Quilting is given in the morning, then which one of the following workshops CANNOT be given on Thursday?

    (A) Jewelry
    (B) Kite-making
    (C) Needlepoint
    (D) Rug-making
    (E) Scrapbooking

6. How many of the workshops are there that could be the one given on Wednesday morning?

    (A) one
    (B) two
    (C) three
    (D) four
    (E) five

GO ON TO THE NEXT PAGE.

Questions 7–12

Exactly six actors—Geyer, Henson, Jhalani, Lin, Mitchell, and Paredes—will appear one after another in the opening credits of a television program. Their contracts contain certain restrictions that affect the order in which they can appear. Given these restrictions, the order in which the actors appear, from first to sixth, must conform to the following:

Both Lin and Mitchell appear earlier than Henson.
Both Lin and Paredes appear earlier than Jhalani.
If Mitchell appears earlier than Paredes, then Henson appears earlier than Geyer.
Geyer does not appear last.

7. Which one of the following could be the order, from first to last, in which the actors appear?

(A)   Geyer, Lin, Jhalani, Paredes, Mitchell, Henson
(B)   Geyer, Mitchell, Paredes, Lin, Henson, Jhalani
(C)   Henson, Lin, Paredes, Jhalani, Geyer, Mitchell
(D)   Lin, Paredes, Mitchell, Henson, Jhalani, Geyer
(E)   Paredes, Mitchell, Lin, Jhalani, Geyer, Henson

8. Which one of the following CANNOT be true?

(A)   Henson appears earlier than Geyer.
(B)   Henson appears sixth.
(C)   Lin appears fifth.
(D)   Paredes appears earlier than Mitchell.
(E)   Paredes appears second.

9. Exactly how many of the actors are there any one of whom could appear sixth?

(A)   5
(B)   4
(C)   3
(D)   2
(E)   1

10. If Jhalani appears earlier than Mitchell, then which one of the following could be the order in which the other four actors appear, from earliest to latest?

(A)   Geyer, Lin, Paredes, Henson
(B)   Geyer, Paredes, Henson, Lin
(C)   Lin, Henson, Geyer, Paredes
(D)   Lin, Paredes, Henson, Geyer
(E)   Paredes, Lin, Henson, Geyer

11. If Lin appears immediately before Geyer, then which one of the following must be true?

(A)   Geyer appears no later than third.
(B)   Henson appears last.
(C)   Lin appears no later than third.
(D)   Mitchell appears earlier than Geyer.
(E)   Paredes appears first.

12. If Mitchell appears first, then which one of the following must be true?

(A)   Geyer appears fifth.
(B)   Henson appears third.
(C)   Jhalani appears sixth.
(D)   Lin appears second.
(E)   Paredes appears fourth.

GO ON TO THE NEXT PAGE.

Questions 13–17

Over the course of one day, a landscaper will use a truck to haul exactly seven loads—three loads of mulch and four loads of stone. The truck's cargo bed will be cleaned in between carrying any two loads of different materials. To meet the landscaper's needs as efficiently as possible, the following constraints apply:

The cargo bed cannot be cleaned more than three times.
The fifth load must be mulch.

13. Which one of the following is a pair of loads that can both be mulch?

(A) the first and the third
(B) the second and the third
(C) the second and the sixth
(D) the third and the sixth
(E) the fourth and the sixth

14. Which one of the following must be true?

(A) The second load is stone.
(B) The first and second loads are the same material.
(C) The second and third loads are different materials.
(D) At least two loads of mulch are hauled consecutively.
(E) At least three loads of stone are hauled consecutively.

15. If the third load is mulch, which one of the following must be true?

(A) The sixth load is a different material than the seventh load.
(B) The first load is a different material than the second load.
(C) The seventh load is mulch.
(D) The sixth load is mulch.
(E) The first load is stone.

16. If the cargo bed is cleaned exactly twice, which one of the following must be true?

(A) The second load is stone.
(B) The third load is mulch.
(C) The third load is stone.
(D) The sixth load is mulch.
(E) The seventh load is mulch.

17. If no more than two loads of the same material are hauled consecutively, then which one of the following could be true?

(A) The first load is stone.
(B) The fourth load is stone.
(C) The third load is mulch.
(D) The sixth load is mulch.
(E) The seventh load is mulch.

GO ON TO THE NEXT PAGE.

Questions 18–23

A travel magazine has hired six interns—Farber, Gombarick, Hall, Jackson, Kanze, and Lha—to assist in covering three stories—Romania, Spain, and Tuscany. Each intern will be trained either as a photographer's assistant or as a writer's assistant. Each story is assigned a team of two interns—one photographer's assistant and one writer's assistant—in accordance with the following conditions:

Gombarick and Lha will be trained in the same field.
Farber and Kanze will be trained in different fields.
Hall will be trained as a photographer's assistant.
Jackson is assigned to Tuscany.
Kanze is not assigned to Spain.

18. Which one of the following could be an acceptable assignment of photographer's assistants to stories?

(A)   Romania: Farber
        Spain: Hall
        Tuscany: Jackson
(B)   Romania: Gombarick
        Spain: Hall
        Tuscany: Farber
(C)   Romania: Gombarick
        Spain: Hall
        Tuscany: Lha
(D)   Romania: Gombarick
        Spain: Lha
        Tuscany: Kanze
(E)   Romania: Hall
        Spain: Kanze
        Tuscany: Jackson

19. If Farber is assigned to Romania, then which one of the following must be true?

(A)   Gombarick is assigned to Spain.
(B)   Hall is assigned to Spain.
(C)   Kanze is assigned to Tuscany.
(D)   Lha is assigned to Spain.
(E)   Lha is assigned to Tuscany.

20. If Farber and Hall are assigned to the same story as each other, then which one of the following could be true?

(A)   Farber is assigned to Tuscany.
(B)   Gombarick is assigned to Romania.
(C)   Hall is assigned to Romania.
(D)   Kanze is assigned to Tuscany.
(E)   Lha is assigned to Spain.

21. If Farber is a writer's assistant, then which one of the following pairs could be the team of interns assigned to Romania?

(A)   Farber and Gombarick
(B)   Gombarick and Hall
(C)   Hall and Kanze
(D)   Kanze and Lha
(E)   Lha and Hall

22. If Gombarick and Kanze are assigned to the same story as each other, then which one of the following could be true?

(A)   Farber is assigned to Romania.
(B)   Gombarick is assigned to Spain.
(C)   Hall is assigned to Romania.
(D)   Kanze is assigned to Tuscany.
(E)   Lha is assigned to Spain.

23. Which one of the following interns CANNOT be assigned to Tuscany?

(A)   Farber
(B)   Gombarick
(C)   Hall
(D)   Kanze
(E)   Lha

S T O P

IF YOU FINISH BEFORE TIME IS CALLED, YOU MAY CHECK YOUR WORK ON THIS SECTION ONLY.
DO NOT WORK ON ANY OTHER SECTION IN THE TEST.

SECTION III

Time—35 minutes

25 Questions

Directions: The questions in this section are based on the reasoning contained in brief statements or passages. For some questions, more than one of the choices could conceivably answer the question. However, you are to choose the best answer; that is, the response that most accurately and completely answers the question. You should not make assumptions that are by commonsense standards implausible, superfluous, or incompatible with the passage. After you have chosen the best answer, blacken the corresponding space on your answer sheet.

1. A research study revealed that, in most cases, once existing highways near urban areas are widened and extended in an attempt to reduce traffic congestion and resulting delays for motorists, these problems actually increase rather than decrease.

   Which one of the following, if true, most helps to explain the discrepancy between the intended results of the highway improvements and the results revealed in the study?

   (A) Widened and extended roads tend to attract many more motorists than used them before their improvement.

   (B) Typically, road widening or extension projects are undertaken only after the population near the road in question has increased and then leveled off, leaving a higher average population level.

   (C) As a general rule, the greater the number of lanes on a given length of highway, the lower the rate of accidents per 100,000 vehicles traveling on it.

   (D) Rural, as compared to urban, traffic usually includes a larger proportion of trucks and vehicles used by farmers.

   (E) Urban traffic generally moves at a slower pace and involves more congestion and delays than rural and suburban traffic.

2. A study found that consumers reaching supermarket checkout lines within 40 minutes after the airing of an advertisement for a given product over the store's audio system were significantly more likely to purchase the product advertised than were consumers who checked out prior to the airing. Apparently, these advertisements are effective.

   Which one of the following, if true, most strengthens the argument?

   (A) During the study, for most of the advertisements more people went through the checkout lines after they were aired than before they were aired.

   (B) A large proportion of the consumers who bought a product shortly after the airing of an advertisement for it reported that they had not gone to the store intending to buy that product.

   (C) Many of the consumers reported that they typically bought at least one of the advertised products every time they shopped at the store.

   (D) Many of the consumers who bought an advertised product and who reached the checkout line within 40 minutes of the advertisement's airing reported that they could not remember hearing the advertisement.

   (E) Many of the consumers who bought an advertised product reported that they buy that product only occasionally.

GO ON TO THE NEXT PAGE.

3. Unless the building permit is obtained by February 1 of this year or some of the other activities necessary for construction of the new library can be completed in less time than originally planned, the new library will not be completed on schedule. It is now clear that the building permit cannot be obtained by February 1, so the new library will not be completed on schedule.

The conclusion drawn follows logically from the premises if which one of the following is assumed?

(A)   All of the other activities necessary for construction of the library will take at least as much time as originally planned.

(B)   The officials in charge of construction of the new library have admitted that it probably will not be completed on schedule.

(C)   The application for a building permit was submitted on January 2 of this year, and processing building permits always takes at least two months.

(D)   The application for a building permit was rejected the first time it was submitted, and it had to be resubmitted with a revised building plan.

(E)   It is not possible to convince authorities to allow construction of the library to begin before the building permit is obtained.

4. In a study of patients who enrolled at a sleep clinic because of insomnia, those who inhaled the scent of peppermint before going to bed were more likely to have difficulty falling asleep than were patients who inhaled the scent of bitter orange. Since it is known that inhaling bitter orange does not help people fall asleep more easily, this study shows that inhaling the scent of peppermint makes insomnia worse.

Which one of the following, if true, most seriously weakens the argument above?

(A)   Several studies have shown that inhaling the scent of peppermint tends to have a relaxing effect on people who do not suffer from insomnia.

(B)   The patients who inhaled the scent of bitter orange were, on average, suffering from milder cases of insomnia than were the patients who inhaled the scent of peppermint.

(C)   Because the scents of peppermint and bitter orange are each very distinctive, it was not possible to prevent the patients from knowing that they were undergoing some sort of study of the effects of inhaling various scents.

(D)   Some of the patients who enrolled in the sleep clinic also had difficulty staying asleep once they fell asleep.

(E)   Several studies have revealed that in many cases inhaling certain pleasant scents can dramatically affect the degree to which a patient suffers from insomnia.

5. Dogs learn best when they are trained using both voice commands and hand signals. After all, a recent study shows that dogs who were trained using both voice commands and hand signals were twice as likely to obey as were dogs who were trained using only voice commands.

The claim that dogs learn best when they are trained using both voice commands and hand signals figures in the argument in which one of the following ways?

(A)   It is an explicit premise of the argument.

(B)   It is an implicit assumption of the argument.

(C)   It is a statement of background information offered to help facilitate understanding the issue in the argument.

(D)   It is a statement that the argument claims is supported by the study.

(E)   It is an intermediate conclusion that is offered as direct support for the argument's main conclusion.

6. Of the many test pilots who have flown the new plane, none has found it difficult to operate. So it is unlikely that the test pilot flying the plane tomorrow will find it difficult to operate.

The reasoning in which one of the following arguments is most similar to the reasoning in the argument above?

(A)   All of the many book reviewers who read Rachel Nguyen's new novel thought that it was particularly well written. So it is likely that the average reader will enjoy the book.

(B)   Many of the book reviewers who read Wim Jashka's new novel before it was published found it very entertaining. So it is unlikely that most people who buy the book will find it boring.

(C)   Neither of the two reviewers who enjoyed Sharlene Lo's new novel hoped that Lo would write a sequel. So it is unlikely that the review of the book in next Sunday's newspaper will express hope that Lo will write a sequel.

(D)   Many reviewers have read Kip Landau's new novel, but none of them enjoyed it. So it is unlikely that the reviewer for the local newspaper will enjoy the book when she reads it.

(E)   None of the reviewers who have read Gray Ornsby's new novel were offended by it. So it is unlikely that the book will offend anyone in the general public who reads it.

GO ON TO THE NEXT PAGE.

7. Scientist: Any theory that is to be taken seriously must affect our perception of the world. Of course, this is not, in itself, enough for a theory to be taken seriously. To see this, one need only consider astrology.

The point of the scientist's mentioning astrology in the argument is to present

(A) an example of a theory that should not be taken seriously because it does not affect our perception of the world

(B) an example of something that should not be considered a theory

(C) an example of a theory that should not be taken seriously despite its affecting our perception of the world

(D) an example of a theory that affects our perception of the world, and thus should be taken seriously

(E) an example of a theory that should be taken seriously, even though it does not affect our perception of the world

8. Clark: Our local community theater often produces plays by critically acclaimed playwrights. In fact, the production director says that critical acclaim is one of the main factors considered in the selection of plays to perform. So, since my neighbor Michaela's new play will be performed by the theater this season, she must be a critically acclaimed playwright.

The reasoning in Clark's argument is most vulnerable to criticism on the grounds that the argument

(A) takes a condition necessary for a playwright's being critically acclaimed to be a condition sufficient for a playwright's being critically acclaimed

(B) fails to consider that several different effects may be produced by a single cause

(C) treats one main factor considered in the selection of plays to perform as though it were a condition that must be met in order for a play to be selected

(D) uses as evidence a source that there is reason to believe is unreliable

(E) provides no evidence that a playwright's being critically acclaimed is the result rather than the cause of his or her plays being selected for production

9. Legal theorist: Governments should not be allowed to use the personal diaries of an individual who is the subject of a criminal prosecution as evidence against that individual. A diary is a silent conversation with oneself and there is no relevant difference between speaking to oneself, writing one's thoughts down, and keeping one's thoughts to oneself.

Which one of the following principles, if valid, provides the most support for the legal theorist's argument?

(A) Governments should not be allowed to compel corporate officials to surrender interoffice memos to government investigators.

(B) When crime is a serious problem, governments should be given increased power to investigate and prosecute suspected wrongdoers, and some restrictions on admissible evidence should be relaxed.

(C) Governments should not be allowed to use an individual's remarks to prosecute the individual for criminal activity unless the remarks were intended for other people.

(D) Governments should not have the power to confiscate an individual's personal correspondence to use as evidence against the individual in a criminal trial.

(E) Governments should do everything in their power to investigate and prosecute suspected wrongdoers.

10. A ring of gas emitting X-rays flickering 450 times per second has been observed in a stable orbit around a black hole. In light of certain widely accepted physical theories, that rate of flickering can best be explained if the ring of gas has a radius of 49 kilometers. But the gas ring could not maintain an orbit so close to a black hole unless the black hole was spinning.

The statements above, if true, most strongly support which one of the following, assuming that the widely accepted physical theories referred to above are correct?

(A) Black holes that have orbiting rings of gas with radii greater than 49 kilometers are usually stationary.

(B) Only rings of gas that are in stable orbits around black holes emit flickering X-rays.

(C) The black hole that is within the ring of gas observed by the astronomers is spinning.

(D) X-rays emitted by rings of gas orbiting black holes cause those black holes to spin.

(E) A black hole is stationary only if it is orbited by a ring of gas with a radius of more than 49 kilometers.

GO ON TO THE NEXT PAGE.

11. A mass of "black water" containing noxious organic material swept through Laurel Bay last year. Some scientists believe that this event was a naturally occurring but infrequent phenomenon. The black water completely wiped out five species of coral in the bay, including mounds of coral that were more than two centuries old. Therefore, even if this black water phenomenon has struck the bay before, it did not reach last year's intensity at any time in the past two centuries.

Which one of the following is an assumption required by the argument?

(A) Masses of black water such as that observed last summer come into the bay more frequently than just once every two centuries.

(B) Every species of coral in the bay was seriously harmed by the mass of black water that swept in last year.

(C) The mass of black water that swept through the bay last year did not decimate any plant or animal species that makes use of coral.

(D) The mounds of centuries-old coral that were destroyed were not in especially fragile condition just before the black water swept in last year.

(E) Older specimens of coral in the bay were more vulnerable to damage from the influx of black water than were young specimens.

12. Many nurseries sell fruit trees that they label "miniature." Not all nurseries, however, use this term in the same way. While some nurseries label any nectarine trees of the Stark Sweet Melody variety as "miniature," for example, others do not. One thing that is clear is that if a variety of fruit tree is not suitable for growing in a tub or a pot, no tree of that variety can be correctly labeled "miniature."

Which one of the following can be properly inferred from the information above?

(A) Most nurseries mislabel at least some of their fruit trees.

(B) Some of the nurseries have correctly labeled nectarine trees of the Stark Sweet Melody variety only if the variety is unsuitable for growing in a tub or a pot.

(C) Any nectarine tree of the Stark Sweet Melody variety that a nursery labels "miniature" is labeled incorrectly.

(D) Some nectarine trees that are not labeled "miniature" are labeled incorrectly.

(E) Unless the Stark Sweet Melody variety of nectarine tree is suitable for growing in a tub or a pot, some nurseries mislabel this variety of tree.

13. Psychologist: Identical twins are virtually the same genetically. Moreover, according to some studies, identical twins separated at birth and brought up in vastly different environments show a strong tendency to report similar ethical beliefs, dress in the same way, and have similar careers. Thus, many of our inclinations must be genetic in origin, and not subject to environmental influences.

Which one of the following, if true, would most weaken the psychologist's argument?

(A) Many people, including identical twins, undergo radical changes in their lifestyles at some point in their lives.

(B) While some studies of identical twins separated at birth reveal a high percentage of similar personality traits, they also show a few differences.

(C) Scientists are far from being able to link any specific genes to specific inclinations.

(D) Identical twins who grow up together tend to develop different beliefs, tastes, and careers in order to differentiate themselves from each other.

(E) Twins who are not identical tend to develop different beliefs, tastes, and careers.

14. Human beings can live happily only in a society where love and friendship are the primary motives for actions. Yet economic needs can be satisfied in the absence of this condition, as, for example, in a merchant society where only economic utility motivates action. It is obvious then that human beings _____.

Which one of the following most logically completes the argument?

(A) can live happily only when economic utility is not a motivator in their society

(B) cannot achieve happiness unless their economic needs have already been satisfied

(C) cannot satisfy economic needs by means of interactions with family members and close friends

(D) can satisfy their basic economic needs without obtaining happiness

(E) cannot really be said to have satisfied their economic needs unless they are happy

GO ON TO THE NEXT PAGE.

15. Technologically, it is already possible to produce nonpolluting cars that burn hydrogen rather than gasoline. But the national system of fuel stations that would be needed to provide the hydrogen fuel for such cars does not yet exist. However, this infrastructure is likely to appear and grow rapidly. A century ago no fuel-distribution infrastructure existed for gasoline-powered vehicles, yet it quickly developed in response to consumer demand.

Which one of the following most accurately expresses the conclusion drawn in the argument?

(A) It is already technologically possible to produce nonpolluting cars that burn hydrogen rather than gasoline.

(B) The fuel-distribution infrastructure for hydrogen-powered cars still needs to be created.

(C) If a new kind of technology is developed, the infrastructure needed to support that technology is likely to quickly develop in response to consumer demands.

(D) The fuel-distribution infrastructure for hydrogen-powered cars is likely to appear and grow rapidly.

(E) Hydrogen-powered vehicles will be similar to gasoline-powered vehicles with regard to the amount of consumer demand for their fuel-distribution infrastructure.

16. Wildlife management experts should not interfere with the natural habitats of creatures in the wild, because manipulating the environment to make it easier for an endangered species to survive in a habitat invariably makes it harder for nonendangered species to survive in that habitat.

The argument is most vulnerable to criticism on the grounds that it

(A) fails to consider that wildlife management experts probably know best how to facilitate the survival of an endangered species in a habitat

(B) fails to recognize that a nonendangered species can easily become an endangered species

(C) overlooks the possibility that saving an endangered species in a habitat is incompatible with preserving the overall diversity of species in that habitat

(D) presumes, without providing justification, that the survival of each endangered species is equally important to the health of the environment

(E) takes for granted that preserving a currently endangered species in a habitat does not have higher priority than preserving species in that habitat that are not endangered

17. Any food that is not sterilized and sealed can contain disease-causing bacteria. Once sterilized and properly sealed, however, it contains no bacteria. There are many different acceptable food-preservation techniques; each involves either sterilizing and sealing food or else at least slowing the growth of disease-causing bacteria. Some of the techniques may also destroy natural food enzymes that cause food to spoil or discolor quickly.

If the statements above are true, which one of the following must be true?

(A) All food preserved by an acceptable method is free of disease-causing bacteria.

(B) Preservation methods that destroy enzymes that cause food to spoil do not sterilize the food.

(C) Food preserved by a sterilization method is less likely to discolor quickly than food preserved with other methods.

(D) Any nonsterilized food preserved by an acceptable method can contain disease-causing bacteria.

(E) If a food contains no bacteria, then it has been preserved by an acceptable method.

GO ON TO THE NEXT PAGE.

18. Activities that pose risks to life are acceptable if and only if each person who bears the risks either gains some net benefit that cannot be had without such risks, or bears the risks voluntarily.

Which one of the following judgments most closely conforms to the principle above?

(A) A door-to-door salesperson declines to replace his older car with a new model with more safety features; this is acceptable because the decision not to replace the car is voluntary.

(B) A smoker subjects people to secondhand smoke at an outdoor public meeting; the resulting risks are acceptable because the danger from secondhand smoke is minimal outdoors, where smoke dissipates quickly.

(C) A motorcyclist rides without a helmet; the risk of fatal injury to the motorcyclist thus incurred is acceptable because the motorcyclist incurs this risk willingly.

(D) Motor vehicles are allowed to emit certain low levels of pollution; the resulting health risks are acceptable because all users of motor vehicles share the resulting benefit of inexpensive, convenient travel.

(E) A nation requires all citizens to spend two years in national service; since such service involves no risk to life, the policy is acceptable.

19. Ecologist: One theory attributes the ability of sea butterflies to avoid predation to their appearance, while another attributes this ability to various chemical compounds they produce. Recently we added each of the compounds to food pellets, one compound per pellet. Predators ate the pellets no matter which one of the compounds was present. Thus the compounds the sea butterflies produce are not responsible for their ability to avoid predation.

The reasoning in the ecologist's argument is flawed in that the argument

(A) presumes, without providing justification, that the two theories are incompatible with each other

(B) draws a conclusion about a cause on the basis of nothing more than a statistical correlation

(C) treats a condition sufficient for sea butterflies' ability to avoid predators as a condition required for this ability

(D) infers, from the claim that no individual member of a set has a certain effect, that the set as a whole does not have that effect

(E) draws a conclusion that merely restates material present in one or more of its premises

20. Principle: One should criticize the works or actions of another person only if the criticism will not seriously harm the person criticized and one does so in the hope or expectation of benefiting someone other than oneself.

Application: Jarrett should not have criticized Ostertag's essay in front of the class, since the defects in it were so obvious that pointing them out benefited no one.

Which one of the following, if true, justifies the above application of the principle?

(A) Jarrett knew that the defects in the essay were so obvious that pointing them out would benefit no one.

(B) Jarrett's criticism of the essay would have been to Ostertag's benefit only if Ostertag had been unaware of the defects in the essay at the time.

(C) Jarrett knew that the criticism might antagonize Ostertag.

(D) Jarrett hoped to gain prestige by criticizing Ostertag.

(E) Jarrett did not expect the criticism to be to Ostertag's benefit.

21. Safety consultant: Judged by the number of injuries per licensed vehicle, minivans are the safest vehicles on the road. However, in carefully designed crash tests, minivans show no greater ability to protect their occupants than other vehicles of similar size do. Thus, the reason minivans have such a good safety record is probably not that they are inherently safer than other vehicles, but rather that they are driven primarily by low-risk drivers.

Which one of the following, if true, most strengthens the safety consultant's argument?

(A) When choosing what kind of vehicle to drive, low-risk drivers often select a kind that they know to perform particularly well in crash tests.

(B) Judged by the number of accidents per licensed vehicle, minivans are no safer than most other kinds of vehicles are.

(C) Minivans tend to carry more passengers at any given time than do most other vehicles.

(D) In general, the larger a vehicle is, the greater its ability to protect its occupants.

(E) Minivans generally have worse braking and emergency handling capabilities than other vehicles of similar size.

GO ON TO THE NEXT PAGE.

22. Consumer advocate: There is no doubt that the government is responsible for the increased cost of gasoline, because the government's policies have significantly increased consumer demand for fuel, and as a result of increasing demand, the price of gasoline has risen steadily.

Which one of the following is an assumption required by the consumer advocate's argument?

(A) The government can bear responsibility for that which it indirectly causes.

(B) The government is responsible for some unforeseen consequences of its policies.

(C) Consumer demand for gasoline cannot increase without causing gasoline prices to increase.

(D) The government has an obligation to ensure that demand for fuel does not increase excessively.

(E) If the government pursues policies that do not increase the demand for fuel, gasoline prices tend to remain stable.

23. A species in which mutations frequently occur will develop new evolutionary adaptations in each generation. Since species survive dramatic environmental changes only if they develop new evolutionary adaptations in each generation, a species in which mutations frequently occur will survive dramatic environmental changes.

The flawed pattern of reasoning in which one of the following is most closely parallel to that in the argument above?

(A) In a stone wall that is properly built, every stone supports another stone. Since a wall's being sturdy depends upon its being properly built, only walls that are composed entirely of stones supporting other stones are sturdy.

(B) A play that is performed before a different audience every time will never get the same reaction from any two audiences. Since no plays are performed before the same audience every time, no play ever gets the same reaction from any two audiences.

(C) A person who is perfectly honest will tell the truth in every situation. Since in order to be a morally upright person one must tell the truth at all times, a perfectly honest person will also be a morally upright person.

(D) An herb garden is productive only if the soil that it is planted in is well drained. Since soil that is well drained is good soil, an herb garden is not productive unless it is planted in good soil.

(E) A diet that is healthful is well balanced. Since a well-balanced diet includes fruits and vegetables, one will not be healthy unless one eats fruits and vegetables.

GO ON TO THE NEXT PAGE.

24. Music critic: How well an underground rock group's recordings sell is no mark of that group's success as an underground group. After all, if a recording sells well, it may be because some of the music on the recording is too trendy to be authentically underground; accordingly, many underground musicians consider it desirable for a recording not to sell well. But weak sales may simply be the result of the group's incompetence.

Which one of the following principles, if valid, most helps to justify the music critic's argument?

(A) If an underground rock group is successful as an underground group, its recordings will sell neither especially well nor especially poorly.

(B) An underground rock group is unsuccessful as an underground group if it is incompetent or if any of its music is too trendy to be authentically underground, or both.

(C) Whether an underground group's recordings meet criteria that many underground musicians consider desirable is not a mark of that group's success.

(D) An underground rock group is successful as an underground group if the group is competent but its recordings nonetheless do not sell well.

(E) For an underground rock group, competence and the creation of authentically underground music are not in themselves marks of success.

25. Graham: The defeat of the world's chess champion by a computer shows that any type of human intellectual activity governed by fixed principles can be mastered by machines and thus that a truly intelligent machine will inevitably be devised.

Adelaide: But you are overlooking the fact that the computer in the case you cite was simply an extension of the people who programmed it. It was their successful distillation of the principles of chess that enabled them to defeat a chess champion using a computer.

The statements above provide the most support for holding that Graham and Adelaide disagree about whether

(A) chess is the best example of a human intellectual activity that is governed by fixed principles

(B) chess is a typical example of the sorts of intellectual activities in which human beings characteristically engage

(C) a computer's defeat of a human chess player is an accomplishment that should be attributed to the computer

(D) intelligence can be demonstrated by the performance of an activity in accord with fixed principles

(E) tools can be designed to aid in any human activity that is governed by fixed principles

S T O P

IF YOU FINISH BEFORE TIME IS CALLED, YOU MAY CHECK YOUR WORK ON THIS SECTION ONLY.
DO NOT WORK ON ANY OTHER SECTION IN THE TEST.

SECTION IV

Time—35 minutes

27 Questions

<u>Directions:</u> Each set of questions in this section is based on a single passage or a pair of passages. The questions are to be answered on the basis of what is <u>stated</u> or <u>implied</u> in the passage or pair of passages. For some of the questions, more than one of the choices could conceivably answer the question. However, you are to choose the <u>best</u> answer; that is, the response that most accurately and completely answers the question, and blacken the corresponding space on your answer sheet.

Over the past 50 years, expansive, low-density communities have proliferated at the edges of many cities in the United States and Canada, creating a phenomenon known as suburban sprawl. Andres
(5) Duany, Elizabeth Plater-Zyberk, and Jeff Speck, a group of prominent town planners belonging to a movement called New Urbanism, contend that suburban sprawl contributes to the decline of civic life and civility. For reasons involving the flow of
(10) automobile traffic, they note, zoning laws usually dictate that suburban homes, stores, businesses, and schools be built in separate areas, and this separation robs people of communal space where they can interact and get to know one another. It is as difficult
(15) to imagine the concept of community without a town square or local pub, these town planners contend, as it is to imagine the concept of family independent of the home.

Suburban housing subdivisions, Duany and his
(20) colleagues add, usually contain homes identical not only in appearance but also in price, resulting in a de facto economic segregation of residential neighborhoods. Children growing up in these neighborhoods, whatever their economic
(25) circumstances, are certain to be ill prepared for life in a diverse society. Moreover, because the widely separated suburban homes and businesses are connected only by "collector roads," residents are forced to drive, often in heavy traffic, in order to
(30) perform many daily tasks. Time that would in a town center involve social interaction within a physical public realm is now spent inside the automobile, where people cease to be community members and instead become motorists, competing for road space,
(35) often acting antisocially. Pedestrians rarely act in this manner toward each other. Duany and his colleagues advocate development based on early-twentieth-century urban neighborhoods that mix housing of different prices and offer residents a "gratifying
(40) public realm" that includes narrow, tree-lined streets, parks, corner grocery stores, cafes, small neighborhood schools, all within walking distance. This, they believe, would give people of diverse backgrounds and lifestyles an opportunity to interact
(45) and thus develop mutual respect.

Opponents of New Urbanism claim that migration to sprawling suburbs is an expression of people's legitimate desire to secure the enjoyment and personal mobility provided by the automobile and the
(50) lifestyle that it makes possible. However, the New Urbanists do not question people's right to their own values; instead, they suggest that we should take a more critical view of these values and of the sprawl-

conducive zoning and subdivision policies that reflect
(55) them. New Urbanists are fundamentally concerned with the long-term social costs of the now-prevailing attitude that individual mobility, consumption, and wealth should be valued absolutely, regardless of their impact on community life.

1. Which one of the following most accurately expresses the main point of the passage?

   (A) In their critique of policies that promote suburban sprawl, the New Urbanists neglect to consider the interests and values of those who prefer suburban lifestyles.

   (B) The New Urbanists hold that suburban sprawl inhibits social interaction among people of diverse economic circumstances, and they advocate specific reforms of zoning laws as a solution to this problem.

   (C) The New Urbanists argue that most people find that life in small urban neighborhoods is generally more gratifying than life in a suburban environment.

   (D) The New Urbanists hold that suburban sprawl has a corrosive effect on community life, and as an alternative they advocate development modeled on small urban neighborhoods.

   (E) The New Urbanists analyze suburban sprawl as a phenomenon that results from short-sighted traffic policies and advocate changes to these traffic policies as a means of reducing the negative effects of sprawl.

2. According to the passage, the New Urbanists cite which one of the following as a detrimental result of the need for people to travel extensively every day by automobile?

   (A) It imposes an extra financial burden on the residents of sprawling suburbs, thus detracting from the advantages of suburban life.

   (B) It detracts from the amount of time that people could otherwise devote to productive employment.

   (C) It increases the amount of time people spend in situations in which antisocial behavior occurs.

   (D) It produces significant amounts of air pollution and thus tends to harm the quality of people's lives.

   (E) It decreases the amount of time that parents spend in enjoyable interactions with their children.

GO ON TO THE NEXT PAGE.

3. The passage most strongly suggests that the New Urbanists would agree with which one of the following statements?

  (A) The primary factor affecting a neighborhood's conduciveness to the maintenance of civility is the amount of time required to get from one place to another.

  (B) Private citizens in suburbs have little opportunity to influence the long-term effects of zoning policies enacted by public officials.

  (C) People who live in suburban neighborhoods usually have little difficulty finding easily accessible jobs that do not require commuting to urban centers.

  (D) The spatial configuration of suburban neighborhoods both influences and is influenced by the attitudes of those who live in them.

  (E) Although people have a right to their own values, personal values should not affect the ways in which neighborhoods are designed.

4. Which one of the following most accurately describes the author's use of the word "communities" in line 2 and "community" in line 15?

  (A) They are intended to be understood in almost identical ways, the only significant difference being that one is plural and the other is singular.

  (B) The former is intended to refer to dwellings—and their inhabitants—that happen to be clustered together in particular areas; in the latter, the author means that a group of people have a sense of belonging together.

  (C) In the former, the author means that the groups referred to are to be defined in terms of the interests of their members; the latter is intended to refer generically to a group of people who have something else in common.

  (D) The former is intended to refer to groups of people whose members have professional or political ties to one another; the latter is intended to refer to a geographical area in which people live in close proximity to one another.

  (E) In the former, the author means that there are informal personal ties among members of a group of people; the latter is intended to indicate that a group of people have similar backgrounds and lifestyles.

5. Which one of the following, if true, would most weaken the position that the passage attributes to critics of the New Urbanists?

  (A) Most people who spend more time than they would like getting from one daily task to another live in central areas of large cities.

  (B) Most people who often drive long distances for shopping and entertainment live in small towns rather than in suburban areas surrounding large cities.

  (C) Most people who have easy access to shopping and entertainment do not live in suburban areas.

  (D) Most people who choose to live in sprawling suburbs do so because comparable housing in neighborhoods that do not require extensive automobile travel is more expensive.

  (E) Most people who vote in municipal elections do not cast their votes on the basis of candidates' positions on zoning policies.

6. The passage most strongly suggests that which one of the following would occur if new housing subdivisions in suburban communities were built in accordance with the recommendations of Duany and his colleagues?

  (A) The need for zoning laws to help regulate traffic flow would eventually be eliminated.

  (B) There would be a decrease in the percentage of suburban buildings that contain two or more apartments.

  (C) The amount of time that residents of suburbs spend traveling to the central business districts of cities for work and shopping would increase.

  (D) The need for coordination of zoning policies between large-city governments and governments of nearby suburban communities would be eliminated.

  (E) There would be an increase in the per capita number of grocery stores and schools in those suburban communities.

7. The second paragraph most strongly supports the inference that the New Urbanists make which one of the following assumptions?

  (A) Most of those who buy houses in sprawling suburbs do not pay drastically less than they can afford.

  (B) Zoning regulations often cause economically uniform suburbs to become economically diverse.

  (C) City dwellers who do not frequently travel in automobiles often have feelings of hostility toward motorists.

  (D) Few residents of suburbs are aware of the potential health benefits of walking, instead of driving, to carry out daily tasks.

  (E) People generally prefer to live in houses that look very similar to most of the other houses around them.

GO ON TO THE NEXT PAGE.

Passage A

In ancient Greece, Aristotle documented the ability of foraging honeybees to recruit nestmates to a good food source. He did not speculate on how the communication occurred, but he and naturalists since

(5) then have observed that a bee that finds a new food source returns to the nest and "dances" for its nestmates. In the 1940s, von Frisch and colleagues discovered a pattern in the dance. They observed a foraging honeybee's dance, deciphered it, and thereby

(10) deduced the location of the food source the bee had discovered. Yet questions still remained regarding the precise mechanism used to transmit that information.

In the 1960s, Wenner and Esch each discovered independently that dancing honeybees emit low-

(15) frequency sounds, which we now know to come from wing vibrations. Both researchers reasoned that this might explain the bees' ability to communicate effectively even in completely dark nests. But at that time many scientists mistakenly believed that

(20) honeybees lack hearing, so the issue remained unresolved. Wenner subsequently proposed that smell rather than hearing was the key to honeybee communication. He hypothesized that honeybees derive information not from sound, but from odors the

(25) forager conveys from the food source.

Yet Gould has shown that foragers can dispatch bees to sites they had not actually visited, something that would not be possible if odor were in fact necessary to bees' communication. Finally, using a

(30) honeybee robot to simulate the forager's dance, Kirchner and Michelsen showed that sounds emitted during the forager's dance do indeed play an essential role in conveying information about the food's location.

Passage B

(35) All animals communicate in some sense. Bees dance, ants leave trails, some fish emit high-voltage signals. But some species—bees, birds, and primates, for example—communicate symbolically. In an experiment with vervet monkeys in the wild,

(40) Seyfarth, Cheney, and Marler found that prerecorded vervet alarm calls from a loudspeaker elicited the same response as did naturally produced vervet calls alerting the group to the presence of a predator of a particular type. Vervets looked upward upon hearing

(45) an eagle alarm call, and they scanned the ground below in response to a snake alarm call. These responses suggest that each alarm call represents, for vervets, a specific type of predator.

Karl von Frisch was first to crack the code of the

(50) honeybee's dance, which he described as "language." The dance symbolically represents the distance, direction, and quality of newly discovered food. Adrian Wenner and others believed that bees rely on olfactory cues, as well as the dance, to find a food

(55) source, but this has turned out not to be so.

While it is true that bees have a simple nervous system, they do not automatically follow just any information. Biologist James Gould trained foraging

(60) bees to find food in a boat placed in the middle of a lake and then allowed them to return to the hive to indicate this new location. He found that hive members ignored the foragers' instructions, presumably because no pollinating flowers grow in such a place.

8. The passages have which one of the following aims in common?

(A) arguing that certain nonhuman animals possess human-like intelligence

(B) illustrating the sophistication with which certain primates communicate

(C) describing certain scientific studies concerned with animal communication

(D) airing a scientific controversy over the function of the honeybee's dance

(E) analyzing the conditions a symbolic system must meet in order to be considered a language

9. Which one of the following statements most accurately characterizes a difference between the two passages?

(A) Passage A is concerned solely with honeybee communication, whereas passage B is concerned with other forms of animal communication as well.

(B) Passage A discusses evidence adduced by scientists in support of certain claims, whereas passage B merely presents some of those claims without discussing the support that has been adduced for them.

(C) Passage B is entirely about recent theories of honeybee communication, whereas passage A outlines the historic development of theories of honeybee communication.

(D) Passage B is concerned with explaining the distinction between symbolic and nonsymbolic communication, whereas passage A, though making use of the distinction, does not explain it.

(E) Passage B is concerned with gaining insight into human communication by considering certain types of nonhuman communication, whereas passage A is concerned with these types of nonhuman communication in their own right.

GO ON TO THE NEXT PAGE.

10. Which one of the following statements is most strongly supported by Gould's research, as reported in the two passages?

(A) When a forager honeybee does not communicate olfactory information to its nestmates, they will often disregard the forager's directions and go to sites of their own choosing.

(B) Forager honeybees instinctively know where pollinating flowers usually grow and will not dispatch their nestmates to any other places.

(C) Only experienced forager honeybees are able to locate the best food sources.

(D) A forager's dances can draw other honeybees to sites that the forager has not visited and can fail to draw other honeybees to sites that the forager has visited.

(E) Forager honeybees can communicate with their nestmates about a newly discovered food source by leaving a trail from the food source to the honeybee nest.

11. It can be inferred from the passages that the author of passage A and the author of passage B would accept which one of the following statements?

(A) Honeybees will ignore the instructions conveyed in the forager's dance if they are unable to detect odors from the food source.

(B) Wenner and Esch established that both sound and odor play a vital role in most honeybee communication.

(C) Most animal species can communicate symbolically in some form or other.

(D) The work of von Frisch was instrumental in answering fundamental questions about how honeybees communicate.

(E) Inexperienced forager honeybees that dance to communicate with other bees in their nest learn the intricacies of the dance from more experienced foragers.

12. Which one of the following most accurately describes a relationship between the two passages?

(A) Passage A discusses and rejects a position that is put forth in passage B.

(B) Passage A gives several examples of a phenomenon for which passage B gives only one example.

(C) Passage A is concerned in its entirety with a phenomenon that passage B discusses in support of a more general thesis.

(D) Passage A proposes a scientific explanation for a phenomenon that passage B argues cannot be plausibly explained.

(E) Passage A provides a historical account of the origins of a phenomenon that is the primary concern of passage B.

GO ON TO THE NEXT PAGE.

Most scholars of Mexican American history mark César Chávez's unionizing efforts among Mexican and Mexican American farm laborers in California as the beginning of Chicano political activism in the
(5) 1960s. By 1965, Chávez's United Farm Workers Union gained international recognition by initiating a worldwide boycott of grapes in an effort to get growers in California to sign union contracts. The year 1965 also marks the birth of contemporary
(10) Chicano theater, for that is the year Luis Valdez approached Chávez about using theater to organize farm workers. Valdez and the members of the resulting Teatro Campesino are generally credited by scholars as having initiated the Chicano theater
(15) movement, a movement that would reach its apex in the 1970s.

In the fall of 1965, Valdez gathered a group of striking farm workers and asked them to talk about their working conditions. A former farm worker
(20) himself, Valdez was no stranger to the players in the daily drama that was fieldwork. He asked people to illustrate what happened on the picket lines, and the less timid in the audience delighted in acting out their ridicule of the strikebreakers. Using the farm
(25) workers' basic improvisations, Valdez guided the group toward the creation of what he termed "actos," skits or sketches whose roots scholars have traced to various sources that had influenced Valdez as a student and as a member of the San Francisco Mime
(30) Troupe. Expanding beyond the initial setting of flatbed-truck stages at the fields' edges, the acto became the quintessential form of Chicano theater in the 1960s. According to Valdez, the acto should suggest a solution to the problems exposed in the
(35) brief comic statement, and, as with any good political theater, it should satirize the opposition and inspire the audience to social action. Because actos were based on participants' personal experiences, they had palpable immediacy.
(40) In her book El Teatro Campesino, Yolanda Broyles-González rightly criticizes theater historians for having tended to credit Valdez individually with inventing actos as a genre, as if the striking farm workers' improvisational talent had depended entirely
(45) on his vision and expertise for the form it took. She traces especially the actos' connections to a similar genre of informal, often satirical shows known as carpas that were performed in tents to mainly working-class audiences. Carpas had flourished
(50) earlier in the twentieth century in the border area of Mexico and the United States. Many participants in the formation of the Teatro no doubt had substantial cultural links to this tradition and likely adapted it to their improvisations. The early development of the
(55) Teatro Campesino was, in fact, a collective accomplishment; still, Valdez's artistic contribution was a crucial one, for the resulting actos were neither carpas nor theater in the European tradition of Valdez's academic training, but a distinctive genre
(60) with connections to both.

13. Which one of the following most accurately expresses the main point of the passage?

(A) Some theater historians have begun to challenge the once widely accepted view that in creating the Teatro Campesino, Luis Valdez was largely uninfluenced by earlier historical forms.

(B) In crediting Luis Valdez with founding the Chicano theater movement, theater historians have neglected the role of César Chávez in its early development.

(C) Although the creation of the early material of the Teatro Campesino was a collective accomplishment, Luis Valdez's efforts and expertise were essential factors in determining the form it took.

(D) The success of the early Teatro Campesino depended on the special insights and talents of the amateur performers who were recruited by Luis Valdez to participate in creating actos.

(E) Although, as Yolanda Broyles-González has pointed out, the Teatro Campesino was a collective endeavor, Luis Valdez's political and academic connections helped bring it recognition.

14. The author uses the word "immediacy" (line 39) most likely in order to express

(A) how little physical distance there was between the performers in the late 1960s actos and their audiences

(B) the sense of intimacy created by the performers' technique of addressing many of their lines directly to the audience

(C) the ease with which the Teatro Campesino members were able to develop actos based on their own experiences

(D) how closely the director and performers of the Teatro Campesino worked together to build a repertoire of actos

(E) how vividly the actos conveyed the performers' experiences to their audiences

GO ON TO THE NEXT PAGE.

15. The second sentence of the passage functions primarily in which one of the following ways?

(A) It helps explain both a motivation of those who developed the first *actos* and an important aspect of their subject matter.

(B) It introduces a major obstacle that Valdez had to overcome in gaining public acceptance of the work of the Teatro Campesino.

(C) It anticipates and counters a possible objection to the author's view that the *actos* developed by Teatro Campesino were effective as political theater.

(D) It provides an example of the type of topic on which scholars of Mexican American history have typically focused to the exclusion of theater history.

(E) It helps explain why theater historians, in their discussions of Valdez, have often treated him as though he were individually responsible for inventing *actos* as a genre.

16. The passage indicates that the early *actos* of the Teatro Campesino and the *carpas* were similar in that

(A) both had roots in theater in the European tradition

(B) both were studied by the San Francisco Mime Troupe

(C) both were initially performed on farms

(D) both often involved satire

(E) both were part of union organizing drives

17. It can be inferred from the passage that Valdez most likely held which one of the following views?

(A) As a theatrical model, the *carpas* of the early twentieth century were ill-suited to the type of theater that he and the Teatro Campesino were trying to create.

(B) César Chávez should have done more to support the efforts of the Teatro Campesino to use theater to organize striking farm workers.

(C) Avant-garde theater in the European tradition is largely irrelevant to the theatrical expression of the concerns of a mainly working-class audience.

(D) Actors do not require formal training in order to achieve effective and artistically successful theatrical performances.

(E) The aesthetic aspects of a theatrical work should be evaluated independently of its political ramifications.

18. Based on the passage, it can be concluded that the author and Broyles-González hold essentially the same attitude toward

(A) the influences that shaped *carpas* as a dramatic genre

(B) the motives of theater historians in exaggerating the originality of Valdez

(C) the significance of *carpas* for the development of the genre of the *acto*

(D) the extent of Valdez's acquaintance with *carpas* as a dramatic form

(E) the role of the European tradition in shaping Valdez's contribution to the development of *actos*

19. The information in the passage most strongly supports which one of the following statements regarding the Teatro Campesino?

(A) Its efforts to organize farm workers eventually won the acceptance of a few farm owners in California.

(B) It included among its members a number of individuals who, like Valdez, had previously belonged to the San Francisco Mime Troupe.

(C) It did not play a major role in the earliest efforts of the United Farm Workers Union to achieve international recognition.

(D) Although its first performances were entirely in Spanish, it eventually gave some performances partially in English, for the benefit of non-Spanish-speaking audiences.

(E) Its work drew praise not only from critics in the United States but from critics in Mexico as well.

20. The passage most strongly supports which one of the following?

(A) The *carpas* tradition has been widely discussed and analyzed by both U.S. and Mexican theater historians concerned with theatrical performance styles and methods.

(B) Comedy was a prominent feature of Chicano theater in the 1960s.

(C) In directing the *actos* of the Teatro Campesino, Valdez went to great lengths to simulate or recreate certain aspects of what audiences had experienced in the *carpas*.

(D) Many of the earliest *actos* were based on scripts composed by Valdez, which the farm-worker actors modified to suit their own diverse aesthetic and pragmatic interests.

(E) By the early 1970s, Valdez was using *actos* as the basis for other theatrical endeavors and was no longer directly associated with the Teatro Campesino.

GO ON TO THE NEXT PAGE.

In October 1999, the Law Reform Commission of Western Australia (LRCWA) issued its report, "Review of the Civil and Criminal Justice System." Buried within its 400 pages are several important

(5) recommendations for introducing contingency fees for lawyers' services into the state of Western Australia. Contingency-fee agreements call for payment only if the lawyer is successful in the case. Because of the lawyer's risk of financial loss, such charges generally

(10) exceed regular fees.

Although there are various types of contingency-fee arrangements, the LRCWA has recommended that only one type be introduced: "uplift" fee arrangements, which in the case of a successful

(15) outcome require the client to pay the lawyer's normal fee plus an agreed-upon additional percentage of that fee. This restriction is intended to prevent lawyers from gaining disproportionately from awards of damages and thus to ensure that just compensation to

(20) plaintiffs is not eroded. A further measure toward this end is found in the recommendation that contingency-fee agreements should be permitted only in cases where two conditions are satisfied: first, the contingency-fee arrangement must be used only as a

(25) last resort when all means of avoiding such an arrangement have been exhausted; and second, the lawyer must be satisfied that the client is financially unable to pay the fee in the event that sufficient damages are not awarded.

(30) Unfortunately, under this recommendation, lawyers wishing to enter into an uplift fee arrangement would be forced to investigate not only the legal issues affecting any proposed litigation, but also the financial circumstances of the potential client

(35) and the probable cost of the litigation. This process would likely be onerous for a number of reasons, not least of which is the fact that the final cost of litigation depends in large part on factors that may change as the case unfolds, such as strategies adopted

(40) by the opposing side.

In addition to being burdensome for lawyers, the proposal to make contingency-fee agreements available only to the least well-off clients would be unfair to other clients. This restriction would unjustly

(45) limit freedom of contract and would, in effect, make certain types of litigation inaccessible to middle-income people or even wealthy people who might not be able to liquidate assets to pay the costs of a trial. More importantly, the primary reasons for entering

(50) into contingency-fee agreements hold for all clients. First, they provide financing for the costs of pursuing a legal action. Second, they shift the risk of not recovering those costs, and of not obtaining a damages award that will pay their lawyer's fees, from

(55) the client to the lawyer. Finally, given the convergence of the lawyer's interest and the client's interest under a contingency-fee arrangement, it is reasonable to assume that such arrangements increase lawyers' diligence and commitment to their cases.

21. As described in the passage, the uplift fee agreements that the LRCWA's report recommends are most closely analogous to which one of the following arrangements?

(A) People who join together to share the costs of purchasing lottery tickets on a regular basis agree to share any eventual proceeds from a lottery drawing in proportion to the amounts they contributed to tickets purchased for that drawing.

(B) A consulting firm reviews a company's operations. The consulting firm will receive payment only if it can substantially reduce the company's operating expenses, in which case it will be paid double its usual fee.

(C) The returns that accrue from the assumption of a large financial risk by members of a business partnership formed to develop and market a new invention are divided among them in proportion to the amount of financial risk each assumed.

(D) The cost of an insurance policy is determined by reference to the likelihood and magnitude of an eventual loss covered by the insurance policy and the administrative and marketing costs involved in marketing and servicing the insurance policy.

(E) A person purchasing a property receives a loan for the purchase from the seller. In order to reduce risk, the seller requires the buyer to pay for an insurance policy that will pay off the loan if the buyer is unable to do so.

22. The passage states which one of the following?

(A) Contingency-fee agreements serve the purpose of transferring the risk of pursuing a legal action from the client to the lawyer.

(B) Contingency-fee agreements of the kind the LRCWA's report recommends would normally not result in lawyers being paid larger fees than they deserve.

(C) At least some of the recommendations in the LRCWA's report are likely to be incorporated into the legal system in the state of Western Australia.

(D) Allowing contingency-fee agreements of the sort recommended in the LRCWA's report would not affect lawyers' diligence and commitment to their cases.

(E) Usually contingency-fee agreements involve an agreement that the fee the lawyer receives will be an agreed-upon percentage of the client's damages.

GO ON TO THE NEXT PAGE.

23. The author's main purpose in the passage is to

(A) defend a proposed reform against criticism
(B) identify the current shortcomings of a legal system and suggest how these should be remedied
(C) support the view that a recommended change would actually worsen the situation it was intended to improve
(D) show that a legal system would not be significantly changed if certain proposed reforms were enacted
(E) explain a suggested reform and critically evaluate it

24. Which one of the following is given by the passage as a reason for the difficulty a lawyer would have in determining whether—according to the LRCWA's recommendations—a prospective client was qualified to enter into an uplift agreement?

(A) The length of time that a trial may last is difficult to predict in advance.
(B) Not all prospective clients would wish to reveal detailed information about their financial circumstances.
(C) Some factors that may affect the cost of litigation can change after the litigation begins.
(D) Uplift agreements should only be used as a last resort.
(E) Investigating whether a client is qualified to enter into an uplift agreement would take time away from investigating the legal issues of the case.

25. The phrase "gaining disproportionately from awards of damages" (lines 18–19) is most likely intended by the author to mean

(A) receiving a payment that is of greater monetary value than the legal services rendered by the lawyer
(B) receiving a higher portion of the total amount awarded in damages than is reasonable compensation for the professional services rendered and the amount of risk assumed
(C) receiving a higher proportion of the damages awarded to the client than the client considers fair
(D) receiving a payment that is higher than the lawyer would have received had the client's case been unsuccessful
(E) receiving a higher proportion of the damages awarded to the client than the judge or the jury that awarded the damages intended the lawyer to receive

26. According to the passage, the LRCWA's report recommended that contingency-fee agreements

(A) be used only when it is reasonable to think that such arrangements will increase lawyers' diligence and commitment to their cases
(B) be used only in cases in which clients are unlikely to be awarded enormous damages
(C) be used if the lawyer is not certain that the client seeking to file a lawsuit could pay the lawyer's regular fee if the suit were to be unsuccessful
(D) not be used in cases in which another type of arrangement is practicable
(E) not be used except in cases where the lawyer is reasonably sure that the client will win damages sufficiently large to cover the lawyer's fees

27. Which one of the following, if true, most seriously undermines the author's criticism of the LRCWA's recommendations concerning contingency-fee agreements?

(A) The proportion of lawsuits filed by the least well-off litigants tends to be higher in areas where uplift fee arrangements have been widely used than in areas in which uplift agreements have not been used.
(B) Before the LRCWA's recommendations, lawyers in Western Australia generally made a careful evaluation of prospective clients' financial circumstances before accepting cases that might involve complex or protracted litigation.
(C) There is strong opposition in Western Australia to any legal reform perceived as favoring lawyers, so it is highly unlikely that the LRCWA's recommendations concerning contingency-fee agreements will be implemented.
(D) The total fees charged by lawyers who successfully litigate cases under uplift fee arrangements are, on average, only marginally higher than the total fees charged by lawyers who litigate cases without contingency agreements.
(E) In most jurisdictions in which contingency-fee agreements are allowed, those of the uplift variety are used much less often than are other types of contingency-fee agreements.

S T O P

IF YOU FINISH BEFORE TIME IS CALLED, YOU MAY CHECK YOUR WORK ON THIS SECTION ONLY.
DO NOT WORK ON ANY OTHER SECTION IN THE TEST.

Wait for the supervisor's instructions before you open the page to the topic.
Please print and sign your name and write the date in the designated spaces below.

Time: 35 Minutes

General Directions

You will have 35 minutes in which to plan and write an essay on the topic inside. Read the topic and the accompanying directions carefully. You will probably find it best to spend a few minutes considering the topic and organizing your thoughts before you begin writing. In your essay, be sure to develop your ideas fully, leaving time, if possible, to review what you have written. **Do not write on a topic other than the one specified. Writing on a topic of your own choice is not acceptable.**

No special knowledge is required or expected for this writing exercise. Law schools are interested in the reasoning, clarity, organization, language usage, and writing mechanics displayed in your essay. How well you write is more important than how much you write.

Confine your essay to the blocked, lined area on the front and back of the separate Writing Sample Response Sheet. Only that area will be reproduced for law schools. Be sure that your writing is legible.

Both this topic sheet and your response sheet must be turned over to the testing staff before you leave the room.

Topic Code	Print Your Full Name Here		
083119	Last	First	M.I.

Date	Sign Your Name Here
/ /	

LSAC®

Scratch Paper
Do not write your essay in this space.

LSAT® Writing Sample Topic

> <u>Directions</u>: The scenario presented below describes two choices, either one of which can be supported on the basis of the information given. Your essay should consider both choices and argue for one over the other, based on the two specified criteria and the facts provided. There is no "right" or "wrong" choice: a reasonable argument can be made for either.

In a total solar eclipse, the moon completely covers the sun and casts a rolling shadow along a track on the Earth's surface a few hundred kilometers wide. The eclipse lasts for a few minutes at any location within this track. The Ortegas are planning a trip to observe an upcoming eclipse during their family vacation. They have narrowed the possibilities down to two countries. Using the facts below, write an essay in which you argue in favor of one country over the other based on the following two criteria:

- The Ortegas want to minimize the chance that cloudiness will obscure the eclipse for them.
- The Ortegas want the trip to be worthwhile even if the eclipse is obscured by clouds.

For the first country, climatic data indicate that the probability of cloudiness in the area of the eclipse track is about 75 percent. The family would fly to the capital, which is a cultural center of almost unparalleled richness. Some members of the family have visited the capital before. On some days, they would drive their rental car to other cultural locations in the country. Having a rental car allows some adjustment of eclipse-viewing location according to weather forecasts.

The second country is about twice as far from the family's home as the first country, with correspondingly greater travel expense and inconvenience. No family member has been in the country before. Climatic data indicate that the probability of cloudiness in the area of the eclipse track in the country is about 25 percent. Because the country has some political instability, the family would travel on an eclipse tour organized by a respected company. Visits to several cultural sites are included.

WP-Q083A

Scratch Paper
Do not write your essay in this space.

COMPUTING YOUR SCORE

Directions:

1. Use the Answer Key on the next page to check your answers.

2. Use the Scoring Worksheet below to compute your raw score.

3. Use the Score Conversion Chart to convert your raw score into the 120–180 scale.

Scoring Worksheet

1. Enter the number of questions you answered correctly in each section.

	Number Correct
SECTION I..................	_____
SECTION II.................	_____
SECTION III................	_____
SECTION IV	_____

2. Enter the sum here: _____

This is your Raw Score.

Conversion Chart
For Converting Raw Score to the 120–180 LSAT Scaled Score
LSAT Form 1LSN84

Reported Score	Raw Score Lowest	Raw Score Highest
180	97	99
179	96	96
178	—*	—*
177	95	95
176	94	94
175	93	93
174	92	92
173	91	91
172	90	90
171	89	89
170	87	88
169	86	86
168	85	85
167	83	84
166	82	82
165	80	81
164	79	79
163	77	78
162	75	76
161	74	74
160	72	73
159	70	71
158	68	69
157	67	67
156	65	66
155	63	64
154	62	62
153	60	61
152	58	59
151	56	57
150	55	55
149	53	54
148	51	52
147	50	50
146	48	49
145	47	47
144	45	46
143	43	44
142	42	42
141	40	41
140	39	39
139	37	38
138	36	36
137	35	35
136	33	34
135	32	32
134	31	31
133	29	30
132	28	28
131	27	27
130	26	26
129	25	25
128	24	24
127	23	23
126	22	22
125	21	21
124	20	20
123	19	19
122	18	18
121	17	17
120	0	16

*There is no raw score that will produce this scaled score for this form.

ANSWER KEY

SECTION I

1.	D	8.	E	15.	B	22.	A
2.	E	9.	D	16.	C	23.	E
3.	B	10.	D	17.	A	24.	C
4.	D	11.	C	18.	E	25.	C
5.	C	12.	A	19.	*		
6.	B	13.	C	20.	D		
7.	C	14.	D	21.	B		

SECTION II

1.	B	8.	C	15.	E	22.	E
2.	D	9.	D	16.	A	23.	C
3.	A	10.	A	17.	B		
4.	A	11.	C	18.	A		
5.	E	12.	C	19.	B		
6.	C	13.	E	20.	B		
7.	E	14.	D	21.	D		

SECTION III

1.	A	8.	C	15.	D	22.	A
2.	B	9.	C	16.	E	23.	C
3.	A	10.	C	17.	D	24.	B
4.	B	11.	D	18.	C	25.	C
5.	D	12.	E	19.	D		
6.	D	13.	D	20.	A		
7.	C	14.	D	21.	E		

SECTION IV

1.	D	8.	C	15.	A	22.	A
2.	C	9.	A	16.	D	23.	E
3.	D	10.	D	17.	D	24.	C
4.	B	11.	D	18.	C	25.	B
5.	D	12.	C	19.	C	26.	D
6.	E	13.	C	20.	B	27.	B
7.	A	14.	E	21.	B		

*Item removed from scoring.

THE OFFICIAL LSAT
PREPTEST®

61

- PrepTest 61
- Form 0LSN86

OCTOBER 2010

SECTION I

Time—35 minutes

27 Questions

Directions: Each set of questions in this section is based on a single passage or a pair of passages. The questions are to be answered on the basis of what is stated or implied in the passage or pair of passages. For some of the questions, more than one of the choices could conceivably answer the question. However, you are to choose the best answer; that is, the response that most accurately and completely answers the question, and blacken the corresponding space on your answer sheet.

The Universal Declaration of Human Rights (UDHR), approved by the United Nations General Assembly in 1948, was the first international treaty to expressly affirm universal respect for human rights.
(5) Prior to 1948 no truly international standard of humanitarian beliefs existed. Although Article 1 of the 1945 UN Charter had been written with the express purpose of obligating the UN to "encourage respect for human rights and for fundamental
(10) freedoms for all without distinction as to race, sex, language, or religion," there were members of delegations from various small countries and representatives of several nongovernmental organizations who felt that the language of Article 1
(15) was not strong enough, and that the Charter as a whole did not go far enough in its efforts to guarantee basic human rights. This group lobbied vigorously to strengthen the Charter's human rights provisions and proposed that member states be
(20) required "to take separate and joint action and to co-operate with the organization for the promotion of human rights." This would have implied an obligation for member states to act on human rights issues. Ultimately, this proposal and others like it were not
(25) adopted; instead, the UDHR was commissioned and drafted.

The original mandate for producing the document was given to the UN Commission on Human Rights in February 1946. Between that time and the General
(30) Assembly's final approval of the document, the UDHR passed through an elaborate eight-stage drafting process in which it made its way through almost every level of the UN hierarchy. The articles were debated at each stage, and all 30 articles were
(35) argued passionately by delegates representing diverse ideologies, traditions, and cultures. The document as it was finally approved set forth the essential principles of freedom and equality for everyone— regardless of sex, race, color, language, religion,
(40) political or other opinion, national or social origin, property, birth or other status. It also asserted a number of fundamental human rights, including among others the right to work, the right to rest and leisure, and the right to education.
(45) While the UDHR is in many ways a progressive document, it also has weaknesses, the most regrettable of which is its nonbinding legal status. For all its strong language and high ideals, the UDHR remains a resolution of a purely programmatic nature.
(50) Nevertheless, the document has led, even if belatedly, to the creation of legally binding human rights

conventions, and it clearly deserves recognition as an international standard-setting piece of work, as a set of aspirations to which UN member states are
(55) intended to strive, and as a call to arms in the name of humanity, justice, and freedom.

1. By referring to the Universal Declaration of Human Rights as "purely programmatic" (line 49) in nature, the author most likely intends to emphasize

   (A) the likelihood that the document will inspire innovative government programs designed to safeguard human rights
   (B) the ability of the document's drafters to translate abstract ideals into concrete standards
   (C) the compromises that went into producing a version of the document that would garner the approval of all relevant parties
   (D) the fact that the guidelines established by the document are ultimately unenforceable
   (E) the frustration experienced by the document's drafters at stubborn resistance from within the UN hierarchy

2. The author most probably quotes directly from both the UN Charter (lines 8–11) and the proposal mentioned in lines 20–22 for which one of the following reasons?

   (A) to contrast the different definitions of human rights in the two documents
   (B) to compare the strength of the human rights language in the two documents
   (C) to identify a bureaucratic vocabulary that is common to the two documents
   (D) to highlight what the author believes to be the most important point in each document
   (E) to call attention to a significant difference in the prose styles of the two documents

3. The author's stance toward the Universal Declaration of Human Rights can best be described as

   (A) unbridled enthusiasm
   (B) qualified approval
   (C) absolute neutrality
   (D) reluctant rejection
   (E) strong hostility

GO ON TO THE NEXT PAGE.

4. According to the passage, each of the following is true of the Universal Declaration of Human Rights EXCEPT:

(A) It asserts a right to rest and leisure.
(B) It was drafted after the UN Charter was drafted.
(C) The UN Commission on Human Rights was charged with producing it.
(D) It has had no practical consequences.
(E) It was the first international treaty to explicitly affirm universal respect for human rights.

5. The author would be most likely to agree with which one of the following statements?

(A) The human rights language contained in Article 1 of the UN Charter is so ambiguous as to be almost wholly ineffectual.
(B) The weaknesses of the Universal Declaration of Human Rights generally outweigh the strengths of the document.
(C) It was relatively easy for the drafters of the Universal Declaration of Human Rights to reach a consensus concerning the contents of the document.
(D) The drafters of the Universal Declaration of Human Rights omitted important rights that should be included in a truly comprehensive list of basic human rights.
(E) The Universal Declaration of Human Rights would be truer to the intentions of its staunchest proponents if UN member countries were required by law to abide by its provisions.

6. Suppose that a group of independent journalists has uncovered evidence of human rights abuses being perpetrated by a security agency of a UN member state upon a group of political dissidents. Which one of the following approaches to the situation would most likely be advocated by present-day delegates who share the views of the delegates and representatives mentioned in lines 11–14?

(A) The UN General Assembly authenticates the evidence and then insists upon prompt remedial action on the part of the government of the member state.
(B) The UN General Assembly stipulates that any proposed response must be unanimously accepted by member states before it can be implemented.
(C) The UN issues a report critical of the actions of the member state in question and calls for a censure vote in the General Assembly.
(D) The situation is regarded by the UN as an internal matter that is best left to the discretion of the government of the member state.
(E) The situation is investigated further by nongovernmental humanitarian organizations that promise to disclose their findings to the public via the international media.

GO ON TO THE NEXT PAGE.

It is commonly assumed that even if some forgeries have aesthetic merit, no forgery has as much as an original by the imitated artist would. Yet even the most prominent art specialists can be duped by a (5) talented artist turned forger into mistaking an almost perfect forgery for an original. For instance, artist Han van Meegeren's *The Disciples at Emmaus* (1937)—painted under the forged signature of the acclaimed Dutch master Jan Vermeer (1632–1675)— (10) attracted lavish praise from experts as one of Vermeer's finest works. The painting hung in a Rotterdam museum until 1945, when, to the great embarrassment of the critics, van Meegeren revealed its origin. Astonishingly, there was at least one highly (15) reputed critic who persisted in believing it to be a Vermeer even after van Meegeren's confession.

Given the experts' initial enthusiasm, some philosophers argue that van Meegeren's painting must have possessed aesthetic characteristics that, in a (20) Vermeer original, would have justified the critics' plaudits. Van Meegeren's *Emmaus* thus raises difficult questions regarding the status of superbly executed forgeries. Is a forgery inherently inferior as art? How are we justified, if indeed we are, in revising (25) downwards our critical assessment of a work unmasked as a forgery? Philosopher of art Alfred Lessing proposes convincing answers to these questions.

A forged work is indeed inferior as art, Lessing (30) argues, but not because of a shortfall in aesthetic qualities strictly defined, that is to say, in the qualities perceptible on the picture's surface. For example, in its composition, its technique, and its brilliant use of color, van Meegeren's work is flawless, even (35) beautiful. Lessing argues instead that the deficiency lies in what might be called the painting's intangible qualities. All art, explains Lessing, involves technique, but not all art involves origination of a new vision, and originality of vision is one of the (40) fundamental qualities by which artistic, as opposed to purely aesthetic, accomplishment is measured. Thus Vermeer is acclaimed for having inaugurated, in the seventeenth century, a new way of seeing, and for pioneering techniques for embodying this new way of (45) seeing through distinctive treatment of light, color, and form.

Even if we grant that van Meegeren, with his undoubted mastery of Vermeer's innovative techniques, produced an aesthetically superior (50) painting, he did so about three centuries after Vermeer developed the techniques in question. Whereas Vermeer's origination of these techniques in the seventeenth century represents a truly impressive and historic achievement, van Meegeren's production (55) of *The Disciples at Emmaus* in the twentieth century presents nothing new or creative to the history of art. Van Meegeren's forgery therefore, for all its aesthetic merits, lacks the historical significance that makes Vermeer's work artistically great.

7. Which one of the following most accurately expresses the main point of the passage?

(A) *The Disciples at Emmaus*, van Meegeren's forgery of a Vermeer, was a failure in both aesthetic and artistic terms.

(B) The aesthetic value of a work of art is less dependent on the work's visible characteristics than on certain intangible characteristics.

(C) Forged artworks are artistically inferior to originals because artistic value depends in large part on originality of vision.

(D) The most skilled forgers can deceive even highly qualified art experts into accepting their work as original.

(E) Art critics tend to be unreliable judges of the aesthetic and artistic quality of works of art.

8. The passage provides the strongest support for inferring that Lessing holds which one of the following views?

(A) The judgments of critics who pronounced *The Disciples at Emmaus* to be aesthetically superb were not invalidated by the revelation that the painting is a forgery.

(B) The financial value of a work of art depends more on its purely aesthetic qualities than on its originality.

(C) Museum curators would be better off not taking art critics' opinions into account when attempting to determine whether a work of art is authentic.

(D) Because it is such a skilled imitation of Vermeer, *The Disciples at Emmaus* is as artistically successful as are original paintings by artists who are less significant than Vermeer.

(E) Works of art that have little or no aesthetic value can still be said to be great achievements in artistic terms.

9. In the first paragraph, the author refers to a highly reputed critic's persistence in believing van Meegeren's forgery to be a genuine Vermeer primarily in order to

(A) argue that many art critics are inflexible in their judgments

(B) indicate that the critics who initially praised *The Disciples at Emmaus* were not as knowledgeable as they appeared

(C) suggest that the painting may yet turn out to be a genuine Vermeer

(D) emphasize that the concept of forgery itself is internally incoherent

(E) illustrate the difficulties that skillfully executed forgeries can pose for art critics

GO ON TO THE NEXT PAGE.

10. The reaction described in which one of the following scenarios is most analogous to the reaction of the art critics mentioned in line 13?

(A)   lovers of a musical group contemptuously reject a tribute album recorded by various other musicians as a second-rate imitation

(B)   art historians extol the work of a little-known painter as innovative until it is discovered that the painter lived much more recently than was originally thought

(C)   diners at a famous restaurant effusively praise the food as delicious until they learn that the master chef is away for the night

(D)   literary critics enthusiastically applaud a new novel until its author reveals that its central symbols are intended to represent political views that the critics dislike

(E)   movie fans evaluate a particular movie more favorably than they otherwise might have because their favorite actor plays the lead role

11. The passage provides the strongest support for inferring that Lessing holds which one of the following views?

(A)   It is probable that many paintings currently hanging in important museums are actually forgeries.

(B)   The historical circumstances surrounding the creation of a work are important in assessing the artistic value of that work.

(C)   The greatness of an innovative artist depends on how much influence he or she has on other artists.

(D)   The standards according to which a work is judged to be a forgery tend to vary from one historical period to another.

(E)   An artist who makes use of techniques developed by others cannot be said to be innovative.

12. The passage most strongly supports which one of the following statements?

(A)   In any historical period, the criteria by which a work is classified as a forgery can be a matter of considerable debate.

(B)   An artist who uses techniques that others have developed is most likely a forger.

(C)   A successful forger must originate a new artistic vision.

(D)   Works of art created early in the career of a great artist are more likely than those created later to embody historic innovations.

(E)   A painting can be a forgery even if it is not a copy of a particular original work of art.

13. Which one of the following, if true, would most strengthen Lessing's contention that a painting can display aesthetic excellence without possessing an equally high degree of artistic value?

(A)   Many of the most accomplished art forgers have had moderately successful careers as painters of original works.

(B)   Reproductions painted by talented young artists whose traditional training consisted in the copying of masterpieces were often seen as beautiful, but never regarded as great art.

(C)   While experts can detect most forgeries, they can be duped by a talented forger who knows exactly what characteristics experts expect to find in the work of a particular painter.

(D)   Most attempts at art forgery are ultimately unsuccessful because the forger has not mastered the necessary techniques.

(E)   The criteria by which aesthetic excellence is judged change significantly from one century to another and from one culture to another.

GO ON TO THE NEXT PAGE.

Passage A

One function of language is to influence others' behavior by changing what they know, believe, or desire. For humans engaged in conversation, the
(5) perception of another's mental state is perhaps the most common vocalization stimulus.

While animal vocalizations may have evolved because they can potentially alter listeners' behavior to the signaler's benefit, such communication is—in contrast to human language—inadvertent, because
(10) most animals, with the possible exception of chimpanzees, cannot attribute mental states to others. The male *Physalaemus* frog calls because calling causes females to approach and other males to retreat, but there is no evidence that he does so because he attributes knowledge
(15) or desire to other frogs, or because he knows his calls will affect their knowledge and that this knowledge will, in turn, affect their behavior. Research also suggests that, in marked contrast to humans, nonhuman primates do not produce vocalizations in response to perception
(20) of another's need for information. Macaques, for example, give alarm calls when predators approach and coo calls upon finding food, yet experiments reveal no evidence that individuals were more likely to call about these events when they were aware of them but their offspring
(25) were clearly ignorant; similarly, chimpanzees do not appear to adjust their calling to inform ignorant individuals of their own location or that of food. Many animal vocalizations whose production initially seems goal-directed are not as purposeful as they first appear.

Passage B

(30) Many scientists distinguish animal communication systems from human language on the grounds that the former are rigid responses to stimuli, whereas human language is spontaneous and creative.

In this connection, it is commonly stated that no
(35) animal can use its communication system to lie. Obviously, a lie requires intention to deceive: to judge whether a particular instance of animal communication is truly prevarication requires knowledge of the animal's intentions. Language philosopher H. P. Grice explains
(40) that for an individual to mean something by uttering x, the individual must intend, in expressing x, to induce an audience to believe something and must also intend the utterance to be recognized as so intended. But conscious intention is a category of mental experience
(45) widely believed to be uniquely human. Philosopher Jacques Maritain's discussion of the honeybee's elaborate "waggle-dance" exemplifies this view. Although bees returning to the hive communicate to other bees the distance and direction of food sources,
(50) such communication is, Maritain asserts, merely a conditioned reflex: animals may use communicative signs but lack conscious intention regarding their use.

But these arguments are circular: conscious intention is ruled out a priori and then its absence
(55) taken as evidence that animal communication is fundamentally different from human language. In fact, the narrowing of the perceived gap between animal communication and human language revealed by recent research with chimpanzees and other animals
(60) calls into question not only the assumption that the difference between animal and human communication is qualitative rather than merely quantitative, but also the accompanying assumption that animals respond mechanically to stimuli, whereas humans speak with
(65) conscious understanding and intent.

14. Both passages are primarily concerned with addressing which one of the following questions?

(A) Are animals capable of deliberately prevaricating in order to achieve specific goals?

(B) Are the communications of animals characterized by conscious intention?

(C) What kinds of stimuli are most likely to elicit animal vocalizations?

(D) Are the communication systems of nonhuman primates qualitatively different from those of all other animals?

(E) Is there a scientific consensus about the differences between animal communication systems and human language?

15. In discussing the philosopher Maritain, the author of passage B seeks primarily to

(A) describe an interpretation of animal communication that the author believes rests on a logical error

(B) suggest by illustration that there is conscious intention underlying the communicative signs employed by certain animals

(C) present an argument in support of the view that animal communication systems are spontaneous and creative

(D) furnish specific evidence against the theory that most animal communication is merely a conditioned reflex

(E) point to a noted authority on animal communication whose views the author regards with respect

GO ON TO THE NEXT PAGE.

16. The author of passage B would be most likely to agree with which one of the following statements regarding researchers who subscribe to the position articulated in passage A?

(A) They fail to recognize that humans often communicate without any clear idea of their listeners' mental states.

(B) Most of them lack the credentials needed to assess the relevant experimental evidence correctly.

(C) They ignore well-known evidence that animals do in fact practice deception.

(D) They make assumptions about matters that should be determined empirically.

(E) They falsely believe that all communication systems can be explained in terms of their evolutionary benefits.

17. Which one of the following assertions from passage A provides support for the view attributed to Maritain in passage B (lines 50–52)?

(A) One function of language is to influence the behavior of others by changing what they think.

(B) Animal vocalizations may have evolved because they have the potential to alter listeners' behavior to the signaler's benefit.

(C) It is possible that chimpanzees may have the capacity to attribute mental states to others.

(D) There is no evidence that the male *Physalaemus* frog calls because he knows that his calls will affect the knowledge of other frogs.

(E) Macaques give alarm calls when predators approach and coo calls upon finding food.

18. The authors would be most likely to disagree over

(A) the extent to which communication among humans involves the ability to perceive the mental states of others

(B) the importance of determining to what extent animal communication systems differ from human language

(C) whether human language and animal communication differ from one another qualitatively or merely in a matter of degree

(D) whether chimpanzees' vocalizations suggest that they may possess the capacity to attribute mental states to others

(E) whether animals' vocalizations evolved to alter the behavior of other animals in a way that benefits the signaler

19. Passage B differs from passage A in that passage B is more

(A) optimistic regarding the ability of science to answer certain fundamental questions

(B) disapproving of the approach taken by others writing on the same general topic

(C) open-minded in its willingness to accept the validity of apparently conflicting positions

(D) supportive of ongoing research related to the question at hand

(E) circumspect in its refusal to commit itself to any positions with respect to still-unsettled research questions

GO ON TO THE NEXT PAGE.

In contrast to the mainstream of U.S. historiography during the late nineteenth and early twentieth centuries, African American historians of the period, such as George Washington Williams and
(5) W. E. B. DuBois, adopted a transnational perspective. This was true for several reasons, not the least of which was the necessity of doing so if certain aspects of the history of African Americans in the United States were to be treated honestly.
(10)   First, there was the problem of citizenship. Even after the adoption in 1868 of the Fourteenth Amendment to the U.S. Constitution, which defined citizenship, the question of citizenship for African Americans had not been genuinely resolved. Because
(15) of this, emigrationist sentiment was a central issue in black political discourse, and both issues were critical topics for investigation. The implications for historical scholarship and national identity were enormous. While some black leaders insisted on their right to U.S.
(20) citizenship, others called on black people to emigrate and find a homeland of their own. Most African Americans were certainly not willing to relinquish their claims to the benefits of U.S. citizenship, but many had reached a point of profound pessimism and had
(25) begun to question their allegiance to the United States.
        Mainstream U.S. historiography was firmly rooted in a nationalist approach during this period; the glorification of the nation and a focus on the nation-state as a historical force were dominant. The
(30) expanding spheres of influence of Europe and the United States prompted the creation of new genealogies of nations, new myths about the inevitability of nations, their "temperaments," their destinies. African American intellectuals who
(35) confronted the nationalist approach to historiography were troubled by its implications. Some argued that imperialism was a natural outgrowth of nationalism and its view that a state's strength is measured by the extension of its political power over colonial territory;
(40) the scramble for colonial empires was a distinct aspect of nationalism in the latter part of the nineteenth century.
        Yet, for all their distrust of U.S. nationalism, most early black historians were themselves engaged in a
(45) sort of nation building. Deliberately or not, they contributed to the formation of a collective identity, reconstructing a glorious African past for the purposes of overturning degrading representations of blackness and establishing a firm cultural basis for a
(50) shared identity. Thus, one might argue that black historians' internationalism was a manifestation of a kind of nationalism that posits a diasporic community, which, while lacking a sovereign territory or official language, possesses a single culture, however
(55) mythical, with singular historical roots. Many members of this diaspora saw themselves as an oppressed "nation" without a homeland, or they imagined Africa as home. Hence, these historians understood their task to be the writing of the history
(60) of a people scattered by force and circumstance, a history that began in Africa.

20. Which one of the following most accurately expresses the main idea of the passage?

(A) Historians are now recognizing that the major challenge faced by African Americans in the late nineteenth and early twentieth centuries was the struggle for citizenship.

(B) Early African American historians who practiced a transnational approach to history were primarily interested in advancing an emigrationist project.

(C) U.S. historiography in the late nineteenth and early twentieth centuries was characterized by a conflict between African American historians who viewed history from a transnational perspective and mainstream historians who took a nationalist perspective.

(D) The transnational perspective of early African American historians countered mainstream nationalist historiography, but it was arguably nationalist itself to the extent that it posited a culturally unified diasporic community.

(E) Mainstream U.S. historians in the late nineteenth and early twentieth centuries could no longer justify their nationalist approach to history once they were confronted with the transnational perspective taken by African American historians.

21. Which one of the following phrases most accurately conveys the sense of the word "reconstructing" as it is used in line 47?

(A) correcting a misconception about
(B) determining the sequence of events in
(C) investigating the implications of
(D) rewarding the promoters of
(E) shaping a conception of

22. Which one of the following is most strongly supported by the passage?

(A) Emigrationist sentiment would not have been as strong among African Americans in the late nineteenth century had the promise of U.S. citizenship been fully realized for African Americans at that time.

(B) Scholars writing the history of diasporic communities generally do not discuss the forces that initially caused the scattering of the members of those communities.

(C) Most historians of the late nineteenth and early twentieth centuries endeavored to make the histories of the nations about which they wrote seem more glorious than they actually were.

(D) To be properly considered nationalist, a historical work must ignore the ways in which one nation's foreign policy decisions affected other nations.

(E) A considerable number of early African American historians embraced nationalism and the inevitability of the dominance of the nation-state.

23. As it is described in the passage, the transnational approach employed by African American historians working in the late nineteenth and early twentieth centuries would be best exemplified by a historical study that

(A) investigated the extent to which European and U.S. nationalist mythologies contradicted one another

(B) defined the national characters of the United States and several European nations by focusing on their treatment of minority populations rather than on their territorial ambitions

(C) recounted the attempts by the United States to gain control over new territories during the late nineteenth and early twentieth centuries

(D) considered the impact of emigrationist sentiment among African Americans on U.S. foreign policy in Africa during the late nineteenth century

(E) examined the extent to which African American culture at the turn of the century incorporated traditions that were common to a number of African cultures

24. The passage provides information sufficient to answer which one of the following questions?

(A) Which African nations did early African American historians research in writing their histories of the African diaspora?

(B) What were some of the African languages spoken by the ancestors of the members of the African diasporic community who were living in the United States in the late nineteenth century?

(C) Over which territories abroad did the United States attempt to extend its political power in the latter part of the nineteenth century?

(D) Are there textual ambiguities in the Fourteenth Amendment that spurred the conflict over U.S. citizenship for African Americans?

(E) In what ways did African American leaders respond to the question of citizenship for African Americans in the latter part of the nineteenth century?

25. The author of the passage would be most likely to agree with which one of the following statements?

(A) Members of a particular diasporic community have a common country of origin.

(B) Territorial sovereignty is not a prerequisite for the project of nation building.

(C) Early African American historians who rejected nationalist historiography declined to engage in historical myth-making of any kind.

(D) The most prominent African American historians in the late nineteenth and early twentieth centuries advocated emigration for African Americans.

(E) Historians who employed a nationalist approach focused on entirely different events from those studied and written about by early African American historians.

26. The main purpose of the second paragraph of the passage is to

(A) explain why early African American historians felt compelled to approach historiography in the way that they did

(B) show that governmental actions such as constitutional amendments do not always have the desired effect

(C) support the contention that African American intellectuals in the late nineteenth century were critical of U.S. imperialism

(D) establish that some African American political leaders in the late nineteenth century advocated emigration as an alternative to fighting for the benefits of U.S. citizenship

(E) argue that the definition of citizenship contained in the Fourteenth Amendment to the U.S. Constitution is too limited

27. As it is presented in the passage, the approach to history taken by mainstream U.S. historians of the late nineteenth and early twentieth centuries is most similar to the approach exemplified in which one of the following?

(A) An elected official writes a memo suggesting that because a particular course of action has been successful in the past, the government should continue to pursue that course of action.

(B) A biographer of a famous novelist argues that the precocity apparent in certain of the novelist's early achievements confirms that her success was attributable to innate talent.

(C) A doctor maintains that because a certain medication was developed expressly for the treatment of an illness, it is the best treatment for that illness.

(D) A newspaper runs a series of articles in order to inform the public about the environmentally hazardous practices of a large corporation.

(E) A scientist gets the same result from an experiment several times and therefore concludes that its chemical reactions always proceed in the observed fashion.

S T O P

IF YOU FINISH BEFORE TIME IS CALLED, YOU MAY CHECK YOUR WORK ON THIS SECTION ONLY.
DO NOT WORK ON ANY OTHER SECTION IN THE TEST.

SECTION II

Time—35 minutes

25 Questions

Directions: The questions in this section are based on the reasoning contained in brief statements or passages. For some questions, more than one of the choices could conceivably answer the question. However, you are to choose the best answer; that is, the response that most accurately and completely answers the question. You should not make assumptions that are by commonsense standards implausible, superfluous, or incompatible with the passage. After you have chosen the best answer, blacken the corresponding space on your answer sheet.

1. Mary to Jamal: You acknowledge that as the legitimate owner of this business I have the legal right to sell it whenever I wish. But also you claim that because loyal employees will suffer if I sell it, I therefore have no right to do so. Obviously, your statements taken together are absurd.

Mary's reasoning is most vulnerable to the criticism that she

(A) overlooks the possibility that when Jamal claims that she has no right to sell the business, he simply means she has no right to do so at this time

(B) overlooks the possibility that her employees also have rights related to the sale of the business

(C) provides no evidence for the claim that she does have a right to sell the business

(D) overlooks the possibility that Jamal is referring to two different kinds of right

(E) attacks Jamal's character rather than his argument

2. Since there is no survival value in an animal's having an organ that is able to function when all its other organs have broken down to such a degree that the animal dies, it is a result of the efficiency of natural selection that no organ is likely to evolve in such a way that it greatly outlasts the body's other organs.

Of the following, which one illustrates a principle that is most similar to the principle illustrated by the passage?

(A) A store in a lower-income neighborhood finds that it is unable to sell its higher-priced goods and so stocks them only when ordered by a customer.

(B) The body of an animal with a deficient organ is often able to compensate for that deficiency when other organs perform the task the deficient one normally performs.

(C) One car model produced by an automobile manufacturer has a life expectancy that is so much longer than its other models that its great popularity requires the manufacturer to stop producing some of the other models.

(D) Athletes occasionally overdevelop some parts of their bodies to such a great extent that other parts of their bodies are more prone to injury as a result.

(E) Automotive engineers find that it is not cost-effective to manufacture a given automobile part of such high quality that it outlasts all other parts of the automobile, as doing so would not raise the overall quality of the automobile.

GO ON TO THE NEXT PAGE.

3. Commentator: If a political administration is both economically successful and successful at protecting individual liberties, then it is an overall success. Even an administration that fails to care for the environment may succeed overall if it protects individual liberties. So far, the present administration has not cared for the environment but has successfully protected individual liberties.

If all of the statements above are true, then which one of the following must be true?

(A) The present administration is economically successful.

(B) The present administration is not an overall success.

(C) If the present administration is economically successful, then it is an overall success.

(D) If the present administration had been economically successful, it would have cared for the environment.

(E) If the present administration succeeds at environmental protection, then it will be an overall success.

4. The legislature is considering a proposed bill that would prohibit fishing in Eagle Bay. Despite widespread concern over the economic effect this ban would have on the local fishing industry, the bill should be enacted. The bay has one of the highest water pollution levels in the nation, and a recent study of the bay's fish found that 80 percent of them contained toxin levels that exceed governmental safety standards. Continuing to permit fishing in Eagle Bay could thus have grave effects on public health.

The argument proceeds by presenting evidence that

(A) the toxic contamination of fish in Eagle Bay has had grave economic effects on the local fishing industry

(B) the moral principle that an action must be judged on the basis of its foreseeable effects is usually correct

(C) the opponents of the ban have failed to weigh properly its foreseeable negative effects against its positive ones

(D) failure to enact the ban would carry with it unacceptable risks for the public welfare

(E) the ban would reduce the level of toxins in the fish in Eagle Bay

5. Vandenburg: This art museum is not adhering to its purpose. Its founders intended it to devote as much attention to contemporary art as to the art of earlier periods, but its collection of contemporary art is far smaller than its other collections.

Simpson: The relatively small size of the museum's contemporary art collection is appropriate. It's an art museum, not an ethnographic museum designed to collect every style of every period. Its contemporary art collection is small because its curators believe that there is little high-quality contemporary art.

Which one of the following principles, if valid, most helps to justify the reasoning in Simpson's response to Vandenburg?

(A) An art museum should collect only works that its curators consider to be of high artistic quality.

(B) An art museum should not collect any works that violate the purpose defined by the museum's founders.

(C) An art museum's purpose need not be to collect every style of every period.

(D) An ethnographic museum's purpose should be defined according to its curators' beliefs.

(E) The intentions of an art museum's curators should not determine what is collected by that museum.

6. Over the last five years, every new major alternative-energy initiative that initially was promised government funding has since seen that funding severely curtailed. In no such case has the government come even close to providing the level of funds initially earmarked for these projects. Since large corporations have made it a point to discourage alternative-energy projects, it is likely that the corporations' actions influenced the government's funding decisions.

Which one of the following, if true, most strengthens the reasoning above?

(A) For the past two decades, most alternative-energy initiatives have received little or no government funding.

(B) The funding initially earmarked for a government project is always subject to change, given the mechanisms by which the political process operates.

(C) The only research projects whose government funding has been severely curtailed are those that large corporations have made it a point to discourage.

(D) Some projects encouraged by large corporations have seen their funding severely curtailed over the last five years.

(E) All large corporations have made it a point to discourage some forms of research.

7. Talbert: Chess is beneficial for school-age children. It is enjoyable, encourages foresight and logical thinking, and discourages carelessness, inattention, and impulsiveness. In short, it promotes mental maturity.

   Sklar: My objection to teaching chess to children is that it diverts mental activity from something with societal value, such as science, into something that has no societal value.

   Talbert's and Sklar's statements provide the strongest support for holding that they disagree with each other over whether

   (A)   chess promotes mental maturity
   (B)   many activities promote mental maturity just as well as chess does
   (C)   chess is socially valuable and science is not
   (D)   children should be taught to play chess
   (E)   children who neither play chess nor study science are mentally immature

8. Marcia: Not all vegetarian diets lead to nutritional deficiencies. Research shows that vegetarians can obtain a full complement of proteins and minerals from nonanimal foods.

   Theodora: You are wrong in claiming that vegetarianism cannot lead to nutritional deficiencies. If most people became vegetarians, some of those losing jobs due to the collapse of many meat-based industries would fall into poverty and hence be unable to afford a nutritionally adequate diet.

   Theodora's reply to Marcia's argument is most vulnerable to criticism on the grounds that her reply

   (A)   is directed toward disproving a claim that Marcia did not make
   (B)   ignores the results of the research cited by Marcia
   (C)   takes for granted that no meat-based industries will collapse unless most people become vegetarians
   (D)   uses the word "diet" in a nontechnical sense whereas Marcia's argument uses this term in a medical sense
   (E)   takes for granted that people losing jobs in meat-based industries would become vegetarians

9. Musicologist: Classification of a musical instrument depends on the mechanical action through which it produces music. So the piano is properly called a percussion instrument, not a stringed instrument. Even though the vibration of the piano's strings is what makes its sound, the strings are caused to vibrate by the impact of hammers.

   Which one of the following most accurately expresses the main conclusion of the musicologist's argument?

   (A)   Musical instruments should be classified according to the mechanical actions through which they produce sound.
   (B)   Musical instruments should not be classified based on the way musicians interact with them.
   (C)   Some people classify the piano as a stringed instrument because of the way the piano produces sound.
   (D)   The piano should be classified as a stringed instrument rather than as a percussion instrument.
   (E)   It is correct to classify the piano as a percussion instrument rather than as a stringed instrument.

10. In a vast ocean region, phosphorus levels have doubled in the past few decades due to agricultural runoff pouring out of a large river nearby. The phosphorus stimulates the growth of plankton near the ocean surface. Decaying plankton fall to the ocean floor, where bacteria devour them, consuming oxygen in the process. Due to the resulting oxygen depletion, few fish can survive in this region.

   Which one of the following can be properly inferred from the information above?

   (A)   The agricultural runoff pouring out of the river contributes to the growth of plankton near the ocean surface.
   (B)   Before phosphorus levels doubled in the ocean region, most fish were able to survive in that region.
   (C)   If agricultural runoff ceased pouring out of the river, there would be no bacteria on the ocean floor devouring decaying plankton.
   (D)   The quantity of agricultural runoff pouring out of the river has doubled in the past few decades.
   (E)   The amount of oxygen in a body of water is in general inversely proportional to the level of phosphorus in that body of water.

GO ON TO THE NEXT PAGE.

11. Psychologists observing a shopping mall parking lot found that, on average, drivers spent 39 seconds leaving a parking space when another car was quietly waiting to enter it, 51 seconds if the driver of the waiting car honked impatiently, but only 32 seconds leaving a space when no one was waiting. This suggests that drivers feel possessive of their parking spaces even when leaving them, and that this possessiveness increases in reaction to indications that another driver wants the space.

Which one of the following, if true, most weakens the reasoning?

(A) The more pressure most drivers feel because others are waiting for them to perform maneuvers with their cars, the less quickly they are able to perform them.

(B) The amount of time drivers spend entering a parking space is not noticeably affected by whether other drivers are waiting for them to do so, nor by whether those other drivers are honking impatiently.

(C) It is considerably more difficult and time-consuming for a driver to maneuver a car out of a parking space if another car waiting to enter that space is nearby.

(D) Parking spaces in shopping mall parking lots are unrepresentative of parking spaces in general with respect to the likelihood that other cars will be waiting to enter them.

(E) Almost any driver leaving a parking space will feel angry at another driver who honks impatiently, and this anger will influence the amount of time spent leaving the space.

12. Shark teeth are among the most common vertebrate fossils; yet fossilized shark skeletons are much less common—indeed, comparatively rare among fossilized vertebrate skeletons.

Which one of the following, if true, most helps to resolve the apparent paradox described above?

(A) Unlike the bony skeletons of other vertebrates, shark skeletons are composed of cartilage, and teeth and bone are much more likely to fossilize than cartilage is.

(B) The rare fossilized skeletons of sharks that are found are often found in areas other than those in which fossils of shark teeth are plentiful.

(C) Fossils of sharks' teeth are quite difficult to distinguish from fossils of other kinds of teeth.

(D) Some species of sharks alive today grow and lose many sets of teeth during their lifetimes.

(E) The physical and chemical processes involved in the fossilization of sharks' teeth are as common as those involved in the fossilization of shark skeletons.

13. Critic: Photographers, by deciding which subjects to depict and how to depict them, express their own worldviews in their photographs, however realistically those photographs may represent reality. Thus, photographs are interpretations of reality.

The argument's conclusion is properly drawn if which one of the following is assumed?

(A) Even representing a subject realistically can involve interpreting that subject.

(B) To express a worldview is to interpret reality.

(C) All visual art expresses the artist's worldview.

(D) Any interpretation of reality involves the expression of a worldview.

(E) Nonrealistic photographs, like realistic photographs, express the worldviews of the photographers who take them.

14. Geologists recently discovered marks that closely resemble worm tracks in a piece of sandstone. These marks were made more than half a billion years earlier than the earliest known traces of multicellular animal life. Therefore, the marks are probably the traces of geological processes rather than of worms.

Which one of the following, if true, most weakens the argument?

(A) It is sometimes difficult to estimate the precise age of a piece of sandstone.

(B) Geological processes left a substantial variety of marks in sandstone more than half a billion years before the earliest known multicellular animal life existed.

(C) There were some early life forms other than worms that are known to have left marks that are hard to distinguish from those found in the piece of sandstone.

(D) At the place where the sandstone was found, the only geological processes that are likely to mark sandstone in ways that resemble worm tracks could not have occurred at the time the marks were made.

(E) Most scientists knowledgeable about early animal life believe that worms are likely to have been among the earliest forms of multicellular animal life on Earth, but evidence of their earliest existence is scarce because they are composed solely of soft tissue.

GO ON TO THE NEXT PAGE.

15. Often a type of organ or body structure is the only physically feasible means of accomplishing a given task, so it should be unsurprising if, like eyes or wings, that type of organ or body structure evolves at different times in a number of completely unrelated species. After all, whatever the difference of heritage and habitat, as organisms animals have fundamentally similar needs and so _____.

Which one of the following most logically completes the last sentence of the passage?

(A) will often live in the same environment as other species quite different from themselves
(B) will in many instances evolve similar adaptations enabling them to satisfy these needs
(C) will develop adaptations allowing them to satisfy these needs
(D) will resemble other species having different biological needs
(E) will all develop eyes or wings as adaptations

16. Engineer: Thermophotovoltaic generators are devices that convert heat into electricity. The process of manufacturing steel produces huge amounts of heat that currently go to waste. So if steel-manufacturing plants could feed the heat they produce into thermophotovoltaic generators, they would greatly reduce their electric bills, thereby saving money.

Which one of the following is an assumption on which the engineer's argument depends?

(A) There is no other means of utilizing the heat produced by the steel-manufacturing process that would be more cost effective than installing thermophotovoltaic generators.
(B) Using current technology, it would be possible for steel-manufacturing plants to feed the heat they produce into thermophotovoltaic generators in such a way that those generators could convert at least some of that heat into electricity.
(C) The amount steel-manufacturing plants would save on their electric bills by feeding heat into thermophotovoltaic generators would be sufficient to cover the cost of purchasing and installing those generators.
(D) At least some steel-manufacturing plants rely on electricity as their primary source of energy in the steel-manufacturing process.
(E) There are at least some steel-manufacturing plants that could greatly reduce their electricity bills only if they used some method of converting wasted heat or other energy from the steel-manufacturing process into electricity.

17. Herbalist: While standard antibiotics typically have just one active ingredient, herbal antibacterial remedies typically contain several. Thus, such herbal remedies are more likely to retain their effectiveness against new, resistant strains of bacteria than are standard antibiotics. For a strain of bacteria, the difficulty of developing resistance to an herbal antibacterial remedy is like a cook's difficulty in trying to prepare a single meal that will please all of several dozen guests, a task far more difficult than preparing one meal that will please a single guest.

In the analogy drawn in the argument above, which one of the following corresponds to a standard antibiotic?

(A) a single guest
(B) several dozen guests
(C) the pleasure experienced by a single guest
(D) a cook
(E) the ingredients available to a cook

18. To find out how barn owls learn how to determine the direction from which sounds originate, scientists put distorting lenses over the eyes of young barn owls before the owls first opened their eyes. The owls with these lenses behaved as if objects making sounds were farther to the right than they actually were. Once the owls matured, the lenses were removed, yet the owls continued to act as if they misjudged the location of the source of sounds. The scientists consequently hypothesized that once a barn owl has developed an auditory scheme for estimating the point from which sounds originate, it ceases to use vision to locate sounds.

The scientists' reasoning is vulnerable to which one of the following criticisms?

(A) It fails to consider whether the owls' vision was permanently impaired by their having worn the lenses while immature.
(B) It assumes that the sense of sight is equally good in all owls.
(C) It attributes human reasoning processes to a nonhuman organism.
(D) It neglects to consider how similar distorting lenses might affect the behavior of other bird species.
(E) It uses as evidence experimental results that were irrelevant to the conclusion.

GO ON TO THE NEXT PAGE.

19. As often now as in the past, newspaper journalists use direct or indirect quotation to report unsupported or false claims made by newsmakers. However, journalists are becoming less likely to openly challenge the veracity of such claims within their articles.

Each of the following, if true, helps to explain the trend in journalism described above EXCEPT:

(A) Newspaper publishers have found that many readers will cancel a subscription simply because a view they take for granted has been disputed by the publication.

(B) The areas of knowledge on which journalists report are growing in specialization and diversity, while journalists themselves are not becoming more broadly knowledgeable.

(C) Persons supporting controversial views more and more frequently choose to speak only to reporters who seem sympathetic to their views.

(D) A basic principle of journalism holds that debate over controversial issues draws the attention of the public.

(E) Journalists who challenge the veracity of claims are often criticized for failing their professional obligation to be objective.

20. When people show signs of having a heart attack an electrocardiograph (EKG) is often used to diagnose their condition. In a study, a computer program for EKG diagnosis of heart attacks was pitted against a very experienced, highly skilled cardiologist. The program correctly diagnosed a significantly higher proportion of the cases that were later confirmed to be heart attacks than did the cardiologist. Interpreting EKG data, therefore, should be left to computer programs.

Which one of the following, if true, most weakens the argument?

(A) Experts agreed that the cardiologist made few obvious mistakes in reading and interpreting the EKG data.

(B) The practice of medicine is as much an art as a science, and computer programs are not easily adapted to making subjective judgments.

(C) The cardiologist correctly diagnosed a significantly higher proportion of the cases in which no heart attack occurred than did the computer program.

(D) In a considerable percentage of cases, EKG data alone are insufficient to enable either computer programs or cardiologists to make accurate diagnoses.

(E) The cardiologist in the study was unrepresentative of cardiologists in general with respect to skill and experience.

21. A government study indicates that raising speed limits to reflect the actual average speeds of traffic on level, straight stretches of high-speed roadways reduces the accident rate. Since the actual average speed for level, straight stretches of high-speed roadways tends to be 120 kilometers per hour (75 miles per hour), that should be set as a uniform national speed limit for level, straight stretches of all such roadways.

Which one of the following principles, if valid, most helps to justify the reasoning above?

(A) Uniform national speed limits should apply only to high-speed roadways.

(B) Traffic laws applying to high-speed roadways should apply uniformly across the nation.

(C) A uniform national speed limit for high-speed roadways should be set only if all such roadways have roughly equal average speeds of traffic.

(D) Long-standing laws that are widely violated are probably not good laws.

(E) Any measure that reduces the rate of traffic accidents should be implemented.

GO ON TO THE NEXT PAGE.

22. Psychiatrist: In treating first-year students at this university, I have noticed that those reporting the highest levels of spending on recreation score at about the same level on standard screening instruments for anxiety and depression as those reporting the lowest levels of spending on recreation. This suggests that the first-year students with high levels of spending on recreation could reduce that spending without increasing their anxiety or depression.

Each of the following, if true, strengthens the psychiatrist's argument EXCEPT:

(A) At other universities, first-year students reporting the highest levels of spending on recreation also show the same degree of anxiety and depression as do those reporting the lowest levels of such spending.

(B) Screening of first-year students at the university who report moderate levels of spending on recreation reveals that those students are less anxious and depressed than both those with the highest and those with the lowest levels of spending on recreation.

(C) Among adults between the ages of 40 and 60, increased levels of spending on recreation are strongly correlated with decreased levels of anxiety and depression.

(D) The screening instruments used by the psychiatrist are extremely accurate in revealing levels of anxiety and depression among university students.

(E) Several of the psychiatrist's patients who are first-year students at the university have reduced their spending on recreation from very high levels to very low levels without increasing their anxiety or depression.

23. Every brick house on River Street has a front yard. Most of the houses on River Street that have front yards also have two stories. So most of the brick houses on River Street have two stories.

Which one of the following is most appropriate as an analogy demonstrating that the reasoning in the argument above is flawed?

(A) By that line of reasoning, we could conclude that most politicians have run for office, since all legislators are politicians and most legislators have run for office.

(B) By that line of reasoning, we could conclude that most public servants are legislators, since most legislators have run for office and most politicians who have run for office are public servants.

(C) By that line of reasoning, we could conclude that not every public servant has run for office, since every legislator is a public servant but some public servants are not legislators.

(D) By that line of reasoning, we could conclude that most legislators have never run for office, since most public servants have never run for office and all legislators are public servants.

(E) By that line of reasoning, we could conclude that most legislators are not public servants, since most public servants have not run for office and most legislators have run for office.

GO ON TO THE NEXT PAGE.

24. Historian: It is unlikely that someone would see history as the working out of moral themes unless he or she held clear and unambiguous moral beliefs. However, one's inclination to morally judge human behavior decreases as one's knowledge of history increases. Consequently, the more history a person knows, the less likely that person is to view history as the working out of moral themes.

The conclusion of the argument is properly drawn if which one of the following is assumed?

(A) Historical events that fail to elicit moral disapproval are generally not considered to exemplify a moral theme.

(B) The less inclined one is to morally judge human behavior, the less likely it is that one holds clear and unambiguous moral beliefs.

(C) Only those who do not understand human history attribute moral significance to historical events.

(D) The more clear and unambiguous one's moral beliefs, the more likely one is to view history as the working out of moral themes.

(E) People tend to be less objective regarding a subject about which they possess extensive knowledge than regarding a subject about which they do not possess extensive knowledge.

25. A recent poll revealed that most students at our university prefer that the university, which is searching for a new president, hire someone who has extensive experience as a university president. However, in the very same poll, the person most students chose from among a list of leading candidates as the one they would most like to see hired was someone who has never served as a university president.

Which one of the following, if true, most helps to account for the apparent discrepancy in the students' preferences?

(A) Because several of the candidates listed in the poll had extensive experience as university presidents, not all of the candidates could be differentiated on this basis alone.

(B) Most of the candidates listed in the poll had extensive experience as university presidents.

(C) Students taking the poll had fewer candidates to choose from than were currently being considered for the position.

(D) Most of the students taking the poll did not know whether any of the leading candidates listed in the poll had ever served as a university president.

(E) Often a person can be well suited to a position even though they have relatively little experience in such a position.

S T O P

IF YOU FINISH BEFORE TIME IS CALLED, YOU MAY CHECK YOUR WORK ON THIS SECTION ONLY.
DO NOT WORK ON ANY OTHER SECTION IN THE TEST.

SECTION III
Time—35 minutes
23 Questions

<u>Directions:</u> Each group of questions in this section is based on a set of conditions. In answering some of the questions, it may be useful to draw a rough diagram. Choose the response that most accurately and completely answers each question and blacken the corresponding space on your answer sheet.

Questions 1–5

Exactly six workers—Faith, Gus, Hannah, Juan, Kenneth, and Lisa—will travel to a business convention in two cars—car 1 and car 2. Each car must carry at least two of the workers, one of whom will be assigned to drive. For the entire trip, the workers will comply with an assignment that also meets the following constraints:
    Either Faith or Gus must drive the car in which Hannah travels.
    Either Faith or Kenneth must drive the car in which Juan travels.
    Gus must travel in the same car as Lisa.

1. Which one of the following is a possible assignment of the workers to the cars?

    (A)   car 1: Faith (driver), Hannah, and Juan
           car 2: Gus (driver), Kenneth, and Lisa
    (B)   car 1: Faith (driver), Hannah, and Kenneth
           car 2: Lisa (driver), Gus, and Juan
    (C)   car 1: Faith (driver), Juan, Kenneth, and Lisa
           car 2: Gus (driver) and Hannah
    (D)   car 1: Faith (driver) and Juan
           car 2: Kenneth (driver), Gus, Hannah, and Lisa
    (E)   car 1: Gus (driver), Hannah, and Lisa
           car 2: Juan (driver), Faith, and Kenneth

2. The two workers who drive the cars CANNOT be

    (A)   Faith and Gus
    (B)   Faith and Kenneth
    (C)   Faith and Lisa
    (D)   Gus and Kenneth
    (E)   Kenneth and Lisa

3. If Lisa drives one of the cars, then which one of the following could be true?

    (A)   Faith travels in the same car as Kenneth.
    (B)   Faith travels in the same car as Lisa.
    (C)   Gus travels in the same car as Hannah.
    (D)   Gus travels in the same car as Juan.
    (E)   Hannah travels in the same car as Lisa.

4. If Faith travels with two other workers in car 1, and if Faith is not the driver, then the person in car 1 other than Faith and the driver must be

    (A)   Gus
    (B)   Hannah
    (C)   Juan
    (D)   Kenneth
    (E)   Lisa

5. Which one of the following CANNOT be true?

    (A)   Gus is the only person other than the driver in one of the cars.
    (B)   Hannah is the only person other than the driver in one of the cars.
    (C)   Juan is the only person other than the driver in one of the cars.
    (D)   Kenneth is the only person other than the driver in one of the cars.
    (E)   Lisa is the only person other than the driver in one of the cars.

GO ON TO THE NEXT PAGE.

Questions 6–11

An archaeologist has six ancient artifacts—a figurine, a headdress, a jar, a necklace, a plaque, and a tureen—no two of which are the same age. She will order them from first (oldest) to sixth (most recent). The following has already been determined:

The figurine is older than both the jar and the headdress.
The necklace and the jar are both older than the tureen.
Either the plaque is older than both the headdress and the necklace, or both the headdress and the necklace are older than the plaque.

6. Which one of the following could be the artifacts in the order of their age, from first to sixth?

(A) figurine, headdress, jar, necklace, plaque, tureen
(B) figurine, jar, plaque, headdress, tureen, necklace
(C) figurine, necklace, plaque, headdress, jar, tureen
(D) necklace, jar, figurine, headdress, plaque, tureen
(E) plaque, tureen, figurine, necklace, jar, headdress

7. Exactly how many of the artifacts are there any one of which could be first?

(A) one
(B) two
(C) three
(D) four
(E) five

8. Which one of the following artifacts CANNOT be fourth?

(A) figurine
(B) headdress
(C) jar
(D) necklace
(E) plaque

9. If the figurine is third, which one of the following must be second?

(A) headdress
(B) jar
(C) necklace
(D) plaque
(E) tureen

10. If the plaque is first, then exactly how many artifacts are there any one of which could be second?

(A) one
(B) two
(C) three
(D) four
(E) five

11. Which one of the following, if substituted for the information that the necklace and the jar are both older than the tureen, would have the same effect in determining the order of the artifacts?

(A) The tureen is older than the headdress but not as old as the figurine.
(B) The figurine and the necklace are both older than the tureen.
(C) The necklace is older than the tureen if and only if the jar is.
(D) All of the artifacts except the headdress and the plaque must be older than the tureen.
(E) The plaque is older than the necklace if and only if the plaque is older than the tureen.

GO ON TO THE NEXT PAGE.

Questions 12–17

The coach of a women's track team must determine which four of five runners—Quinn, Ramirez, Smith, Terrell, and Uzoma—will run in the four races of an upcoming track meet. Each of the four runners chosen will run in exactly one of the four races—the first, second, third, or fourth. The coach's selection is bound by the following constraints:

If Quinn runs in the track meet, then Terrell runs in the race immediately after the race in which Quinn runs.

Smith does not run in either the second race or the fourth race.

If Uzoma does not run in the track meet, then Ramirez runs in the second race.

If Ramirez runs in the second race, then Uzoma does not run in the track meet.

12. Which one of the following could be the order in which the runners run, from first to fourth?

(A) Uzoma, Ramirez, Quinn, Terrell
(B) Terrell, Smith, Ramirez, Uzoma
(C) Smith, Ramirez, Terrell, Quinn
(D) Ramirez, Uzoma, Smith, Terrell
(E) Quinn, Terrell, Smith, Ramirez

13. Which one of the following runners must the coach select to run in the track meet?

(A) Quinn
(B) Ramirez
(C) Smith
(D) Terrell
(E) Uzoma

14. The question of which runners will be chosen to run in the track meet and in what races they will run can be completely resolved if which one of the following is true?

(A) Ramirez runs in the first race.
(B) Ramirez runs in the second race.
(C) Ramirez runs in the third race.
(D) Ramirez runs in the fourth race.
(E) Ramirez does not run in the track meet.

15. Which one of the following CANNOT be true?

(A) Ramirez runs in the race immediately before the race in which Smith runs.
(B) Smith runs in the race immediately before the race in which Quinn runs.
(C) Smith runs in the race immediately before the race in which Terrell runs.
(D) Terrell runs in the race immediately before the race in which Ramirez runs.
(E) Uzoma runs in the race immediately before the race in which Terrell runs.

16. If Uzoma runs in the first race, then which one of the following must be true?

(A) Quinn does not run in the track meet.
(B) Smith does not run in the track meet.
(C) Quinn runs in the second race.
(D) Terrell runs in the second race.
(E) Ramirez runs in the fourth race.

17. If both Quinn and Smith run in the track meet, then how many of the runners are there any one of whom could be the one who runs in the first race?

(A) one
(B) two
(C) three
(D) four
(E) five

GO ON TO THE NEXT PAGE.

Questions 18–23

From the 1st through the 7th of next month, seven nurses—Farnham, Griseldi, Heany, Juarez, Khan, Lightfoot, and Moreau—will each conduct one information session at a community center. Each nurse's session will fall on a different day. The nurses' schedule is governed by the following constraints:

At least two of the other nurses' sessions must fall in between Heany's session and Moreau's session.
Griseldi's session must be on the day before Khan's.
Juarez's session must be on a later day than Moreau's.
Farnham's session must be on an earlier day than Khan's but on a later day than Lightfoot's.
Lightfoot cannot conduct the session on the 2nd.

18. Which one of the following could be the order of the nurses' sessions, from first to last?

(A) Farnham, Griseldi, Khan, Moreau, Juarez, Lightfoot, Heany
(B) Heany, Lightfoot, Farnham, Moreau, Juarez, Griseldi, Khan
(C) Juarez, Heany, Lightfoot, Farnham, Moreau, Griseldi, Khan
(D) Lightfoot, Moreau, Farnham, Juarez, Griseldi, Khan, Heany
(E) Moreau, Lightfoot, Heany, Juarez, Farnham, Griseldi, Khan

19. Juarez's session CANNOT be on which one of the following days?

(A) the 2nd
(B) the 3rd
(C) the 5th
(D) the 6th
(E) the 7th

20. If Juarez's session is on the 3rd, then which one of the following could be true?

(A) Moreau's session is on the 1st.
(B) Khan's session is on the 5th.
(C) Heany's session is on the 6th.
(D) Griseldi's session is on the 5th.
(E) Farnham's session is on the 2nd.

21. If Khan's session is on an earlier day than Moreau's, which one of the following could conduct the session on the 3rd?

(A) Griseldi
(B) Heany
(C) Juarez
(D) Lightfoot
(E) Moreau

22. If Griseldi's session is on the 5th, then which one of the following must be true?

(A) Farnham's session is on the 3rd.
(B) Heany's session is on the 7th.
(C) Juarez's session is on the 4th.
(D) Lightfoot's session is on the 1st.
(E) Moreau's session is on the 2nd.

23. Lightfoot's session could be on which one of the following days?

(A) the 3rd
(B) the 4th
(C) the 5th
(D) the 6th
(E) the 7th

S T O P

IF YOU FINISH BEFORE TIME IS CALLED, YOU MAY CHECK YOUR WORK ON THIS SECTION ONLY.
DO NOT WORK ON ANY OTHER SECTION IN THE TEST.

SECTION IV

Time—35 minutes

26 Questions

<u>Directions:</u> The questions in this section are based on the reasoning contained in brief statements or passages. For some questions, more than one of the choices could conceivably answer the question. However, you are to choose the <u>best</u> answer; that is, the response that most accurately and completely answers the question. You should not make assumptions that are by commonsense standards implausible, superfluous, or incompatible with the passage. After you have chosen the best answer, blacken the corresponding space on your answer sheet.

1. Among Trinidadian guppies, males with large spots are more attractive to females than are males with small spots, who consequently are presented with less frequent mating opportunities. Yet guppies with small spots are more likely to avoid detection by predators, so in waters where predators are abundant only guppies with small spots live to maturity.

   The situation described above most closely conforms to which one of the following generalizations?

   (A)   A trait that helps attract mates is sometimes more dangerous to one sex than to another.
   (B)   Those organisms that are most attractive to the opposite sex have the greatest number of offspring.
   (C)   Those organisms that survive the longest have the greatest number of offspring.
   (D)   Whether a trait is harmful to the organisms of a species can depend on which sex possesses it.
   (E)   A trait that is helpful to procreation can also hinder it in certain environments.

2. Programmer: We computer programmers at Mytheco are demanding raises to make our average salary comparable with that of the technical writers here who receive, on average, 20 percent more in salary and benefits than we do. This pay difference is unfair and intolerable.

   Mytheco executive: But many of the technical writers have worked for Mytheco longer than have many of the programmers. Since salary and benefits at Mytheco are directly tied to seniority, the 20 percent pay difference you mention is perfectly acceptable.

   Evaluating the adequacy of the Mytheco executive's response requires a clarification of which one of the following?

   (A)   whether any of the technical writers at Mytheco once worked as programmers at the company
   (B)   how the average seniority of programmers compares with the average seniority of technical writers
   (C)   whether the sorts of benefits an employee of Mytheco receives are tied to the salary of that employee
   (D)   whether the Mytheco executive was at one time a technical writer employed by Mytheco
   (E)   how the Mytheco executive's salary compares with that of the programmers

3. Cable TV stations have advantages that enable them to attract many more advertisers than broadcast networks attract. For example, cable stations are able to target particular audiences with 24-hour news, sports, or movies, whereas broadcast networks must offer a variety of programming. Cable can also offer lower advertising rates than any broadcast network can, because it is subsidized by viewers through subscriber fees. Additionally, many cable stations have expanded worldwide with multinational programming.

   The statements above, if true, provide support for each of the following EXCEPT:

   (A)   Some broadcast networks can be viewed in several countries.
   (B)   Broadcast networks do not rely on subscriber fees from viewers.
   (C)   Low costs are often an important factor for advertisers in selecting a station or network on which to run a TV ad.
   (D)   Some advertisers prefer to have the opportunity to address a worldwide audience.
   (E)   The audiences that some advertisers prefer to target watch 24-hour news stations.

4. In polluted industrial English cities during the Industrial Revolution, two plant diseases—black spot, which infects roses, and tar spot, which infects sycamore trees—disappeared. It is likely that air pollution eradicated these diseases.

   Which one of the following, if true, most strengthens the reasoning above?

   (A)   Scientists theorize that some plants can develop a resistance to air pollution.
   (B)   Certain measures help prevent infection by black spot and tar spot, but once infection occurs, it is very difficult to eliminate.
   (C)   For many plant species, scientists have not determined the effects of air pollution.
   (D)   Black spot and tar spot returned when the air in the cities became less polluted.
   (E)   Black spot and tar spot were the only plant diseases that disappeared in any English cities during the Industrial Revolution.

GO ON TO THE NEXT PAGE.

5. Many scholars are puzzled about who created the seventeenth-century abridgment of Shakespeare's *Hamlet* contained in the First Quarto. Two facts about the work shed light on this question. First, the person who undertook the abridgment clearly did not possess a copy of *Hamlet*. Second, the abridgment contains a very accurate rendering of the speeches of one of the characters, but a slipshod handling of all the other parts.

Which one of the following statements is most supported by the information above?

(A) The abridgment was prepared by Shakespeare.
(B) The abridgment was created to make *Hamlet* easier to produce on stage.
(C) The abridgment was produced by an actor who had played a role in *Hamlet*.
(D) The abridgement was prepared by a spectator of a performance of *Hamlet*.
(E) The abridgment was produced by an actor who was trying to improve the play.

6. Musicologist: Many critics complain of the disproportion between text and music in Handel's *da capo* arias. These texts are generally quite short and often repeated well beyond what is needed for literal understanding. Yet such criticism is refuted by noting that repetition serves a vital function: it frees the audience to focus on the music itself, which can speak to audiences whatever their language.

Which one of the following sentences best expresses the main point of the musicologist's reasoning?

(A) Handel's *da capo* arias contain a disproportionate amount of music.
(B) Handel's *da capo* arias are superior to most in their accessibility to diverse audiences.
(C) At least one frequent criticism of Handel's *da capo* arias is undeserved.
(D) At least some of Handel's *da capo* arias contain unnecessary repetitions.
(E) Most criticism of Handel's *da capo* arias is unwarranted.

7. Baxe Interiors, one of the largest interior design companies in existence, currently has a near monopoly in the corporate market. Several small design companies have won prestigious awards for their corporate work, while Baxe has won none. Nonetheless, the corporate managers who solicit design proposals will only contract with companies they believe are unlikely to go bankrupt, and they believe that only very large companies are unlikely to go bankrupt.

The statements above, if true, most strongly support which one of the following?

(A) There are other very large design companies besides Baxe, but they produce designs that are inferior to Baxe's.
(B) Baxe does not have a near monopoly in the market of any category of interior design other than corporate interiors.
(C) For the most part, designs that are produced by small companies are superior to the designs produced by Baxe.
(D) At least some of the corporate managers who solicit design proposals are unaware that there are designs that are much better than those produced by Baxe.
(E) The existence of interior designs that are superior to those produced by Baxe does not currently threaten its near monopoly in the corporate market.

GO ON TO THE NEXT PAGE.

8. The giant Chicxulub crater in Mexico provides indisputable evidence that a huge asteroid, about six miles across, struck Earth around the time many of the last dinosaur species were becoming extinct. But this catastrophe was probably not responsible for most of these extinctions. Any major asteroid strike kills many organisms in or near the region of the impact, but there is little evidence that such a strike could have a worldwide effect. Indeed, some craters even larger than the Chicxulub crater were made during times in Earth's history when there were no known extinctions.

Which one of the following, if true, would most weaken the argument?

(A) The vast majority of dinosaur species are known to have gone extinct well before the time of the asteroid impact that produced the Chicxulub crater.

(B) The size of a crater caused by an asteroid striking Earth generally depends on both the size of that asteroid and the force of its impact.

(C) Fossils have been discovered of a number of dinosaurs that clearly died as a result of the asteroid impact that produced the Chicxulub crater.

(D) There is no evidence that any other asteroid of equal size struck Earth at the same time as the asteroid that produced the Chicxulub crater.

(E) During the period immediately before the asteroid that produced the Chicxulub crater struck, most of the world's dinosaurs lived in or near the region of the asteroid's impending impact.

9. In a sample containing 1,000 peanuts from lot A and 1,000 peanuts from lot B, 50 of the peanuts from lot A were found to be infected with *Aspergillus*. Two hundred of the peanuts from lot B were found to be infected with *Aspergillus*. Therefore, infection with *Aspergillus* is more widespread in lot B than in lot A.

The reasoning in which one of the following is most similar to the reasoning in the argument above?

(A) Every one of these varied machine parts is of uniformly high quality. Therefore, the machine that we assemble from them will be of equally high quality.

(B) If a plant is carelessly treated, it is likely to develop blight. If a plant develops blight, it is likely to die. Therefore, if a plant is carelessly treated, it is likely to die.

(C) In the past 1,000 experiments, whenever an experimental fungicide was applied to coffee plants infected with coffee rust, the infection disappeared. The coffee rust never disappeared before the fungicide was applied. Therefore, in these experiments, application of the fungicide caused the disappearance of coffee rust.

(D) Three thousand registered voters—1,500 members of the Liberal party and 1,500 members of the Conservative party—were asked which mayoral candidate they favored. Four hundred of the Liberals and 300 of the Conservatives favored Pollack. Therefore, Pollack has more support among Liberals than among Conservatives.

(E) All of my livestock are registered with the regional authority. None of the livestock registered with the regional authority are free-range livestock. Therefore, none of my livestock are free-range livestock.

GO ON TO THE NEXT PAGE.

10. Economist: If the belief were to become widespread that losing one's job is not a sign of personal shortcomings but instead an effect of impersonal social forces (which is surely correct), there would be growth in the societal demand for more government control of the economy to protect individuals from these forces, just as the government now protects them from military invasion. Such extensive government control of the economy would lead to an economic disaster, however.

The economist's statements, if true, most strongly support which one of the following?

(A) Increased knowledge of the causes of job loss could lead to economic disaster.

(B) An individual's belief in his or her own abilities is the only reliable protection against impersonal social forces.

(C) Governments should never interfere with economic forces.

(D) Societal demand for government control of the economy is growing.

(E) In general, people should feel no more responsible for economic disasters than for military invasions.

11. A development company has proposed building an airport near the city of Dalton. If the majority of Dalton's residents favor the proposal, the airport will be built. However, it is unlikely that a majority of Dalton's residents would favor the proposal, for most of them believe that the airport would create noise problems. Thus, it is unlikely that the airport will be built.

The reasoning in the argument is flawed in that the argument

(A) treats a sufficient condition for the airport's being built as a necessary condition

(B) concludes that something must be true, because most people believe it to be true

(C) concludes, on the basis that a certain event is unlikely to occur, that the event will not occur

(D) fails to consider whether people living near Dalton would favor building the airport

(E) overlooks the possibility that a new airport could benefit the local economy

12. After the rush-hour speed limit on the British M25 motorway was lowered from 70 miles per hour (115 kilometers per hour) to 50 miles per hour (80 kilometers per hour), rush-hour travel times decreased by approximately 15 percent.

Which one of the following, if true, most helps to explain the decrease in travel times described above?

(A) After the decrease in the rush-hour speed limit, the average speed on the M25 was significantly lower during rush hours than at other times of the day.

(B) Travel times during periods other than rush hours were essentially unchanged after the rush-hour speed limit was lowered.

(C) Before the rush-hour speed limit was lowered, rush-hour accidents that caused lengthy delays were common, and most of these accidents were caused by high-speed driving.

(D) Enforcement of speed limits on the M25 was quite rigorous both before and after the rush-hour speed limit was lowered.

(E) The number of people who drive on the M25 during rush hours did not increase after the rush-hour speed limit was lowered.

13. An art critic, by ridiculing an artwork, can undermine the pleasure one takes in it; conversely, by lavishing praise upon an artwork, an art critic can render the experience of viewing the artwork more pleasurable. So an artwork's artistic merit can depend not only on the person who creates it but also on those who critically evaluate it.

The conclusion can be properly drawn if which one of the following is assumed?

(A) The merit of an artistic work is determined by the amount of pleasure it elicits.

(B) Most people lack the confidence necessary for making their own evaluations of art.

(C) Art critics understand what gives an artwork artistic merit better than artists do.

(D) Most people seek out critical reviews of particular artworks before viewing those works.

(E) The pleasure people take in something is typically influenced by what they think others feel about it.

GO ON TO THE NEXT PAGE.

14. The number of automobile thefts has declined steadily during the past five years, and it is more likely now than it was five years ago that someone who steals a car will be convicted of the crime.

Which one of the following, if true, most helps to explain the facts cited above?

(A) Although there are fewer car thieves now than there were five years ago, the proportion of thieves who tend to abandon cars before their owners notice that they have been stolen has also decreased.

(B) Car alarms are more common than they were five years ago, but their propensity to be triggered in the absence of any criminal activity has resulted in people generally ignoring them when they are triggered.

(C) An upsurge in home burglaries over the last five years has required police departments to divert limited resources to investigation of these cases.

(D) Because of the increasingly lucrative market for stolen automobile parts, many stolen cars are quickly disassembled and the parts are sold to various buyers across the country.

(E) There are more adolescent car thieves now than there were five years ago, and the sentences given to young criminals tend to be far more lenient than those given to adult criminals.

15. Legislator: My staff conducted a poll in which my constituents were asked whether they favor high taxes. More than 97 percent answered "no." Clearly, then, my constituents would support the bill I recently introduced, which reduces the corporate income tax.

The reasoning in the legislator's argument is most vulnerable to criticism on the grounds that the argument

(A) fails to establish that the opinions of the legislator's constituents are representative of the opinions of the country's population as a whole

(B) fails to consider whether the legislator's constituents consider the current corporate income tax a high tax

(C) confuses an absence of evidence that the legislator's constituents oppose a bill with the existence of evidence that the legislator's constituents support that bill

(D) draws a conclusion that merely restates a claim presented in support of that conclusion

(E) treats a result that proves that the public supports a bill as a result that is merely consistent with public support for that bill

16. Many nursing homes have prohibitions against having pets, and these should be lifted. The presence of an animal companion can yield health benefits by reducing a person's stress. A pet can also make one's time at a home more rewarding, which will be important to more people as the average life span of our population increases.

Which one of the following most accurately expresses the conclusion drawn in the argument above?

(A) As the average life span increases, it will be important to more people that life in nursing homes be rewarding.

(B) Residents of nursing homes should enjoy the same rewarding aspects of life as anyone else.

(C) The policy that many nursing homes have should be changed so that residents are allowed to have pets.

(D) Having a pet can reduce one's stress and thereby make one a healthier person.

(E) The benefits older people derive from having pets need to be recognized, especially as the average life span increases.

17. Near many cities, contamination of lakes and rivers from pollutants in rainwater runoff exceeds that from industrial discharge. As the runoff washes over buildings and pavements, it picks up oil and other pollutants. Thus, water itself is among the biggest water polluters.

The statement that contamination of lakes and rivers from pollutants in rainwater runoff exceeds that from industrial discharge plays which one of the following roles in the argument?

(A) It is a conclusion for which the claim that water itself should be considered a polluter is offered as support.

(B) It is cited as evidence that pollution from rainwater runoff is a more serious problem than pollution from industrial discharge.

(C) It is a generalization based on the observation that rainwater runoff picks up oil and other pollutants as it washes over buildings and pavements.

(D) It is a premise offered in support of the conclusion that water itself is among the biggest water polluters.

(E) It is stated to provide an example of a typical kind of city pollution.

GO ON TO THE NEXT PAGE.

18. Wong: Although all countries are better off as democracies, a transitional autocratic stage is sometimes required before a country can become democratic.

Tate: The freedom and autonomy that democracy provides are of genuine value, but the simple material needs of people are more important. Some countries can better meet these needs as autocracies than as democracies.

Wong's and Tate's statements provide the most support for the claim that they disagree over the truth of which one of the following?

(A) There are some countries that are better off as autocracies than as democracies.

(B) Nothing is more important to a country than the freedom and autonomy of the individuals who live in that country.

(C) In some cases, a country cannot become a democracy.

(D) The freedom and autonomy that democracy provides are of genuine value.

(E) All democracies succeed in meeting the simple material needs of people.

19. Principle: When none of the fully qualified candidates for a new position at Arvue Corporation currently works for that company, it should hire the candidate who would be most productive in that position.

Application: Arvue should not hire Krall for the new position, because Delacruz is a candidate and is fully qualified.

Which one of the following, if true, justifies the above application of the principle?

(A) All of the candidates are fully qualified for the new position, but none already works for Arvue.

(B) Of all the candidates who do not already work for Arvue, Delacruz would be the most productive in the new position.

(C) Krall works for Arvue, but Delacruz is the candidate who would be most productive in the new position.

(D) Several candidates currently work for Arvue, but Krall and Delacruz do not.

(E) None of the candidates already works for Arvue, and Delacruz is the candidate who would be most productive in the new position.

20. Many important types of medicine have been developed from substances discovered in plants that grow only in tropical rain forests. There are thousands of plant species in these rain forests that have not yet been studied by scientists, and it is very likely that many such plants also contain substances of medicinal value. Thus, if the tropical rain forests are not preserved, important types of medicine will never be developed.

Which one of the following is an assumption required by the argument?

(A) There are substances of medicinal value contained in tropical rain forest plants not yet studied by scientists that differ from those substances already discovered in tropical rain forest plants.

(B) Most of the tropical rain forest plants that contain substances of medicinal value can also be found growing in other types of environment.

(C) The majority of plant species that are unique to tropical rain forests and that have been studied by scientists have been discovered to contain substances of medicinal value.

(D) Any substance of medicinal value contained in plant species indigenous to tropical rain forests will eventually be discovered if those species are studied by scientists.

(E) The tropical rain forests should be preserved to make it possible for important medicines to be developed from plant species that have not yet been studied by scientists.

GO ON TO THE NEXT PAGE.

21. In modern deep-diving marine mammals, such as whales, the outer shell of the bones is porous. This has the effect of making the bones light enough so that it is easy for the animals to swim back to the surface after a deep dive. The outer shell of the bones was also porous in the ichthyosaur, an extinct prehistoric marine reptile. We can conclude from this that ichthyosaurs were deep divers.

Which one of the following, if true, most weakens the argument?

(A)   Some deep-diving marine species must surface after dives but do not have bones with porous outer shells.

(B)   In most modern marine reptile species, the outer shell of the bones is not porous.

(C)   In most modern and prehistoric marine reptile species that are not deep divers, the outer shell of the bones is porous.

(D)   In addition to the porous outer shells of their bones, whales have at least some characteristics suited to deep diving for which there is no clear evidence whether these were shared by ichthyosaurs.

(E)   There is evidence that the bones of ichthyosaurs would have been light enough to allow surfacing even if the outer shells were not porous.

22. Librarian: Some argue that the preservation grant we received should be used to restore our original copy of our town's charter, since if the charter is not restored, it will soon deteriorate beyond repair. But this document, although sentimentally important, has no scholarly value. Copies are readily available. Since we are a research library and not a museum, the money would be better spent preserving documents that have significant scholarly value.

The claim that the town's charter, if not restored, will soon deteriorate beyond repair plays which one of the following roles in the librarian's argument?

(A)   It is a claim that the librarian's argument attempts to show to be false.

(B)   It is the conclusion of the argument that the librarian's argument rejects.

(C)   It is a premise in an argument whose conclusion is rejected by the librarian's argument.

(D)   It is a premise used to support the librarian's main conclusion.

(E)   It is a claim whose truth is required by the librarian's argument.

23. Columnist: Although much has been learned, we are still largely ignorant of the intricate interrelationships among species of living organisms. We should, therefore, try to preserve the maximum number of species if we have an interest in preserving any, since allowing species toward which we are indifferent to perish might undermine the viability of other species.

Which one of the following principles, if valid, most helps to justify the columnist's argument?

(A)   It is strongly in our interest to preserve certain plant and animal species.

(B)   We should not take any action until all relevant scientific facts have been established and taken into account.

(C)   We should not allow the number of species to diminish any further than is necessary for the flourishing of present and future human populations.

(D)   We should not allow a change to occur unless we are assured that that change will not jeopardize anything that is important to us.

(E)   We should always undertake the course of action that is likely to have the best consequences in the immediate future.

24. One is likely to feel comfortable approaching a stranger if the stranger is of one's approximate age. Therefore, long-term friends are probably of the same approximate age as each other since most long-term friendships begin because someone felt comfortable approaching a stranger.

The reasoning in the argument is flawed in that it

(A)   presumes, without warrant, that one is likely to feel uncomfortable approaching a person only if that person is a stranger

(B)   infers that a characteristic is present in a situation from the fact that that characteristic is present in most similar situations

(C)   overlooks the possibility that one is less likely to feel comfortable approaching someone who is one's approximate age if that person is a stranger than if that person is not a stranger

(D)   presumes, without warrant, that one never approaches a stranger unless one feels comfortable doing so

(E)   fails to address whether one is likely to feel comfortable approaching a stranger who is not one's approximate age

GO ON TO THE NEXT PAGE.

25. There can be no individual freedom without the rule of law, for there is no individual freedom without social integrity, and pursuing the good life is not possible without social integrity.

The conclusion drawn above follows logically if which one of the following is assumed?

(A) There can be no rule of law without social integrity.

(B) There can be no social integrity without the rule of law.

(C) One cannot pursue the good life without the rule of law.

(D) Social integrity is possible only if individual freedom prevails.

(E) There can be no rule of law without individual freedom.

26. Economist: Countries with an uneducated population are destined to be weak economically and politically, whereas those with an educated population have governments that display a serious financial commitment to public education. So any nation with a government that has made such a commitment will avoid economic and political weakness.

The pattern of flawed reasoning in which one of the following arguments is most similar to that in the economist's argument?

(A) Animal species with a very narrow diet will have more difficulty surviving if the climate suddenly changes, but a species with a broader diet will not; for changes in the climate can remove the traditional food supply.

(B) People incapable of empathy are not good candidates for public office, but those who do have the capacity for empathy are able to manipulate others easily; hence, people who can manipulate others are good candidates for public office.

(C) People who cannot give orders are those who do not understand the personalities of the people to whom they give orders. Thus, those who can give orders are those who understand the personalities of the people to whom they give orders.

(D) Poets who create poetry of high quality are those who have studied traditional poetry, because poets who have not studied traditional poetry are the poets most likely to create something shockingly inventive, and poetry that is shockingly inventive is rarely fine poetry.

(E) People who dislike exercise are unlikely to lose weight without sharply curtailing their food intake; but since those who dislike activity generally tend to avoid it, people who like to eat but dislike exercise will probably fail to lose weight.

S T O P

IF YOU FINISH BEFORE TIME IS CALLED, YOU MAY CHECK YOUR WORK ON THIS SECTION ONLY.
DO NOT WORK ON ANY OTHER SECTION IN THE TEST.

Wait for the supervisor's instructions before you open the page to the topic.
Please print and sign your name and write the date in the designated spaces below.
Time: 35 Minutes

General Directions

You will have 35 minutes in which to plan and write an essay on the topic inside. Read the topic and the accompanying directions carefully. You will probably find it best to spend a few minutes considering the topic and organizing your thoughts before you begin writing. In your essay, be sure to develop your ideas fully, leaving time, if possible, to review what you have written. **Do not write on a topic other than the one specified. Writing on a topic of your own choice is not acceptable.**

No special knowledge is required or expected for this writing exercise. Law schools are interested in the reasoning, clarity, organization, language usage, and writing mechanics displayed in your essay. How well you write is more important than how much you write.

Confine your essay to the blocked, lined area on the front and back of the separate Writing Sample Response Sheet. Only that area will be reproduced for law schools. Be sure that your writing is legible.

Both this topic sheet and your response sheet must be turned over to the testing staff before you leave the room.

Topic Code	Print Your Full Name Here		
097214	Last	First	M.I.

Date	Sign Your Name Here
/ /	

LSAT® Writing Sample Topic

> **Directions:** The scenario presented below describes two choices, either one of which can be supported on the basis of the information given. Your essay should consider both choices and argue for one over the other, based on the two specified criteria and the facts provided. There is no "right" or "wrong" choice: a reasonable argument can be made for either.

The attorneys for the plaintiffs in a lawsuit against a major pharmaceutical company are choosing an expert scientific witness to testify that a drug produced by the company was responsible for serious side effects. The attorneys have narrowed their choices down to two people. Using the facts below, write an essay in which you argue for choosing one person over the other based on the following two criteria:

- The attorneys want a witness who will be able to communicate technical information in a clear and effective manner to the jury.
- The attorneys want a witness who is highly knowledgeable in the field of pharmacology.

Dr. Rosa Benally has qualifications similar to those of the defense team's expert witness in that she has a PhD in pharmacology, teaches at a university, and is highly respected for her scientific research. Dr. Benally recently led a series of studies investigating the side effects of the class of drugs that will be under discussion during the trial. She has served effectively as an expert witness in a number of similar trials over the last five years.

Dr. Josephine Rickman is a medical doctor who also has a PhD in pharmacology. She has a busy medical practice. Dr. Rickman sometimes serves as a medical news correspondent on a national news program. She is the author of three best-selling books on medical topics, including one on the pharmaceutical industry. Dr. Rickman prescribed the drug in question to a number of patients who appeared to have experienced side effects like those to be discussed during the trial.

WP-S097A

Scratch Paper
Do not write your essay in this space.

COMPUTING YOUR SCORE

Directions:

1. Use the Answer Key on the next page to check your answers.

2. Use the Scoring Worksheet below to compute your raw score.

3. Use the Score Conversion Chart to convert your raw score into the 120–180 scale.

Scoring Worksheet

1. Enter the number of questions you answered correctly in each section.

	Number Correct
SECTION I................	_____
SECTION II...............	_____
SECTION III..............	_____
SECTION IV	_____

2. Enter the sum here: _____
   This is your Raw Score.

Conversion Chart
For Converting Raw Score to the 120–180 LSAT Scaled Score
LSAT Form 0LSN86

Reported Score	Raw Score Lowest	Raw Score Highest
180	99	101
179	98	98
178	97	97
177	96	96
176	—*	—*
175	95	95
174	94	94
173	93	93
172	92	92
171	91	91
170	89	90
169	88	88
168	87	87
167	85	86
166	84	84
165	82	83
164	81	81
163	79	80
162	78	78
161	76	77
160	74	75
159	73	73
158	71	72
157	69	70
156	67	68
155	66	66
154	64	65
153	62	63
152	60	61
151	58	59
150	57	57
149	55	56
148	53	54
147	52	52
146	50	51
145	48	49
144	47	47
143	45	46
142	43	44
141	42	42
140	40	41
139	39	39
138	37	38
137	36	36
136	34	35
135	33	33
134	31	32
133	30	30
132	29	29
131	27	28
130	26	26
129	25	25
128	24	24
127	22	23
126	21	21
125	20	20
124	19	19
123	18	18
122	16	17
121	—*	—*
120	0	15

*There is no raw score that will produce this scaled score for this form.

ANSWER KEY

SECTION I

1.	D	8.	A	15.	A	22.	A
2.	B	9.	E	16.	D	23.	E
3.	B	10.	C	17.	D	24.	E
4.	D	11.	B	18.	C	25.	B
5.	E	12.	E	19.	B	26.	A
6.	A	13.	B	20.	D	27.	B
7.	C	14.	B	21.	E		

SECTION II

1.	D	8.	A	15.	B	22.	C
2.	E	9.	E	16.	C	23.	D
3.	C	10.	A	17.	A	24.	B
4.	D	11.	A	18.	A	25.	D
5.	A	12.	A	19.	D		
6.	C	13.	B	20.	C		
7.	D	14.	D	21.	E		

SECTION III

1.	A	8.	A	15.	A	22.	B
2.	E	9.	C	16.	E	23.	A
3.	A	10.	B	17.	B		
4.	C	11.	D	18.	D		
5.	D	12.	D	19.	C		
6.	A	13.	D	20.	D		
7.	C	14.	B	21.	B		

SECTION IV

1.	E	8.	E	15.	B	22.	C
2.	B	9.	D	16.	C	23.	D
3.	A	10.	A	17.	D	24.	E
4.	D	11.	A	18.	A	25.	B
5.	C	12.	C	19.	E	26.	B
6.	C	13.	A	20.	A		
7.	E	14.	A	21.	C		

LSAC LawHub®

What You Need for Your Journey, from Prelaw Through Practice

At LSAC, we believe everyone should have the support they need to succeed on their journey to law school and beyond.

Tens of thousands of law school candidates already **rely on LawHub** and its growing portfolio of information and resources to support that journey from prelaw to practice. From LSAT preparation in the authentic test interface to education programs designed to prepare you for the modern law practice, discover what LawHub has to offer to help you develop the confidence and skills needed to achieve your academic and professional goals.

Sign up today at **LSAC.org**.

Connect with Us

 @LawSchoolAdmissionCouncil

 @LSAC_Official

 @official_lsac

 Law School Admission Council

 Law School Admission Council

General Directions for the LSAT Answer Sheet

This portion of the test consists of five multiple-choice sections, each with a time limit of 35 minutes. The supervisor will tell you when to begin and end each section. If you finish a section before time is called, you may check your work on that section **only**; do not turn to any other section of the test book and do not work on any other section either in the test book or on the answer sheet.

There are several different types of questions on the test, and each question type has its own directions. **Be sure you understand the directions for each question type before attempting to answer any questions in that section.**

Not everyone will finish all the questions in the time allowed. Do not hurry, but work steadily and as quickly as you can without sacrificing accuracy. You are advised to use your time effectively. If a question seems too difficult, go on to the next one and return to the difficult question after completing the section. **MARK THE BEST ANSWER YOU CAN FOR EVERY QUESTION. NO DEDUCTIONS WILL BE MADE FOR WRONG ANSWERS. YOUR SCORE WILL BE BASED ONLY ON THE NUMBER OF QUESTIONS YOU ANSWER CORRECTLY.**

ALL YOUR ANSWERS MUST BE MARKED ON THE ANSWER SHEET. Answer spaces for each question are lettered to correspond with the letters of the potential answers to each question in the test book. After you have decided which of the answers is correct, blacken the corresponding space on the answer sheet. **BE SURE THAT EACH MARK IS BLACK AND COMPLETELY FILLS THE ANSWER SPACE.** Give only one answer to each question. If you change an answer, be sure that all previous marks are **erased completely.** Since the answer sheet is machine scored, incomplete erasures may be interpreted as intended answers. **ANSWERS RECORDED IN THE TEST BOOK WILL NOT BE SCORED.**

There may be more question numbers on this answer sheet than there are questions in a section. Do not be concerned, but be certain that the section and number of the question you are answering matches the answer sheet section and question number. Additional answer spaces in any answer sheet section should be left blank. Begin your next section in the number one answer space for that section.

LSAC takes various steps to ensure that answer sheets are returned from test centers in a timely manner for processing. In the unlikely event that an answer sheet is not received, LSAC will permit the examinee either to retest at no additional fee or to receive a refund of his or her LSAT fee. **THESE REMEDIES ARE THE ONLY REMEDIES AVAILABLE IN THE UNLIKELY EVENT THAT AN ANSWER SHEET IS NOT RECEIVED BY LSAC.**

HOW DID YOU PREPARE FOR THE LSAT?
(Select all that apply.)

Responses to this item are voluntary and will be used for statistical research purposes only.

○ By using Khan Academy's official LSAT practice material.
○ By taking the free sample questions and/or free sample LSAT available on LSAC's website.
○ By working through official LSAT *PrepTest* and/or other LSAC test prep products.
○ By using LSAT prep books or software **not** published by LSAC.
○ By attending a commercial test preparation or coaching course.
○ By attending a test preparation or coaching course offered through an undergraduate institution.
○ Self study.
○ Other preparation.
○ No preparation.

CERTIFYING STATEMENT

Please write the following statement. Sign and date.

I certify that I am the examinee whose name appears on this answer sheet and that I am here to take the LSAT for the sole purpose of being considered for admission to law school. I further certify that I will neither assist nor receive assistance from any other candidate, and I agree not to copy, retain, or transmit examination questions in any form or discuss them with any other person.

_____
_____
_____
_____
_____
_____
_____
_____

SIGNATURE: _____   TODAY'S DATE: ___/___/___
                                                        MONTH DAY YEAR

DO NOT WRITE IN THIS BOX.

FOR LSAC USE ONLY

INSTRUCTIONS FOR COMPLETING THE BIOGRAPHICAL AREA ARE ON THE BACK COVER OF YOUR TEST BOOKLET.
USE ONLY A NO. 2 OR HB PENCIL TO COMPLETE THIS ANSWER SHEET. DO NOT USE INK.

1 LAST NAME | FIRST NAME | MI

(Grid of bubbles A–Z for Last Name, First Name, and MI)

2 LAST 4 DIGITS OF SOCIAL SECURITY/ SOCIAL INSURANCE NO.

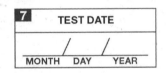

L

(Bubbles 0–9)

3 LSAC ACCOUNT NUMBER

(Bubbles 0–9)

4 CENTER NUMBER

(Bubbles 0–9)

5 DATE OF BIRTH

MONTH	DAY	YEAR
Jan		
Feb		
Mar		
Apr		
May		
June		
July		
Aug		
Sept		
Oct		
Nov		
Dec		

(Bubbles 0–9)

6 TEST FORM CODE

(Bubbles 0–9)

7 TEST DATE

MONTH / DAY / YEAR

8 TEST FORM

═ Law School Admission Test ═

Mark one and only one answer to each question. Be sure to fill in completely the space for your intended answer choice. If you erase, do so completely. Make no stray marks.

SECTION 1 — Questions 1–30, each with answer choices (A) (B) (C) (D) (E)

SECTION 2 — Questions 1–30, each with answer choices (A) (B) (C) (D) (E)

SECTION 3 — Questions 1–30, each with answer choices (A) (B) (C) (D) (E)

SECTION 4 — Questions 1–30, each with answer choices (A) (B) (C) (D) (E)

SECTION 5 — Questions 1–30, each with answer choices (A) (B) (C) (D) (E)

9 TEST BOOK SERIAL NO.

(Grid of bubbles A–T and 0–9)

10 PLEASE PRINT INFORMATION

LAST NAME

FIRST NAME

DATE OF BIRTH

● Ⓑ

SCANTRON. EliteView™ EM-295665-4:654321

INSTRUCTIONS FOR COMPLETING THE BIOGRAPHICAL AREA ARE ON THE BACK COVER OF YOUR TEST BOOKLET.
USE ONLY A NO. 2 OR HB PENCIL TO COMPLETE THIS ANSWER SHEET. DO NOT USE INK.

A

1 LAST NAME | FIRST NAME | MI

2 LAST 4 DIGITS OF SOCIAL SECURITY/ SOCIAL INSURANCE NO.

3 LSAC ACCOUNT NUMBER

4 CENTER NUMBER

5 DATE OF BIRTH
MONTH | DAY | YEAR
○ Jan ○ Feb ○ Mar ○ Apr ○ May ○ June ○ July ○ Aug ○ Sept ○ Oct ○ Nov ○ Dec

6 TEST FORM CODE

7 TEST DATE
MONTH / DAY / YEAR

8 TEST FORM

Law School Admission Test

Mark one and only one answer to each question. Be sure to fill in completely the space for your intended answer choice. If you erase, do so completely. Make no stray marks.

9 TEST BOOK SERIAL NO.

SECTION 1 | SECTION 2 | SECTION 3 | SECTION 4 | SECTION 5

(Questions 1–30, each with answer choices A B C D E, in each of the five sections)

10 PLEASE PRINT INFORMATION

LAST NAME

FIRST NAME

DATE OF BIRTH

SCANTRON. EliteView™ EM-295665-4:654321

INSTRUCTIONS FOR COMPLETING THE BIOGRAPHICAL AREA ARE ON THE BACK COVER OF YOUR TEST BOOKLET.

USE ONLY A NO. 2 OR HB PENCIL TO COMPLETE THIS ANSWER SHEET. DO NOT USE INK.

1 LAST NAME | FIRST NAME | MI

2 LAST 4 DIGITS OF SOCIAL SECURITY/ SOCIAL INSURANCE NO.

3 LSAC ACCOUNT NUMBER

4 CENTER NUMBER

5 DATE OF BIRTH

MONTH	DAY	YEAR
○ Jan		
○ Feb		
○ Mar		
○ Apr		
○ May		
○ June		
○ July		
○ Aug		
○ Sept		
○ Oct		
○ Nov		
○ Dec		

6 TEST FORM CODE

7 TEST DATE

MONTH / DAY / YEAR

8 TEST FORM

═══ Law School Admission Test ═══

Mark one and only one answer to each question. Be sure to fill in completely the space for your intended answer choice. If you erase, do so completely. Make no stray marks.

9 TEST BOOK SERIAL NO.

SECTION 1 | SECTION 2 | SECTION 3 | SECTION 4 | SECTION 5

(Questions 1–30, each with answer bubbles A B C D E)

10 PLEASE PRINT INFORMATION

LAST NAME

FIRST NAME

DATE OF BIRTH

© 2018 BY LAW SCHOOL ADMISSION COUNCIL.
ALL RIGHTS RESERVED. PRINTED IN USA.

SCANTRON. EliteView™ EM-295665-4:654321

A

INSTRUCTIONS FOR COMPLETING THE BIOGRAPHICAL AREA ARE ON THE BACK COVER OF YOUR TEST BOOKLET.
USE ONLY A NO. 2 OR HB PENCIL TO COMPLETE THIS ANSWER SHEET. DO NOT USE INK.

1 LAST NAME | FIRST NAME | MI

2 LAST 4 DIGITS OF SOCIAL SECURITY/ SOCIAL INSURANCE NO.

L

3 LSAC ACCOUNT NUMBER

4 CENTER NUMBER

5 DATE OF BIRTH
MONTH | DAY | YEAR

- Jan
- Feb
- Mar
- Apr
- May
- June
- July
- Aug
- Sept
- Oct
- Nov
- Dec

6 TEST FORM CODE

7 TEST DATE
MONTH / DAY / YEAR

8 TEST FORM

Law School Admission Test

Mark one and only one answer to each question. Be sure to fill in completely the space for your intended answer choice. If you erase, do so completely. Make no stray marks.

9 TEST BOOK SERIAL NO.

SECTION 1 | **SECTION 2** | **SECTION 3** | **SECTION 4** | **SECTION 5**

(Questions 1–30, answer choices A B C D E for each section)

10 PLEASE PRINT INFORMATION

LAST NAME

FIRST NAME

DATE OF BIRTH

© 2018 BY LAW SCHOOL ADMISSION COUNCIL.
ALL RIGHTS RESERVED. PRINTED IN USA.

INSTRUCTIONS FOR COMPLETING THE BIOGRAPHICAL AREA ARE ON THE BACK COVER OF YOUR TEST BOOKLET.
USE ONLY A NO. 2 OR HB PENCIL TO COMPLETE THIS ANSWER SHEET. DO NOT USE INK.

1 LAST NAME · FIRST NAME · MI

2 LAST 4 DIGITS OF SOCIAL SECURITY/ SOCIAL INSURANCE NO.

L

3 LSAC ACCOUNT NUMBER

4 CENTER NUMBER

5 DATE OF BIRTH — MONTH · DAY · YEAR
Jan, Feb, Mar, Apr, May, June, July, Aug, Sept, Oct, Nov, Dec

6 TEST FORM CODE

7 TEST DATE — MONTH / DAY / YEAR

8 TEST FORM

Law School Admission Test

Mark one and only one answer to each question. Be sure to fill in completely the space for your intended answer choice. If you erase, do so completely. Make no stray marks.

9 TEST BOOK SERIAL NO.

SECTION 1 · SECTION 2 · SECTION 3 · SECTION 4 · SECTION 5
(Questions 1–30, answer choices A B C D E for each)

10 PLEASE PRINT INFORMATION

LAST NAME

FIRST NAME

DATE OF BIRTH

Ⓐ B

SCANTRON. EliteView™ EM-295665-4:654321

INSTRUCTIONS FOR COMPLETING THE BIOGRAPHICAL AREA ARE ON THE BACK COVER OF YOUR TEST BOOKLET.
USE ONLY A NO. 2 OR HB PENCIL TO COMPLETE THIS ANSWER SHEET. DO NOT USE INK.

1 LAST NAME | FIRST NAME | MI

2 LAST 4 DIGITS OF SOCIAL SECURITY/ SOCIAL INSURANCE NO.

L

3 LSAC ACCOUNT NUMBER

4 CENTER NUMBER

(Bubble grids A–Z for name fields; numeric grids 0–9 for fields 2, 3, and 4)

5 DATE OF BIRTH

MONTH	DAY	YEAR
Jan		
Feb		
Mar		
Apr		
May		
June		
July		
Aug		
Sept		
Oct		
Nov		
Dec		

6 TEST FORM CODE

(Numeric grid 0–9)

7 TEST DATE

____ / ____ / ____
MONTH   DAY   YEAR

8 TEST FORM

Law School Admission Test

Mark one and only one answer to each question. Be sure to fill in completely the space for your intended answer choice. If you erase, do so completely. Make no stray marks.

9 TEST BOOK SERIAL NO.

(Grid A–T and 0–9)

SECTION 1	SECTION 2	SECTION 3	SECTION 4	SECTION 5
1 A B C D E	1 A B C D E	1 A B C D E	1 A B C D E	1 A B C D E
2 A B C D E	2 A B C D E	2 A B C D E	2 A B C D E	2 A B C D E
3 A B C D E	3 A B C D E	3 A B C D E	3 A B C D E	3 A B C D E
4 A B C D E	4 A B C D E	4 A B C D E	4 A B C D E	4 A B C D E
5 A B C D E	5 A B C D E	5 A B C D E	5 A B C D E	5 A B C D E
6 A B C D E	6 A B C D E	6 A B C D E	6 A B C D E	6 A B C D E
7 A B C D E	7 A B C D E	7 A B C D E	7 A B C D E	7 A B C D E
8 A B C D E	8 A B C D E	8 A B C D E	8 A B C D E	8 A B C D E
9 A B C D E	9 A B C D E	9 A B C D E	9 A B C D E	9 A B C D E
10 A B C D E	10 A B C D E	10 A B C D E	10 A B C D E	10 A B C D E
11 A B C D E	11 A B C D E	11 A B C D E	11 A B C D E	11 A B C D E
12 A B C D E	12 A B C D E	12 A B C D E	12 A B C D E	12 A B C D E
13 A B C D E	13 A B C D E	13 A B C D E	13 A B C D E	13 A B C D E
14 A B C D E	14 A B C D E	14 A B C D E	14 A B C D E	14 A B C D E
15 A B C D E	15 A B C D E	15 A B C D E	15 A B C D E	15 A B C D E
16 A B C D E	16 A B C D E	16 A B C D E	16 A B C D E	16 A B C D E
17 A B C D E	17 A B C D E	17 A B C D E	17 A B C D E	17 A B C D E
18 A B C D E	18 A B C D E	18 A B C D E	18 A B C D E	18 A B C D E
19 A B C D E	19 A B C D E	19 A B C D E	19 A B C D E	19 A B C D E
20 A B C D E	20 A B C D E	20 A B C D E	20 A B C D E	20 A B C D E
21 A B C D E	21 A B C D E	21 A B C D E	21 A B C D E	21 A B C D E
22 A B C D E	22 A B C D E	22 A B C D E	22 A B C D E	22 A B C D E
23 A B C D E	23 A B C D E	23 A B C D E	23 A B C D E	23 A B C D E
24 A B C D E	24 A B C D E	24 A B C D E	24 A B C D E	24 A B C D E
25 A B C D E	25 A B C D E	25 A B C D E	25 A B C D E	25 A B C D E
26 A B C D E	26 A B C D E	26 A B C D E	26 A B C D E	26 A B C D E
27 A B C D E	27 A B C D E	27 A B C D E	27 A B C D E	27 A B C D E
28 A B C D E	28 A B C D E	28 A B C D E	28 A B C D E	28 A B C D E
29 A B C D E	29 A B C D E	29 A B C D E	29 A B C D E	29 A B C D E
30 A B C D E	30 A B C D E	30 A B C D E	30 A B C D E	30 A B C D E

10 PLEASE PRINT INFORMATION

LAST NAME

FIRST NAME

DATE OF BIRTH

INSTRUCTIONS FOR COMPLETING THE BIOGRAPHICAL AREA ARE ON THE BACK COVER OF YOUR TEST BOOKLET.
USE ONLY A NO. 2 OR HB PENCIL TO COMPLETE THIS ANSWER SHEET. DO NOT USE INK.

1 LAST NAME FIRST NAME MI

2 LAST 4 DIGITS OF SOCIAL SECURITY/ SOCIAL INSURANCE NO.

3 LSAC ACCOUNT NUMBER

4 CENTER NUMBER

5 DATE OF BIRTH

MONTH	DAY	YEAR
Jan		
Feb		
Mar		
Apr		
May		
June		
July		
Aug		
Sept		
Oct		
Nov		
Dec		

6 TEST FORM CODE

7 TEST DATE
MONTH / DAY / YEAR

8 TEST FORM

Law School Admission Test

Mark one and only one answer to each question. Be sure to fill in completely the space for your intended answer choice. If you erase, do so completely. Make no stray marks.

9 TEST BOOK SERIAL NO.

SECTION 1 | SECTION 2 | SECTION 3 | SECTION 4 | SECTION 5

(Questions 1–30, each with answer choices A B C D E)

10 PLEASE PRINT INFORMATION

LAST NAME

FIRST NAME

DATE OF BIRTH

INSTRUCTIONS FOR COMPLETING THE BIOGRAPHICAL AREA ARE ON THE BACK COVER OF YOUR TEST BOOKLET.
USE ONLY A NO. 2 OR HB PENCIL TO COMPLETE THIS ANSWER SHEET. DO NOT USE INK.

A

1 LAST NAME / FIRST NAME / MI

2 LAST 4 DIGITS OF SOCIAL SECURITY/ SOCIAL INSURANCE NO.

3 LSAC ACCOUNT NUMBER

4 CENTER NUMBER

5 DATE OF BIRTH

MONTH	DAY	YEAR
Jan		
Feb		
Mar		
Apr		
May		
June		
July		
Aug		
Sept		
Oct		
Nov		
Dec		

6 TEST FORM CODE

7 TEST DATE

MONTH / DAY / YEAR

8 TEST FORM

Law School Admission Test

Mark one and only one answer to each question. Be sure to fill in completely the space for your intended answer choice. If you erase, do so completely. Make no stray marks.

9 TEST BOOK SERIAL NO.

SECTION 1 | SECTION 2 | SECTION 3 | SECTION 4 | SECTION 5

(Questions 1–30, each with answer choices A B C D E)

10 PLEASE PRINT INFORMATION

LAST NAME

FIRST NAME

DATE OF BIRTH

INSTRUCTIONS FOR COMPLETING THE BIOGRAPHICAL AREA ARE ON THE BACK COVER OF YOUR TEST BOOKLET.
USE ONLY A NO. 2 OR HB PENCIL TO COMPLETE THIS ANSWER SHEET. DO NOT USE INK.

1 LAST NAME / FIRST NAME / MI

(Bubble grid A–Z for Last Name, First Name, and MI)

2 LAST 4 DIGITS OF SOCIAL SECURITY/ SOCIAL INSURANCE NO.

L (Bubble grid 0–9)

3 LSAC ACCOUNT NUMBER

(Bubble grid 0–9)

4 CENTER NUMBER

(Bubble grid 0–9)

5 DATE OF BIRTH

MONTH	DAY	YEAR
○ Jan		
○ Feb		
○ Mar		
○ Apr		
○ May		
○ June		
○ July		
○ Aug		
○ Sept		
○ Oct		
○ Nov		
○ Dec		

(Bubble grid 0–9)

6 TEST FORM CODE

(Bubble grid 0–9)

7 TEST DATE

_____ / _____ / _____
MONTH   DAY   YEAR

8 TEST FORM

9 TEST BOOK SERIAL NO.

(Bubble grid A–T, 0–9)

Law School Admission Test

Mark one and only one answer to each question. Be sure to fill in completely the space for your intended answer choice. If you erase, do so completely. Make no stray marks.

SECTION 1 / SECTION 2 / SECTION 3 / SECTION 4 / SECTION 5

Each section: questions 1–30, answer choices (A) (B) (C) (D) (E)

10 PLEASE PRINT INFORMATION

LAST NAME

FIRST NAME

DATE OF BIRTH

(B)

SCANTRON. EliteView™ EM-295665-4:654321

INSTRUCTIONS FOR COMPLETING THE BIOGRAPHICAL AREA ARE ON THE BACK COVER OF YOUR TEST BOOKLET.
USE ONLY A NO. 2 OR HB PENCIL TO COMPLETE THIS ANSWER SHEET. DO NOT USE INK.

1 LAST NAME | FIRST NAME | MI

2 LAST 4 DIGITS OF SOCIAL SECURITY/ SOCIAL INSURANCE NO.

3 LSAC ACCOUNT NUMBER

4 CENTER NUMBER

5 DATE OF BIRTH

MONTH	DAY	YEAR
Jan		
Feb		
Mar		
Apr		
May		
June		
July		
Aug		
Sept		
Oct		
Nov		
Dec		

6 TEST FORM CODE

7 TEST DATE

/ /

MONTH   DAY   YEAR

8 TEST FORM

Law School Admission Test

Mark one and only one answer to each question. Be sure to fill in completely the space for your intended answer choice. If you erase, do so completely. Make no stray marks.

9 TEST BOOK SERIAL NO.

SECTION 1	SECTION 2	SECTION 3	SECTION 4	SECTION 5

10 PLEASE PRINT INFORMATION

LAST NAME

FIRST NAME

DATE OF BIRTH

© 2018 BY LAW SCHOOL ADMISSION COUNCIL.
ALL RIGHTS RESERVED. PRINTED IN USA.